ISBN 978-0-483-38205-3
PIBN 10834386

CURRICULUM RECORDS OF THE CHILDREN'S SCHOOL

National College of Education

The School and Its Neighborhood

Curriculum Records
of the Children's School

NATIONAL COLLEGE OF
EDUCATION

BY MEMBERS OF THE STAFF

CLARA BELLE BAKER, *Director of the Children's School*
DAVID W. RUSSELL, *Assistant Director*
LOUISE FARWELL DAVIS, *Director of Research*

SARA LOFFLER BLACK   JAMES GRIGGS
ARTHUR WITT BLAIR   EDITH MADDOX
MAURINE BREDESON   MARGARET McPHERSON
LYNN E. BROWN, JR.   JEAN RUMRY
MIRIAM BRUBAKER   ALIDA SHINN
ANNE DE BLOIS   ELIZABETH SPRINGSTUN
EDITH FORD   DOROTHY WELLER
VIOLET RUSH GEIGER   NELLIE BALL WHITAKER

MIRIAM WIGGENHORN

Bureau of Publications

NATIONAL COLLEGE OF EDUCATION

EVANSTON, ILLINOIS

FOREWORD

THE Children's School of the National College of Education was established in 1926, for the purpose of studying and guiding the development of boys and girls from the nursery school to the high school period. The school includes the six elementary grades, a nursery school for children two and three years of age, a junior kindergarten for four-year-olds, and a senior kindergarten for five-year-olds. Boys and girls completing the sixth grade enter the junior high school of National College of Education.

The children come for the most part from the homes of teachers, physicians, and other professional people who are keenly interested in the problems of education. The National College of Education conducts courses for parents, and the Children's School sponsors a program of activities in which teachers and parents coöperate. The school is organized for demonstration and informal investigation. Each group is under the direction of an experienced teacher, who is assisted by two or more senior students.

The attack on curriculum problems has been experimental. Teachers have made use of children's spontaneous interests in developing projects, and have also initiated enterprises, observing and recording pupil responses. Group and individual records of progress have been made, and checks have been used in the form of educational tests and informal rating sheets. A careful study of each child's development is made by the room teacher, with the help of physician, psychologist, and a staff of specialists.

Members of the staff have worked together to formulate certain aims and principles for creative curriculum-making, to collect source material for children's enterprises, to build a bibliography for both teachers and pupils, and to organize certain forms for recording units of experience and also for recording group and individual progress in various types of activities.

This volume of records is presented in the hope that it may be helpful to other schools engaged in the adventure of creative curriculum making.

ACKNOWLEDGMENT

INDEBTEDNESS *is acknowledged to several groups who have given aid in the preparation of this volume: for helpful suggestions concerning certain phases of curriculum making and record keeping, to Edna Dean Baker, Laura Hooper, Harriet Howard, Frances Kern and Caroline Crawford McLean, of the staff of National College of Education; for aid in developing children's enterprises and in recording progress of individual children, to Viggo Bovbjerg, George Wilson, Martha Fink, Nellie MacLennan, Ruth Wendelken, Etta Mount, Mary H. Pope, M. D., specialists on the staff of the Children's School; for assistance in preparing bibliographies, to Clarence R. Graham, librarian of National College of Education, and to Marjorie Walker Davis, secretary to the director of the Children's School.*

The staff wishes also to acknowledge indebtedness to that larger group of philosophers, scientists, and creative teachers in American education who are doing so much at the present time to clarify our thinking and to inspire us all to greater effort. The names of many of these leaders are listed in the Bibliography for Teachers at the end of the book.

CONTENTS

PART I. TEACHERS' GUIDES

PAGE

SOME GENERAL AIMS AND PRINCIPLES 3

SOURCE MATERIAL FOR CURRICULUM MAKING 5

Living in the Complete Modern Home 7

Living in the Modern Community 10

Activities Involved in the Arts and Industries Which Support Home and Community 13

Experiences of Various Peoples in Adapting to Environment 15

Experiences Involved in the Discovery and Development of Our Own Country and Our Own Community . . 18

Experiences Involved in the Development of the Modern World and the Contribution of Certain Peoples to Civilization 22

PART II. SOME TYPICAL UNITS OF EXPERIENCE

DEVELOPING AND RECORDING GROUP ENTERPRISES . . . 27

UNITS OF EXPERIENCE IN KINDERGARTEN 31

Raising Animal Families 33

Traveling by Train 37

Traveling by Boat 42

Traveling in the Air 46

Playing with the Leaves 50

Helping the Birds 52

UNITS OF EXPERIENCE IN FIRST GRADE 54

Enjoying and Using Autumn Treasures 57

Creating an Autumn Festival 63

Enjoying and Caring for Pets 66

Using Cars and Filling Stations 72

Conducting a Post Office 77

Conducting a Toy Store 82

UNITS OF EXPERIENCE IN SECOND GRADE 86

Living in a Trailer 88

Developing a Harbor 93

Carrying the Mail 102

Developing Pottery and a Pottery Shop 109

Living on a Farm 114

Creating a Garden and a Garden Market 119

UNITS OF EXPERIENCE IN THIRD GRADE .
    Conducting an Art Gallery .
    Traveling in Old and New Ways .
    Visiting the Indians
    Visiting Mexico .
    Following Hobbies in Science

UNITS OF EXPERIENCE IN FOURTH GRADE
    Making a Trip Around the World
    How America Was Discovered and Explored
    How Chicago Grew from Wigwams to Skyscrapers
    Learning to Choose Healthful Lunches .
    Making a Star Observatory .
    How Baby Chicks Are Developed .

UNITS OF EXPERIENCE IN FIFTH GRADE .
    What Other Sections of the United States Share with
        Chicago .
    How Chicago Obtains and Uses Iron .
    How Chicago Obtains and Uses Lumber
    Enjoying Playgrounds of the United States .
    How New York Became Our Greatest City .
    How the United States Moved West from New York to San
        Francisco
    Learning to Use and Control Water

UNITS OF EXPERIENCE IN SIXTH GRADE .
    Planning a Community
    How Architecture Has Developed
    What Is Our Heritage from the Middle Ages?
    What Has Modern Europe Contributed to the United
        States? .
    Behind the News in China and Japan .
    Sharing the Earth with Insects .
    Maintaining an Aquarium .

PART III. THE DAY'S PROCEDURE

ARRANGING THE PROGRAM .
    The Changing Schedule, Provision for Individual Interests,
        Provision for Inter-class Assemblies, Provision for Use
        of Community Resources .

PAGE

ARRANGING THE PROGRAM—continued

Daily Procedure in the Nursery School, Junior Kindergarten, Senior Kindergarten, First Grade, Second Grade . 296

Tentative Weekly Program for Third Grade, Fourth Grade, Fifth Grade, Sixth Grade 303

SKETCHES OF VARIOUS DAYS 307

Nursery School: A Day in September, A November Day, A Rainy Day in April 308

Junior Kindergarten: An October Day, A Snowy Day in January, A Day in June 317

Senior Kindergarten: A Day in December 323

First Grade: A Morning in March 328

Second Grade: An October Day 332

Third Grade: A Tuesday in May 335

Fourth Grade: A Morning in November 338

Fifth Grade: A Morning in the Summer Session . . . 341

Sixth Grade: A Wednesday in April (including a description of *The National News*) 344

PART IV.   GROUP RECORDS OF PROGRESS IN A FEW IMPORTANT SKILLS

RECORDING PROGRESS IN TERMS OF SPECIFIC SKILLS . . . 355

ENGLISH RECORDS

Development of Reading Readiness in the Kindergarten . 356

Language and Literature Experience in the Senior Kindergarten 358

Provision for Language Progress in the Elementary Grades . 364

Language, Writing and Spelling in First Grade, Second Grade, Third Grade, Fourth Grade, Fifth Grade, Sixth Grade 365

READING RECORDS

Provision for Reading Progress in the Elementary Grades . 409

Reading and Literature in First Grade, Second Grade, Third Grade, Fourth Grade, Fifth Grade, Sixth Grade . . 411

ARITHMETIC RECORDS

Development of Number Concepts in the Kindergarten . 466

Number Experience in the Senior Kindergarten . . . 466

Provision for Arithmetic Progress in the Elementary Grades . 471

Arithmetic in the First Grade, Second Grade, Third Grade, Fourth Grade, Fifth Grade, Sixth Grade . . . 472

PART V. INDIVIDUAL RECORDS AND
THEIR USE

		PAGE
MEETING THE NEEDS OF THE INDIVIDUAL		513

PARENTS' AND TEACHERS' RECORDS

Relationship of Parents to the School 515
Child's Original Enrollment Record 517
Initial Conference with Parents (Nursery School and
    Kindergarten) 520
Key and Typical Reports from Nursery School and Kinder-
    garten 522
Key and Typical Reports from Primary Grades . . . 534
Key and Typical Reports from Intermediate Grades . . 540

PHYSICIAN'S RECORDS

Functions of the Health Department 554
Health History (Contributed by Parent and Family
    Physician) 556
Health Record (Kept by School Physician) 557
Physician's Report to Parents 558

RECORDS OF THE GUIDANCE LABORATORY 559
Personnel of the Laboratory, Description of the Laboratory,
    Types of Tests Used, Major Responsibilities . . . 559
Intelligence Tests and Personality Studies 563
Policies Related to Evaluation of Achievement and the Im-
    provement of Learning 570
Standardized Achievement Tests, Achievement Test In-
    ventory and Interpretation, Letters of Transfer, Indi-
    vidual Profile Graphs 574
Reading Aptitude Tests, Positive Traits of Children Basic
    to Learning 586
Research Studies in Status and Improvement of Learning . 590
Summary Record of a Pupil Attending the School for Eight
    Years 592

BIBLIOGRAPHY FOR TEACHERS 597

LIST OF ILLUSTRATIONS

From Photographs

THE SCHOOL AND ITS NEIGHBORHOOD . . . . . *Fron*

THANKSGIVING BRINGS FRESH GIFTS AND OLD TALES . . .

CHICKENS ARE AMUSING FRIENDS . . . .

SERVICE IS GOOD ON THIS TRAIN . . . .

THE WIND IS NORTH BY EAST . . . .

WATCHING MECHANICS INSTALL A MOTOR IN A PLANE . . .

BULBS NOW AND TULIPS BY AND BY . . . . . .

YOUNG RABBITS SHOW GROWTH IN WEIGHT . . . .

HOODED RATS ARE INTERESTING . . . .

A STOP IS MADE AT THE FILLING STATION . . . . .

GIFTS ARE EXCHANGED THROUGH THE POST OFFICE . . .

THE LAKE TESTS WATER TOYS . . . .

A TRAILER FAMILY MEETS WOOD FOLK . . . . .

NEW BOATS WILL SOON BE LAUNCHED . . . . .

IMPORTANT LETTERS ARE POSTED . . . . . .

IT'S FUN TO MODEL . . . .

POTTERY IS PRODUCED TO SELL . . . .

MOTHERS ARE GOOD CUSTOMERS . . . . . .

ART ENRICHES LIVING . . . .

OLD TIME VESSELS REAPPEAR . . . .

INDIAN ARTS ARE PRACTICED . . . .

MEXICAN CURIOS STIMULATE CRAFTS . . . . . .

EXPERIMENTS PROVE INTERESTING FACTS . . . . .

CREW OF SANTA MARIA SIGHTS LAND . . . . . .

FORT DEARBORN PROTECTS EARLY SETTLERS . . . . .

COOKING STIMULATES WHOLESOME APPETITES . . . .

A PICNIC IS ENJOYED AT THE CAMPUS FIREPLACE . . . .

SCHOOL TELESCOPE IS INVESTIGATED . . . . . .

OBSERVATORY SHOWS MYSTERIES OF THE SKY . . . .

AN INCUBATOR REQUIRES SCIENTIFIC CARE . . . . .

A JIG-SAW PUZZLE MAP INTRIGUES ITS MAKERS . . . .

THE COVERED WAGON SPELLS ADVENTURE . . . .

TEMPERATURE OF WATER IS TESTED . . . . .

LOCAL OFFICERS BECOME TEACHERS . . . . .

Sixth Graders Evaluate City's Fire Protection . .
Neighborhood Airport Is Approved . . . : .
Jean Is Made Knight of the Cathedral . . . .
Each Contributes to World's Fair . . . . .
Notes Are Taken on Radio Travel Talks . . .
Water Creatures Fascinate . . . . . .
Individual Interests . . . .
Camera Club Develops and Enlarges Photographs .
Dressing Is a Big Task . . . .
Pets Are Fed Each Morning . . . . . .
Logs and Boxes Prevent Unemployment . . . .
Soap Bubbles Are Enjoyed on Rainy Days . . .
The Pony Is a Favorite at the Farm . . . .
Snow Brings Jolly Fun . . . .
Home-Making Consumes Much Time . . . .
Rhythm Instruments Add to Joy in Music . . .
Summer School Brings Water Play . . . .
Boys Develop Skill in Baseball . . . . .
Sixth Grade Publishes a Newspaper . . . .
Stories and Pictures Provide Stimulus for Conversation
Language and Art Join Hands in Creating a Play .
Puppets Show School Courtesies . . . . .
Drama Develops Language -Powers . . . .
A Radio Broadcast Is Presented . . . . .
Children Share Vacation Trips . . . . .
It Is Fun to Read . . . .
Getting Acquainted with the Library . . . .
The Library Leads to New Adventure . . . .
First Aid to Librarians . . . .
Facts from Reading Are Used in Writing and Art . .
Buying Is Enthusiastic at Play Time . . . .
Scales Show Satisfactory Gains . . . . .
Balancing Prices and Vitamins . . . . .
Study of Temperature and Humidity Affords Problems
Managing the National News Involves Mathematics . .

PART I

Teachers' Guides

MORNING

Far off the Fairy Horns are blowing
Through the morning, through the dew.
Above the emerald green and blue
The windy clouds are white and new.
We'll carry through this windy morn
Hearts fit to meet the Fairy Horn.

E. G. (age ten)
Children's School.

SOME GENERAL AIMS AND PRINCIPLES

THE school shares the belief that a chief purpose of the curriculum is to habituate the children to ways of living that are satisfying and worth while now and that will lead them into rich and productive living as they grow more mature. With this purpose in view, the school wishes for the individual these attainments, which should grow gradually from year to year:

1. Such development and integration of personality as can come only through the individual's active and enthusiastic response to a challenging yet flexible curriculum and standards of achievement.

2. An understanding of the important activities of the home and the community and of the arts and industries which support the home and the community, and also the significant experiences of the race, the nation and the modern world, in so far as these influence or explain present ways of living and trends of creative thinking.

3. The ability to think constructively, to evaluate, compare and form sane judgments, developed through a curriculum that presents unanswered questions and unsolved problems and encourages research, experiment and discussion.

4. The habit of working purposefully toward a goal with the recognition of the need for added knowledge and skill emerging in the effort.

5. The mastery of essential skills and techniques (such as reading, arithmetic, spelling) with the aid of scientific data now available, and with the stimulus of practical application.

6. A readiness to participate in worthy social living, cultivated by actual contacts and experiences with the institutions of real life and a continuance of such experiences through a variety of life-like activities in the school.

7. A recognition that the social order is continually changing, and a willingness to participate in building a better school and a better community.

3

8. Such social attitudes or traits that the individual can make the best possible use of his own powers and can enter into the fullest coöperation with other people.

9. The development of power to understand and appreciate the artistic resources of our race inheritance and of the present age, in art, literature, music, and related fields.

10. The urge to create art forms that represent the individual's finest skill and his own evaluation of the meaning of experience.

11. Through these experiences and through the practice of desirable health habits, such physical development that the body becomes the finest possible instrument for expression.

With these aims in view the school seeks to provide for the children a program of dynamic living. In such a program there is a continuous stream of experiences and enterprises which are real and vital to the children, and therefore challenge their wholehearted effort. Information is gained through the study of real problems, and practice in the mastery of skills is provided as there is readiness on the part of the child.

Since education has a responsibility both for guiding the developing life of the child and also for molding the future of society, the experiences and enterprises in which the children engage can not be left entirely to chance. Rather the teachers as they work with their groups must guide in the selection of activities which will bring to the children all desirable forms of experience, and at the same time provide the true conditions for effective learning. Conditions for learning are most favorable when the children enter into all experiences freely and joyously.

In this volume, the familiar phrase "unit of work" has been omitted as it has been widely used to refer either to an extended lesson plan in a particular subject, or to a complex correlation of activities around a topic selected by the curriculum maker. The "unit of experience" described in the present volume has been defined by the authors as "any series of activities and experiences occurring is the pursuit of a vital interest or purpose by an individual or a group." The terms "enterprise," "project," and "study of a problem" are all used at times in referring to such units of experience.

SOURCE MATERIAL
FOR CURRICULUM MAKING

IN CREATING a curriculum, it seems desirable that teachers should have some guide further than the interests of the children in the group. What constitutes valuable curriculum material for the present decade? Many methods of approach to this problem are being made; and the "source material" here presented suggests one possible method of approach. If the purpose of the curriculum is to habituate the children to ways of living that are satisfying and worth while, then it is important that they become familiar with desirable ways of living in the modern home and community and also that they understand ways of living in other parts of the world and in earlier times, in so far as these explain or interpret their own experiences.

The outline which follows lists significant experiences or activities of the well-equipped modern home and community, and of the arts and industries that support the home and the community. It also lists experiences of the race, the nation and the modern world, which help to explain present-day activities and to shape present trends of creative thinking. These experiences involve meanings, appreciations, habits and skills which must have worth for education.

The outline provides "source material" for curriculum making in all grades of the elementary school. It not only integrates history, geography and civics, and provides material for a program in the social studies, but also suggests activities in the sciences and in all the arts.

While the outline includes much more material than could be covered in any one year in any one school, it has given to teachers perspective in formulating problems with the children. The selection and development of units of study in this school over a period of years tend to show that the most valuable and interesting studies throughout the elementary school are those that concern the child's own environment and provide opportunity for firsthand investigation. Experiment has shown, however, that studies relating to distant times and places may in middle and upper grades prove of high interest if action and adventure are involved and opportunities are provided for dramatic play, and that such studies may prove valuable in helping the child to understand and enjoy our own heritage of song and story, science and art. Studies tracing the development of certain social customs from early times to the present, as the development of architecture, communication, transportation, and lighting, have also proved successful in developing understandings and appreciations. Choices of units of study by the children and teachers are highly desirable, since the curriculum is richer if many different types of projects are undertaken, and if enterprises vary in each grade from year to year. Thus boys and girls in each group may have an enriched experience through school assemblies and through observing exhibits and dramatizations in other rooms. Opportunities for following individual as well as group interests should be provided.

Much study of children's readiness for the various learnings listed in the following outlines has been made. Spontaneous interests in each group have been observed, and also children's responses to activities initiated by the teacher. The brief introductions to the different outlines indicate the age levels at which certain material has been found suitable. Problems related to the child's own environment are of vital interest and importance at all levels, since these can always be wholly or partly solved by firsthand investigation. Older children are ready for more complex organization and more intense and prolonged study of the questions involved. Problems relating to remote periods and places may well be postponed until the child has developed sufficient reading ability to use the library and sufficient background of real experience to interpret what he finds in books and pictures. Actual units of study which have been chosen and developed by children and teachers at various age levels are included in Part II.

Living in the Complete Modern Home

SINCE the school becomes the home of the children for many hours each day, home activities have a vital place in the school program. The school also seeks contacts with each child's real home and through parent education, endeavors to unify his experience in the school home and in the actual home. Because the modern home is often limited in space, materials and activities, it becomes increasingly necessary that the school supplement the home in providing all desirable forms of experience.

These activities begin in nursery school and kindergarten and continue with gradually expanding appreciations and skills through the elementary school. At times, the play house or doll house becomes the scene of desirable experience. Again, the school room, the school building and school ground form the background for carrying on home activities.

These include all the simple everyday acts that build the habits and attitudes, arts and skills, fundamental to good daily living.

I. Providing and maintaining a house.
1. Building the house.
2. Decorating the house.
3. Furnishing the house.
4. Care of the house—order, cleanliness, careful usage.
5. Improving the house in convenience and beauty.

II. Living in the home.
1. Provision and preparation of foods.
2. Provision and use of suitable clothing.
3. Development of proper health habits: diet, clothing, sleep, cleanliness, self-control.
4. Development of proper attitudes toward self, family, events, things.
5. Sharing of responsibilities among members of the family.

III. Social life in the home.
1. Entertainment of guests; planning parties.
2. Participating in games.
3. Visiting other people's homes.
4. Writing letters and notes to friends; receiving letters.

IV. Reading in the home.
  1. Selection of books, magazines, papers.
  2. Reading silently for personal satisfaction, and to gain information on specific problems.
  3. Reading aloud to children, older people, or for pleasure of family group.
  4. Listening to stories read or told.
  5. Discussion of books and articles read.

V. Music in the home.
  1. Selection of musical instruments; as, piano, victrola, radio.
  2. Selection of music books and records.
  3. Listening to music for enjoyment.
  4. Reproducing or composing music for personal satisfaction and for pleasure of family and friends.

VI. Creative work in language and art.
  1. Providing materials for writing, drawing, painting, and other arts.
  2. Providing and enjoying magazines, books, pictures, objects, that give inspiration and background for expression.
  3. Adding design and decoration in house furnishings and clothing.
  4. Writing and drawing to commemorate or interpret experiences.
  5. Writing and drawing for publication or for other social purposes.

VII. Plants and pets in the home.
  1. Making a garden
     a. Selection of vegetables, flowers, shrubs, trees.
     b. Planting a garden.
     c. Care of garden.
  2. Attracting birds to garden.
  3. Contact with insects in garden.
  4. Use and care of flowers and plants in home decoration.
  5. Provision for pets.
  6. Care of pets.

VIII. Adaptation to changing weather and seasons in the home.
  1. Studying causes and signs of changes in weather and seasons.
  2. Reading thermometer and hygrometer.
  3. Adapting clothing and food to weather conditions,

4. Enjoying sports for different seasons.
5. Noting effect of weather and seasons on plants and animals in garden. Providing protection and care as needed.

IX. Use of time in the home.

1. Recognition of the divisions of time, and scientific reasons.
2. Telling time by natural phenomena: sun, moon, stars.
3. Telling time by instruments: hourglass, sundial, clock, calendar.
4. Planning wise use of time, with consideration of physical needs.
5. Making records and reminders: time schedule, date book, calendar, diary.
6. Using time so that all responsibilities are discharged promptly and all appointments kept punctually.

X. Celebration of festivals in the home.

1. Searching for the meaning of each festival.
2. Continuing old traditions—jack-o'-lantern, Christmas trees, valentines, May baskets, birthday candles.
3. Enjoyment of the traditional art forms in song, story, picture, costume, decoration.
4. Expressing the meaning of the festival through creative activities.
5. Coöperating with a group in the school, church, or neighborhood in a creative art expression of the meaning of the festival.

XI. Thrift in the home.

1. Careful spending of money to secure the greatest possible value.
2. Saving for worthy purposes.
3. Generous use of whatever is available to make living most worth while.
4. Avoidance of unnecessary waste.
5. Conservation by careful usage, making needed repairs and replacements.

Living in the Modern Community

THE school is itself a small community, and many community activities are carried forward within the school. The school also develops contacts with the larger community, helping the children to learn its institutions and share with increasing understanding the responsibilities and privileges of citizenship.

Experiences in certain phases of community activity are provided in nursery school and kindergarten, and these experiences are enlarged in first and second and later grades. The historical development of the community and its institutions has been studied in the intermediate grades. A study of community planning has been of vital interest in the upper grades.

I. **Buying and selling.**
  1. Construction and furnishing of shops; as, clothing, grocery, florist, toy shop, gift shop, book shop, pottery shop, garden market.
  2. Providing capital and securing the initial stock.
  3. Organization into departments.
  4. Obtaining and arranging supplies, goods for sale.
  5. Decorating and displaying wares attractively.
  6. Making inventories.
  7. Handling of money: fixing prices, making change, making bills, keeping accounts.
  8. Advertising by means of newspapers, posters, dodgers.
  9. Coöperating with all engaged in the enterprise: owner, manager, salesperson, cashier, floorman.

II. **Transportation in the community.**
  1. Obtaining vehicles for family or community use.
  2. Assembling and repairing vehicles—providing fuel and oil.
  3. Operating vehicles:
    a. Cars for family use.
    b. Delivery wagons, trucks, freight cars and boats, for transportation of supplies.
    c. Buses, trains, boats, airplanes, streetcars, for carrying passengers.
  4. Training officers and mechanics for operating conveyances.
  5. Providing for comfort and pleasure of passengers on long trips: food, sleep, entertainment, communication.

6. Providing stopping and starting points for vehicles: garages, car barns, hangars, stations, yards, docks.
7. Developing traffic regulations and safety rules—insuring against accidents.
8. Financing public transportation.

III. Public service.
1. Organization of institutions to meet needs:
   Education—School, library, church, summer camp.
   Communication—Newspaper, printing shop, post office, telephone, telegraph, radio.
   Health—Medical and dental offices, hospital, health department.
   Sanitation and Comfort—Filtration plant, street cleaning, light and fuel plants, drainage.
   Protection—Police department, fire department, military camp, lighthouse, lifesaving station.
   Government and Finance—Town assembly, law court, bank.
2. Providing suitable buildings and equipment.
3. Choosing officers and dividing responsibilities.
4. Enlisting coöperation of citizens.
5. Studying to improve quality of service.
6. Keeping records of activities.
7. Financing these institutions.

IV. Recreation.
1. Organization of centers:
   Sports—Bathing beach, swimming or wading pool, skating rink, golf course, tennis court, stadium for games, playground, toboggan.
   Arts—Art gallery, museum, theatre, motion picture theatre, concert hall, bandstand, circus, broadcasting studio.
   Exhibits—Fair, baby show, flower show, stock show, pet show, automobile show, aviation show, parade.
2. Providing buildings and equipment.
3. Securing contributions of artists, coaches, directors, workmen.
4. Creating new art forms for public enjoyment.
5. Arranging programs, guidebooks, sporting events.
6. Participating as actor or audience.
7. Working to improve skill as performer or participant.
8. Evaluating and discriminating in choice of recreations.
9. Securing funds to support public recreation centers.

10. Securing funds through benefit entertainments to support other worthy projects.

V. Opportunities for study of nature.
1. Setting aside of centers: forest preserve, park, lake or pool, conservatory, zoo, birdhouse, aquarium, observatory, planetarium.
2. Preserving and introducing interesting varieties of plants, animals, rocks, shells.
3. Providing conditions and care for growth and propagation.
4. Observing habits and characteristics of plants and animals.
5. Sketching, photographing and recording interesting phases of plant and animal life, earth formation, and astral bodies.
6. Safeguarding natural resources while enjoying these experiences.
7. Securing funds for enlarging such opportunities in the community.

VI. Improving the community in convenience and beauty.
1. Zoning for residence, business and factory areas and for parks.
2. Laying out and widening streets and boulevards; building bridges and subways.
3. Beautifying streets and parks with trees, plants, fountains, monuments.
4. Removing any unnecessary sources of ugliness or untidiness.

Activities Involved in the Arts and Industries which Support Home and Community

KINDERGARTEN, first and second grade children often wish to investigate the industries that are carried on in the community or nearby. Unusual interest is shown in all phases of transportation. The study of the farm has proved successful when actual farm activities could be observed and could be carried on at school.

Children of the intermediate grades have traced to their sources some of the materials and products which we use daily, and have studied the development of certain modern industries from early times to the present.

I. Providing food.
1. Maintenance of sources of food supply—truck farm, fruit grove, poultry and cattle ranches, fishery, grain farms, sugar plantation, dairy farm.
2. Adapting production to natural conditions; as, climate, soil.
3. Studying plants and animals—their habits and development.
4. Developing methods of culture, propagation, using machines.
5. Studying birds and insects which help or hinder food production.
6. Keeping records and spreading information concerning plant and animal culture.
7. Studying the cycle of seasons in the country, what each season brings in beauty and in produce—interpretation of the seasons in art, music and literature.
8. Provision for workers in these situations—their duties and recreations, songs and stories.
9. Preparation of food stuffs for market—cannery, mill, factory.
10. Transportation and marketing of food stuffs.

II. Providing clothing.
1. Maintenance of sources of supply—sheep ranch, cotton plantation, fur farm, raising of silkworms, mining for silver, gold, jewels.
2. Adapting labor to natural resources and limitations.
3. Studying to improve amount and quality of production.
4. Keeping records and preparing books and magazines for spread of information.

13

5. Originating and improving processes of making cloth—weaving, dyeing; use of machinery.
6. Making jewelry: metalwork, cutting gems.
7. Making of clothing with help of designers, dressmakers, tailors, factory workers.
8. Development of fashions, styles, and patterns.
9. Financing business enterprises.

III. Providing buildings, tools, utensils.

1. Preparation of materials—lumber, glass, steel, stone, brick, plaster, china, tile, cement, rubber, paper.
2. Adventures of workers in contact with nature—forest, mine, quarry.
3. Developing processes of molding and beautifying raw materials—mill, kiln, pottery.
4. Making of plans and designs by architects, artists.
5. Practical construction by contractors, mechanics, artisans.
6. Financing building enterprises.
7. Preparation of books and magazines containing information and creative suggestions for building and decorating.
8. Studying to conserve and extend natural resources.

IV. Providing transportation.

1. Engineering of railroads, bridges, tunnels, roads, canals.
2. Construction of boats, trains, automobiles, airplanes.
3. Originating and improving means of locomotion.
4. Training of workers in technique of handling vehicles.
5. Adventures of those who control and use vehicles.
6. Making records of experiments and achievements.
7. Financing the production and running of vehicles.

V. Providing light and power.

1. Experimenting with the forces of nature,—water, coal, oil, gas, steam, electricity, radio.
2. Harnessing natural forces to provide light and power.
3. Adventures of pioneers—discovery and mastery of these forces.
4. Originating and improving machinery for various industries.
5. Keeping records and spreading information on science and invention.
6. Conserving natural resources.

Experiences of Various Peoples in Adapting to Environment

THROUGH their own vacation experiences and through hearing travel stories from parents and friends, children have become interested in studying living conditions in other parts of the world. Home and community life under varying environmental conditions has proved a fascinating study in the middle grades. One fourth grade group enjoyed an imaginary trip around the world.

I. **Types of environment to which simple independent peoples have adjusted.**
 1. Cold climates.
 2. Hot climates—deserts, jungles, volcanic regions.
 3. Temperate climates—mountains, lowlands, seaside, forest.

II. **Providing shelter, tools and utensils.**
 1. Seeking protection from natural discomforts, dangers, difficulties inherent in the geographic situation: cold, heat, storms, earthquakes, wild beasts.
 2. Discovery of available materials and forces in the environment: clay, ice, snow, reeds, skins, bones, wood, stone, fire.
 3. Experimenting with materials and adapting to meet needs peculiar to locality.
 4. Adventures in overcoming obstacles and dangers.
 5. Improving types of construction.

III. **Providing food.**
 1. Discovering edible plant and animal foods in the environment.
 2. Devising means of securing foods—hunting, trapping, fishing, digging, gathering.
 3. Adventures in hunting and foraging.
 4. Discovering ways and means of preparing foods.
 5. Domesticating plants and animals as food supply.
 6. Developing methods of culture and propagation suited to the environment: clearing, draining, irrigation, building dikes.

IV. Providing clothing.

1. Seeking bodily protection from changing weather conditions; also seeking personal adornment.
2. Discovering and using available materials in the environment—skins, foliage, grasses, feathers; also teeth, bones, shells, berries, minerals, and precious stones.
3. Systematic hunting, trapping or raising of animals; also the raising of certain plants as clothing supply.
4. Originating and improving processes of making clothing and ornament—weaving, dyeing, sewing, metalwork.
5. Developing costumes suited to the environment and occupations of the people, and reflecting racial characteristics.

V. Development of transportation.

1. Migrating because of changes in climatic conditions or exhaustion of local resources.
2. Seeking easier ways of bearing burdens and quicker means of travel.
3. Devising and developing receptacles and vehicles for carrying burdens and for traveling on water and land: vehicles carried, drawn or pushed by men, vehicles drawn or borne by animals, vehicles or vessels propelled by natural forces; as, water, wind.
4. Improving natural trails by marking, removing obstacles, shortening, leveling, bridging, dredging.
5. Adventures in learning to control and use beasts and vehicles on land and water.
6. Devising instruments to guide travel; as, maps, compass.
7. Explorations and discoveries.

VI. Developing social organization.

1. Forming groups for defense and for supply of needs: family, tribe, clan, village, state.
2. Developing traditions, customs, mores, laws, for regulating social interaction; as, trade, property, government, conservation of resources.
3. Developing ceremonials for the celebration of noteworthy events.
4. Devising methods of exchanging goods—trade, barter, monetary system, with founding of trading centers; as, post, market, shop.
5. Building for common use—meeting hall, church, fort.

VII. Developing communication and education.

1. Growth in use of speech and development of oral expression.
2. Devising signs and signals for communication.
3. Originating and improving forms of keeping and transmitting records: pictures, symbols, alphabet, figures, transcribed with suitable implements and materials.
4. Growth in written expression and in book-making.
5. Educating the young in traditions of the group and in its skills and arts.

VIII. Expression through the arts.

1. Seeking to express the meaning of experience through the various arts.
2. Making pictures to commemorate significant experiences.
3. Depicting detail in the environment through design and decoration in costumes and in household articles; as, pottery, baskets, rugs, blankets.
4. Expressing values and meanings through architectural design.
5. Creating and telling stories to commemorate interesting events, and to afford symbolic interpretation of experience— the crystallizing of many of these into permanent artistic forms.
6. Originating and using songs and dances to express emotions accompanying various experiences.
7. Development of musical instruments for the accompaniment of song and dance.
8. Originating and using games and sports to express exuberance of spirits and to develop skill in use of body.

Experiences Involved in the Discovery and Development of Our Own Country and Our Own Community

IN AN effort to understand our patriotic holidays, our American traditional stories and songs, the treasures of homespun days in our houses, the children have become curious about the development of life in America. In fourth and fifth grades studies have been made of pioneer days and the development of our own community and some other areas in the United States. A fuller study of the development of American culture has been made in the junior high school.

I. **Beginnings of our country.**
  A. *Discovery and settlement.*
    1. Seeking a shorter route to the East.
    2. Discovering the western hemisphere.
    3. Exploration to gain wealth, adventure and glory.
    4. Surmounting natural barriers and obstacles: ocean, mountains, forests, lakes, rivers.
    5. Claiming the land in the name of the mother country.
    6. Planting forts, missions and trading posts.
    7. Founding colonies to better religious, social or economic conditions.
    8. Establishing contacts with the Indians and repelling hostile attacks.

  B. *Life in colonial times.*
    1. Importation of customs, traditions, and industrial processes from the mother country.
    2. Adaptation of manner of living to the new environment—climate, topography, natural resources.
    3. Development of characteristic home life, arts, and industries, local government, and forms of worship in each colonial group.
    4. Development of devices and materials for education, and extension of educational opportunity.
    5. Service of leaders in situations of need.
    6. Influences of the colonial period in modern American life.

C. *Growth into a nation.*

1. Expansion of English possessions in the new world, and corresponding spread of English civilization.
2. Gradual growth of democratic ideas of government and consequent dissatisfaction with autocratic rule.
3. Unification of the colonists under skillful leadership in the struggle for independence and in the establishment of a democracy.
4. Winning of recognition and respect from other nations.

II. Development of our own community.

A. *Founding the community.*

1. Early explorations in this section of the country.
2. Contacts with local tribes of Indians.
3. Discovering in this locality suitable geographic features for the meeting of certain needs; as lake, harbor, river, mineral deposits, fertility of soil.
4. Building of explorers' huts, trading post, fort, mission.
5. Settling of pioneers, traveling westward, seeking new homes.
6. Hardships endured in travel and in establishing homes.
7. Solution of early problems in gaining a livelihood and protecting the community in the new environment.

B. *Expansion and change in the community.*

1. Growth in population, due to the coming of immigrants from various parts of the world, attracted by commercial and industrial opportunities.
2. Development of architecture to meet changing needs and attitudes of the people.
3. Changes in transportation by land, water, air; inventions and improvements of vehicles; construction of bridges, roads, and railroads; building of railway stations, docks, and airports; influence of improved methods of transportation on growth of the city.
4. Development of means of communication through expanding postal service, and through invention of telephone, telegraph, wireless, radio.
5. Development of natural resources and changes in geographic features; as, straightening the river, building the canal, deepening the harbor, "filling in" to increase available land, leveling.
6. Improvement and expansion of industry and commerce

through the application of growing scientific knowledge; the invention of machinery and the development of power.

7. Changes in government as the community grows from a village into a city; provision for financing public utilities.
8. Growing provision for the welfare and safety of the community; water supply, sanitation, light and fuel supply, police and fire protection.
9. Changes in education and growth in educational facilities.
10. Development of institutions for the unfortunate; as, hospitals, settlements, homes for the needy.
11. Increase in the standard of living and the amount of leisure, with consequent expansion of recreational facilities; as, parks, playgrounds, theatres, museums.
12. Contributions of gifted citizens in art, music, literature, science.

C. *Looking forward.*

1. Recognition of possibilities for future growth in commerce, industry, education, and other fields.
2. Effort to solve the city's problems; as, traffic congestion, accidents, smoke, noise, ugliness and untidiness.
3. Creative planning for a "city beautiful."

III. **Development of different sections of the country and their contributions: the South, the East, the Middle West, the Far West.**

A. *Story of each section.*

1. Exploring and acquiring the territory.
2. Settlement by people of various nationalities, attracted by natural resources and favorable geographic factors; as, climate, soil, topography, mineral deposits.
3. Development of avenues of transportation; as, trails, roads, canals, railways, highways, air routes.
4. Improvement of vehicles from early times to present: wagons, boats, automobiles, trains, airplanes.
5. Adventures of pioneers in various fields of activity, influencing expansion and growth.

B. *Modes of living and contributions of each section.*

1. Utilization of climate, topography and soil in the production of typical crops; as, cotton, fruit, grain.
2. Selecting and propagating animals suited to the region; as, sheep, bees, fish.

3. Obtaining raw materials from regional sources of supply: lumber, coal, iron, oil, tin, copper, zinc, gold, silver.
4. Development of industries, transforming the raw products of the section.
5. Utilization of transportation facilities in' importing and exporting raw products and manufactured goods.
6. Use of power resources in the section and development of machinery.
7. Conservation and extension of natural resources.
8. Modes of living and characteristics of the people influenced by climate, occupations and relative wealth.
9. Growth of cities and reasons for this growth in geographic factors and type of service rendered.
10. Expression of attitudes and appreciations in the arts: characteristic stories, songs, architecture, beauty in manufactured products.

C. *Interdependence and interchange of ideas of people in different sections.*
1. Growing specialization and dependence of each region upon others for products.
2. Constantly increasing ease and rapidity of communication: mail service, telegraph, telephone, radio, daily papers, moving and talking pictures.
3. Continued improvement of transportation facilities and growing use of these: national conventions, traveling business agencies, sight-seeing tours.
4. Sharing and conserving the nation's playgrounds: ocean and lake resorts, national parks, scenic wonders.
5. Sharing the benefits and responsibilities of national government.
6. Common responsibilities in helping to solve national problems; as, education, public health, taxation, coöperation with law.

Experiences Involved in the Development of the Modern World and the Contribution of Certain Peoples to Civilization

IN THE upper grades, boys and girls have shown a growing interest in current events, with which they have become acquainted through the radio, daily and weekly newspapers, news reels in motion picture programs, and discussions in their homes. This interest has led to a desire to learn more about certain foreign countries and their relations to our country and to one another.

At the sixth grade level and in junior high school some countries have been chosen for detailed study, with stress upon their contribution to our own civilization.

I. **Various continents and countries that have influenced modern civilization:**

   1. Countries or city-states famous for early contributions to present civilization; as, Egypt, Palestine, Greece, Rome, China.
   2. Countries that have exercised leadership in medieval and modern times; as, Great Britain, France, Germany, Italy, Spain, Japan, Russia.
   3. Younger countries that are at present contributing; as, Canada, Mexico, South American countries.

II. **Story of the country.**

   1. Influence of natural conditions and resources upon development: location, climate, topography, soil, mineral resources.
   2. Characteristics of people as determined by ancestral background and environment.
   3. Exploits of heroes in dramatic incidents or episodes.
   4. Activities of great leaders and their influence in shaping destiny.
   5. Changes in occupations and modes of living at different periods.

III. **Economic contributions.**

   1. Raising crops and animal products peculiar to that region; as, flax, coffee, rubber, rice.

2. Mining and quarrying of minerals and stones; as, marble, diamonds.
3. Manufacturing of articles of beauty and utility characteristic of the country; as, Italian leather, Swiss watches, Japanese silks, Persian rugs.
4. Work of scientists and inventors in forwarding progress; as, Marconi of Italy, James Watt of England.

IV. Cultural contributions.
1. Development of dances, games and sports expressive of the environment and characteristics of the people.
2. Development of the stage and drama; work of famous actors.·
3. Expression in literature: folk lore, classic and modern compositions.
4. Evolution of musical forms and instruments; service of artists in rendering and composing music.
5. Evolution of traditions, customs, fashions; as, celebration of festivals, design in costume, social courtesies and conventions.
6. Creative work in architecture, painting, sculpture.

V. Interdependence and interchange of ideas between nations.
1. Exchange of products through exports and imports.
2. Intermingling of people through emigration and immigration.
3. Sharing of art treasures through reproduction and exchange.
4. Appreciation of cultural contributions and natural beauty through travel.
5. Interchange of ideas through various means of communication: books, plays, magazines, newspapers, radio, cable, postal service, moving and talking pictures.

PART II

Some Typical Units of Experience

DEVELOPING AND RECORDING GROUP ENTERPRISES

Selecting the Problems

THE Staff of the Children's School, working as a curriculum committee, have, after considerable experiment and study, selected tentatively certain large aims and certain large areas of experience which seem appropriate at different age levels. Specific enterprises, however, are selected and planned by the teachers and the children together. Outstanding interests in the community, children's vacation experiences, problems that arise in the homes, all influence the selection and trends of particular units of experience. The teacher studies the records of previous enterprises in which these children have engaged, and also the records of successful projects carried on by other groups of children at this age level; and she endeavors to provide experiences which will lead the children into studies rich in values for their development.

The teachers of the youngest children provide orientation by arranging excursions and introducing suggestive pictures, stories and materials. Problems usually arise one at a time as the children work and talk together.

As the children grow older, they assist not only in selecting the unit, but in making the preliminary plans. They suggest excursions, list questions, collect books, pictures and other materials; and often initiate experiments and constructive activities. Usually the group divides itself into small groups or committees for certain phases of the work, and each child is helped to choose the group where he can work effectively.

The length of time spent upon any enterprise depends upon the continuance of keen interest on the part of the children, and the unfolding of valuable new problems and new forms of expression as the work progresses.

Classroom Enterprises

Observation and analysis of what actually occurs in carrying on a unit of experience has led to the organization of the outline form

27

used here. Any successful unit of learning is preceded and accompanied by certain enriching experiences which rouse and foster
interest and give background for various types of activity. These
experiences may include excursions, collection and exhibit of illustrative materials, study of photographs, films and slides, and recall
of past experiences of members of the group gained through social
contacts, travel, and other opportunities.

As the children enjoy these shared experiences, certain questions
arise which lead to pursuit of further and more detailed information. These questions may be listed at the beginning of the unit
by the teacher and the group, or they may arise one at a time
as the class works together. The solution of these problems may
involve oral discussion, study of books for added facts, and constructive activities for the purpose of experiment and illustration.

In the kindergarten and primary grades, construction is often
of supreme importance and may be the starting point of the whole
enterprise. Many of the problems that arise at this level are practical problems in construction, and their solution involves discussion,
observation, experiment, and use of the picture-story library, with
the teacher as guide and interpreter. In almost every enterprise
at every age level, arithmetic is needed to give more accurate information concerning size, time and distance, and to aid in construction and dramatization.

As knowledge and experience grow, attitudes and appreciations
are acquired that relate to the subject of study, and these attitudes
and appreciations find expression in the arts. The skilful teacher
introduces appropriate songs, poems and dances from her art collections, and the child finds expression in the reproduction of
these forms. Often as the work proceeds, there is a spontaneous
blossoming into picture-making or into composition of original
song or verse or story.

With the kindergarten-primary children, the climax of the
project is often dramatic play, making use of the buildings and
equipment that have been constructed. With older children, the
final expression may be a sharing of experiences with others,
through dramatization, assembly program, gift-giving or a room
exhibit of constructive and creative work. If the enterprise has

been valuable, new interests have arisen which suggest other lines of activity or new topics of study.

In a school year, at every level, many interests arise, which may involve only one child or a group of two or three. It is perhaps desirable to record in detailed fashion only units in which a fairly large group of children take part, in which the time covers several days or weeks, and the outcomes in child development are significant. No detailed units of learning occur in the nursery school or junior kindergarten. These children tend to work individually or in small groups, and any social enterprises which are undertaken, are short-lived and fragmentary. Beginning with the five-year-old kindergarten, group enterprises grow in organization and duration, as the children show greater social readiness.

The units of experience in this volume were recorded first in parallel column form, and later for convenience in reading and printing were recast into outline form. The worth of an outline form like the one used here, is that it enables the teacher to compare different units for possibilities and values. The danger of a set form of recording is that it may encourage a forced correlation which represents no fundamental need or relationship. It will seldom occur that every type of activity is linked up with a particular unit of experience, and certainly the form of art expression will depend on the attitudes and capacities of the individuals within the group, and may vary with different children and different topics of study.

The units of experience which follow were developed in two or three different years. It is hoped that in each successive year many new units of learning will be developed, reflecting the varying interests of the children and the outstanding new developments in the community. If certain units are occasionally repeated, these should be expanded and enriched by the growing experience and continued study of the teacher, and the suggestions and questions of each new group of children.

SCHOOL ENTERPRISES

In addition to projects in each grade, there have been some enterprises in which the whole school participated. The building

THANKSGIVING BRINGS FRESH GIFTS AND OLD TALES

up of the Children's Library has been a common goal which has captivated the interest of both parents and children. Library Gift Day was planned by mothers, children and teachers together, and gave everyone who wished the opportunity to join in a processional bearing books to the Library. Mothers with the coöperation of local bookstores and the school librarian, sold desirable books at the school, and children from their individual savings made their own selections of books to give.

At Thanksgiving all the children have joined in a processional bearing harvest gifts for a settlement nursery school, and at Christmas several groups have coöperated in a festival to which parents have been invited. A gift of toys and puzzles for the Children's Memorial Hospital was an enterprise in the workshop which interested the children from several grades. A song and rhythm assembly in the spring, and a field day of games and sports events have been enjoyed by boys and girls of various age levels.

UNITS OF EXPERIENCE IN KINDERGARTEN

MAINTAINING an environment and a program suitable for promoting and retaining both physical and mental health, is one of the first considerations of the kindergarten. A comfortable, happy atmosphere, free from tension and strain yet stimulating to thought, action, and all-round growth, is considered to be of utmost importance. Other objectives of the kindergarten have been, to help the children to understand better their own immediate environment, and to provide the opportunity for social living in a way acceptable in the worthy modern home and community. The children have in the main initiated their own enterprises, guided by materials, pictures, stories and conversations. The interest in construction and dramatic play has been encouraged by the availability of large floor blocks, workbenches and tools, large materials of many kinds for use in art and industrial enterprises, and ample space for freedom of bodily movement.

Transportation has frequently been a center of interest. The keen interest in all phases of transportation is explained by the school environment. The school is situated just one block from Lake Michigan, where small boats of many sorts may be seen at any time of the year. In front of the school is Sheridan Road, the favorite lake-shore drive between Chicago and Fort Sheridan. Two large airports are located in the vicinity, and stations for steam and electric railway systems are only a few blocks away. The children's individual experience records show that many of them have traveled extensively. In each group several have traveled by airplane, and most of them have taken trips by boat, automobile and train. Three units of experience dealing with transportation are included in this volume, and all of these occurred in a single year.

There has been a continuing interest also in activities related to nature. The community is one of homes and gardens, with many parks available, and forest preserves and farms not far distant. The seasons and the festivals have had their share in suggesting activities. A few short units of experience dealing with nature problems are

31

included in this volume. The raising of animal families has been of special interest.

A corner equipped with a few pieces of playhouse furniture and some durable dolls has been available for housekeeping activities, and playing house has also been a live interest. Frequently the house has been combined with transportation projects, and has been the point of departure for journeys by land, air and sea.

Much of the activity in kindergarten occurs in small groups. Usually several centers of interest may be noted at one time. The units of experience described in this section interested the entire group at times.

Outcomes in social meanings and appreciations peculiar to each unit are included with the unit. All of the experiences described have afforded opportunity for growth in desirable social attitudes and habits; as, coöperation in making plans and solving problems, consideration for others, respect for the opinions of others, appreciation of the need for dependability, willingness to give and take helpful suggestions, joy in individual and group successes. These experiences have also afforded opportunity for growth in expression in the various arts and for an awakening interest in the attainment of certain needed skills. Outcomes in terms of certain arts and skills are summarized under Group Records of Progress, in Part IV.

Raising Animal Families

A Series of Experiences in Senior Kindergarten

I. **Enriching experiences which roused and fostered interest.**
  A. One child whose father was a physician brought white rats to school from the hospital laboratories.
  B. The teacher encouraged bringing any form of animal life to school, which resulted in a variety of fish, insects, snails, turtles, caterpillars, and household pets being present in the schoolroom from time to time.
  C. Children were encouraged to handle and observe these as much as possible.
  D. Teachers provided rabbits, guinea pigs, canaries, and a hen at various times.

II. **Some of the questions which led to investigation.**
  A. Where shall we keep our various animals?
  B. What kind of shelter will they need? Size? Materials?
  C. Who will take care of them?
  D. What do they eat?
  E. Where will we get the food?
  F. How do the tracks of the various pets differ?
  G. Why do hens and canaries need gravel?
  H. How long does it take for the eggs to hatch?
  I. How can we keep an accurate account of the days?
  J. Where are the young before birth?
  K. Why must the male be removed to another cage (in some cases)?
  L. What shall we do with the young?

III. **Finding solution of problems and answers to questions.**
  A. Through experience.
    1. Playing with the animals indoors and out.
    2. Watching their habits.
    3. Excursions to the country to learn from farmers.
    4. Caring for animals.
    5. Opening a hen's egg from time to time to see what was happening.
    6. Opening a cocoon to see the chrysalis.
    7. Gathering clover, digging worms, and so on, to obtain food for pets.

CHICKENS ARE AMUSING FRIENDS

B. Through constructive activities.
1. Making pens and shelters.
2. Making carriers to take pets back and forth to school.
3. Making feed boxes.
C. Through books.
1. Older children searched through picture books for suggestions concerning shelters.
2. Teacher read extracts from government bulletins.

Picture and Story Books for Children and Teachers

Barlow, Ruth C.	Fun At Happy Acres	1935	Crowell
Bianco, Margery	All About Pets	1929	Macmillan
Bianco, Margery	The Good Friends	1934	Viking
Ets, Marie Hall	Mr. Penny	1935	Viking
Gág Wanda	A. B. C. Bunny	1933	Coward-McCann
Howard, Constance	The Twins and Tabiffa	1923	Macrae Smith
Kunhardt, Dorothy	Little Ones	1935	Viking
Lathrop, Dorothy	Who Goes There?	1935	Macmillan
Lord, Isabel	Picture Book of Animals	1931	Macmillan
Newbery, Clare T.	Mittens	1936	Harper
Piper, Watty	Animal Friends Story Book	1928	Platt & Munk

Picture Books

Book of Animals	Saalfield Pub. Co (Illustrations by C. M. Burd)
Friends of Fur and Feather	Samuel Gabriel and Sons
The Second Picture Book of Animals	(Photographs) Macmillan

References for Teachers

Comstock, Anna B. Handbook of Nature Study 1939 Comstock

Russell, David W. Suggestions for the Care of Pets in the Elementary Classroom. Reprinted from School Science and Mathematics, April 1939. (Bulletins from the United States Department of Agriculture, Washington, D. C., proved most up-to-date and reliable for authentic information.)

D. Through discussions concerning:
1. Differences and similarities in young rats, guinea pigs, rabbits.
2. Differences and similarities in nests of canaries and chickens.
3. Differences and similarities in eggs of canaries and chickens.
4. Methods and materials of constructing shelters.
5. Undue handling of the young.
6. Disposition to be made of the young.

E. Through use of numbers.
1. Use of rulers by some children to measure wood for pens and shelters.
2. Counting days before the arrival of the young to find the date, and checking these off the calendar.
3. Some slight attention to cost, to justify the sale of the young.

IV. Social meanings, attitudes, and appreciations gained through the experiences.
A. Knowledge of the importance of care in:
1. Providing food and water.
2. Shelter.
3. Cleanliness.

B. Interest in providing these.

C. Realization of our dependence on sources of information, such as farmer, science teacher, printed material.

D. Appreciation of the joy which pets bring.

E. Information concerning reproduction.

F. Wholesome attitude toward process of reproduction.

V. Interpretation and expression of attitudes and appreciations.
A. Through story telling.
1. Many creative stories were told by the children.

2. Stories of pets (see list above), were told by the teacher.
B. Through picture making and clay modelling.
1. Paintings and drawings were made of various pets.
2. Clay was an especially good material for expression.
C. Through music.
1. Some creative songs were sung by individuals.
2. Songs were used also from the teacher's collection.
D. Through dramatization.
1. Rhythmic expression, (such as rabbits hopping), was supplemented by music.
2. Loosely organized dramatic play, not especially rhythmic in nature, was enjoyed from time to time.
E. Through poetry.
Such collections were used as:

Baruch, Dorothy	I Like Animals	1933 Harper
Lear, Edward	The Alphabet Book	- 1915 Reilly & Lee
Untermeyer, Louis	Rainbow in the Sky	1935 Harcourt, Brace

Traveling by Train

A Center of Interest in Senior Kindergarten

I. **Enriching experiences which roused interest and provided background for activities.**
   A. The interest grew out of the contribution of one child who had just had his first experience of riding on a train. His enthusiasm for his trip to New York on "The Century" spread to the group with the result that a large train was built of the Hill floor blocks.
   B. As many of our children go by motor when traveling, we found that some of the group had never had any train experience. We asked that they be given that experience even though it could be only a ride on the suburban train into Chicago. The parents responded very well to our request and made the most of the opportunity to show the children the engine, coal car, and other parts of a train.
   C. Pictures of trains of all kinds, interiors of sleeping cars, parlor cars, diners, helped provide background.

II. **Problems and questions which led to experiment and investigation. Many questions arose which necessitated our asking questions of the fathers and using encyclopedias.**
   A. Of what use is the sand dome? The steam dome?
   B. Why did the older types of engines have tall stacks and new ones low stacks?
   C. Why must trains have water?
   D. How do trains on long runs "pick up" water?
   E. How long is the run for an engineer on a train?
   F. When is the bell used?
   G. When is the whistle blown?
   H. What do the different uses of the whistle mean?
   I. Why do some trains have automatic stokers?
   J. What do different colored signals mean?
   K. Where do trains go when they are not making a run?
   L. How does a turntable operate?
   M. Why are electric engines sometimes used?
   N. When does the train crew eat and sleep?
   O. How are the Pullman seats made into beds?

III. **Finding solution of problems and answers to questions.**
   A. Through correlative construction.
      1. The interest centered about the construction of a large

37

SERVICE IS GOOD ON THIS TRAIN

train made of the Hill blocks. The engine, coal car and one passenger car comprised the original train. Each day as dramatic play developed there was need for more detail. More cars were added—a Pullman car, diner and baggage car.

2. Blocks proved unsatisfactory as seats. Kindergarten chairs were substituted. Light weight boards (12 inches by 3 feet) were used across the chairs in the Pullman.

3. The doll dishes were used in the diner.

4. A station and ticket office were made after the play had continued for two weeks.

B. Through conversation.

Many conversations in small groups and in the whole group took place concerning the train. Each day brought new problems for discussion. There was much freedom of verbal expression in the discussions. The children sought information at home and made valuable contributions to the group on their findings.

C. Through use of books.

The children gained a feeling for the use of books which would give necessary information. While the teachers did the reading and interpreted what was read, the children had the experience of going to the library to get the books and seeing them used.

Picture and Story Books for Children and Teacher

Kuh, Charlotte	The Engineer	1929	Macmillan
Lent, H. B.	Clear Track Ahead!	1932	Macmillan
Pryor, W. C.	The Train Book	1933	Harcourt
Read, Helen S.	An Engine's Story	1928	Scribner
Smith, E. B.	The Railway Book	1925	Samuel Gabriel

Books for the Teacher

Dalgliesh, Alice	America Travels	1933	Macmillan
Eaton, J.	The Story of Transportation	1927	Harper
Henry, R. S.	Trains	1938	Bobbs-Merrill
Reed, Brian	Railway Engines of the World	1934	Oxford
Van Metre, T. B.	Trains, Tracks and Travel	1931	Simmons-Boardman
Webster, H. H.	Travel by Air, Land and Sea	1933	Houghton

Selected material from Compton's Pictured Encyclopedia and the World Book Encyclopedia.

D. Through use of number.
  1. Time entered in to a small degree. Trains run on scheduled time, and the children gained some feeling for the necessity of promptness.
  2. The problem of too many children for the number of seats came up from time to time.

IV. **Social meanings, attitudes and appreciations developing through these experiences.**
  A. A spirit of coöperation developed as the children shared duties in constructing and operating the train.
  B. An appreciation was gained for the responsibility placed upon the train crew—their interest in the comfort and safety of the passengers.
  C. Knowledge was gained concerning the members of the train crew and the duties of each one.
  D. Understanding and appreciation developed for the various functions of trains and their importance; in carrying passengers, in transporting mail, in shipping provisions to our cities—milk, fruit, vegetables, cattle.
  E. Knowledge was gained of the construction and use of different parts of a train and different kinds of cars; as, engine, coal car, caboose, baggage car, diner, sleeping car, parlor car, oil car, cattle car, mail car.

F. Appreciation developed for the importance of punctuality in running and using trains.

V. Expression and interpretation of attitudes and appreciations.
  A. Through literature.
    Selections were enjoyed from these sources:

Piper, Walty	The Little Engine That Could	1930 Platt
Tippett, James	I Go A-Traveling	1929 Harper

  B. Through picture-making.
    The interest was richly expressed through drawing, painting and through paper cutting and paste work:
    1. Many children did individual drawings and paintings of trains, stations, water tanks, gates at crossing and like subjects.
    2. A few group paintings were made, using four or five full sheets of unprinted newspaper pasted together. This was fastened to the blackboard with adhesive tape. Four or five children worked together on these group pictures, doing coöperative planning, as to what should go into each picture and what part each person should paint.
    3. Several group drawings were made on the blackboard in like manner.
  C. Through music.
    1. The development of train play through rhythmic activity was interesting to note. At first the children were merely trains running at great speed down the tracks. Gradually more organization came into their play: the slow pulling out of the train from the station, the gain in speed and then the slowing down to stop. Music was helpful in supplementing the children's mood and in controlling the play.
    2. Two original songs were created, which were jotted down by the teacher, and given back to the group, and became favorite songs to sing. "The Train Song" from Singing Time by Thorne and Coleman was also used.
  D. Through dramatic play.
    A wealth of dramatic play was carried on each day.
    1. The serving of meals in the diner, the going to bed, the firing of the boiler, the taking of tickets, all came up in the play of each day.
    2. Dolls were taken traveling. There was desirable inter-

play between the doll corner and the train. The engineer and the conductor would go "home" to the doll corner when they were not on their runs.

VI. New interests.

Other means of travel (boats, busses, automobiles and airplanes) were discussed, and were possibilities for future activity.

Traveling by Boat

A Center of Interest in Senior Kindergarten

I. **Enriching experiences which aroused interest and provided background for activities.**

    A. Many pictures were used to help clarify ideas and to provide background. Several parents sent photographs of different kinds of boats.

    B. Excursion to Wilmette harbor gave information about small boats, yachts, motorboats and speedboats.

    C. A trip to the lighthouse enriched ideas of the size and construction of a lighthouse.

    D. One child brought a real compass which opened up a new line of interest in how a captain can find his directions.

II. **Some of the questons which led to investigation.**

    A. What is meant by such terms as: stern, prow, bridge, pilot or wheelhouse, decks, gangplank, anchors, dry dock, crow's-nest, mast, funnel, ventilators, ship's log, captain's flag, buoy, Union Jack, waterline?

    B. How is a ship loaded?

    C. Why are there portholes?

    D. Why are there numbers down near the waterline?

    E. How can sailors tell when a ship is nearing an iceberg?

    F. How do ships send messages?

    G. What does "S.O.S." mean?

    H. How does the captain signal the engine room that the ship is ready to sail?

    I. How does a captain recognize different lighthouses?

    J. How does the fog horn "work"?

    K. What is the principle on which a compass is made?

    L. Why can some ships go faster than others?

    M. Of what are life belts made? How are they adjusted?

III. **Finding solution of problems and answers to questions.**

    A. Through correlative construction.

        1. A boat was built with floor blocks. Boards, boxes and scraps of beaver board were also used.

        2. A Union Jack and captain's flag were added.

        3. A pilot wheel was made and placed so that it could be turned.

THE WIND IS NORTH BY EAST

    4. A lighthouse was built. Colored paper was used over the light to designate which lighthouse it was.

    5. A few children made small boats at the workbench.

B. Through conversations.

    1. There was a wealth of discussion relating to experiences on boats.

    2. Discussion of pictures, excursions, experiments, films, enjoyed by the group, helped to answer questions.

Picture Books for Children

Lent, H. B.	Full Steam Ahead!	1933 Macmillan
Read, H. S.	A Story About Boats	1928 Scribner

Teacher's References

Pamphlets

    Cunard Lines

    French Line—Sectional View of a Great Liner

    Smithsonian Institution—Bulletin No. 127—Catalog of Watercraft Collection

Books

Jackson, O. P. & Evans, F. E.	Book of American Ships	1926 Stokes
Rocheleau, W. F.	Transportation	1928 A. Flanagan
Van Metre, T. W.	Tramps and Liners	1931 Doubleday
Webster, H. H.	Travel by Air, Land and Sea	1933 Houghton

Selected material from Compton's Pictured Encyclopedia and World Book Encyclopedia.

Films

"Queen of the Waves," American Museum of Natural History, New York City

C. Through use of number.

1. A decided interest developed in the use of thermometers in reading the temperature of water for detecting icebergs. This led into a short study of temperature.

2. Interest in numbers at the prow of the ship led to some understanding of the loading and the weight carried on board.

3. The number of passengers was counted following a discussion in which the children learned that each ship has a maximum capacity.

IV. **Social meanings, attitudes and appreciations developed through these experiences.**

A. A fine attitude of coöperation in the play on the ship; in taking turns as captain, mates, mechanics.

B. Knowledge and appreciation of "marine ethics": signaling of another ship; response to calls for help; need for teamwork on the part of a crew as well as coöperation with other crews when need arises.

C. Recognition and appreciation of characteristics of a good captain: steadiness, carefulness, skill, courage.

D. Some knowledge and appreciation of shipbuilding.

E. Recognition of various kinds of boats and different parts of a boat.

V. **Interpretation and expression of attitudes and appreciations.**

A. Through literature.

1. Several original realistic stories were told by children and teachers.

2. These stories and verses were also found interesting:

Goodwin, Myra A.	The Lighthouse Keeper's Daughter
Mitchell, Lucy Sprague	Fog Boat Story
Read, Helen	Story About Boats
Tippett, James	I Go A-Traveling

B. Through picture-making.
1. Pictorial expression was a source of great joy throughout the interest. Incidental drawings of boats, lighthouses, buoys, bridges were made, and also several large group paintings of boats.
2. Large boat posters were made.
C. Through music.
These songs were favorites:

> "A Song of Ships," One Hundred and Forty Folk-Songs, Davison and Surette.
> (This was sung to the children for appreciation, but the swing and rhythm caught their interest and they learned it.)
> "I Had a Little Sail-boat," One Hundred and Forty Folk-Songs, Davison and Surette.

D. Through dramatic activity. This interest offered great outlet in a dramatic way. Every day there was rich dramatic play on the boat: pilot steering ship; mechanics fixing machinery; passengers riding on ship, disembarking.

VI. New interests foreshadowing further activities.
A. Other means of transportation.
B. Other types of boats.

Traveling in the Air

A Center of Interest in Senior Kindergarten

I. **Enriching experiences which aroused interest and provided back-ground for activities.**
   A. A visit to the airport enriched our background and did a great deal in sustaining the interest in aviation. The group spent the morning at the field and saw planes going and coming, taxiing, landing, and banking curves. The children were allowed in the hangar and had a close view of many different kinds of planes.
   B. Some of the children had attended aviation shows with their parents.
   C. Children brought toy planes to school.
   D. Several children had airplane trips during the summer. The relating of their experiences promoted great interest.

II. **Some of the questions which led to investigation.**
   A. Why do some planes have more than one motor?
   B. Why do some planes have one wing and others two?
   C. What kind of fuel does a plane use?
   D. How is an airplane "wound up"?
   E. What is the purpose of such things as: stabilizer, flipper wings, coils on the motor, wind determiner, the "boats"?
   F. What is the fuselage? Why is it shaped like a bird?
   G. Why do pilots wear goggles and helmets at times?
   H. How can a pilot do such things as:
      1. Tell the direction of the wind at night?
      2. Distinguish different fields at night?
      3. Make the plane "bank" when turning a curve?
      4. Know where he is going if he can't see land?
   I. What is the purpose of beacons?
   J. What is done in towns to help pilots tell what town they are passing?
   K. What do the colored lights on planes mean?
   L. How does it look above the clouds?
   M. Why are planes made in different shapes?

III. **Finding solution of problems and answers to questions.**
   A. Through correlative construction.
      1. Airplanes were built with floor blocks.
      2. Small airplanes of wood were made at the workbench.

46

Photographed at the Municipal Airport, Chicago

WATCHING MECHANICS INSTALL A MOTOR IN A TRANSPORT PLANE

3. Some children enjoyed making airplanes of clay.
There was a steady gain in constructive work. New phases
were added and work improved through discussion and
study of pictures. The children themselves commented upon
the improvement shown in the small wooden airplanes.
  B. Through conversations.
    1. The subject was most conducive to valuable language ex-
      pression. Every child was full of the interest and there-
      fore talked freely. The children told of their experiences
      in seeing planes and riding in them.
    2. Pictures and toy models were discussed.

Teacher's References

Pamphlets:

Fairchild Aviation Corporation   Plain Facts for Plain People
Smithsonian Institution   Handbook of National Aircraft
    Collection

Books:

Driggs, L.	Heroes of Aviation	1927 Little, Brown
Floherty, J. J.	'Board the Airliner	1934 Doubleday
Fraser, C. C.	Heroes of the Air	1927 Crowell
Fraser, C. C.	Model Aircraft Builder	1931 Crowell
Post, A.	Skycraft	1933 Oxford
Thomson, Jay E.	Aviation Stories	1929 Longmans, Green
Webster, H. H.	Travel by Air, Land and Sea	1933 Houghton

C. Through use of number.

There was an interest in counting such things as seats in a plane, cylinders, windows.

IV. **Social meanings, attitudes and appreciations developed through these experiences.**

A. Recognition and appreciation of the fact that one must be thoroughly trained for one's job.

B. Recognition and appreciation of the necessity of being dependable. Mechanic must be sure that all is well with the plane before it takes off.

C. Attitude of respect for mail pilots who fly through all kinds of weather to serve the public.

D. Knowledge and appreciation of the piloting of a plane and the qualities which a pilot must possess.

E. Knowledge of the most important facts regarding airplane construction.

F. Some understanding of the purpose and need of maps.

G. Recognition of various kinds of planes and the different parts of a plane.

V. **Interpretation and expression of attitudes and appreciations.**

A. Through literature.

These stories and verses were enjoyed by the children:

Page, Victor	A. B. C. of Aviation
Read, Helen	An Airplane Ride
Tippett, James	My Airplane
	(From I Go A-Traveling)

B. Through creative composition.

The children created some stories about airplanes, based on their own experiences; as,

Monday we went to the airport.
We saw airplanes.

We saw monoplanes.
We saw biplanes.
It was fun when we went to the airport.

. . . .

Airplanes fly at the airport.
They fly through the rain.
They fly through the fog.
They fly through the clouds.
I would like to fly.

C. Through picture-making.
   1. There was much interest in pictorial expression. Several group paintings (involving three or four children) of the airport were created. There were many individual drawings and paintings of planes, hangars, beacons, pilots.
   2. Scrapbooks were made containing cut-out pictures of different kinds of airplanes.
D. Through dramatic activity.
   1. There was a wealth of dramatic play with pilots carrying passengers in their airplanes of large blocks. Dolls were taken for rides. Dramatic feeling ran high in the thrills of air pockets, tail spins, and other adventures.
   2. Children played with small wooden airplanes. Landing fields of blocks were the scene of planes taxiing, landing, taking off.

VI. New interest foreshadowing further activities.

An interest was shown in other forms of air transportation: balloons and gliders.

Playing with the Leaves

An Interest in Senior Kindergarten

I. Enriching experiences which roused and fostered interest.
   A. Excursions were made about the neighborhood to gather leaves and to observe the outstanding differences of the most common trees (five or six in all).
   B. Excursions were made in the spring to see the bursting of buds.
   C. Branches from bushes were brought in to watch the leaves come out, when these were put in water.

II. Some of the questions which led to investigation.
   A. Why do leaves fall?
   B. Why do some trees keep their leaves all winter?
   C. What makes leaves turn different colors?
   D. Why do some trees stay green all winter?
   E. What makes the new leaves grow?
   F. How may falling leaves be used: for fun? for the garden?
   G. What kinds of trees grow in our own gardens?
   H. How do they differ in shape, size and color of leaf?

III. Answering questions.
   A. Through constructive activities.
      1. Hats of colored leaves were made to wear for a "leaf dance."
      2. Leaves were mounted on tagboard.
      3. A few children enjoyed making blueprints of leaves.
   B. Through conversation.
      1. There was much discussion as to how leaves are used: to furnish shade, to cover gardens, to make homes and gardens beautiful.
      2. The children talked about the kinds of trees, their shapes, the kinds and colors of leaves.
      3. Questions were asked and discussion ensued about the causes of the changing colors and the falling of leaves.
      4. The children wished to keep the pretty leaves, and there was discussion about ways to preserve them. Plans were made for a room collection.
      5. There was some discussion of pictures and informational material which were found in the school library, and interpreted to the group by the teacher.

Teacher's References

Comstock, Anna B.	Handbook of Nature Study	1939 Comstock
Downing, Elliot R.	Our Living World	1928 Longmans, Green
Emerson, A. I. & Weed, J. B.	Our Trees	1937 Lippincott
Farquhar, F. F. and others	World·Book Encyclopedia	1936 Quarrie
Ford, A. S., and others	Compton's Pictured Encyclopedia	1938 Compton
Hough, Romeyn B.	Handbook of the Trees	1924 Romeyn B. Hough

IV. **Social meanings, attitudes, appreciations, developed through these experiences.**

   A. Recognition of leaves of a few common trees.

   B. Some understanding of the cycle of growth from spring to fall.

   C. Appreciation of the value of leaves in providing shade, making gardens and parks beautiful, covering the garden in winter.

   D. An understanding that leaves and branches must not be taken from trees on private property.

V. **Interpretation and expression of attitudes and appreciations.**

   A. Through picture-making.
      A few children were interested in drawing different kinds of leaves.

   B. Through songs and rhythm.
      Songs about leaves were enjoyed, and a leaf dance was created.

   C. Through social activity.
      There was much delightful activity in raking and playing in the leaves.

Helping the Birds

An Interest in Senior Kindergarten

I. **Enriching experiences which roused and fostered interest.**
   A. The children were interested in the mating of the kindergarten canaries. They saw the nest put into the cage, and watched the mother and father carry material to line the nest.
   B. The return of the wild birds was a source of delight.
   C. Excursions were arranged about the neighborhood to see birds, birds' nests and birdhouses.
   D. Colored pictures of common birds were enjoyed.

II. **Some of the questions which led to investigation.**
   A. Why do some birds live in houses and some in nests?
   B. Why do some birds like to live in colonies?
   C. What decides the size of the hole?
   D. What materials do the various birds use in making their nests?
   E. Why don't all birds' eggs hatch?
   F. What do birds need besides nesting materials?

III. **Finding answers to problems and questions.**
   A. Through constructive activities.
      1. Cloth and string were cut up for the canaries' nest.
      2. Birdhouses were built.
   B. Through conversation.
      1. The children talked about the birds they had seen, their habits and ways of living, nests that birds had built in their own yards, birdhouses and bird baths in neighboring yards.
      2. The eggs in the canaries' nest formed a topic of question and discussion.
      3. Problems arising in the making of birdhouses were discussed.
   C. Through use of books.
      1. The names of the more common birds were used in connection with the pictures.
      2. Extracts from bird guides were read to the children, giving outstanding facts about our common birds.
      3. Directions for making birdhouses were found in "The Birdhouse Book," put out by the Boy Scouts.

Teacher's References

Allen, A. A.	The Book of Bird Life	1930 Van Nostrand
Baynes, E. H.	Wild Bird Guests	1931 Dutton
Blanchan, Neltje	The Bird Book	1932 Doubleday
Comstock, Anna B.	Handbook of Nature Study	1939 Comstock
King, Julius	Birds	1934 Harter
Pearson, T. G.	Birds of America	1936 Garden City
Peterson, R. T.	Junior Book of Birds	1939 Houghton
Compton's Pictured Encyclopedia		1940 Compton
World Book Encyclopedia		1940 Quarrie

D. Through use of number.
  1. The ruler was used to measure wood for the birdhouses. A few of the children were able to measure independently.
  2. The calendar was used in order to keep a record of when the canary eggs were laid, and when they were due to hatch.

IV. Social meanings, attitudes, and appreciations developing through these experiences.

  A. An attitude of friendliness and protection toward birds.
  B. Some understanding of the needs of birds and a desire to help by providing nesting materials, shelter, food and water.
  C. Some knowledge and appreciation of how carefully nesting birds must be protected:—the cage or house must not be moved, the nest must not be touched with the hands, the birds must not be frightened.
  D. Some knowledge and appreciation of bird life: interesting habits and ways of living, beauty of color and song.

V. Interpretation and expression of attitudes and appreciations.

  A. Through story telling.
    1. Many creative stories were given by the children.
    2. The teachers told some realistic stories about birds.
  B. Through picture making and modeling.
    1. Many spring pictures were drawn and painted, including birds building their nests, feeding their baby birds, singing in the trees.
    2. Some children spontaneously made birds and birds' nests of clay.
  C. Through music.
    The children created a few songs about birds, and three of these were used over and over again.

UNITS OF EXPERIENCE IN FIRST GRADE

IMPORTANT objectives in first grade, as in kindergarten, have been to help the child to understand more fully his own immediate environment and to provide the opportunity for worthy social living.

The children are still in the period of dramatic play, and they have greatly enjoyed reliving in play the activities of the community. The interest in construction is very keen. Two sets of large floor blocks with roofing pieces have been provided for building, and these have been supplemented by large boxes and composition board. A workbench and tools have been included in the room equipment, and sometimes the help of the teacher of arts and crafts has been sought. The wholesome dramatic activity rendered possible by the large building enterprises, has made the effort and expense of this type of work tremendously worth while.

The children often beg to save one building when starting another, so that as the year progresses, the first-grade room becomes a "street," with many sorts of enterprises going on. Transportation is still a leading interest, but transportation at this level has usually been studied in its relationship to other activities of the community. The play store with its opportunities for dramatization of buying and selling and transporting goods has been a favorite activity. The grocery store, the toy store, and the valentine shop have appeared in different years. Conducting a post office and sending mail by truck, train and airplane has been a favorite enterprise. One group of children thought it fun to have "a school in a school," and they built a schoolhouse and a school bus, and dramatized with glee their own daily experience of going to school. Another group enjoyed building an automobile and a filling station. A bungalow and an apartment house have been enjoyed in different years. At Christmas time a house with a fireplace was built by one class, and a small Santa Claus in a school-made suit arrived with a well-constructed sleigh and a troop of two-legged reindeer. A baby show with dolls for babies, a motion-picture show, an aviation show, and a circus have in different years afforded an opportunity to study community recreation; and in one summer session, the Fourth of July was recognized by a parade of well-constructed floats which was conducted through the corridors, while children from other grades looked on.

The interest in a single such dramatic enterprise may continue anywhere from one to six weeks, or even longer, but as a rule several such enterprises occur in the year's program. Sometimes all of the children are keenly interested in a single enterprise. At other times interest is divided among two or three or many different projects.

In addition to the study of community activities, there has been a continual interest in nature and particularly in the seasonal changes, which in this locality are very marked. The children have enjoyed decorating the room with poster pictures of each season as it comes, and making collections of the season's treasures. The interest in pets has been very keen and many kinds of small animals have found a temporary home in the first-grade room: goldfish, turtles, white mice, baby chicks, squirrel, canary, finches, lovebirds. Through the courtesy of one of the fathers, who has been engaged in experimental work with animals, families of rabbits, guinea pigs and white rats have been loaned to the school for short periods of time. Because it is a common and keen interest of all first-grade children, the topic of pets has been a source of much delightful work in creative language; and songs, stories and verses have been composed, which have later found their way into original reading books. First-grade records show many experiences with individual pets, but for convenience these are summarized here in a single outline.

The enterprises outlined here have been selected from the records of three different years. Outcomes in social meanings and appreciations peculiar to each unit have been included with the unit. All of the experiences described have afforded opportunity for growth in certain desirable social and personal habits and attitudes; as, coöperation in group purposing and planning, responsibility in carrying out group plans, wise use of time and materials, self-control in observing group regulations, respect for the rights and possessions of others, willingness to give and take helpful suggestions, satisfaction in worthy group and individual achievement, appreciation of the efforts of others. These enterprises have also afforded opportunity for growth in art expression and for progress in fundamental skills. Some outcomes of this sort are summarized under Group Records of Progress in Part IV.

Enjoying and Using Autumn Treasures

A First Grade Interest in October

I. **Enriching experiences which aroused and fostered interest and provided background.**
   A. Observation of autumn changes on the school grounds, on walks, in the children's own gardens.
   B. Examination of leaves brought in by the children: oak, elm, maple, catalpa, sumac, horse chestnut, cottonwood.
   C. Enjoyment of other fall treasures contributed by members of the group: milkweed pods, corn and corn stalks, acorns, chestnuts, pumpkins, flowers, bittersweet, cocoons.
   D. Study of pictures placed on bulletin boards: harvesting apples, grapes, corn, wheat; raking, piling, playing in leaves; storing vegetables for winter.
   E. Observation of Halloween decorations in shops and in other schoolrooms.

II. **Problems and questions leading to discussion and experiment.**
   A. How can we make our room look like the out-of-doors in autumn? Through the use of nature materials? Through pictures brought from home? Through pictures and posters made at school?
   B. How can we use the autumn leaves? Where can we find pretty colored leaves? How can we classify and mount them?
   C. What flowers bloom in the garden in autumn?
   D. What can we plant in the garden in autumn?
   E. What fruits and vegetables are gathered in the autumn?
   F. How may we use our autumn collection for Halloween?

III. **Finding answers to questions and problems.**
   A. Through constructive activities.
      1. Collecting autumn leaves and mounting these on big posters.
      2. Arranging an exhibit of seeds and pods, collected on short excursions.
      3. Decorating the room from day to day with flowers, leaves and corn shocks brought from home and from the country.
      4. Bringing bulbs from home and planting these in the school garden.
      5. Stringing acorns for beads by a few skilful children.

6. Making Halloween place cards from leaf designs.
7. Making doilies for a Halloween luncheon.
8. Arranging and decorating tables for the Halloween luncheon.

B. Through oral language.
　1. Discussion related to nature facts and materials.
　　a. Simple discussions of the causes of seasonal changes and which nature treasures belong to the autumn season.
　　b. Discussion of types of autumn activities in the home, the farm, the forest, the animal kingdom.
　　c. Discussion of which autumn treasures will best beautify our room; many discussions as to best placement and arrangement.
　　d. Oral contributions from the children suggesting ways of recognizing oak, maple, elm, cottonwood, sumac leaves.
　　e. Reports of children's autumn experiences outside of school.
　2. Discussion related to Halloween festivities.
　　a. Reports of activities on previous Halloween days.
　　b. Discussions of best ways to plan Halloween fun.
　　c. Making plans for Halloween luncheon.

C. Through factual reading.
　1. Reading of phrases and sentences posted beneath pictures on the bulletin boards.
　2. Making and reading from the blackboard lists of autumn materials suitable for room decorations.
　3. Reading a few labels beside the exhibits.
　4. Reading the place cards to find places at the table.

Teacher's References

Comstock, Anna B.	Handbook of Nature Study	1939 Comstock
Downing, Elliot R.	Our Living World	1928 Longmans, Green
Emerson, A. I.	Our Trees	1937 Lippincott
Farquhar, F. F., and others	World Book Encyclopedia	1940 Quarrie
Ford, A. S., and others	Pictured Encyclopedia	1940 Compton
Fox, Frances M.	Flowers and Their Travels	1936 Bobbs-Merrill
Fultz, Frances M.	The Fly Aways and Other Seed Travelers	1928 Public School
Hough, Romeyn B.	Handbook of the Trees	1924 Romeyn B. Hough
Kenley, Julie C.	Green Magic	1930 Appleton
Parker, B. M. & Cowles, H. C.	The Book of Plants	1925 Houghton Mifflin

Bulbs Now and Tulips By and By

D. Through use of numbers.
  1. Developing a sense of balance.
    a. In placing objects on the posters.
    b. In placing autumn specimens about the room.
    c. In planning size of posters to fit wall space.
  2. Recognizing groups of objects.
    a. Seeing how many groups of corn shocks there are in the corners of the room.
    b. Seeing how many posters are arranged in one space.
    c. Seeing quickly how many acorns or seeds are in each little group in the exhibit.
  3. Counting.
    a. Counting to see of which type leaf we had found the most.
    b. Counting the bulbs each child brought, and the number to be set in each garden bed.
    c. Counting involved in Halloween luncheon preparation: doilies, place cards, glasses.
    Note: Some of these activities were spontaneous, and only part of the children participated.

IV. **Social meanings, attitudes, appreciations, developing through these experiences.**
  A. Some appreciation of the beauty of the autumn time.
  B. The beginning of an understanding of the efforts of the farmers in realizing a plentiful harvest.
  C. Some appreciation of the need for combined effort and unselfishness to create a beautiful room.
  D. The beginning of an ideal of beauty through well-kept, orderly surroundings.
  E. Some development in an attitude of reverence toward the richness of the harvest.
  F. The beginning of an appreciation for the need of appropriate behavior at a party.
  G. An increasing friendliness between children and teachers through working toward one goal.
  H. An increased attitude of possession and feeling at home in the new room.

V. **Interpretation and expression of attitudes and appreciations.**
  A. Through telling and listening to stories.
    The Maple Tree (from The Beginner's Book in Religion, Edna Dean Baker)
    Farmer Brown and the Apples (from The Beginner's Book in Religion, Edna Dean Baker)

The Little Black Cat and the Big Orange Pumpkin (from My Book-house)

B. Through creating original verses, later written and compiled for an autumn booklet; as,

> Flowers, Flowers!
> Gently sway,
> When the autumn winds come,
> To blow you away.

> Pumpkins and witches on Halloween night
> Will frighten everyone
> Who is in sight.

C. Through poster making.
  1. Series for a frieze made by small groups:
     a. Children gathering apples in the orchard.
     b. Children raking falling leaves.
     c. Children and fathers burning leaves.
     d. Halloween night.
     e. Poster of the story—The Little Black Cat and the Big Orange Pumpkin.
  2. One large poster made by a group.
     A corn field with a pumpkin in the shocks, and to the right a glorious group of autumn trees and falling leaves.

D. Through music.
  1. Singing and dramatizing songs such as:

The Gay Leaves.	Jack-o'-lantern.
The Wild Wind.	If I Were a Tiny Elfin.
The Orchard.	The Journey of the Leaves.
The Harvest.	

  2. Playing brownies and goblins with music:
     "Elves Dance"—Grieg, and other suitable music found in excerpts from such composers as Haydn, Wagner, Schumann.

Source Books

Baker and Kohlsaat	Songs for the Little Child	1938 Abingdon Press
Davison and Surette	One Hundred Forty Folk Songs	1922 E. C. Schirmer
McConathy, Meissner, Birge and Bray	Music Hour in Kindergarten and First Grade	1929 Silver Burdett
Robinson, Ethel	School Rhythms	1923 Clayton Summy

E. Through social activity.
  1. Playing out-of-doors with seeds from the milkweed pods.
  2. Preparing and participating in a simple Halloween luncheon as final, complete enjoyment of the room they had beautified.

VI. New interests foreshadowing further activities.
   A. Interest in studying farm and farmer's preparation for fall.
   B. Interest in playing store or fruit market.
   C. Interest in planning an autumn festival.

Creating an Autumn Festival

A First Grade Interest in November

I. **Enriching experiences which aroused and fostered interest and provided background.**
   A. The previous enterprise of beautifying the room for autumn.
   B. The memory of the school festival of the previous year.
   C. The study of pictures: actual photographs of the previous school Thanksgiving festival; pictures brought in of harvest offerings.

II. **Problems and questions which led to discussion and experiment.**
   A. What fruits are harvested in the autumn?
   B. How can we make fruits and vegetables to play with?
   C. How shall we use these objects?
   D. How may we tell in a festival our joy in the harvest?
   E. How may we make costumes for an autumn festival?

III. **Answering questions and solving problems.**
   A. Through constructive activities.
      1. Modeling from clay, apples, pears, corn.
      2. Painting objects with enamel paint to make them more realistic.
      3. Making of grape vines, using cotton, crepe paper, and covered flower wire.
      4. Designing costumes to represent autumn fruits, leaves, and vegetables.
      5. Dyeing cloth for costumes.
      6. Cutting, sewing and decorating apple, leaf, grape and corn costumes.
   B. Through oral language.
      1. After making clay fruits and vegetables, the children suggested a store and a festival. The decision was made to have a festival.
      2. Plans were discussed for the festival. Suggestions were made for costumes to represent fruits; for a dramatization of leaves falling, fruits being picked, corn swaying; for a choir to furnish music.
   C. Through reading.
      Plans were read from the blackboard for costumes, color schemes, activities.

D. Through use of numbers.
   1. Counting and grouping of children for different activities.
   2. Counting of costumes and clay fruits.
   3. Measuring for costumes.

IV. **Social meanings, attitudes, appreciations, developing through these experiences.**
   A. Some understanding and appreciation of the importance of a plentiful harvest.
   B. A spirit of thankfulness for an abundant harvest.
   C. An attitude of joy toward the autumn season.
   D. Joy in participating in a festival, and an appreciation of the beauty of color, music and rhythmic movement in the festival.

V. **Interpretation and expression of attitudes and appreciations.**
   A. Through original verses: as,

   The grapes are blue
   And good for you.

   ───────

   The leaves are falling,
   For it is fall.
   We rake up the leaves
   And heap them all.

   ───────

   Green grapes! Green grapes!
   Yellow corn! Yellow corn!
   Red apples! Red apples!
   Golden pears! Golden pears!
   Beautiful autumn! Beautiful autumn!

   B. Through picture making and design.
      1. Pictures and freehand cuttings as ideas and designs for costumes.
      2. Crayola drawings and water-color paintings of the child's reaction to the festival.
   C. Through music and dramatization.
      The children worked out a simple dramatization in costume. They carried the clay fruits constructed and moved rhythmically (walked, danced, skipped or swayed) to appropriate music. A choir sang the songs or the piano furnished the music as the need arose.

VI. New interests foreshadowing further activity:

Interest in sharing autumn treasures with others. The following week the children brought a Thanksgiving gift of fruits and vegetables for Mary Crane Nursery School at Hull House, and carried their gifts in a processional with other grades.

Enjoying and Caring for Pets

A Series of Experiences in First Grade

I. Enriching experiences which aroused and fostered interest and provided background.
   A. Observation of pets in the room.
     1. Goldfish in the room when children came.
     2. Turtles and finches presented to the room by two children.
     3. A parrot purchased from pet store.
     4. A pair of rabbits given to the room in the spring, and a family of young which arrived one week-end.
     5. A pair of hooded rats loaned to the room in the summer session.
   B. Observation of animal families in other rooms and on the playground: canaries, guinea pigs, baby chicks, ducks, tadpoles.
   C. Trips to pet stores to buy parrot, to secure supplies for pets, and to observe their care.
   D. Children's stories of pets at home: dogs, kittens, rabbits, birds.
   E. Trips to Children's Library to secure pictures and stories about pets.
   F. Pictures of children and their pets on bulletin boards from time to time.

II. Problems and questions which led to discussion and experiment. For pets studied, such questions as these arose:
   A. What kind of a house is needed? As, cage, aquarium, house.
   B. What materials are needed in the home?
   C. How shall the home be kept sanitary?
   D. What kinds of food are needed?
   E. How often should the pet be fed and what amount?
   F. How can friendship of pets best be gained?
   G. What interesting habits does the pet show: responses to persons; to other animals; to food; to objects; to noises; care of young?
   H. Where can pets be purchased?
   I. How are pets raised and handled at the pet store?
   J. How are different pets valued in selling?
   K. Where can supplies for pets be obtained?
   L. How can information be secured as to proper care of pets?

III. **Finding answers to problems and questions.**
  A. Through constructive activities.
    1. Provision and equipment of suitable homes for school pets.
    2. Provision and preparation of food for school pets.
    3. Mounting of colored pictures of children and pets for bulletin boards.
    4. Construction of a series of reading books to record information about pets.
  B. Through oral language.
    1. Discussion of needs of pets in room.
    2. Plans for responsibility in care of room pets.
    3. Oral stories of pets at home: their habits, tricks and care.
    4. Oral reports of information gained from visits at pet store.
    5. Oral reports of observation of pets in other rooms.
    6. Composition of factual stories about different pets, which were written on the board by teacher and later placed on bulletins, or duplicated for children's books.
  C. Through reading.
    1. Reading of short factual stories of school and home pets, first from the blackboard, later from charts and from little books made by the children: fish book, finch book, turtle book, kitten book, dog book.
    2. Reading later from pre-primers and primers realistic stories about children's activities with their pets.

Baker and Reed	Playmates	1938 Bobbs-Merrill
Baker and Baker	Toots in School	1938 Bobbs-Merrill
Baker and Baker	The Pet Pony	1938 Bobbs-Merrill
Hardy, Marjorie	Wag and Puff	1926 Wheeler
Hill and Martin	Bob and Baby Pony	1934 Scribner
Lewis and Gehres	Tots and Toys	1931 Winston
Stevens, Avis	Nippy	1936 Webster
Storm, Grace E.	Nip and Tuck	1936 Lyons and Carnahan

Teacher's References

Bianco, Margery	All About Pets	1929 Macmillan
Comstock, Anna B.	Handbook of Nature Study	1939 Comstock
Downing, Elliot R.	Our Living World	1928 Longmans, Green
Johnson, Constance	When Mother Lets Us Keep Pets	1926 Dodd Mead
Mathiews, F. K.	Boy Scouts Book of Indoor Hobby Trails	1939 Appleton
Russell, David W.	Suggestions for the Care of Pets	

(Reprinted from School Science and Mathematics, April, 1939)

YOUNG RABBITS SHOW GROWTH IN WEIGHT

D. Through use of numbers.
1. Adjustment of size of living quarters to size of pet.
2. Estimate of quantity of food needed according to number and size of pets.
3. Inquiry at pet store as to money value of different pets.
4. Decision to buy a parrot because funds available would provide one.
5. Purchase of food and supplies needed for pets.
6. Counting number in different animal families at school.
7. Weighing baby animals to check diet.

IV. Social meanings, attitudes, appreciations, probably developed through these experiences.
A. Appreciation and knowledge of some small animals:— their coloring, texture of covering, their habits and cunning responses to new situations.
B. Readiness to give needed care and protection to small friendly animals.
C. Willingness to share with others the responsibility of care and the privilege of observation of pets.
D. Appreciation of need for scientific information concerning the correct care of pets.

HOODED RATS ARE INTERESTING

E. Appreciation of need for responsible and regular care of pets.

V. Interpretation and expression of attitudes and appreciations.
  A. Through literature.
    1. Spontaneous memorization of certain favorite poems.

Aldis, Dorothy	The Gold Fish
Farrar, John	Wish
Lindsay, Vachel	The Turtle

    2. Enjoying with the teacher picture-story books found in library:

Ets, Marie	Mr. Penny	1935 Viking Press
Gág, Wanda	A. B. C. Bunny	1933 Coward-McCann
Gág, Wanda	Millions of Cats	1928 Coward-McCann
Hill and Max-well	Charlie and His Puppy Bingo	1927 Macmillan
Hill, Mabel B.	Big, Little, Smaller and Least	1936 Stokes
Hogan, Inez	The White Kitten and the Blue Plate	1930 Macmillan
Lofting, Hugh	The Story of Mrs. Tubbs	1923 Stokes
Newbery, Clare	Mittens	1936 Harper

B. Through creative composition. Original verses were composed; as,

> Singing, singing,
> The birds are singing
> And I will sing to you.

> Swinging, swinging,
> The doves are swinging
> And I will swing with you.

C. Through picture-making, design, decoration.
  1. Free drawing of pictures of different pets, with their homes, with children feeding them, engaged in play.
  2. Free cutting of some pictures which were mounted to make "poster pictures."
  3. Designs made for covers of animal books.

D. Through music.
  1. Through songs related to pets of particular interest; as,

> Pretty Pussy
> Bunny, Pretty Bunny
> The Squirrel
> Dusty Bob
> Naughty Bird
> Oh, Where Is My Little Dog Gone
> My Big Black Dog
> The Proper Kitten

  2. Pantomiming and dramatizing such songs as:

> Little Chickens
> The Pony Ride
> On a Frosty Morning (About a family of squirrels)

  3. Altering words of songs to fit pets at school. Creating new verses to familiar songs; as,

> Oh, I am little Susie Finch,
> Susie Finch, Susie Finch,
> Oh, I am little Susie Finch,
> I like you.

  4. Rhythmic pantomime such as:

> Ducks
> Frogs—teacher at the piano improvised music to suit the rhythm and tempo set by the children.

Music References

Baker and Kohlsaat	Songs for the Little Child	1938 Abingdon Press
Hofer, Mari	Old Tunes, New Rimes and Games	1917 A. Flanagan
Surette	Songs from Many Lands	1937 Houghton Mifflin
Foresman	A Child's Book of Songs	1937 American Book
Davison and Surette	One Hundred and Forty Folk Songs	1921 E. C. Schirmer
Whitlock	Come and Caper	1932 G. Schirmer

E. Through social activity: sharing room pets with children of other grades who came to see them.

VI. New interests foreshadowing further units of work.

A. Interest in owning pets at home and 'caring for them properly.
B. Interest in wild animals and their care and protection; as, wild birds and squirrels.
C. Interest in animals at zoo, and how they are kept and cared for.
D. Interest in the training of animals for circus or animal show.

Using Cars and Filling Stations

A First Grade Interest in the First Semester

I. **Enriching experiences which aroused and fostered interest and provided background.**

  A. Trips to filling station to see gas, oil and water put in a car; car greased; oil changed; tire changed and mended; bulk truck deliver gas.
  B. Identifying types of cars in nearby parking lot.
  C. Watching traffic being controlled at busy corner—by policeman and traffic light.
  D. Trip to garage to see mechanic at work on motor.
  E. Riding past freight trains and identifying oil cars.
  F. Riding on a city bus.

II. **Problems and questions which led to discussion and investigation.**

  A. How can we make a car to ride in?
  B. How can we make it go?

A STOP IS MADE AT THE FILLING STATION

C. Where can we get gas?

D. How does a real filling station get gas?

E. How can we make a filling station with gas pumps, air pumps, oil, etc.?

F. How can we raise our car to work on the engine?

G. What does a garage man do to fix a flat tire?

H. How do they get old oil out of a car?

I. Why does Ethyl gas cost more than regular?

J. What does a filling station handle besides gas?

III. Finding answers to problems and questions.

A. Through constructive activities.

1. Big car of wood, boxes, steel rods for axles and wheels—strong enough to carry children.

2. Filling station of blocks and boxes, including:

a. gas pumps.

b. air pump.

c. hoist of ropes and pulleys.

d. oil bottles

e. tires—wheels from blocks.

3. Small wooden cars for floor play.

4. Small cars of cardboard boxes for floor play.

5. Accessories for above—small filling stations, traffic lights, bridges, etc., of wood, boxes, and odds and ends.

B. Through oral language.

1. Conferences to decide about such problems of construction as:

a. What shall we use for lights, tail lights, bumpers, steering wheel, axles?

b. Where is a good place to ride a car?

c. How high does the filling station need to be?

d. How can we make it light enough to see inside the filling station?

2. Conferences to plan the dramatic play.

a. Who is the filling station attendant to-day?

b. Who takes care of washing the car?

c. What does the garage mechanic do?

d. Who is responsible for putting the car away?

3. Free conversation during the dramatic play expressive of the activities being portrayed.

a. The family on a trip.

b. Being towed by the wrecker.

c. Fixing a flat tire.

    d. Engine trouble.

    e. Buying gas.

    f. Bringing home vegetables from the farm.

C. Through written language.

  1. Memoranda of things needed and how they are to be obtained.

  2. Listing of groups for certain purposes—those building the filling station, those playing car to-day, etc.

  3. Writing of stories about group experiences, such as letters to absent children or stories for our own enjoyment.

D. Through factual reading.

  1. Reading of experience stories about trips made by the group.

  2. Reading of riddles about cars and filling stations made by small groups of children.

  3. Reading of cards sent by children away on trip—finding where they are on map.

  4. Dramatic play with road maps, with some location of nearby or important places.

  5. Use of picture material to get some knowledge of process of oil refining and delivering, car assembling, etc., from various sources; as,

    a. Auto show.

    b. Magazine advertising.

    c. Advertising departments of gasoline companies.

    d. Book: Lent, H. B., Wide Road Ahead, 1933, Macmillan.

  6. Identifying names of popular cars—Ford, Buick, Cadillac, De Soto, etc.

  7. Reading license numbers on cars.

  8. Making and reading signs for use in play—Ethyl Gas, Free Air, etc.

E. Through the use of number.

  1. Measuring floor space and height of filling station.

  2. Measuring wood and boxes to make car large enough and symmetrical.

  3. Counting the number of gallons of gasoline or quarts of oil put in car.

  4. Some concept of quantity in liquid measure—quart, gallon, 200 gallon storage tanks.

  5. Growing knowledge of money values—penny, nickel, dime, quarter, half dollar, dollar, five dollars.

  6. Some concept of relative cost of gas, oil, new tires, new car.

7. Some concept of distance covered in cross country travel—in terms of days on the road, miles traveled per day.

IV. Social meanings, attitudes and appreciations developing through these experiences.

A. A knowledge that gas comes from underground.

B. A knowledge that gas is transported in various ways—by train, boat, truck.

C. A knowledge that gas is used as fuel for many kinds of engines—boats, trains, cars, airplanes.

D. An appreciation of the fact that a filling station attendant is well-trained, courteous, responsible.

E. An appreciation of the fact that many workers contribute to make possible what we consider very ordinary experiences.

F. Growing knowledge of how to make auto traffic safe—motorists and pedestrians obey signals, motorists have good brakes, children riding in cars should remain seated, etc.

G. A knowledge that the use to which a car is put determines its construction; as, dump truck, van, bus, pleasure car.

H. Appreciation of the fact that driving demands a specialized technique, especially if the vehicle is a heavy one.

I. A concept that automobiles have changed through the years as they have developed.

J. A knowledge that travel is a means of learning about people.

V. Interpretation and expression of attitudes and appreciations.

A. Through literature.

1. Stories.

From Coöperative School Pamphlet No. 2—"Streets"
Story of Little Old Car.
Red Gasoline Pump.
Big Street in Big City.
Taxi that Hurried.
Boy Who Thought with His Ears.
From Here and Now Story Book—Lucy S. Mitchell
Speed.

2. Verse.

From Coöperative School Pamphlet No. 2—"Streets"
Three Autos.
Police Cop Man.
From Golden Flute—Hubbard and Babbitt.
Cars Go Fast—Annette Wynne.
Old Coach Road—Rachel Field.
From Here and Now Story Book—Lucy S. Mitchell.
Automobile Song.

From I Go A-traveling—James Tippett.
    Traffic Sounds.
    My Taxicab.
    Taxicabs.
    Hurrying.
    Our Automobile.
    Green Bus.
    Tracks.
    River Streets.
From Taxis and Toadstools—Rachel Field.
    Good Green Bus.
    Taxis.

B. Through picture making.
   1. Spontaneous drawing and painting of individual and group experiences, such as:
      a. Family going for a ride.
      b. Moving day.
      c. Wrecker coming to tow car.
      d. A grocery truck.
C. Through dramatic play.
   1. Individual and small group play centering around small cars and accessories depicting such things as:
      a. A busy street.
      b. Delivering coal.
      c. Auto race.
   2. Play centering around big car and filling station on such themes as:
      a. Fixing a flat tire.
      b. Engine trouble.
      c. A trip to New York.
      d. Helping the flood victims.
      e. Driving a bus.

VI. **New interests foreshadowing further activities.**
   A. How people touring by car get food, leading to grocery store, restaurant or tourist home.
   B. Kinds of automobiles—leading to study of bus or truck transportation.
   C. How people get word to family at home when on a trip—leading to a study of mail.

Conducting a Post Office

A First Grade Interest in the Second Semester

I. **Enriching experiences which aroused and fostered interest and provided background for activities.**
   A. Delivering valentines from the valentine box.
   B. Receiving letters from relatives and friends.
   C. Trips to the local post office with parents.
   D. Observing the mailboxes on the corner.
   E. Observing the mailman collecting mail.
   F. Getting mail from the mailbox at home.
   G. An excursion to the post office with the whole class.
   H. Pictures, stamps, letters mounted on the bulletin boards.
   I. An excursion to the airport.

II. **Problems and questions which led to discussion and investigation.**
   A. Problems which arose concerning the construction of the post office building.
      1. Of what material should it be constructed?

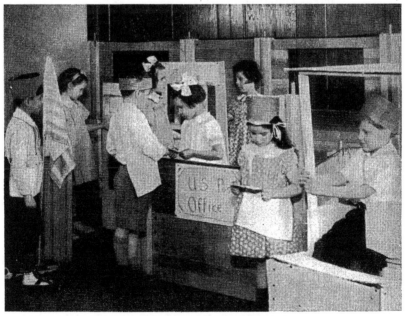

GIFTS ARE EXCHANGED THROUGH THE POST OFFICE

2. What shape is a post office?
3. What type of windows are used in a post office? .
B. Problems which arose concerning interior equipment.
   1. What furniture is needed?
   2. How is mail sorted? Where do people call for their mail?
C. Questions dealing with names, labels, signs.
   1. Where do you see names and signs in a post office?
   2. Is a clock found in a post office?
D. Problems dealing with an organization of the dramatic play.
   1. What officers are needed?
   2. What time shall mail be collected?
   3. What time shall the post office be open?
E. Problems which arose concerning carrying of mail.
   1. How is mail carried from town to town?
   2. How shall we construct a mail truck?
   3. How shall we construct a mail plane?
   4. How and why are stamps used?
F. Problems which arose concerning uniforms worn by different employees.
   1. What type, color, decorations on the real uniforms?
   2. How can we make some simply that would fit our need?

III. Answering questions and solving problems.

A. Through constructive activities. Small groups of children were interested in different phases of the construction.
   1. Construction of buildings.
      a. Constructing a post office of floor blocks and pieces of beaver board.
      b. Providing flag pole and flag.
      c. Constructing a stamp window.
      d. Making chutes for letters and packages.
      e. Constructing individual cubby holes for mail boxes, of cigar boxes nailed together.
   2. Constructing vehicles for carrying the mail.
      a. Building a large truck for collecting mail from boxes.
      b. Building an airplane large enough to carry mail pilot.
   3. Making labels and signs.
      a. Printing signs for the front of the post office, the mail truck, the airplane, the stamp window, the post box.
      b. Printing labels for the letter and package chute.
      c. Printing numbers for individual mail boxes.

4. Making materials to be posted.
   a. Cutting and making picture post cards.
   b. Modeling objects of clay as cats, book ends, paper weights, pencil holders, to mail to friends.
5. Making stamps and envelopes.
   a. Making large envelopes when manufactured ones would not fit.
   b. Making one, two, and three-cent stamps.
   c. Making air mail stamps.
6. Making uniforms.
   a. Constructing blue and gold postman's caps.
   b. Making oil cloth bags for postman's bags.
B. Through oral language.
   1. Oral discussion to solve problems suggested.
   2. Discussion of visits to the local post office and to the airport.
   3. Oral reports of trips to the corner post boxes to find out what was printed on them.
   4. Discussion to decide upon color schemes; size and type of equipment; officers and employees of the post office.
   5. Reports on information gleaned from parents, books, friends, on the rules for stamping letters, addressing letters, amounts of postage, and transportation of mail.
C. Through factual reading.
   1. Blackboard reading.
      a. Reading daily plans for work for the day.
      b. Reading names of postal employees and their duties.
      c. Reading plans for the trip to the post office and the airport.
   2. Bulletin boards.
      a. Reading captions beneath pictures.
      b. Reading names and amounts from a stamp chart.

Picture-Story Books for Children's Use

Kuh, Charlotte	The Postman	1929 Macmillan
Park, Dorothea	Here Comes the Postman	1936 Houghton
Read, Helen S.	Billy's Letter	1928 Scribner

Teacher's References

Harlow, A. F.	Old Post Bags	1928 Appleton
McSpadden, J. W.	How They Carried the Mail	1930 Dodd, Mead
Storm, Grace E.	The Social Studies in the Primary Grades	1931 Lyons and Carnahan
Webster, H. H.	Travel by Air, Land and Sea	1933 Houghton

   D. Through the use of arithmetic.
      1. Measuring: framework for the post office; sides and roof
         for the post office; windows for the post office; chassis
         for automobile; wings and body for airplane; tagboard
         for signs; paper for stamps.
      2. Recognition of numbers.
         a. Reading time on the clock.
         b. Reading numbers on the post boxes.
         c. Reading numbers on stamps.
         d. Reading time of collections.
      3. Counting.
         a. Counting stamps.
         b. Counting pennies by 1's and by 2's to $1.00.
         c. Counting nickels to $1.00.
      4. Computing.
         a. Computing the cost of mailing 2 or 3 letters or
             post cards.
         b. Computing cost of sending package at 5c a pound.
      5. Weighing.
         a. Weighing packages to ascertain postage needed.
         b. Weighing letters to see if more than one stamp is
             needed.

IV. **Social meanings, attitudes, appreciations, developing through these
    experiences.**
   A. An understanding and appreciation of the importance and
      value of the post office in a community.
   B. An appreciation of the efficiency of mail service.
   C. An appreciation of the privilege of communication by let-
      ters.
   D. Some knowledge and appreciation of the work of the post
      office, and the responsibility borne by its employees.
   E. Some knowledge and appreciation of the responsibility
      borne by those who transport mail; their faithfulness,
      courage and skill.
   F. An appreciation of the need for orderliness, accuracy, and
      speed on the part of post-office employees.
   G. An appreciation of the need for honesty and care in han-
      dling property belonging to another.
   H. A partial understanding of correct form in writing and
      mailing letters, and need for accuracy, legibility and neat-
      ness.

V. **Interpretation and expression of attitudes and appreciations.**
  A. Through creative composition.
    1. Some composition of short messages for post cards.

> Dear Sue:
>   Do you like the picture?
> I made it.
>   John

> Dear Phillip:
>   I like the spring. I like the birds.
> I like the flowers. Do you?
>   Herbert

  2. Some original composition in letter writing, by a few capable writers.

> Dear Peter:
> Can you guess my riddle?
> It has a head.
> It has four feet.
> But it cannot walk. What is it?
>   Marilyn

  B. Through picture making.
    1. Making pictures with crayolas on post cards to send to friends.
    2. Painting and drawing pictures to send to friends.
  C. Through singing.

> The Postman
> The Engine
> The Aeroplane
>   (In Baker, Clara Belle, and Kohlsaat, Caroline. Songs for the Little Child. 1938 Abingdon)
> The Mailbox
>   (In Davison, A. T., and Surette, T. W. One Hundred and Forty Folk Songs. 1922 E. C. Schirmer)

  D. Through dramatic play.
    1. Playing postman: delivering mail, collecting mail, taking it by truck or airplane to the post office.
    2. Playing clerk: cancelling the stamps, sorting the mail, waiting on customers.
    3. The play of sending letters, picture post cards, and gifts. The children spent most of their free time for some weeks in this play.

VI. **New interests foreshadowing further activities.**
  A. An interest in the different methods of transportation.
  B. A broader interest in the community and its various public institutions.

Conducting a Toy Store

An Enterprise in the First Grade Summer Session

I. Enriching experiences which aroused and fostered interest and provided background for activities.
   A. Boats and sand toys used in the children's summer play on the lake shore.
   B. Water toys brought to school by various children.
   C. Children's stories of playing on the lake shore.
   D. Pictures placed on the bulletin boards: children playing with toys; children playing in the water.

II. Problems and questions which led to discussion and experiment.
   A. Problems of construction.
      1. Which toys are most salable in the summer?
      2. What qualities in a toy do people look for when buying?
      3. Of what materials are store buildings made?
      4. What material is most practical for our store?
      5. What shape and size are good for store buildings?
      6. How can a delivery truck be made?
   B. Problems of organization.
      1. What employees are needed in a toy store?
      2. What are the duties of each?
      3. Will there be delivery service?
   C. Problems related to buying and selling.
      1. How does one fix the prices?
      2. Do prices change from customer to customer?
      3. How does a customer know the price?
      4. Whom does one pay?
   D. Problems related to money.
      1. What shall we use for money?
      2. Under what conditions may we use another's money? (It was decided to borrow $5 from the school bank in nickels, dimes, and pennies to use in playing store.)

III. Answering questions and solving problems.
   A. Through constructive activities. Different children were interested in different phases of construction.
      1. Construction of buildings.
         a. Store built of double set of floor blocks.
         b. Show cases outside built of blocks.
         c. Counters inside built of orange crates.

      d. Cashier's booth built on as an extra wing.
2. Construction of toys.
      a. Building of wood: hydroplanes, boats, steamers, tug boats, barges, sail boats, motor boats, engines and trains, wooden spades.
      b. Painting large gallon tomato cans for sand pails.
      c. Cutting from oiled cardboard toy ducks, frogs, fish, turtles, and mounting them on large corks.
3. Constructing a large auto from packing boxes for delivery truck.
4. Constructing incidentals for the store.
      a. Making labels, price tags, price lists, checks.
      b. Making tagboard and raffia purses.

B. Through oral language.
  1. Related to construction and organization.
      a. Solving problems through discussions, relating to children's experiences in stores.
      b. Selecting clerks, cashiers, janitors, delivery boys to run the store.
      c. Deciding duties and responsibilities of each.
  2. Related to buying and selling.
      a. Listing rules to assure good usage of money.
      b. Deciding how much to charge for articles, according to size, amount of labor.
      c. Working out procedure:
          Get money from the bank; write withdrawal slip.
          Select toys with help of a clerk.
          Get bill from clerk.
          Pay the cashier.

C. Through factual reading.
  1. Blackboard reading.
      a. Reading lists of toys suggested for construction.
      b. Reading names of employees and children's names.
  2. Reading charts and lists.
      a. Reading price lists, labels, price tags.
      b. Reading name, date, amount on withdrawal slip.

D. Through use of number.
  1. Developing a sense of the value of money.
      a. Using and caring for real money.
      b. Fixing fair prices for the toys.
  2. Counting and using money.
      a. Counting nickels and dimes to find amount needed to make purchases.

THE LAKE TESTS WATER TOYS

    b. Counting nickels and dimes by cashier to see if he is given right amount.

3. Measuring.
    a. Measuring wood to be used for toys.
    b. Measuring floor space to build store right size.
    c. Measuring paper for withdrawal slips, price tags, signs.

IV. Social meanings, attitudes, appreciations, developing through these experiences.

    A. Some understanding and appreciation of toy manufacturers.
    B. Some understanding and appreciation of the skill required to organize, equip and manage a store.
    C. More appreciation of attractive, well-made toys; and more joy in playing with toys.
    D. Better understanding of the value of toys and the value of money.
    E. Some understanding and appreciation of the responsibility accepted by a clerk and cashier, in a store.
    F. Some appreciation of honest, careful workmanship in manufactured articles.
    G. Eagerness to be fair and honest in business endeavors.
    H. Some development toward an attitude of thrift.
    I. A desire to be polite and courteous when serving people.

V. Interpretation and expression of attitudes and appreciations.
    A. Through literature.
        1. Stories told by the teacher and by the children.

> The Doll's Boat
>   (In Baker, C. B. and E. D. Fifty Flags. 1938 Bobbs-Merrill)
> Lindsay, Maud The Toy Shop. 1926 Lothrop
> Dicky's Birthday
>   (In Baker, C. B. and E. D. The Sailing Tub. 1938 Bobbs-Merrill)

        2. Verses memorized by some of the children.

Stevenson, Robert L.	When I Was Down Beside the Sea
Lindsay, Vachel	The Little Turtle
Aldis, Dorothy	The Goldfish
Stevenson, Robert L.	Dark Brown Is the River

    B. Through music.
    Singing and dramatizing such songs as:

> The Engine
> The Aeroplane
>   (In Baker, C. B. and Kohlsaat, C. Songs for the Little Child.
>   1938 Abingdon)
> The Sailboat
> The Little Ship
>   (In Davison, A. T. and Surette, T. W. One Hundred and Forty
> Folk Songs. 1922 E. C. Schirmer)

    C. Through dramatic activity and social activity.
        1. Playing with toys in the room after they had been purchased.
        2. The variety of playing bank and store.
        3. A trip to the lake shore to sail boats and hydroplanes, to play with the turtle and fish floats, and to play in the sand with the trains and buckets.

VI. New interests foreshadowing further units of work.
    A. Interest in other types of stores.
    B. Interest in the wider activities of the community.
    C. Interest in other industries.

UNITS OF EXPERIENCE IN
SECOND GRADE

PARTICULAR objectives in the second grade have been to extend the children's knowledge of their own community, and to help them to appreciate more fully their own responsibilities and privileges as citizens. The dependence of the community on nearby industries has also been emphasized.

The interest in clay modeling led to an excursion to the Haeger pottery and art shop in Dundee where the potter's wheel and the making of clay articles in molds were observed. A pottery unit followed which culminated in a Christmas gift shop.

The interest in transportation is still keen at this level. A study of travel by trailer, and a harbor unit have been particularly successful. A dramatization of carrying the mail, using puppets and models of vehicles was the center of interest for an extended period.

Through excursions and stories, an interest in farming has sometimes been created, and the dairy farm, the poultry farm, and the wheat farm have been studied in different years. One of the parents presented the school with an incubator, so that it has been possible to experiment with the hatching of hens' eggs and ducks' eggs. The investigation of methods in farming has led to much experimental study of the germination of seeds, and to the making of a garden on the school grounds. A garden market was a successful spring enterprise of two different years.

The enterprises included in this volume have been selected from the records of three different years, and are some that have been attended by special success. Outcomes in social meanings and appreciations peculiar to the particular unit are included with the unit. All of the enterprises have proved valuable in developing certain desirable social and personal habits and attitudes; as, the habit of planning work before beginning, good use of time and of materials, neatness and carefulness in using tools and materials, desire to improve quality of work, persistence in finishing work begun, sharing of ideas and materials, respect for rights and opinions of others, sympathy and appreciation for the efforts of others.

readiness to give and receive constructive criticism, self-control in observing the rules of the group, pride in worthy individual and group attainments. The enterprises have also provided opportunity for growth in the powers of expression through music, dramatization, fine and industrial arts, and creative language, and for progress in fundamental skills. Outcomes in terms of particular arts and skills are summarized under Group Records of Progress in Part IV.

Living In a Trailer

An Enterprise in Second Grade in the Fall

I. **Enriching experiences which aroused and fostered interest and provided background for activities.**

    A. Summer traveling experiences of the children: seeing trailers in the road; seeing trailer camps.

    B. A trip into the city to a trailer distributor to examine real trailers and to seek answers to questions.

    C. A trip to a trailer camp in Evanston.

    D. A trip to the lake shore to cook lunch on the beach.

    E. Sending for and showing to the school a March of Time film on the history, construction, and use of trailers.

II. **Problems and questions which led to investigation.**

    A. What is the approximate size of a real trailer?

    B. What equipment is needed in a trailer to make housekeeping and living possible?

    C. How can the needs of a family be met in such a small amount of space?

    D. Is it healthy to live in a trailer?

    E. Why do some people prefer living in a trailer?

    F. Will trailers some day take the place of permanent homes?

    G. What are the good points and the bad points of trailer life?

    H. How can we put electric lights in our trailer?

    I. Where will we get power? How do ocean liners and trains and automobiles get electric power?

    J. Are trailers used for any purposes other than homes?

    K. Why do cities object to trailer homes?

    L. How much do trailers cost?

III. **Answering questions and solving problems.**

    A. Through oral and written language.

        1. Relating observations of trailers seen on the road and owned by friends.

        2. Discussion of plans for the building of a trailer: size, number of windows, material to use.

        3. Discussion of the trip to inspect a trailer.

        4. Planning a healthful luncheon to be prepared outdoors.

        5. Composing letters and sending them to various trailer companies for pamphlets, pictures and information.

A TRAILER FAMILY MEETS WOOD FOLK

6. Writing road signs; writing the name of the trailer on it; writing signs for the various parts of their play.
7. Writing letters to parents, other classes, and faculty friends to come and see their trailer play.

B. Through constructive activities.
   1. Building a large trailer six feet high, five feet wide, and ten feet long.
   2. Making furniture: table and benches, sofa, stove, icebox, and cupboards.
   3. Making curtains for the windows.
   4. Wiring the trailer for electric lights.
   5. Connecting and using dry cell batteries.
   6. Cutting and painting large trees, bushes, and ponds for their trailer play.
   7. Making dishes to use in the trailer.

C. Through writing letters; as,

The United States Coach Company.
Dear Sirs:
    Please send us some pictures of trailers. Please tell us something about trailers. We want to build one in our room. We are going to Mr. Zepp's to see trailers.   **Stephen.**

D. Through making of a trailer scrapbook.
   1. Many illustrations, painted and drawn.
   2. Original verses, stories, and songs.
   3. Newspaper and magazine clippings.
   4. Newspaper and magazine illustrations.
   5. Letters written to trailer companies.
   6. Letters received from trailer companies.
   7. Pamphlets and booklets about trailers.
   8. Records of their own activities.
E. Through factual reading.
   1. Reading letters from various trailer companies.
   2. Reading parts of trailer pamphlets.
   3. Reading parts of newspaper and magazine articles about trailers.
   4. Reading class plans from charts, blackboard.
   5. Reading titles on the March of Time film on trailers.
   6. Reading plans for the class play.

Teacher's References

Sims, Blackburn. The Trailer Home. 1937 Longmans.
Compton's Pictured Encyclopedia. 1938 Compton.
World Book Encyclopedia. 1936 Quarrie.

F. Through arithmetic.
   1. Measuring lumber and beaverboard used in constructing the trailer.
   2. Estimating the number of lights needed for the trailer.
   3. Shopping for food for lunch.
      a. Keeping within a budget allowed them.
      b. Keeping a record of amount spent.
      c. Making a report to the dietitian on money spent.
   4. Getting some idea of various expenditures involved in supporting a family.
   5. Getting some idea of comparative cost of living in a trailer and living in a home.

IV. **Meanings, attitudes, and appreciations probably developed through these experiences.**
   A. An appreciation of a permanent home.
   B. An appreciation of the climate and natural beauty of various parts of our country.
   C. Some appreciation for sanitation and its part in the community health program.
   D. An increasing appreciation for nature and outdoor experiences.

E. A willingness to share experiences with other classes; as, March of Time film.

F. The beginning of an understanding of the cost of keeping a family.

G. Willingness to share responsibilities in family living.

V. Interpretation and expression of attitudes and appreciations.

A. Through composition, as:

> We rode on the North Shore and then we rode on the elevated when we went to see trailers. We saw the elevated round house. We saw a car that didn't have any wheels on it. I guess it is used for a house now. Yes, a work house where they keep the tools.
>
> We went up, up in the air on the "L". We saw the tops of houses and old shoes on the roof tops and sign boards on the roof tops. We went down, down again.
>
> We rode over two bridges that went over rivers. And we walked across a bridge that went over the "L" tracks. Then we waited for the North Shore train to come.
>
> Peter thought the train would tip over rocking back and forth.
>
> > Tippity, Tippity,
> > Sideways and straight,
> > Sideways and straight.
>
> It was fun looking out of the windows. We passed many stations and read the signs on them. Some were funny. Some were big. Some were good.

B. Through verse and song writing, as:

I had a little trailer;	I went down by a river
Nothing would it bear,	To catch a little fish;
But a little table	I cooked him and I fried him;
And some little chairs.	I put him in a dish.
One day I went a-riding	I put him on the table;
Down the road afar,	I ate him with a swish;
With my trailer hooked on	And that was the end
Behind my little car.	Of my poor little fish!

(Tune: I Had a Little Nut Tree)

C. Through design and picture making.

1. Many pictures were made of trailers in various geographical settings, pictures of trailer camps, and outdoor experiences.

2. Simple scenery for the play was designed and painted.

3. Simple costumes were designed and decorated.

D. Through making a trailer scrapbook including finger-painted cover.

1. Illustrations painted and drawn.

2. Story for original play.

E. Through dramatic play: playing house; traveling in a trailer.

F. Through the creation of an original play on trailer life in the summer.

Scene I. In the family automobile with trailer attached. Looking for a place to spend the night.

Scene II. Animal life at a trailer camp. Watching active squirrels, rabbits, birds, frogs.

Scene III. Dinner time in the trailer. Walking in the sunset at the camp.

VI. New interests foreshadowing further projects.

A. An interest in nature, animal and bird life in the autumn.

B. An interest in sanitation—the city's problem.

C. A desire to know more about different kinds of homes.

Developing a Harbor

An Enterprise in Second Grade

I. **Enriching experiences which aroused and fostered interest and provided background.**

    A. Stories were told of vacation experiences at lakes where children had ridden in various kinds of small craft. Some had had trips on the Great Lakes on yachts and on the lake steamers.

    B. Frequent trips were made to Wilmette Harbor and the drainage canal to see small lake craft.

    C. A trip to see the "lookout" tower at the harbor and a visit to the U. S. Coast Guard Station were made.

    D. Children brought in pictures of boats, bridges, buoys, and also some ship models.

    E. A trip to the Navy Pier in Chicago to see various kinds of boats and the way they are put in winter storage, to see tugs take ore-boats into the Chicago River, and the operating of the new boulevard link bridge, and to make a tour through the coast guard cutter *Rush,* proved rich in building background.

    F. The Evanston Lighthouse was visited.

    G. Seeing a dredge and barge at work in the canal during the first week of school was an incentive for further study of boats.

II. **Problems and questions which led to investigation.**

    A. Relating to the making of boats.

        1. What kinds of boats to make and what sizes should they be for best play use?

        2. Which boats are large and which ones are small?

        3. Why are some boats pointed at the prow and others straight across the front?

        ·. How can an even point be made on the keel?

        . How can boats be made to look as real as possible?

        6. How do the new streamlined liners differ from older models of steamships?

        7. What are the various parts of a boat called?

        8. What do the colors on funnels of steamships signify?

        9. Why is the pilothouse on an airplane carrier on one side of the boat? What makes the boat balance?

      10. Why is its funnel so tall?

11. Where are its cabins?
12. Where are lifeboats carried? Is the position the same on all boats?

B. Relating to the different purposes of boats.
  1. What does a liner carry besides people?
  2. What are tugs used for? How does their crew know when and where they are needed?
  3. Why do barges have no engines?
  4· What is a tramp steamer and how does it differ from a freighter?
  5. What is a police boat and what is it used for?
  6. Why do large harbors have fire boats?
  7. Where do the ore boats come from and why do they come to Chicago?
  8. Of what use is a coast guard cutter?
  9. Why does our government have a navy?
  10. What is a lightship?
  11. Why does the government have airplane carriers?
  12. Why are ferryboats used in some places instead of building bridges?
  13. Do boats have traffic laws like cars have?

C. Relating to the responsibilities of a crew.
  1. What does the captain do?
  2. Who are his helpers?
  3. Why does he wear brass braid on his sleeves?
  4. Who operates the radio and who gives signals with the "ship's flags"?
  5. What is a steward?
  6. Who stays in the crow's-nest and why?
  7. Who blows the foghorn and the boat's whistles?
  8. What do the whistles mean?
  9. What do deep sea divers do?
  10. How can the crew detect icebergs?
  11. Why do liners have "harbor pilots"?
  12. How does the compass help the captain?
  13. On which side do ships pass one another?
  14. How are icebergs detected?
  15. How does an ice cutter cut through the ice?
  16. What happens to stowaways?
  17. What happens if some one falls overboard?
  18. How do the men on deck know when a deep sea diver wants to come up?

D. Relating to lighthouses.
  1. What is their purpose?

2. Where are they located?
3. Why does each lighthouse have certain flashes?
4. Why is a lighthouse built round?
5. How does one go to the top?
6. What kind of a light does it have?
7. Why cannot it be seen in the daylight?
8. Where does the lighthouse keeper live?
9. Why doesn't the Evanston Lighthouse use a foghorn?

E. Relating to harbors.
  1. Why are some places better than others to build harbors?
  2. Why do some harbors need breakwaters?
  3. What are breakwaters made of?
   . What are slips or berths?
  4. What is the purpose of buoys and what kinds of buoys are there?
  6. Why are they made in different shapes?
  7. What happens to boats in winter? Are all boats stored?
  8. What is the purpose of a dry dock?

F. Relating to bridges.
  1. Why are some bridges stationary and some movable?
  2. What kinds of bridges are there?
  3. What makes them move?
  4. Why cannot a swing span bridge be used in a narrow river?
  5. What are the sections that lift up called?

G. Relating to locks.
  1. Why are there locks at Wilmette Harbor?
  2. How do they work?

III. Finding answers to questions and problems.

A. Through firsthand experiences.
Trips were made to the harbors, coast guard cutters, yacht, lighthouse, coast guard station locks, etc.

B. Through oral expression.
  1. Told stories of experiences on boats.
  2. Discussed group experiences and information gained through this means.
  3. Discussed conversations held with parents at home about problems that arose at school in connection with study.
  4. Discussed pictures found in books and shown to group.
  5. Gained firsthand information from captain of the *Rush*, and from a father of one of the group who deals in boats.

C. Through factual reading.
  1. Read simple books about boats.

2. Teachers read more difficult books, extracts from encyclopedia, etc.

Children's Picture-Story Books

Beaty, John Y.	Story Pictures of Transportation	1939	Beckley-Cardy
Bourgeois, Florence	Beachcomber Bobbie	1935	Doubleday Doran
Curtis, Nell	Boats	1927	Rand McNally
Dalgleish, Alice	Sailor Sam	1935	Scribners
DuBois, William	Otto at Sea	1936	The Viking Press
Petersham, Maud & Miska	The Story of Boats	1935	Winston
Starbuck, Wilson	Liners and Freighters	1934	Thomas Nelson

Books for the Teacher

Branie, Sheila E.	Merchant Ships and What They Bring Us	1931	Dutton
Cartwright, Charles E.	The Boys' Book of Ships	1925	Dutton
Collins, Francis Arnold	Sentinels Along Our Coast	1922	Century
Curtis, Nell C.	Boats	1927	Rand McNally
Dukelow, Jean H. & Webster H.	The Ship Book	1931	Houghton
Reck, F. M.	Romance of American Transportation	1938	Crowell
Romer, Ralph & Margaret	Sky Travel	1930	Houghton

Material on Airplane Carriers

Van Metre, T. W.	Tramps and Liners	1931	Doubleday Doran
Webster, Hanson Hart	Travel by Air, Land and Sea	1933	Houghton

Bulletin

Burrow, Clayton   Community Life in the Harbor, Curriculum Units for
Elementary Schools, No. 1, Department of Education,
Sacramento, California, 1935

D. Through constructive activities.
1. Built boats.
2. Laid out harbors.
3. Made lighthouses and breakwaters.
4. Built bridges of various kinds.
E. Through use of arithmetic.
1. Compared sizes of various kinds of boats.
2. Used linear measurement in construction of keels, making of prows, making of funnels, making of bridges.
3. Used liquid measurement in the making of cement for
breakwaters. (Children gained a valuable lesson in making one section of a breakwater. They were careless in
measuring the cement and dumped in an extra quantity,
and the result was that the section cracked into several

NEW BOATS WILL SOON BE LAUNCHED

pieces. Accuracy in measuring was an important factor after that experience.)

4. Discussed "water line" and its meaning—how it showed the weight on board, etc.

IV. Social meanings, attitudes, appreciations, probably developed through these experiences.

A. Some understanding of water travel and shipping.

B. Appreciation for the responsibilities of a crew, lighthouse keepers, coast guard man, bridge tenders, keepers of the locks.

C. Some realization of what is needed to make water travel safe.

D. A dawning realization of distance.

E. A knowledge of different kinds of boats and their uses.

F. A feeling for the life of seamen, the thrill of adventure, and the joy of travel.

G. An emotional thrill in seeing the beauty of water, the rolling of waves, lights on the water, etc.

H. An emotional thrill in hearing the swish of waves, the whistles of boats, calls of seamen.

V. **Interpretation and expressions of attitudes and appreciations.**
  A. Through literature.
    1. Oral reading of selected stories from school readers.
    2. Oral reading of a few poems, such as

Bennett, Rowena	"Boats"	
	from *The Golden Flute*	John Day
Fyleman, Rose	"The Boat" and "The Deck Steward"	
	from *Gay Go Up*	Doubleday
Fyleman, Rose	"Fairies by the Sea"	
	from *Fairies and Friends*	Doubleday
Field, Rachel	"I'd Like to Be a Lighthouse"	
	from *Taxis and Toadstools*	Doubleday
Field, Rachel	"Whistles"	
	from *The Pointed People*	Macmillan
Sandburg, Carl	"Fog"	
	from *Early Morn*	Harcourt
Tippett, James	"Motor Boats" and "Sand Boats"	
	from *I Spend the Summer*	Harper
Tippett, James	"Ferry Boats" and "Freight Boats"	
	from *I Go A-Traveling*	Harper

  B. Through creative composition.
    1. Poems were created by the group.
    2. Charts were composed by the children.
  C. Through picture making.
    1. Pictures were drawn by individuals of various kinds of boats.
    2. Group pictures made of harbor life depicted ships, cargo being loaded, lighthouses, deep sea divers, life under the sea, etc.
  D. Through music.
    1. Rhythmic pantomime.
      a. Rowing boats.
      b. Ploughing liners through the water. Out of several types of music, the children chose music in three-two meter with a majestic swing.
    2. Songs were sung of boats and sea life; as,

By Boat.
Blow the Man Down
The Tarpaulin Jacket
I Had a Little Sailboat
A Song of Ships
The Lighthouse
The Sea Gull
Sailing
Our Motor Boat (Rhythmic activity followed the singing.)
Sailors on Shore (Rhythmic activity followed the singing.)
Song of the Boisterous Sailors
I Wish I Were a Sailor

Music References

Surette, T. W.	Songs from Many Lands	1937	Houghton Mifflin
Palmer, W. B.	American Songs for Children	1931	Macmillan
Davison and Surette	One Hundred and Forty Folk-Songs	1921	E. C. Schirmer
	Favorite Songs of the People	1927	Theodore Presser
Hofer, Mari	Old Tunes, New Rimes and Games	1917	A. Flanagan
Perham, Beatrice	Songs of Travel and Transport	1937	Keil Kjos

E. Through dramatic interests, using small dolls.

Shipping of cargo; carrying of passengers; rescuing of boats in trouble; docking of ships at dry dock; diving; the fire and police boats in action; operating the various kinds of bridges as boats pass through.

VI. New interests foreshadowing further units of work.

A. A developing of a community where the crews and the people who travel on the boats may live.

B. An interest in sea specimens—whales, starfish, octopus, etc.

C. An interest in mail through some discussion of mail boats and carrying of mail on ocean liners.

D. An interest in map making—beginning with a local map of points of interest, such as, National College, the Wilmette Harbor, Coast Guard Station, Lighthouse, the homes of the children, elevated railroad and North Shore electric lines.

Stories and Poems Created in the Study of Harbors

The Sinking Ship

In the harbor there is a horrible racket.
The whistles of boats are blowing.
The sirens of fire boats are ringing.
One loud fire alarm rings.
Away dashes the fire boat No. 84.
A whistle blows—
Up come four tugs—
Another whistle blows.
Away goes the police boat.
A coast guard cutter follows.
They are going to the rescue of a sinking ship.
There must have been two sinking ships.
A steamer came bounding out of its dock at a hundred knots an hour instead of 18.
All the tugs and everything started leaping out of the harbor, for they know if they hear an S.O.S. call they should not stand around.
They answered the S.O.S. call and they went plenty fast—don't worry.
Down the river went all the harbor boats.
Soon they came to a few masts sticking out of the water.

The boats stopped suddenly.
They heard the S.O.S. coming out of the water.
They knew that was the boat they had come to rescue.
A steamer sent a radio call out for a submarine.
Down the harbor came the submarine and all the boats saved the
    sinking ship.

—Keith

Out of the harbor goes the tramp steamer.
It is going to Florida.
Ding, dong goes the bell buoy.
It is warning the steamer of dangerous rocks.
She is carrying a cargo of wheat to Florida.

—Jeanne

The beacon light shines over the water.
It is beautiful, so beautiful.
The harbor is very big.
The lighthouse looks very far away.

—Jeanne

See the boats
Afloating on the rippling sea
And the bell buoy
Sings dingedy-dong.
When the sea
Goes up and down
The light
Of the lighthouse
Flickers in the night.

—Meredith

In the harbor a freighter is coming in.
It has come from Canada.
The captain is on the bridge.
He signals to the engine room to shut off the engine.
The engineer shuts off the engine.
The boat stops.
A harbor boat drives up.
The harbor pilot climbs up a rope ladder.
Tugs whistle to the freighter.
The freighter whistles back.
Soon little tugs drive up.
The tugs go puff-puff-puff, pulling the freighter.
The tugs pull the freighter into its dock.

—Keith

Some boats are out on the sea,
It looks as if they were going too fast to me,
Its sails are swinging wide and free,
And the people on it laugh with glee.

—Carol

When the waves go up.
The bell buoy says "Ding."
When the waves go down,
The bell buoy says "Dong."
"Dingety-dong, dingety-dong,"
Goes the bell buoy's lonesome,
Lonesome song.

—Richard

It's a very foggy night
And a ship is out at sea.
The ship is brightly lighted
On this foggy, foggy night.
The captain drops the anchor.
The fog horn blows and blows.
Out of the dark comes its "To-o-ot, to-o-ot, to-o"
Wait, captain, wait
Until it's safe to travel.
—A Group Poem.

The lighthouse stands in the rock sea
And along comes a tug boat out to sea.
The bell buoy rocks to and fro,
While the south wind blows soft and low.
The bell buoy tells of dangerous rocks,
"Oh, captain brave, look out, look out!
For there are rocks ahead."
—A Group Poem

The sun shines down on the greenish blue,
And far, far down in the deep, deep sea,
Sea divers go in search of pearls
And I hope they'll bring some pearls to me.
—A Group Poem

Carrying the Mail

An Enterprise in Second Grade

I. **Enriching experiences which aroused and fostered interest and provided background for activities.**

    A. Cards were sent to members of the group by the teacher on her vacation trip. These were mailed from different parts of the country. Cards received by the children from other sources, during the summer, were brought in.

    B. Group visited the old post office in Evanston; also visited the new one in the process of construction.

    C. Two letters were mailed by the group, addressed to the group at the school. One was sent by regular delivery and the other by special delivery to determine difference in amount of time for delivery.

    D. Letter was written to postmaster to gain permission to visit post office.

    E. Excursion was made through new post office. A guide was supplied. Children followed the processes a local letter goes through from time it was brought in on truck from a street box to placing the letter in bag of carrier. A letter was also mailed to a second grade group in another city. Group saw letter placed in bag and put on truck, then followed truck to railroad station two blocks away and saw bag put on mail train.

    F. Stamps were collected. Two foreign children in the group and one or two fathers whose business brought foreign mail added much to the room collection. Emphasis was on United States stamps at first. Later as foreign stamps were collected the children were interested in looking up places where foreign stamps came from.

    G. Children wrote letters to parents who were out of town. Exchanged letters with two other second grade groups—one in a private school in Chicago, another in Michigan. Wrote letters to absent members of the group from time to time.

    H. Made a collection of pictures and interesting newspaper clippings that told of how mail was carried in various parts of the world.

    I. Rode on suburban train to Northwestern Station in Chicago to see mail trains loaded and unloaded—to see mail dumped on conveyor belts between tracks. Visited mail room in station.

IMPORTANT LETTERS ARE POSTED

J. Visited municipal airport to see mail received and loaded.
K. Some members of group were taken by parents to Historical Society to see setup of country store containing post-office boxes, and to see collection of early stamps.
L. Neighborhood excursions were made to see carriers get mail from storage boxes and to see trucks pick up mail.

II. Problems and questions which led to investigation.

A. Problems relating to the delivery of mail.
1. How does mail reach its destination?
2. How should a letter be addressed?
3. In how many ways does mail travel?
·. How was it carried long ago?
. How is mail picked up in small towns?
6. Why do people in small towns call for their mail?
7. Why do not all cities have air service?
8. Why is not the autogyro used in delivering mail in all large cities?
9. Why do some people have "curb service" instead of boxes on their homes?

10. Where must rural boxes be placed?
    What kind of boxes must they be?
11. How far does a rural carrier have to ride and how far
    does a city carrier have to walk?
12. How far did the Pony Express rider have to ride and
    how fast did the horses go?
13. What happens to dead letters and smashed packages?
14. How does a sorting clerk know which sorting box a letter
    should go in for city delivery?
15. How do the employees unlock street boxes? Why must
    their keys for these be turned in at the office each night?
16. How is registered and special delivery mail different from
    other mail?

B. Questions concerning responsibility towards mail.
   1. Why is it considered serious to open other people's mail?
   2. Why is it serious for an employee to tamper with mail?
   3. Why do larger post offices have a "catwalk"?
   4. What happens to dishonest employees?
   5. Must mail be delivered in any kind of weather?

C. Questions relative to postal savings and money orders.
   1. What are money orders and what is their advantage?
   2. Why does the post office have a postal savings depart-
      ment?
   3. How is it different from a bank?

D. Problems relative to the building of a post office in the
   room.
   1. What material can be used for building it?
   2. What size should it be in relation to floor space in the
      room? (Due to limited floor space and the children's
      desire to correlate other activities such as planes, trains,
      boats, trucks, etc., to carry mail, it was the unanimous
      decision of the group to construct the post office on a
      small scale and carry on dramatic play through dolls.)
   3. What will be needed in the post office?
   4. What means of transportation will be needed?

E. Problems concerning dramatic play.
   1. What are the activities and responsibilities of those
      working in the post office?
   2. What are the activities and responsibilities of those who
      handle mail on planes, boats, trucks, trains, etc.?

F. Questions concerning the post office as a government building.
   1. Why does it belong to the government?
   2. Why does it fly the American flag?

3. When is the flag put up and taken down?

4. Why does it hang at half-mast at times?

III. **Answering questions and solving problems.**

  A. Through constructive activities. Several small groups worked on the building of the post office and its furnishings. Others made the small houses and furnishings and laid out the streets in the community—built the harbor, docks, airport and railroad station. Many children contributed their individual constructions of trucks, trains, boats, planes, etc.

    1. Building of the post office. This was made of scrap wood, boxes, beaver board and other scrap material.

      a. Post office was constructed so as to leave part of it open, making possible play within the building.

      b. Pulley arrangement was made to raise and lower flag. (This seemed an important part of the post office. The children were delighted one morning to find their pet parrot had gotten out of his cage and was perched on the top of this flag pole. "Now we have a bird on our flag pole, just like the brass eagle down at the real post office!")

      c. Stamp windows, mail chutes, sorting tables, boxes, mailbags and corner mailboxes were constructed.

    2. Constructing of boats, mail boats, trains and airplanes to carry mail bags.

    3. Building of houses using boxes, orange crates and heavy cardboard cartons.

    4. Making of people—clothespin dolls and pipe cleaner dolls.

    5. Laying out of community.

  B. Through oral and written language.

    1. Group discussions pertaining to questions that arose during construction periods, and relative to knowledge sought.

    2. Discussions relative to excursions, their purpose and outcomes.

    3. Individual contributions relative to experiences concerning mail, trips to post office, etc., or information gained outside of school.

    4. Making of labels and signs.

      a. Signs on post office, mail trucks, boats, trains and airplanes.

      b. Labels for windows in post office, on mailbox, etc.

C. Through reading.

1. Reading from blackboard material, answering questions the members of the group wanted answered.
2. Sharing with one another stories in readers dealing with the post office.
3. Reading of letters from one another. (Children would often write letters at home to one another and have on desks to surprise one another.) Reading of letters from other groups with whom they corresponded.
4. Bulletin board material—interesting bits written by the teacher concerning mail. Labels on new or unusual stamps.

Books Read By Children

Park, Dorothea	Here Comes the Postman	1936	Houghton
Read, Helen S.	Billy's Letter	1929	Scribner
Smith, Nila B.	The Postman	1935	Silver Burdett

Stories Told to Children

Ingersoll, M. I. Owney of the Mail Bags (In Baker, C. B. and E. D. Dinty the Porcupine and Other Stories. 1938 Bobbs-Merrill)

Lyvers, Helen The Mail goes Through (In Baker, C. B. and E. D. Our World and Others. 1938 Bobbs-Merrill)

Bibliography for Teacher

Chapman, Arthur	The Pony Express	1932	Putnam
Hall, C. G.	Mail Comes Through	1938	Macmillan
Hall, C. G.	Skyways	1938	Macmillan
Hall, C. G.	Through by Rail	1938	Macmillan
Harlow, Alvin F.	Old Post Bags	1928	Appleton
Hughes, Avah	Carrying the Mail	1933	Teachers College
McSpadden, J. W.	How They Carried the Mail	1930	Dodd, Mead

United States Post Office Department. A Brief History of the United States Postal Service. 1938, Government Printing Office

D. Through the use of arithmetic.

1. Measuring carefully all construction work whenever there was a real need.
2. Recognizing need for good proportion in making building, means of conveyance, etc.
3. Recognizing of numbers on clock and stamps of various denominations, time collections on boxes.
4. Counting and computing.
   a. Playing games with stamps mounted on cards.
   b. Playing games with the above stamp cards plus using real coins to "buy" the stamps. Amounts up to 50 cents were used.

    c. Comparing cost of sending letters today with cost of transportation by Pony Express.

    d. Learning the number of miles traveled by an Express rider.

  5. Weighing.

    Experimenting with scales to determine the weight of various size packages.

IV. Social meanings, attitudes, appreciations, developing through these experiences.

  A. Some understanding of how the postal system operates.

  B. An appreciation of the need for the dependability of those working for the postal system.

  C. Some conception of the need for accuracy and speed on the part of employees.

  D. Some understanding of the inter-relationships involved in transporting mail.

  E. An interest in various cities and in foreign countries and their location.

  F. Some conception of the route of the Pony Express.

  G. Some understanding of how to write a letter and address an envelope in proper form.

V. Interpretation and expression of attitudes and appreciations.

  A. Through creative expression.

    1. Many letters written by individuals.

    2. Group letters composed to postmaster.

    3. Stories written by individuals about carrying the mail.

    4. Poems created by individuals; as,

The Mail Plane

Br-r-r- The airplane
  is carrying mail
  through the sky;
Far below the airport's lights
  are gleaming.
She roars down to a landing.
The mail trucks are waiting.
Off to the post office with the mail.
The men sort the mail and—
Off to the houses it goes.

The Mail Plane

The wonderful bird gets ready to fly.
She goes over mountains and cities.
Away goes the mail plane with its
  passengers and all.

Through night and day it flies—
    snow or no snow
She goes on and on—
On she flies.

Drop, drop the letters in the slot,
Air mails and special deliveries.
Fast they must go—
Fast on their way.

    B. Through picture making.
      1. Drawing of pictures by individuals.
      2. Painting of pictures relative to processes in handling mail. The incentive for these was to share with others at an assembly the group's experience in finding out what happens to a letter when it is mailed.
    C. Through dramatic play.
      1. Delivering and collecting mail, using small dolls as puppets.
      2. Loading and unloading mail from trains, trucks, boats, planes and busses.
      3. Dramatization of Owney the Postal Dog—using a toy dog and having him travel with the mail on various conveyances.

VI. New interests foreshadowing further units of work.

    A. A desire to go more deeply into a study of the Pony Express and Indian life in the west.
    B. An interest in the life of Buffalo Bill and Kit Carson and other pioneers of the west.

Developing Pottery and a Pottery Shop

An Enterprise in the Second Grade

I. Enriching experiences which aroused and fostered interest and provided background.

    A. Moist clay was available in the room for the children's use, and modeling became a favorite occupation. Discussion of the children's work led to an interest in pottery.

    B. Pictures of beautifully designed clay bowls were studied from the bulletin board.

    C. An exhibit of pottery made by college students increased the children's interest.

    D. A trip to Haeger Pottery at Dundee enabled the children to see various ways of making pottery.

    E. The group visited the pottery shop run in connection with the Haeger Pottery at Dundee, and purchased a vase and a bowl for their room.

    F. The making of plaster of Paris molds at school provided a means of producing many bowls, and the idea occurred to the children that these might be sold in a pottery shop of their own.

    G. A bazaar held by the college students gave suggestions to the children of ways of organizing a sale.

II. Problems and questions which led to investigation.

    A. Concerning the making of pottery.

        1. Where does clay come from? How do we get it?

        2. What makes clay harden? How can we keep unfinished clay objects moist?

        3. How are the dishes in our homes made and decorated?

        4. How can dishes which are exactly alike be made?

        5. What are the different ways of making clay objects?

            a. How are molds made?

            b. How is the potter's wheel operated?

            c. How is liquid clay used?

        6. By what process is pottery fired and decorated?

    B. Concerning the operation of a gift shop.

        1. What shall we do with the molds we have made? Could we make many bowls and plates and sell them?

        2. What might be sold in a gift shop? What articles shall we make for our shop?

        3. What persons are needed to conduct a gift shop?

4. How is the value of articles determined? How shall our pottery be priced?
5. What does the shopkeeper do with his money? Where does money go from a bazaar? What shall we do with our money?
6. How shall we build our booths?

III. Answering questions and solving problems.
A. Through group discussions.
1. Discussions were held concerning the children's clay modeling, how the work could be improved, how unfinished clay objects could be kept, how finished articles could be hardened and decorated.
2. Conversations were held concerning the kinds of dishes the family used at home, where and how these wares were made.
3. Observations at the Haeger Pottery were discussed at length. Many questions were asked and answered both during the excursion and later.

It's Fun to Model

POTTERY IS PRODUCED TO SELL

4. Plans for making molds and duplicating articles were discussed.
5. The decision to conduct a gift shop led to many discussions concerning the making of articles, the construction of booths, the organization for selling, and the prices.

B. Through constructive activities.
  1. The children at first carried on much experimentation with clay, making bowls, candlesticks, inkwells, pencil holders, and plaques.
  2. After the trip to the Haeger Pottery, they experimented with plaster of Paris molds, as follows:
    a. Mixed plaster of Paris with water.
    b. Made molds by placing original object in pan of soft plaster.
    c. Made liquid clay by mixing clay with water to a pouring consistency.
    d. Made duplicate objects by pouring liquid clay into molds.

3. The best objects made were fired and decorated. The children helped to pack and unpack clay articles sent to be fired.

4. Articles were constructed from wood to sell with the clay objects in the gift shop: book ends, bookracks, bookcases, letter openers, door stops, doll furniture, boats.

5. Booths were constructed and decorated.

6. Price tags, lists, posters and signs were made.

C. Through factual reading.

1. Plans and directions were written on the blackboard from time to time and read.

2. Signs, posters, labels and price lists all required reading.

3. Some informational material was simplified by the teacher and placed on charts for the children's reading.

Teacher's References

Bragg, William Henry	Creative Knowledge (Old Trades and New Sciences.)	1927	Harper
Bruce, Marjory	Book of Craftsmen	1937	Dodd, Mead
Cox, George James	Pottery	1926	Macmillan
Parker, Arthur C.	Indian How Book	1927	Doubleday Doran
Scacheri, Maria	Indians Today	1936	Harcourt, Brace
Wheeler, Ida W.	Playing with Clay	1927	Macmillan

D. Through arithmetic.

1. Children learned to judge the quantity of clay needed for a certain object.

2. Measurement was required in pouring liquid clay into molds.

3. Values of pottery were learned from the purchase of articles at the Haeger Pottery Shop.

4. Valuation of the children's work was made in pricing articles for the shop.

5. The sale gave opportunity for application of the following skills:

a. Reading figures on price labels and price lists.

b. Using some addition, subtraction and multiplication facts.

c. Handling coins in making change.

d. Using certain arithmetic terms; as, price, purchase, borrow, lend, equals.

IV. **Meanings, attitudes and appreciations probably developed through these experiences.**

A. Respect for the skillful work of others and for those who create beautiful things.

B. Knowledge and appreciation of what constitutes beauty in pottery: form, color, design.
C. Appreciation of the need for carefulness, patience, skill in making pottery.
D. Knowledge of the commercial process of making pottery and its commercial value.
E. Knowledge and appreciation of fairness and accuracy in buying and selling.
F. Increased understanding of the contribution of the factory and the merchant to the community.
G. Appreciation of the need for courtesy, cheerfulness and helpfulness in conducting a business.

V. **Interpretation and expressions of attitudes and appreciations.**
   A. Through creative composition.
      1. Original stories were written in diaries about the trip to the pottery.
      2. Letters were written to absent children about the trip and about the plans for a shop.
   B. Through picture-making, design, decoration.
      1. Designs were drawn sometimes before objects were decorated.
      2. Many clay articles were decorated with original designs.
      3. Booths and posters were designed and decorated by the children.
   C. Through social activity, sharing experiences with others.
      1. Some of the clay articles made were presented as gifts to mothers at the Christmas party.
      2. Other grades came in to see the booths before the sale was opened.
      3. The children enjoyed both buying and selling. Parents, friends, teachers and college students were patrons of the gift shop.

VI. **New interests, foreshadowing other activities.**
   A study of designs on Indian pottery led to an interest in Indians.

Living on a Farm

A Spring Interest in Second Grade

I. **Enriching experiences which aroused and fostered interest and provided background.**

    A. One of the children related frequently stories of his summer on a farm, arousing an interest in farm life.

    B. The class took an excursion to a farm.

    C. Many farm pictures were brought to school.

    D. A college student brought six baby ducks to visit for a few days.

    E. A mother presented the room with a small incubator.

II. **Problems and questions which led to investigation.**

    A. Concerning farm buildings.

        1. In making a farm, what are some of the buildings we should have?

        2. Why is the barn usually larger than the house? For what purposes is the barn used?

        3. Why does the farmer like to have a cement floor for the barn?

        4. Where are the hay and corn kept?

        5. Why is the silo placed near the barn?

        6. What kind of house should the farmer have?

        7. What color are farm buildings usually painted and why?

    B. Concerning the farm animals.

        1. What space is needed for large animals to roam?

        2. Why does gravel make a good covering for the barnyard?

        3. What is a pasture? What animals go to the pasture?

        4. What kind of fence is best to have on a farm?

        5. What care must be given to cows? How is milk protected and used?

        6. Why do sheep need a different type of shelter than cows and horses?

    C. Concerning the raising of poultry.

        1. What is an incubator? What is a brooder?

        2. What kind of eggs do we have to get for hatching?

        3. What temperature must the incubator be set? Should the eggs be moist or dry? How often should the eggs be turned?

        4. How long does it take the eggs to hatch?

        5. What care must be given to baby chicks and ducks?

III. Answering questions and solving problems.

    A. Through discussion.

        1. Children told of their personal experiences in living on farms.

        2. There was much discussion of the class excursion to a farm. Reference was made to this trip as problems arose in constructing a farm.

        3. Pictures stimulated discussion and aided in solving problems.

        4. Planning for building the farm involved comparison of suggestions and sometimes real debate.

        5. The gift to the room of an incubator stimulated questions and discussions concerning the raising of baby chicks and ducks.

    B. Through constructive activities.

        1. A farm was constructed on the floor along one side of the room. Buildings and vehicles were built of boxes and lumber: house, barn, silo, hen house, chicken coop, dog house, wagon, hayrack.

        2. Spaces were measured off for yard, barnyard and pastures. Fences were constructed and installed.

        3. The barnyard was covered with gravel, and a well and trough were constructed.

        4. The yard and pasture were covered with earth, over a heavy piece of linoleum. Grass seed was planted.

        5. A pool and swing were made for the yard.

        6. Many farm animals were made of wood and clay.

        7. Dolls were dressed to represent the farmer, his wife and child.

        8. The children wished to experiment with the incubator which had been presented to the room. Eggs were purchased and the incubator was watched and tended with great care.

        9. Children tried the experiment of making butter.

    C. Through factual reading.

        1. Accounts of the children's actual farm experiences were read from the blackboard.

        2. Plans for constructing the farm were also read.

        3. Material from government bulletins on the raising and care of poultry and other farm animals was simplified by the teacher and placed on charts.

        4. The care of the incubator required reading of the time and temperature chart; and also the weekly calendar, listing each child's time to turn the eggs.

References for Children and Teacher

Bulletin from the Department of Agriculture, Washington, D. C.

Beaty, John Y.	Story Pictures of Farm Animals	1934	Beckley-Cardy
Beaty, John Y.	Story Pictures of Farm Foods	1935	Beckley-Cardy
Beaty, John Y.	Story Pictures of Farm Work	1936	Beckley-Cardy
Comstock, Anna B.	Handbook of Nature Study	1939	Comstock
Lawson, J. G.	Farm Animals	1935	Rand McNally
Lent, H. B.	The Farmer	1937	Macmillan
Mason, M. E.	Smiling Hill Farm	1937	Ginn
Miller, M.	Dean and Don at the Dairy	1936	Houghton Mifflin
Petersham, Maud and Miska	The Story Book of Foods	1936	Winston
Sherman, H. C.	Food Products	1924	Macmillan
Webster, H. H. and Polkinghorne, A. R.	What the World Eats.	1938	Houghton Mifflin

Compton's Pictured Encyclopedia. 1940 Compton.
World Book Encyclopedia. 1940 Quarrie.

D. Through use of arithmetic.
1. Measurement was acquired in constructing farm build-ings and fences, and in setting off spaces for yard, barn-yard, pasture.
2. Eggs were purchased and counted for incubator.
3. Thermometer was used in keeping accurate temperature of incubator.
4. Terms pint, quart, pound, were used in butter making.
5. Calendar was kept for timing the hatching of the eggs.

IV. **Meanings, attitudes, appreciations probably developed through these experiences.**
A. Some understanding of what the farmer does for us in pro-viding food.
B. Appreciation of farm animals, their value and service.
C. Some knowledge of the organization of the old-fashioned farm and its varied activities.
D. Some appreciation of the dependence of the city on the sur-rounding farms.
E. Some appreciation of the need for well-kept and sanitary farms.
F. An appreciation of the picturesque charm of a farm, at dif-ferent seasons of the year.
G. Some understanding and appreciation of the farmer's re-sponsibility, in providing proper care for animals and plants, under changing weather conditions.
H. An eagerness to participate in farm activities by raising chickens and making a garden.

V. Interpretation and expression of attitudes and appreciations.

A. By means of picture-story books about farm life. The children enjoyed silent and oral reading from these books:

Agnew, K. E. & Coble, M.	Baby Animals on the Farm	1933 World Book
Baker, C. B. and Reed, M.	Friends Here and Away	1938 Bobbs-Merrill
Hader, Mrs. B.	The Farmer in the Dell	1931 Macmillan
Manly-Griswold	Summer on the Farm	1926 Scribner
Orton, Helen F.	Bobby at Cloverfield Farm	1922 Stokes
Orton, Helen F.	Prancing Pat	1927 Stokes
Orton, Helen F.	The Little Lost Pigs	1925 Stokes
Perkins, Lucy Fitch	The Farm Twins	1928 Houghton Mifflin
Read, E. & Lee, H.	Grandfather's Farm	1928 Scribner
Stong, P. D.	Farm Boy	1934 Doubleday Doran
Tippett, James S.	The Singing Farmer	1927 World Book
Troxell, E. & Dunn, F.	Baby Animals	1928 Row Peterson
Zirbes, Laura	Book of Pets	1936 Keystone

Selected farm stories and poems from several readers.

B. By means of music.
1. The children enjoyed singing about farm life and its activities, such songs as: The Bee, Little Chickens, My Pony, Little Boy and the Sheep, Planting a Garden, Harvest Song, The Shower, Song of Bread.
2. Some nonsense songs were learned, such as: This is how we milk the cow; The milkmaid; Turkey in the straw.
3. Many of the songs suitable for action were dramatized.

Source Books

Baker and Kohlsaat	Songs for the Little Child	1938 Abingdon Press
Coleman, Satis	The Gingerbread Man	1931 John Day
Davison and Surette	One Hundred Forty Folk-Songs	1922 E. C. Schirmer
O'Neill, Norman	A Song Garden for Children	1928 Edward Arnold
Palmer, Winthrop	American Songs for Children	1931 Macmillan
LaSalle, Dorothy	Rhythms and Dances	1930 A. S. Barnes
Robinson, Ethel	School Rhythms	1928 Clayton Summy

C. By means of dramatic activity.
The children greatly enjoyed carrying on farm activities with the dolls as puppets, dramatizing these activities:
1. Carrying hay on the rack and tossing it into the barn.
2. Drawing water from the well, and placing it in the trough for the animals.
3. Taking the cows to pasture and bringing them back to the barn.

4. Hauling farm produce in the wagon.

VI. New interests, foreshadowing further activities.
    A. A keen interest in poultry raising.
    B. An interest in making a garden. A garden on the campus
        was started while the interest in the farm was still high.

Creating a Garden and a Garden Market

A Second Grade Interest During Spring Months

I. **Enriching experiences which aroused and fostered interest and provided background.**
   A. The study of farm life involved listing of different vegetables and fruits raised on a farm.
   B. During the excursion to a farm, the children saw extensive gardens.
   C. A trip to a grocery store afforded observation of many different kinds of vegetables.
   D. Seed catalogs brought by the children stimulated an interest in raising vegetables and flowers.
   E. Planting the garden led to an interest in experimenting with seeds.
   F. Maturing vegetables brought a desire for a garden market.
   G. Another trip to the grocery store was made to learn prices of vegetables and methods of displaying them for sale.

II. **Problems and questions which led to discussion and experiment.**
   A. Concerning preparation for a garden.
      1. How shall we prepare to make a garden?
      2. What kind of soil is needed? Do different plants need different soils?
      3. How does the soil have to be prepared?
      4. What is the best location for a garden?
      5. How should the garden be plotted?
      6. What kind of tools will we need?
   B. Concerning the planting and care of a garden.
      1. What is the best time to plant?
      2. What kind of seeds shall we plant in our garden?
      3. Where will be the best place to plant each kind? Which vegetables grow under the ground and which above? Which grow tall and which short?
      4. What kind of care does a growing garden need?
      5. Who will care for the garden?
   C. Concerning experimentation with seeds.
      1. Do seeds grow best in dark or sunlight?
      2. Do seeds grow best with or without water?
      3. What gives the plants their colors?
   D. Concerning the marketing of produce.
      1. What are we going to do with our vegetables?

MOTHERS ARE GOOD CUSTOMERS

2. What are right prices for vegetables?
3. How are they arranged and prepared for selling?
4. How shall we make our market?
5. Who will be most likely to buy our vegetables? How shall we advertise?
6. What else might be sold in a garden market besides vegetables and flowers?

III. Finding answers to problems and questions.

A. By means of oral discussion.
  1. Many problems as they arose were solved by group discussion.
  2. Particular problems were referred to committees for discussion and investigation. Committees brought reports to the whole group.
  3. Experiences in home gardens and in excursions were recalled and used to throw light on problems.
  4. Much spontaneous conversation developed among the children as they talked over their plans for making the garden and for selling their vegetables.

B. By means of constructive activities.
  1. In making the garden the children engaged in a variety of activities.
     a. Marked out the garden plot.
     b. Turned up the ground, pulverized the dirt, raked it smooth.
     c. Drew a diagram of best places to plant seeds.
     d. Divided the garden plot according to the diagram.
     e. Planted the seeds at correct depth.
     f. Made garden markers for different plants.
     g. Weeded and watered the garden.
  2. The children carried on some experimentation with seeds.
     a. Planted two boxes of peas and beans, one left in dark and one in sunlight.
     b. Planted beans and peas in earth and on wet cotton.
     c. Planted two boxes of beans and peas, one to be watered and one not.
  3. In preparing for the garden market the class carried on these activities.
     a. Made and decorated booths in which to sell vegetables.
     b. Decorated boxes and baskets for holding vegetables; pots for holding flowers.
     c. Made garden markers of wool to sell, and garden kneeling pads of oilcloth.
     d. Pulled up vegetables, sorted and priced them for selling.
     e. Made signs, posters and price tags.
C. By means of factual reading.
  1. Extracts were read from seed catalogs, telling names of vegetables and flowers and how to plant them.
  2. The diagram of the garden plot was read.
  3. The children made and read a chart, recording results of experiments with seeds.

Teacher's References

Comstock, Anna B.	Handbook of Nature Study	1939 Comstock
Dubois, Gertrude and Frances	Peter and Penny Make a Garden	1936 Stokes
Encking, L. F.	The Little Gardeners	1935 Whitman
Fox, Frances M.	Flowers and Their Travels	1936 Bobbs-Merrill
Jenkins, D. H.	The Children Make a Garden	1936 Doubleday
McGill, Janet	The Garden of the World	1930 Follett
Wodell, H. P.	Beginning to Garden	1928 Macmillan

D. By means of arithmetic.
   1. Children used measuring and counting in making the garden.
     a. Measured the garden plot.
     b. Divided the plot into quarter sections.
     c. Measured in drawing garden diagram for the room.
     d. Counted kinds of seeds, and number of rows.
     e. Planted some seeds $\frac{1}{4}$ inch deep; others $\frac{1}{2}$ inch and 1 inch deep.
   2. The market required counting and handling of money.
     a. Sorted vegetables in bunches; as, 6 radishes, 5 onions, 10 lettuce leaves.
     b. Priced vegetables for sale.
     c. Made change in selling.
     d. Counted money and deposited in bank.
   3. The decision was made to use funds for helping in decoration of children's dining room.

IV. **Meanings, attitudes and appreciations probably developed through these experiences.**
   A. Understanding of activities required in raising plants.
   B. Appreciation of thought and time and responsible care which must be given to production of vegetables and flowers.
   C. Understanding of activities involved in marketing vegetables.
   D. Appreciation of service of truck farmer, gardener, grocer, and our dependence on them.
   E. Appreciation of value of sunshine and rain and part they play in gardening.
   F. A respect for scientific experimentation.
   G. A pleasure in the beauty of growing and blooming plants.
   H. A greater readiness to eat and enjoy fresh garden vegetables.

V. **Interpretation and expression of attitudes and appreciations.**
   A. By means of creative composition.
     1. Results of different experiments with beans and peas were written up.
     2. Letters were sent to mothers telling them about the garden market, and inviting them to come.
     3. Spring poems were written about the garden, rain, sunshine, flowers; as,

Spring

Spring is here and I am glad,
'Cause I hear the birds calling,
And see the rain falling,
And hear the wind blowing,
And see the flowers growing.

What Is Coming?

What is coming? What is coming?
Spring is coming. Spring is coming.
What is here? What is here?
Spring is here. Spring is here.
And all the flowers and all the trees are in bloom.

Rain

Rain, rain, coming fast,
It is coming down at last.
When the sun comes out
There is a spluttering sprout.

Rain, rain, do not fall,
Do not make the grass grow tall.
When the rain goes away,
I am going out to play.

The Rainbow

Rainbow, rainbow,
As you stretched across the sky,
The sky was so blue,
The sun was so bright,
And so were the clouds
That went slip-sliding by.

B. By means of picture making.
   1. Farm pictures were drawn with gardens included.
   2. There was spontaneous painting and drawing of flowers and vegetables.
   3. Posters were designed to announce the garden market.
C. By means of music.
   1. Songs of spring and gardens were used, such as:

The Shower	One Hundred Forty Folk Songs
The Apple Tree House	One Hundred Forty Folk Songs
Planting a Garden	One Hundred Forty Folk Songs
The Farm	One Hundred Forty Folk Songs
My Garden of Flowers	One Hundred Forty Folk Songs
Singing	Kindergarten Book of Folk Songs

   2. The class enjoyed selecting and orchestrating, for rhythm instruments, music with a spring-like mood.

In May	One Hundred Forty Folk Songs
Come Lasses and Lads	A Book of Songs
The Sleepy Miller	Kindergarten Book of Folk Songs
Burny-Bee	Kindergarten Book of Folk Songs
Lavender's Blue	Kindergarten Book of Folk Songs

3. Music was found suitable for one of the children's own poems, "Rain." The familiar old song, "Rain, rain, go to Spain" found in the Kindergarten Book of Songs was used.

Source Books

Diller and Page	Rote Songs for Rhythm Bands	1930 Schirmer
Davison and Surette	One Hundred Forty Folk Songs	1922 Schirmer
Davison, Surette, Zanzig	A Book of Songs	1922 Schirmer
Warner	A Kindergarten Book of Folk Songs	1923 Schirmer

D. By means of social activity.
   1. Some of the radishes and lettuce were used for the school luncheon.
   2. The children enjoyed buying and selling at the garden market. The teachers and mothers were patrons of the sale.

VI. New interests foreshadowing further activities.
   A. Study of flowers and flower arrangement.
   B. Preparation of vegetables and other foods for the table.
   C. Hygienic value of vegetables and fruits.

UNITS OF EXPERIENCE IN
THIRD GRADE

OPPORTUNITIES offered by the community for broadening interests and information have been utilized in the third grade.

A delight in picture-making led to the study of the art centers in the community. The children constructed an art gallery in the room and exhibited there many famous pictures loaned from home collections. In one wing their own best art productions were exhibited. A visit to the Chicago Art Institute enabled them to see the originals of some of their favorite prints.

The children have enjoyed constructing a puppet theater or a shadow theater, making or dressing dolls as actors, and dramatizing their favorite stories for other groups in the room and for boys and girls of neighboring rooms. Attendance at children's plays given by professional actors and puppeteers has given background.

As in other grades, the interest in transportation and travel is very keen. The third-grade children have enjoyed reporting on their vacation trips, and sometimes this interest has led to a study of the means of traveling used in different parts of the world today or the development of transportation in our own country. Visits to airports, railway stations, and boat piers have been supplemented by trips to the museum to see models of vehicles used in other countries and in earlier times.

Sometimes the interest in travel has led to the study of a different community; as, American Indians or Mexicans. Such studies have been enriched by many beautiful objects which the children or their parents have collected during vacation trips; and by pictures and motion pictures which parents have loaned.

In addition to these experiences in the social studies, the children have had some live science interests. Individual hobbies in science have been followed for extended periods. A large aquarium was purchased by the third-grade children one year, and a study of water life was inherited by the succeeding group. Many kinds of water creatures have been kept at different times in the room aquarium, and excursions to the new Shedd Aquarium in Chicago have afforded an enriched experience.

An alert third-grade group became curious about the making of maple sugar, through a story read in the room library; and made an intensive study of maple trees and the art of sugar-making. A correspondence was carried on with the owner of a maple sugar farm in Vermont; and the children took orders for maple syrup and sugar and imported a small amount to sell. A picturesque maple sugar camp was erected under the maple trees on the campus, where their wares were displayed.

The studies outlined here were some that provoked particular interest on the part of the group engaged in the study. They have been selected from the work of three or four different years. Outcomes in social meanings and appreciations peculiar to the particular unit are included with the unit. All of the enterprises have afforded opportunity for growth in certain desirable social attitudes and habits; as, coöperation and responsibility in carrying on group activities, independence in working out a small problem alone, respect for the rights and opinions of others in the group, appreciation of the contribution of others, readiness to share ideas and materials with others, courteous conduct at school and on excursions, resourcefulness in using materials at hand, persistence in completing work begun. The studies have contributed, too, in the development of the powers of expression through fine and industrial arts, music, dramatization and other avenues. Outcomes in terms of the specific skills, arithmetic and English, are summarized in Group Records of Progress, Part IV.

Conducting an Art Gallery

An Interest in Third Grade

I. Enriching experiences which aroused and fostered interest and provided background for activities.

    A. Children spontaneously drew and painted pictures at easels and on worktables.

    B. Children's original pictures were exhibited and discussed.

    C. Pictures in the room by great artists were studied.

    D. Children brought from home prints of masterpieces.

    E. Trips were made to the Art Institute by the group and by individual children in company with their parents. It was possible to see originals of some of the prints in the room gallery.

    F. Trips were made around the building to study pictures in different rooms.

II. Problems and questions which led to investigation.

    A. What pictures are master paintings?

    B. Who are some of the master painters?

    C. What is meant by "original paintings"?

    D. Which pictures are copies and which are originals?

    E. Where are originals of famous pictures found?

    F. What is the present valuation of some of these originals?

    G. What are the names of some of the master paintings? Why did the artists name their pictures as they did?

    H. What materials are needed to make an art gallery in our room?

    I. How shall pictures be arranged and hung?

    J. How shall visitors be guided?

III. Answering questions and solving problems.

    A. Through discussion.

        1. Children discussed the permanent pictures in their room; learned the title of the picture and the name of the artist.

        2. As prints were brought in, each picture was studied and talked about. Children reported what their parents had said about the picture; where they had seen copies; why the picture was considered great.

        3. Trips to see pictures stimulated discussions about the

ART ENRICHES LIVING

selection of pictures for a school, a home, a gallery; the
arrangement, hanging and lighting of pictures.
4. Plans were made for building and conducting an art gallery in the room and for making guidebooks.
B. Through constructive activities.
1. An art gallery was constructed of composition boards,
covered with cheesecloth to give a soft background.
2. Prints of master paintings were arranged and hung.
3. Pictures in the art gallery were labeled with title and
name of artist.
4. Guidebooks were constructed containing miniature
copies of the paintings in the room gallery.
5. As gifts for parents, plaques of wood were designed, made
and shellacked. Each child selected and mounted a print
of a master painting upon his plaque.
C. Through factual reading.
1. The children read the cards which recorded the name and
title of each picture.
2. They kept and read a chart recording each child's contribution to the gallery and the guidebook.

3. Articles from magazines about famous pictures and artists were brought in and read by children and teachers.
4. Reference was made to books as questions arose.

References for Teacher and Children

Berry, A. M.	Art for Children	1929	Studio Pubs.
Bulliet, C. J.	Paintings	1934	Reynal
Chandler, Anna C.	Treasure Trails in Art	1937	Hale
Hillyer, V. M.	Child's History of Art	1933	Appleton
Lester, K. M.	Great Pictures and Their Stories (five volumes)	1927	Mentzer
Whitford, W. G.	Art Stories	1935	Scott Foresman

D. Through arithmetic.
1. Children were much interested in the money value of certain master paintings; enjoyed stories of auction sales of these pictures and surprising changes in value when the artist's name was discovered; compared prices of originals and prints.
2. Pictures in the room gallery were counted and numbered.

IV. **Meanings, attitudes and appreciations probably developed through these experiences.**
   A. Understanding and appreciation of a few master paintings: their beauty, color, meaning.
   B. Knowledge and admiration of a few master painters: their lives, greatest works, characteristic technique.
   C. Recognition and appreciation of the artist's contribution to the community and the home.
   D. Greater appreciation of the work of children in creating various art forms.

V. **Interpretation and expression of attitudes and appreciations.**
   A. Through literature and creative composition.
      1. Children listened with pleasure to stories told by teacher about certain pictures and artists.
      2. Children created original stories about the prints hung in the room gallery. Some of these were written and included in the guidebooks.
   B. Through painting and drawing.
      1. The study of famous pictures stimulated greater interest in creative painting and drawing on the part of the children. Much easel painting was done.
      2. Covers were designed for the original books.
      3. Gift cards were designed to accompany the plaques.

C. Through social activity, sharing experiences with others.
1. Parents and other grades were invited from time to time to see the gallery and use the guidebooks.
2. The plaques were presented to the parents as gifts.

VI. New interests, foreshadowing other projects.

Interest in various types of art; as, clay modeling, sketching, block printing, architecture, sculpture.

Traveling in Old and New Ways

An Enterprise in Third Grade

I. **Enriching experiences which aroused and fostered interest and gave background for activities.**
   A. Previous experiences.
      In the reports on summer vacations, the children told of the various ways they traveled during the summer. Thus they glimpsed the many interesting ways one might travel; and then followed organization of this unit.
   B. Conversations.
      Conversation led from familiar types of travel to the older types.
   C. Pictures.
      Snapshots, post cards, picture books, motion pictures, newspaper and magazine clippings, library picture collection, were all brought into use.
   D. Travel stories.
      1. Miss B. told the story of her trip to Alaska.
      2. Miss S. related the story of her travels in Mexico.
   E. Bringing of articles from home.
      1. Models. Pack horses, automobiles, coaches, covered wagons, many types of airplanes, birchbark canoe, kayak, were brought in from homes.
      2. Books. Books brought in by the children included Pictorial Portfolio of the World; The Picture Book of Travel; A Book of Ships; Wheel, Sail and Wing.
      3. Magazines. Magazines brought included copies of National Geographic, Travel, Alaska.

II. **Problems and questions which guided investigations.**
   A. For the group.
      1. What are the kinds of transportation?
      2. What are some of the vehicles used in each kind of travel; land, water, air?
      3. How will it be best to study all about transportation?
      4. Would it be a good idea to have three committees? How should the class be divided into committees?
      5. In what ways can we gain information about transportation?
      6. What would be the best way to use the picture collections and models brought in?

OLD-TIME VESSELS REAPPEAR

7. What can we make that will show different sorts of transportation?
8. How can we share what we learn with other people?

B. For the committee on land transportation.
　1. What were the first kinds of land travel in our country?
　2. Why do the people use dogs and sledges in Alaska?
　3. Why do men still use pack animals in many places to-day?
　4. What did the Pony Express carry?
　5. What was the covered wagon? Who used it and why?
　6. Why do we need bridges and tunnels for travel?
　7. When were the first trains made? What were they like?
　8. When were the first automobiles made? How were they different from ours to-day?

C. For the committee on water transportation.
　1. What was the first way men crossed bodies of water?
　2. How were the first canoes made?
　3. What is a kayak? Why is it suitable for use even today?
　4. What are some important differences between the earliest boats, the sailboats, and the steamers of to-day?
　5. How have different peoples constructed ships?

6. Are submarines ships?
7. Why do ships travel so fast now?
8. How did early ocean trips vary in time of crossing from the ones to-day?

D. For the committee on air transportation.
1. For what purposes are airplanes used?
2. What was the first means of transportation in the air?
3. What makes a balloon rise from the ground?
4. What are the kinds of planes and how do they differ?
5. For what are amphibians used?
6. How are planes equipped differently for landing on land, water, ice?
7. How does an autogiro differ from other air craft?
8. What were some of the famous air trips made by American pilots?

III. Finding answers to problems and questions.

A. Through oral discussion.
1. Group discussions were held concerning general organization of the work.
2. Committee discussions were held on all phases of their study.
3. Individuals reported progress to the teachers.
4. Individuals shared bits of information with other members of the committee.
5. The class organized a report of the unit to be put into a class bulletin for other grades to read.
6. The class planned a program in which the various committees might share with each other and their guests the information they had gained.

B. Through constructive activities.
1. The children prepared an exhibit of pictures and models brought in, labeling each one with a card bearing country, time and purpose.
2. From wood individual children made models to use in connection with their committee reports: dogs and sledges, jinrikisha, pack animals, covered wagon and oxen, carriages, dugout, canoe, Viking ship, airplane and other similar articles.
3. Each committee made large posters on transportation. Freehand cutting from colored paper was done.
4. Animals and boats were modeled from clay.
5. One committee made a block print of a ship and printed it on a muslin square.

6. Individuals made scrapbooks containing collections of pictures and clippings on particular phases of the study, with written explanations.

C. Through factual reading.

   1. Pamphlets on transportation were collected and used for reference.

   2. Books and magazines on travel were collected from the home and school libraries and used for study.

   3. Individuals did much silent reading, followed by oral reports and occasionally oral reading to the committee.

Children's References

Aitchison, A. E. and Uttley, M.	Across Seven Seas to Seven Continents	1937	Bobbs-Merrill
Beaty, John Y.	Story Pictures of Transportation	1939	Beckley-Cardy
Curtis, Nell C.	Boats	1927	Rand McNally
Dalgliesh, Alice	America Travels	1933	Macmillan
Dobias, Frank	Picture Book of Flying	1928	Macmillan
Floherty, J. J.	'Board the Airliner	1934	Doubleday
Fox, Florence C.	How the World Rides	1929	Scribner
Fraser, C. C.	The Model Aircraft Builder	1931	Crowell
Gravatt, Lila	Pioneers of the Air	1928	Mentzer Bush
Hader, B. and E.	Picture Book of Travel	1928	Macmillan
Henry, R. S.	Trains	1938	Bobbs-Merrill
Holland, R. S.	Historic Airplanes	1928	Macrae Smith
Holland, R. S.	Historic Railroads	1927	Macrae Smith
Holland, R. S.	Historic Ships	1926	Macrae Smith
Lent, H. B.	Clear Track Ahead!	1932	Macmillan
Lent, H. B.	Full Steam Ahead!	1933	Macmillan
Nathan, A. and E.	The Iron Horse	1931	Knopf
Stephenson, M. B.	Wheel, Sail and Wing	1930	Rockwell
Swift, Hildegarde	Little Blacknose	1929	Harcourt Brace

Teacher's References

Bridges, T. C.	Young Folks' Book of the Sea	1928	Little Brown
Collins, A. F.	Bird's Eye View of Invention	1926	Crowell
Daniel, H.	Ships of the Seven Seas	1925	Doubleday
Hall, C. G.	Skyways	1938	Macmillan
Hall, C. G.	Through by Rail	1938	Macmillan
Leeming, Joseph	Ships and Cargoes	1926	Doubleday
Post, A.	Skycraft	1933	Oxford
Reck, F. M.	Romance of American Transportation	1938	Crowell
Rocheleau, W. F.	Transportation	1928	Flanagan
Van Metre, T. B.	Trains, Tracks and Travel	1931	Simmons
Van Metre, T. B.	Tramps and Liners	1931	Doubleday
Wade, M. H.	Adventurers All	1927	Appleton
Webster, H. H.	Travel by Air, Land and Sea	1933	Houghton

D. Through use of number.
  1. Careful measuring was required to construct in proportion the dogs, oxen, pack animals; and also sledges, covered wagons, and other vehicles. Attempt was made to work out a fairly accurate scale of sizes.
  2. Much computation was needed in woodwork; as,
      a. If one ox is nine inches long, how long a strip of wood is needed to cut four oxen?
      b. If it takes four minutes to saw one dog, how long a time will be needed to complete six dogs?

IV. **Social meanings, attitudes, appreciations, probably developed through these experiences.**
  A. Some understanding of the development of transportation, of the crude and slow methods used in early times.
  B. Knowledge of how methods of transportation in different countries have depended on geographic conditions.
  C. Understanding and appreciation of the continuous achievements of men in overcoming difficulties in transportation.
  D. Wonder and gratitude for the attainments of modern science in construction of vehicles, bridges, tunnels, highways.
  E. Some appreciation of the changes wrought by growing speed of transportation.
  F. Admiration of the accomplishment of classmates in production of models and gathering of information.

V. **Interpretation and expression of attitudes and appreciations.**
  A. Through creative composition.
      1. Individuals created original narratives to commemorate interesting events in the development of transportation. These were told or read aloud to the group and also incorporated in individual scrapbooks.
      2. Individuals wrote descriptions on such topics as: Covered Wagons, The Jinrikisha, Pack Animals, Carriages of Early Days, Sledges, Canoes, Autogiros. These were used either in scrapbooks or in connection with exhibits.
      3. A class report was composed for a class bulletin.
  B. Through picture-making.
      There was much spontaneous picture-making.
      1. Large pictures on travel were painted.
      2. Large crayon drawings were also made.
      3. Large blackboard drawings were made, several children often working together.

    4. Covers were designed for individual scrapbooks.

C. Through social activity.

    1. At an assembly of the entire class, each committee reported on the results of its study and work. The class was so enthusiastic, that it was decided to share the reports with other groups.

    2. The fourth grade was invited to attend an assembly, to see the exhibits, and hear a review of the study.

    3. A program was arranged for the mothers, and invitations were sent. The chairman of each committee announced the contributions from his committee, together with the names of the speakers.

VI. New interests.

After completing this unit of study, the children were eager to take an imaginary trip together traveling in as many ways as possible.

Visiting the Indians

A Study of Modern Indian Life in Third Grade

I. **Enriching experiences which aroused and fostered interest and provided background.**
  A. A study of "Carrying the Mail" led to an historical survey involving the Pony Express and the encounters the riders had with the Indians.
  B. Several children contributed experiences in visiting Indians in Arizona, New Mexico and Wisconsin.
  C. Some children brought Indian materials from home—some they had gathered in their travels or had been given by parents and friends.
  D. The class made collections of pictures of different tribes of Indians, later placing emphasis on those of the Southwest.
  E. Shared with the whole school at an assembly two excellent motion pictures showing the present modes of living of Indians in the Southwest.
  F. Made an excursion to the Field Museum where observation and study were confined to Indians of the Southwest. (The teachers guided the investigation in order to make a more concentrated study of Indian culture today as found in Hopis, Navajos and Apaches, rather than diffuse interest on any or all Indians.)
  G. Shared with the whole school a dramatization using one chapter of *Dancing Cloud* (see bibliography) which was presented in connection with a Book Week program.
  H. Arranged an exhibit of all Indian material which they collected and placed in the library as part of the Book Week program.
  I. Carried on correspondence with children of an Indian school in northern Wisconsin.
  J. Made Christmas gifts for these children and received from them a box of cones and Christmas greens to decorate the room at school.

II. **Problems and questions which led to investigation.**
  A. Relating to shelter.
    1. Where are Indians living today and in what types of homes?
    2. Why do their homes vary in material and construction?
    3. How are they furnished?

4. Why are some tribes nomadic?
B. Relating to food.
1. What are the problems involved in the food supply in various tribes throughout the country?
2. What do the Indians of the Southwest eat, and how do they prepare their foods?
3. What utensils do they use and how are these made?
C. Relating to clothing.
1. What is the dress of the Indians in different parts of the country today?
2. How does it vary from earlier days and why?
3. How are their dyes made?
4. What variety is seen in their hairdress, and of what significance is this?
5. Why do not Indian men have whiskers?
D. Relating to means of livelihood.
1. How do the Indians make a living?
2. What is the contribution of the Indians of the Southwest to the arts and crafts of today?
3. What meanings have the designs used in rug weaving, sand painting, silver work, and pottery?
4. What are their opportunities for barter and buying and selling?
E. Relating to transportation.
1. By what means do Indians travel today?
2. How did they travel in earlier days?
3. What materials were used and how were dugouts, bull-boats, canoes, and papoose cases made?
4. What animals are used by the Indians in traveling and in conveying materials?
F. Relating to ceremonies and dances.
1. What forms of religion do the Indians have?
2. What meanings have their ceremonies and dances?
3. What part does costume and decoration play in their ceremonies?
4. How do they care for their sick today and previously?
5. What instruments do they use and of what materials are these made?

III. Finding answers to questions and problems.

A. Through oral discussion.
1. Children exchanged firsthand experiences in visiting Indian centers.
2. Teacher (who had rich background of experience among

Indians of the Southwest and Wisconsin) contributed to discussions.

3. Shared stories found in readers, library books, and told stories heard at home and from other adults.
4. Discussed factual material gathered from many sources.
5. Discussed problems involved in use of materials, constructions, arranging exhibit, presentation of dramatic efforts.
6. Discussed questions provoked by use of pictures, motion pictures, and excursion to museum.

B. Through factual reading.

A room library was established with a wealth of books which children used extensively as problems arose. The material varied greatly in difficulty so that all children could participate in carrying on some research either for their own benefit or to share with others their findings.

Bibliography of Children's Books

Armer, Laura Adams	Waterless Mountain	1931	Longmans
Brock, Emma L.	One Little Indian Boy	1932	Knopf
Buff, Mary and Conrad	Dancing Cloud	1937	Viking Press
Deming, Therese O., and Edwin W.	Indians in Winter Camp	1931	Laidlaw
Deming, Therese O., · and Edwin W.	Little Eagle	1931	Laidlaw
Deming, Therese O., and Edwin W.	Red People of the Wooded Country	1932	Whitman
Gifford, J. C.	Red Feather's Adventures	1923	Lyons and Carnahan
Henderson, Rose	Five Little Indians	1931	McBride
Kellogg, Harold and Delaine	Indians of the Southwest	1936	Rand McNally
Lyback, Johanna R.	Nayka	1932	Abingdon
Moon, Grace	The Book of Nah-Wee	1932	Doubleday
Sperry, Armstrong	Little Eagle, A Navajo Boy	1938	Winston
Walker, Hattie Adell	Shining Star	1932	Beckley-Cardy

References for Teachers

Applegate, Frank G.	Indian Stories from the Pueblo	1929	Lippincott
Buttree, Julia M.	The Rhythm of the Redman	1930	Barnes
Coolidge, M. R.	The Rain Makers	1929	Houghton
Goddard, Pliny E.	Indians of the Southwest	1931	American Museum Press
Goddard, Pliny E.	First Families of the Southwest	1928	Fred Harvey
Harrington, Isis L.	Nah-le Kah-de (He Herds His Sheep)	1937	E. P. Dutton
Hunt, W. Ben	Indian and Camp Handicraft	1938	Bruce
Lincoln School Staff	Curriculum Making in an Elementary School	1927	Ginn
Parker, Arthur C.	The Indian How Book	1927	Doubleday
Salomon, Julian H.	Indian Crafts and Indian Lore	1928	Harper
Smith, (Mrs.) White Mountain	Indian Tribes of the Southwest	1933	Stanford Univ.
Wissler, Clark	The American Indian	1938	Oxford Press

Films Used in Study of Indian Civilization
(all rental films)

Cheeka, an Indian Boy	Eastman Kodak Company
Arts and Crafts	Y.M.C.A. Motion Picture Bureau
Dances of the Southwest	American Museum of Natural History, New York City
His Contribution to Modern Civilization	Y.M.C.A. Motion Picture Bureau
Navajo Weaving	American Museum of Natural History, New York City
Indians at Work	Dept of Interior, Office of Indian Affairs, Washington, D. C.
To! Cil! (Water! Grass!)	Dept. of Interior, Division of Information, Photographic Section, Washington, D. C.
Wee Anne Sees the Indians	Cinegraphic Corp., Pasadena, California, or University of Illinois Visual Aids Service

C. Through constructive activities.

1. Clay bowls were made and decorated.

2. Designs were made by a few for bead work, and some children executed small motifs on small commercial looms.

3. A rack for jerk meat was made to use in dramatic setting.

4. The girls made costumes of dyed unbleached muslin to use in the play of *Dancing Cloud*.

INDIAN ARTS ARE PRACTICED

5. The boys made Navajo belts, using circles cut from tin cans as silver on which they put meaningful Indian designs. These were perforated in the tin with nails.
6. Blankets were designed, using powder paints on unbleached muslin.
7. Models in miniature of a hogan, tepee, and pueblo were made, emphasizing the authentic materials and means of construction.
8. Drums and rattles were made and used in dramatic play.

D. Through use of arithmetic.
1. Gained an understanding of relative size of shelters as compared to height of persons, number of people to be accommodated, etc.
2. Compared size of hogan with pueblo.
3. Gained some understanding of barter and the need for it among the Indians of today.
4. Learned something about purpose of trading posts and their operation.
5. Used linear measure in all construction work (pueblos, tepees, hogans, etc.).

IV. **Social meanings, attitudes, appreciations probably developed through these experiences.**

A. Recognition and appreciation of cunning and skill of Indians.
B. Recognition and appreciation of the Indian's contribution in arts and crafts.
C. Understanding of the ability of Indians to adjust and make use of environment.
D. Some knowledge of actual processes used by them.
E. Respect for their courage, loyalty and endurance.
F. Some knowledge of their customs and beliefs.
G. Some appreciation, sympathy and a friendly respect for the "red man."

V. **Interpretation and expression of attitudes and appreciations.**

A. Through creative composition.
1. Stories were composed about Indian customs relative to food, shelter, clothing, transportation, etc. (Each child has his own loose leaf notebook with a stiff cover on which an Indian design was worked out as an art enterprise.)
2. Stories were composed using beautiful colored plates,

depicting Indian life, found in *National Geographic Magazine,* November, 1937.

B. Through picture making, design, decoration.
  1. Designs were made for pottery and book covers. Boys made designs for their Navajo belts; girls cut designs of leather to glue on costumes for play.
  2. Some of the children made a border (twelve inches in width) of Indian designs to frame the doorway of the room as a decoration for Book Week.
  3. Individual children drew and painted many pictures expressing their ideas of Indian life.

C. Through music.
  1. Listened to recordings of native and idealized Indian music such as:

      a. Chant of the Eagle Dance, Hopi Indian Chanters, Victor 20043.
      b. Shawnee Hunting Dance, Suite Primeval, by Skilton, Victor 22144.
      c. Cheyenne War Dance, Suite Primeval, by Skilton, Victor 22144.

  2. Sang Indian songs such as:

      a. At Parting (Dakota). Used the Indian words.
      b. Mooki, Mooki (Hopi Lullaby). Used the Indian words.
      c. Song of the Captive Deer.
      d. Song of the Owl.
      e. Song of the Red Blanket.
      f. Song of the Bear.

  3. Listened to piano arrangements and recordings, noting the thin quality of the melodies, the frequent changes in meter, and characteristic rhythmic patterns.
  4. Selected rhythmic patterns from favorite song and dance music and made scores for percussion instruments.
  5. Made tom-toms and rattles.
  6. Saw exhibits of Indian musical instruments.
  7. Attended programs of music and dance given by small group of professional Indians and by a Boy Scout Troop.

Source Books and References for Music

Botsford	Folk-Songs of Many Peoples		Womans Press
Palmer	American Songs for Children	1931	Macmillan
Gest	North American Tunes for Rhythm Orchestra	1934	Boston Music
Jeanson, Jean	Indian Song Book		Denver Allied Arts
Buttree, Julia	The Rhythm of the Redman	1930	A. S. Barnes
Curtis, Natalie	The Indians' Book	1907	Harper
Whitlock	Come and Caper	1932	G. Schirmer

    D. Through dramatic activity and social activity.
       1. Played Indians on playground.
       2. Dramatize chapter of *Dancing Cloud.*
       3. Wore costumes about the room and "lived" the part of the Navajos.

VI. New interests foreshadowing further studies.
    A. An interest in the Mexican Indians which may lead to a study of Mexico.
    B. Some knowledge gained through this experience of the early days on the western frontier—the days of Kit Carson and Buffalo Bill—may lead to an interest in western expansion.

Visiting Mexico

A Study in Third Grade

I. **Enriching experiences which aroused and fostered interest and provided background for activities.**
   A. A previous study of Indian life in the Southwest.
   B. An interesting talk by a teacher who had taught in a school on the Mexican border.
   C. An exhibit of Mexican handicraft by this same teacher.
   D. Many colorful Mexican curios brought by children from home collections.
   E. A display of attractive books from the school library and from home libraries.
   F. An excursion to the Field Museum to see the Mexican exhibit.
   G. An excursion to the Art Institute.
   H. A large picture map of Mexico.
   I. A colored film on Mexico which was taken and presented by one of the room mothers.
   J. Mexican films presented at the School Assembly.

II. **Problems and questions which led to investigation.**
   A. Concerning the country.
      1. What states touch this southern neighbor?
      2. How can Mexico be reached from Chicago?
      3. Where is the Pan-American Highway?
      4. Why is Mexico sometimes called the "horn of plenty"?
      5. What parts of Mexico are mountainous?
      6. In what part of the country do most of the people live?
      7. What cities should we learn more about?
   B. Concerning home life in Mexico.
      1. How do the natives in the Mexican villages build their houses?
      2. Why do the pictures show so many with tile roofs?
      3. What kind of houses are found in the cities?
      4. Where is the garden of a Mexican house? What is it called?
      5. How does the Mexican food differ from ours?
      6. What are their chief foods?
      7. How are tortillas made?
      8. Do the Mexicans wear the gay colored clothes we see in pictures?

9. How do the people in the cities dress?
10. How are the serapes made? Do the designs woven in them have any meaning?

C. Concerning the people and their activities.
  1. What things do the Mexicans do to earn a living?
  2. What are their important industries?
  3. What kind of valuable mines are found in this country? Who develops the mines?
  4. What products does Mexico send to the United States and other countries?
  5. What kind of government do they have?
  6. What are the arts and crafts of Mexico?
  7. What is sold in a Mexican market?
  8. What kind of money do they use? What is it worth in our money?
  9. How do the Mexicans buy and sell?
  10. What languages are spoken in Mexico?
  11. What kind of schools do the children attend?
  12. What games do they play?
  13. What are some of the festival days in Mexico?
  14. How do the children celebrate Christmas?
  15. What kind of toys do the Mexican children like?
  16. Do the people enjoy singing and dancing?
  17. How do the people travel?

III. Finding answers to problems and questions.

A. Through oral discussion.
  1. Conversations about Mexican pictures, costumes, toys, and art which had been brought in by individual children.
  2. Conversations about group experiences: films, excursions.
  3. Discussions following reading concerning topics of interest.
  4. Comparisons made between life in Mexican villages and life in the city.
  5. Discussion of books which might be used as material for dramatization; selection of *Pablo and Petra*, as a suitable story.
  6. Learning and understanding some common Spanish words.
  7. Discussing plans for dramatization, and offering suggestions as the play developed.

B. Through informational reading.
1. Independent reading in order to answer questions.
2. Reading captions under pictures and posters.
3. Reading to interpret maps, globes and charts in studying location and physical features.
4. Reading newspapers and various clippings brought in by the children.

References for Teacher and Pupil

Aitchison, A. E. and Uttley, M.	North America by Plane and Train	1937	Bobbs-Merrill
Brandeis, M.	Little Mexican Donkey Boy	1931	Flanagan
Decatur, D. D.	Two Young Americans in Mexico	1929	Heath
Holmes, Burton	Mexico	1939	Wheeler
Lee, M. H.	Pablo and Petra	1934	Crowell
May, S. B.	Children of Mexico (10 cent book)	1936	Rand McNally
Morrow, E. R.	Painted Pig	1930	Knopf
Peck, Anne	Young Mexico	1934	McBride
Perdue, H. A.	How Other Children Live	1927	Rand McNally
Smith, S. C.	Made in Mexico	1930	Knopf
Thomas, M. L.	The Burro's Moneybag	1931	Abingdon
Thomas, M. L.	Carlos	1938	Bobbs-Merrill

C. Through constructive activities.
1. Preparing exhibits of articles from Mexico contributed by teachers and children; making labels for use in exhibit.
2. Making tortillas as they are made in Mexico.
3. Planting various kinds of cactus plants in a window box which was made for that purpose.
4. Building a Mexican house to hold exhibit of curios.
5. Building two booths which could be used in a Mexican market scene, in the play.
D. Through the use of arithmetic.
1. Measuring ingredients used in making tortillas.
2. Comparing the size and population of Mexico with that of the United States.
3. Measuring material used in constructing market booths.
4. Measuring material to make serapes.
5. Finding relative values of certain Mexican coins.

IV. Social meanings, attitudes, appreciations, developing through these experiences.
A. An appreciation of the creative ability of the Mexicans.
B. An appreciation of their love of beauty and color.
C. An appreciation of their achievements in the way of art.

MEXICAN CURIOS STIMULATE CRAFTS

D. An understanding of the great resources of Mexico.
E. An understanding of the importance of festival days.
F. An understanding of why more and more people go to visit this neighboring country every year.
G. An understanding of the difference in living conditions found in Mexico and our own country.
H. An understanding of how the people have adapted to their environment.

V. **Interpretation and expression of attitudes and appreciations.**
   A. Through creative composition.
      1. Writing original stories about Mexico.
      2. Writing a play based on one chapter from the book, *Pablo and Petra,* by Melicent Lee. This play was presented at an assembly during Book Week.
   B. Through literature.
   Oral reading and telling parts of favorite books and stories:

Armer, L.	Forest Pool	1938	Longmans
Bannon, L.	Manuela's Birthday	1939	Whitman
Brann, Esther	Lupe Goes to School	1930	Macmillan

Church, P.	The Burro of Angelitos	1936 Suttonhouse
Eliot, Frances	Pablo's Pipe	1936 Dutton
Gay, Zhenya	Pancho and His Burro	1930 Morrow
Humason, M.	Marcos	1937 Whitman
Lee, Melicent	Pablo and Petra	1934 Crowell
Morrow, E. R.	The Painted Pig	1930 Knopf
Purnell, Idella	The Wishing Owl	1931 Macmillan
Russell, Mary	Si, Si, Rosita	1936 American Book

C. Through picture making, design and decoration.
   1. Drawing large pictures, showing Mexican costumes and interpreting Mexican customs.
   2. Making designs for serapes.
   3. Dyeing materials for serapes.
   4. Making border designs for room.
   5. Making and decorating clay pottery.
D. Through music.
   1. Singing typical Mexican songs such as
      Las Golondrinas (The Swallows)
      La Cucaracha (The Cockroach)
      Tecolotito (Little Owl)
      The Bumblebee
      The Pilgrims (Christmas ballad)

   2. Singing and playing the groups' own orchestration for percussion instruments:
      The Peacock
      The Cradle

   3. Observing characteristic patterns of rhythm—stepped them, used them with the instruments, and transcribed them on the blackboard in plane rhythm:
      a. Piano scores:
         The Peasant Girl
         To Jerez We Will Go
         Selections from Mexican Border Songs

      b. Phonograph records such as:
         Spanish Rhapsody—Chabrier—Victor 1337
         Jota (The Lamb's Mother)—Victor 79364

         Music References
         Spanish Folk Songs of New Mexico, Ralph Fletcher Seymour, Chicago.
         Third Book of Songs, Foresman-American Book Company.
         Folk Songs of Many Peoples, Vol. 11, Botsford, Womans Press.
         North American Tunes for Rhythm Orchestra, Gest, Boston Music Company.
         American Songbag, Sandburg, Harcourt, Brace and Company.

VI. **New interests foreshadowing further studies.**
   1. An interest in other neighboring countries particularly those of Central America.

Following Hobbies in Science

Science Interests in Third Grade

I. **Enriching experiences which aroused interest and gave rise to activity.**
   A. Children were encouraged to bring in their individual collection of science materials to form a class museum.
      1. Collection of shells from Florida.
      2. Cigar boxes filled with mounted butterflies and moths collected at camp.
      3. Insect collections from camps and summer outings.
      4. Assortment of seeds.
      5. Snake skin found on the golf course adjoining the playground.
      6. Cotton bolls sent from the South. .
      7. Collection of gourds. ·
      8. Three birds' nests abandoned and found near the playground.
      9. Home aquarium.
   B. Field trips near the school. Children went out in interest groups with a student teacher.
      1. To parks to see autumn flowers and foliage, birds and squirrels.
      2. To vacant lots to gather seeds, fallen leaves, and cocoons.
      3. To the exhibit of the Evanston Garden Club, in order to follow the "Nature Trail."
   C. Field trips to Harms Woods (Forest Preserve) to collect additional information and material to encourage the science hobbies. The class divided into small groups and followed various interests.
      1. Experimenting with the pond water by use of the microscope.
      2. Tracing the small creek to its source to determine the direction of· its flow and observe the living creatures in the water.
      3. Observing the leaves and bark of trees, and also the fungus and lichens growing on trees and dead wood.
      4. Observing different types of seeds.
      5. Studying the cat family and talking to a Forest Ranger. A family of cats was discovered living in a drain pipe emptying into the creek. The cats were friendly, and of course the children wanted to take the kittens home. A

149

Forest Ranger approached and suggested they leave the cats in the woods and help to build protection for the cat house. This they did. The Forest Ranger gave the children some "tips" on forestry and caring for a forest preserve. They did not pick flowers, leaves, and seeds, but looked at them. The Forest Ranger said "Goodby," and invited the group to come back again.

    D. Visits to the Academy of Natural Sciences and the Field Museum.
1. To investigate how museums are arranged.
2. To survey methods of mounting specimens.
3. To notice how museum cases are lighted and protected.
4. To study the methods of labeling specimens.
5. To secure material for the classroom library.

    E. Excursions to the Chicago Zoological Park and the Lincoln Park Zoo, by a group especially interested in live animals.
1. Observing the general living condition of animals in relation to food and shelter.
2. Noticing attitude of people toward animals.
3. Securing material for the classroom library.

    F. Visit to the Hobby Show held at the Evanston Woman's Club to observe and list new ideas in the line of science hobbies. Some of the children had entered materials in the show which is an annual center of interest in the community.

    G. Talks by teachers and outsiders on their science hobbies and interesting things to do in spare time at school and home.

    H. Observing collections of plaster of Paris casts and blueprints made by the upper grade children.

II. Problems and suggestions which led to research and investigation. Not all suggestions were followed, but all were discussed by the class.

    A. Related to the collection of science materials brought by the class and the building of a museum.
1. How shall we build cabinets to display our collections?
2. How shall we display and label our materials?
3. How shall we light our cabinets?
4. How may we improve on the science material already on hand to make the material different and more interesting than most collections?
5. How shall we divide responsibility for constructing and managing the museum?

      6. How can we house properly our exhibits of insects, moths, butterflies, and cocoons?

      7. How shall we classify our collections of seeds, leaves, and shells?

  B. Related to the trip taken to the Garden Club Exhibit, the Forest Preserve, and the Hobby Show.

      1. How can we make a "nature trail" near the school playground?

      2. Shall we plant various kinds of seeds, and have a "guessing contest" when they sprout, to see who can name the most plants correctly?

      3. How can we secure more collections for our museum, like some seen at the Hobby Show?

      4. How shall we record the information given us by the Forest Ranger concerning the care and protection of the forest preserve?

  C. Related to the study of animals. One group of children were interested in live animals rather than in museum collections.

      1. How can we construct shelters for animals, like some seen at the outdoor museums?

      2. How can we encourage better treatment of animals in this vicinity?

      3. How can we prepare a food chart and outline for the care of common household and school pets?

      4. How shall we determine whether the gray squirrels are beneficial or detrimental to the people of Evanston? (Some Evanstonians have objected to the number of gray squirrels that make their homes in the city and have asked to have them exterminated. Many residents like and enjoy the squirrels, and so the problem has become a community issue.)

      5. How can we organize an aquarium and "balance" its contents?

III. Answering questions and solving problems.

Each activity mentioned was not carried on by the entire class, but as a rule was planned by a committee, or interest group, working under the guidance of the teacher who gave individual help in accordance with needs.

  A. Through construction.

      1. Building a museum case in the shop, which was a large 5' x 6' cabinet, with movable shelves for display purposes.

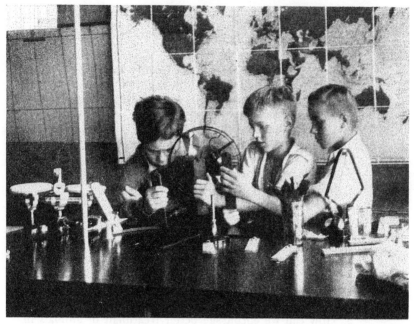

EXPERIMENTS PROVE INTERESTING FACTS

     2. Installing lighting equipment with a storage battery and miniature lamps and sockets.

     3. Making wooden prisms to use as backs for labels of specimens.

     4. Building a small aquarium.

  B. Through experiment and demonstration.

     1. Organizing an aquarium and stocking it with fish.

     2. Demonstrating how oxygen is given off by plants in an aquarium. By use of a glass funnel covering some plants in an aquarium, the oxygen can be captured and its presence shown by the use of a spark on a pine splint.

     3. Arranging leaf and plant specimens for observation.

     4. Conducting experiments in transpiration with leaves collected from the playground. (Leaves are collected and put into a tumbler with their stems passing through a cardboard cover into another glass. The water goes up the stems, into the leaves, out of the leaves, and deposits on the sides of the tumbler, thus illustrating the passage of water from one tumbler to another through the medium of leaves.)

5. Arranging exhibit of insects and cocoons for the museum.
6. Classifying and arranging seeds for observation.
7. Caring for a few pets: tame squirrel; hooded rats; goldfish.

C. Through creative activities.
  1. Making plaster of Paris casts of leaves and footprints.
  2. Making blueprints of leaves and sprays and making spatter prints on colored paper.
  3. Planning and making posters, labels and charts.
  4. Making lists of flower and vegetable seeds, with drawings.
  5. Writing original nature stories and rhymes.
  6. Writing records of excursions, experiments, and other experiences for diaries.
  7. Sketching trees, shrubs, and plants in the open.

D. Through arithmetic and its application.
  1. Measuring material for the display cases and other items built in the shop.
  2. Estimating space necessary for displays.
  3. Estimating time and materials needed for experiments and demonstrations.

E. Through use of the classroom library and the school library.
  1. Collecting pictures and pamphlets during excursions, to add to the classroom library.
  2. Withdrawing pictures from the picture collection in the school library to use in the classroom.
  3. Searching for material in the school library to aid in solving specific problems.
  4. Using encyclopedias and other reference books with the aid of the teacher.

Bibliography for Teachers and Pupils

Beard, Dan	American Boy's Book of Bugs, Butterflies and Beetles	1932	Lippincott
Comstock, John H.	An Introduction to Entomology	1936	Comstock
Comstock, Anna B.	Handbook of Nature Study	1939	Comstock
Emerson, A. I., and Weed, J. B.	Our Trees	1937	Lippincott
Farquhar and others	World Book Encyclopedia	1940	Quarrie
Ford, G. S., and others	Compton's Pictured Encyclopedia	1940	Compton
Fox, M. F.	Flowers and Their Travels	1936	Bobbs-Merrill
Kaempfer, Fred	The Aquarium—Care and Treatment	1930	Kaempfer
Smalley, Janet	Do You Know About Fishes?	1936	Morrow

IV. Social meanings, attitudes, and appreciations probably developed.

A. Becoming better acquainted with the immediate environment and its relation to science and science hobbies.

B. Becoming better acquainted with some interesting institutions in greater Chicago and their relation to science and hobbies.

C. Appreciation of the opportunity to carry on hobbies related to science experiences at school, under guidance.

D. Satisfying curiosity through exploration and investigation.

E. Learning respect for truth by searching for principles of science that affect our everyday living.

F. Developing an enthusiastic attitude toward investigating for information and enjoyment.

G. Learning some facts that are useful and interesting.

H. A beginning of intelligent use of the encyclopedia and other resource materials.

V. Expression of attitudes and appreciations through social sharing.

A. Telling other groups about field trips.

B. Demonstrating some of the science experiments for other groups.

C. Sharing some of the original rhymes, stories, and records with other groups.

D. Inviting other grades to see the museum, and giving explanations to them concerning the exhibits and experiments.

VI. Suggested projects, which may lead to future activity.

A. Building a "nature trail" near the school.

B. Developing an outdoor "zoo" for the school.

UNITS OF EXPERIENCE IN
FOURTH GRADE

TO HELP the children to understand the development of their own community, and to appreciate the marvelous changes that have taken place in the last century, has been one objective in the fourth grade. The teachers have sought also to enlarge the concept of citizenship responsibility within the community. A thorough review and sharing of the children's vacation experiences has afforded an introduction to the history and geography of this region, and indeed of the whole United States.

One fourth-grade class spent a year in an intensive study of the city of Chicago. During the first semester the exploration of the region was studied, the first settlements and life in pioneer days. The second semester's study included the development of sanitation, fire protection, transportation, and communication. Many excursions were arranged, and comparisons were made between early days and our own era.

Another class through a celebration of Columbus Day became interested in the discoveries and explorations of early American history, and developed a study on this topic. Following a review of vacation experiences, one group planned a trip around the world, which involved a study of methods of travel, and ways of living in some typical geographical areas.

When the children reach fourth grade, they are permitted to use the school cafeteria and to choose their own menu each day. It has seemed appropriate, therefore, to include in the fourth-grade curriculum a study of foods and food values, and the planning of a day's menu. This unit has sometimes involved a study of sources and preparation of foods, as well as the hygiene of foods.

As in early grades, interest in natural science is keen, and some studies in science have been included in each year's program. One class after an excursion to the Illinois Garden Show planned a garden show in the fourth-grade room. A successful study in one summer session was based on the birds of this vicinity. A wealth of story, verse and picture material was available, and the topic proved to be a stimulus for some delightful creative language work. One fourth grade group made a star observatory and another conducted an experiment in raising baby chicks.

The teachers of fourth grade have sought in various ways to enlarge the concept of citizenship responsibility within the community. One class made a study of the opportunities for showing consideration in the home and school community, and developed a puppet show on consideration. In some years the fourth grade has participated in the publication of a school magazine or year book.

The outlines which follow were selected from the records of three different years. The outcomes in social meanings and appreciations peculiar to the unit are included with the unit. All of the studies have been found valuable in developing certain desirable social habits and attitudes; as, cooperation in planning and carrying on small group activities; responsibility in caring for materials in the proper way; appreciation of work done by others in the group; willingness to give and receive friendly, helpful criticism; independence in working out individual problems; initiative in suggesting plans for the group; resourcefulness in using materials at hand; respect for the opinions and rights of others; courteous conduct at school and on excursions; persistence in seeing a job completed. The studies have also proved valuable in developing the powers of expression in the fine and industrial arts, music and creative language. Outcomes in terms of fundamental skills in English and arithmetic are summarized under Group Records of Progress, Part IV.

Making a Trip Around the World

An Enterprise in Fourth Grade

I. **Enriching experiences which aroused and fostered interest and provided background for activities.**
   A. Reports on vacation experiences. One child had been to Alaska; others had been in various sections in the United States and Canada. Class decided to take a trip around the world. Stories were read from diary of child who had been in Alaska.
   B. Pictures and objects contributed by teachers, children and parents.
   C. Large new globe which children found in the room after vacation.
   D. Excursions to Field Museum to see exhibits from various places.
   E. Plays given by the college students for children of the school and community.
   F. Motion pictures shown on the school projector.

II. **Problems and questions which led to investigation.**
   A. Related to plans for the trip.
      1. What countries shall be included in the trip?
      2. What continents will be touched? What oceans crossed?
      3. What possible routes can be taken?
      4. What are the best means of transportation?
      . What should be taken in clothing, conveniences?
      6. Which countries are cold? Which are warm?
      7. What is the meaning of equator, zone?
      8. What causes climate, day, night, seasons?
      9. How may records be kept of the trip?
   B. Related to the trip across the United States.
      1. What of interest can be seen crossing the United States?
      2. What states are crossed in going to San Francisco?
      3. What is a country, state, city, village?
      4. What farm areas are passed? What prairies, mountains, rivers? What famous scenic regions?
      5. How much time is needed for the trip to San Francisco?
   C. Related to the ocean voyage.
      1. What sights are seen on the ocean? What kinds of boats, airplanes?
      2. What causes rain, fog, snow, wind, icebergs?

157

D. Related to travel in foreign lands.
    1. What of interest can be seen in countries visited:
    A cold region: Northern Alaska.
    An island region: Hawaii.
    A hot wet region: Jungle of India.
    A hot dry region: The Arabian desert.
    A mountainous region: Norway.
    2. How do the people dress? How are their homes built? How is food produced and prepared?
    3. What plants and animals are seen?
    4. How does climate affect the living conditions?
    5. What are the customs of each country?
    6. How do the people travel?
E. Related to a trip home by airplane.
    1. How much time would be saved by flying home?
    2. What would be the probable expense?
    3. What routes might be followed?

III. Answering questions and solving problems.
A. Through oral discussion.
    1. Discussion of travel possibilities and plans, followed by decision to write letters to travel agencies.
    2. Discussion of how to keep a diary of the trip.
    3. Discussion of how to make a map to trace trips, kinds of maps and map symbols.
    4. Discussion of possible routes to San Francisco.
    5. Discussing of plans for collecting and exhibiting objects of interest.
    6. Oral reports on material read about different countries.
    7. Discussion of objects brought by the class and of the exhibits seen at the Field Museum.
B. Through informational reading.
    1. Reading of pamphlets sent by travel bureaus.
    2. Study of globe to learn continents, oceans, zones, equator, and location of countries to be visited.
    3. Study of geography references to learn more about climate, seasons, weather.
    4. Study of map of United States; learning to read map symbols for highlands, lowlands, water bodies.
    5. Study of railroad maps; tracing trip to San Francisco.
    6. Study of books describing foreign lands; learning to use the library for reference materials.

Children's References

Aitchinson, A. E.	Across Seven Seas to Seven Continents	1937	Bobbs-Merrill
Atwood, W. and Thomas, G.	Home Life in Far Away Lands	1933	Ginn
Baker, C. B., and E. D.	The Earth We Live On	1937	Bobbs-Merrill
Ford, G. S., and others	Compton's Pictured Encyclopedia	1940	Compton
Parker, E. P. & Barrows, H. H.	Journeys in Distant Lands	1936	Silver, Burdett
Shinn, Alida V.	Children of Hawaii	1939	McKay
Smith, N. B.	Near and Far	1935	Silver, Burdett
Smith, N. B; and Bayne, S. F.	Distant Doorways	1940	Silver, Burdett

C. Through constructive activities.
1. Making of large world map upon which to trace trip.
2. Making of individual pictorial maps of some countries.
3. Constructing book for diary.
4. Making sand-pan land and water forms.
5. Arranging exhibit of pictures and objects collected.
6. Making charts showing foods used in different countries.
7. Making charts of plants, animals of different countries.
D. Through the use of arithmetic.
1. Finding the cost of transportation.
2. Finding approximate cost of bags, clothing, accessories for the trip.
3. Measuring and drawing to scale, to make maps.
4. Computing approximate time for trip, changes of time and causes for such.
5. Reading and writing large numbers, used in learning size of population of various countries.
6. Comparing size of other countries with the size of the United States and separate states; also population.
7. Computing mileage.

IV. **Social meanings, attitudes, appreciations, probably developed through these experiences.**
A. Recognition and appreciation of the bigness of the world.
B. Some understanding and appreciation of wonder of forces governing natural conditions around the world.
C. Some knowledge and appreciation of grandeur and beauty in our own country and others.
D. Understanding of the part environment plays in molding habits and customs.
E. Appreciation of gifts given by other countries to us.

F. Appreciation of the unique charm of each country visited, revealed in natural beauty, type of buildings, picturesque costumes, characteristic habits.
G. Gratitude to travel bureaus affording help, and understanding of their service to the community.

V. **Interpretation and expression of attitudes and appreciations.**
A. Through creative composition.
1. Composing letters to absent members of the class telling them about group experiences.
2. Composing a diary describing imaginary journey.
a. Trip on the train.
b. Day in San Francisco; embarking on an ocean liner.
c. Story of interesting sights in each country visited.
d. Story of airplane trip home.
B. Through picture making, design, decoration.
1. Drawing to illustrate diary stories of trip.
2. Making posters for diaries, showing typical scenes of each country visited.
C. Through dramatic activity and social activity in sharing experiences.
1. Holding assemblies with other grades: giving talks, playing phonograph records, showing lantern slides, and motion pictures of places visited.

VI. **New interests foreshadowing further studies.**
A. Explorers and discoverers of the North and South Polar regions.
B. Explorations and settlement of the United States by people of other countries.

How America Was Discovered and Explored

A Study in Fourth Grade

I. **Enriching experiences which aroused and fostered interest and provided background.**

    A. Previous studies of people of other lands.

    B. Pictures of boats of early days; of adventurers of today; as, Byrd and Lindbergh; of adventurers of early days; as, Columbus, Marco Polo; of old maps.

    C. Stories read by the teacher; as, parts of "Little America," "Boys' Life of Marco Polo."

    D. Objects brought in; as, a model of a Viking boat and the Mayflower.

    E. Lantern slides of early explorers.

    F. Excursion to Lincoln Park to see a "Viking Boat."

II. **Problems and questions which led to research.**

    A. Concerning discoveries and explorations.

        1. Why did men wish to reach the countries in the Far East?

        2. Which countries sent out explorers first?

        3. Who was Marco Polo? What did he do? Why was he important?

        4. Who were the Vikings? What did they do?

        5. Who first had the idea that the world is round?

        6. Who were Prince Henry, The Crusaders, Columbus? Why were they important?

        7. How was sailing made safer by the invention of the compass, maps, globes and charts?

        8. What effect did the invention of printing have?

        9. What did the nations especially desire to get from the new world?

      10. Where did the Spanish people explore? What did they want in the new world?

      11. Who were some of the Spanish explorers?

      12. What adventures did they have on the high seas and on land?

      13. How did the other nations feel when Spain was so successful?

      14. What did England, France, and the Dutch people do?

      15. Were they successful in the new world?

16. Who were the most important people who came to the new world?

17. What did each of the countries finally succeed in getting from the new world?

18. What were some of the important events that took place during the period of exploration and discovery?

B. Concerning the first settlements.

1. How did the climate and topography of the land affect the kind of settlements made?

2. Why did the English people come to live in the new world?

3. How did England come to own most of North America instead of Spain or France?

III. Answering questions and solving problems.

A. Through oral composition.

1. Giving reports from individual and group research.

2. Discussing the setting up of goals and standards of work.

3. Planning the making of the time chart of important events.

4. Discussing stories read to the group by the teacher, groups of children, and individual pupils.

5. Planning the making of the large picture map of the early explorations.

6. Planning of dramatizations to be given to groups within the room and to other rooms.

7. Discussing many problems, involved in the display of pictures, stories, graphs, on the bulletin board.

8. Discussing the best means of making individual books and folders, to keep collections in.

9. Beginning to outline for written composition.

·10. Composing captions for pictures painted.

11. Holding informal debates upon topics of interest to the group.

B. Through informational reading.

1. Reading to find answers to specific problems in order to reproduce information in graphic and plastic materials.

2. Reading to verify conclusions by citing authorities.

3. Reading to find the most descriptive phrases describing places and characters.

4. Learning to skim to locate information needed for reports.

5. Reading to take mastery tests of the unit.

6. Reading maps, charts, graphs.
7. Reading to organize material read into simple outline.
8. Study of symbols needed in finding distances on different kinds of maps; tracing routes of the Crusaders, Marco Polo, Spanish, French, Portuguese, English; locating important places with reference to explorations and discoveries.
9. Reading from encyclopedias, reference books; learning to use library facilities.

References for Children

Baker, C. B., and E. D.	The Earth We Live On	1937	Bobbs-Merrill
Barker, E. C., and others	The Story of Our Nation	1933	Row, Peterson
Barker, E. C., and others	Old Europe and Our Nation	1932	Row, Peterson
Barnard, E. F. & Tall, L. L.	How the Old World Found the New	1929	Ginn
Gordy, W. F.	Stories of Early American History	1930	Scribner
Kelty, Mary G.	The Beginning of American People and Nation	1930	Ginn
McGuire, E. & Phillips, C. A.	Adventuring in Young America	1929	Macmillan
Melbo, I. R.	Our America	1937	Bobbs-Merrill
Nida, W. L.	Pilots and Pathfinders	1928	Macmillan
Nida, W. L.	Explorers and Pioneers	1934	Macmillan
Sherwood, H. N.	Makers of the New World	1936	Bobbs-Merrill
Sherwood, H. N.	Our Country's Beginnings	1937	Bobbs-Merrill
Smith, N. B., and Bayne, S. F.	Distant Doorways	1940	Silver, Burdett

C. Through constructive activities.
1. Making of larger world map, upon which voyages of various explorers were traced, resulting in a pictorial map of early discoveries.
2. Organizing and making a time chart, upon a long strip of wrapping paper, showing the dates of important discoveries and their relative importance.
3. Making and binding books, for keeping in permanent form the best work of individuals and of the class.
4. Building an exhibit table for various exhibits brought by children and teachers.
5. Constructing boats, showing early models; as, Mayflower, a Viking boat.
6. Giving of a play by one group of children, depicting the voyage of Columbus.
7. Making of costumes for characters in the play.

CREW OF SANTA MARIA SIGHTS LAND

D. Through the use of arithmetic.
   1. Comparing sizes; as, the square miles of land on the various continents, the vastness of the ocean, the depth of the ocean, and height of mountains.
   2. Comparing dates, length of time, intervals, days, months, years, decades, centuries.
   3. Measuring great distances; as, miles across continents, oceans; making comparisons of relative sizes and distances.
   4. Reading and writing large numbers, of thousands, millions, in dealing with population and area of countries, tonnage of boats, mileage.
   5. Using dollars and cents in computing the cost of voyages.

IV. **Social meanings, attitudes and appreciations probably developed through these experiences.**
   A. A keen appreciation of the bravery of the explorers and their contribution to the world.
   B. A keener appreciation of things which we have, and which have usually been taken for granted; as, sugar, light, maps, comparative safety of travel.

C. A keener appreciation for the contribution of those who have collected interesting facts that we might understand history and geography better.

D. An understanding of how geographical factors influence the habits and lives of various peoples.

E. An understanding of the progress made in methods of communication, transportation by man's use of scientific knowledge.

V. **Interpretation and expression of attitudes and appreciations.**

A. Through literature.

1. Oral reading of selected stories from:

Byrd, R. E.	Little America	1930 Putnam
Coffman, R.	Our America	1930 Dodd
Melbo, I. R.	Our America	1937 Bobbs-Merrill

2. Oral reading of a few poems:

Miller, Joaquin	Columbus
Newbolt, Henry	Drake's Drum
Thackeray, Wm. M.	Pocahontas
Whitman, Walt	O Captain, My Captain

B. Through creative composition.

1. Composing and writing captions for painted scenes from early explorations.

2. Writing scenes for play by individuals and in groups.

3. Composing imaginary letters written by sailors on the boats.

4. Writing descriptions of beauties of nature, the natives, and occupations found in the newly discovered lands.

C. Through picture making, design, decoration.

1. Drawing pictures depicting historical scenes of the discoveries.

2. Painting background for historical tables, set up.

3. Modeling figures of people, animals to be used on the tables.

4. Designing houses, trees, shrubs, to be used on the tables.

5. Painting large friezes for the room, showing historical scenes; as, Columbus on the Sea of Darkness.

6. Decorating charts and posters for exhibits and reports.

D. Through music.

Learning songs that express the struggles of seamen, the daring of explorers, the longing for home. The songs were used at music assemblies.

From the Concord Series No. 4   E. C. Schirmer
Columbus—Italian
My Banjo—Italian
A Mystery of the Sea—Italian
Fair are These Fields—French
Over the Sea—English
The Wanderer—Spanish
From Third Book of Songs—Foresman   American Book
Music of Spain—Spanish
My Native Land—Spanish
Spanish Lullaby—Spanish
Sailing, Sailing—French
From Dido and Aeneas—Henry Purcell   Oxford Press
The Sailor's Song

E. Through dramatic interests.

1. Playing scenes of discoveries on the playground; as, Drake and his trip around the world, Columbus finding America, Cortez and his entrance to Mexico, Champlain discovering the St. Lawrence, Landing of the Pilgrims at Plymouth.

2. Giving of a play by small group for other groups within the room.

3. Presenting pantomimes and charades by small groups for other groups within the room.

VI. New interests foreshadowing further studies.

1. Interest in different kinds of transportation, especially in the evolution of boats.

2. Interest in the life of the peoples across the sea.

3. Interest in how we secured some of the lands we use today.

4. Interest in further study of useful inventions and how they have influenced life as it is today.

5. Interest in the earth as a planet, leading to a study of the solar system and other heavenly bodies.

How Chicago Grew from Wigwams
to Skyscrapers

A Study in Fourth Grade

I. **Enriching experiences which aroused and fostered interest, and provided background for activities.**
   A. Vacation exhibit of places visited during the summer, leading to an interest in the development of our own community.
   B. Pictures and objects exhibited in the room, such as, an old fire bucket, plate from Chicago Fire, pictures from newspaper depicting early history of Chicago.
   C. Excursion to Chicago Historical Society to see objects of interest.
   D. Excursion to Evanston Historical Society.
   E. Excursion to Mandel Brothers' (Chicago) exhibit, showing the growth of Chicago.
   F. Excursion to a pumping station to see method of present day sanitation system.
   G. Excursion to fire department to study modern methods of fighting fire.
   H. Talks given to class by members of the community.

II. **Problems and questions proposed by children which led to research.**
   A. Relating to early days in Chicago.
      1. Who were the first explorers? How did they happen to find the present site of Chicago? What tribes of Indians did they find?
      2. Why did the French come? How was English supremacy established here?
      3. Who were the first people to establish homes here? How was the present site of Chicago chosen?
      4. How did the early settler live?
         a. How did he provide himself with food, clothing, shelter?
         b. How did he amuse himself?
         c. How were other persuaded to come to Chicago?
      5. What was the appearance of Chicago as an early settlement?
   B. Relating to growth and improvement in the city.
      1. Why did Chicago gain so fast when other cities remained small?

167

2. How did Chicago learn to protect itself from fire?
3. How has Chicago developed communication and transportation?
4. How did Chicago solve its sanitation difficulties?
5. How has the architecture in Chicago changed to meet the needs of a big city?
6. How can Chicago become a better city?

III. **Answering questions and solving problems.**

A. Through informational reading.

1. Independent reading of pamphlets on Chicago to solve problems.
2. Reading captions under pictures, current events, press notices and cartoons, relating to growth of Chicago.
3. Reading to interpret maps, globes, charts in studying location and physical features of the Chicago area.
4. Oral reading to report information found as the result of individual and group research.
5. Reading to answer questions in tests, checking the individual's mastery of subject matter.
6. Independent reading for information along interests stimulated by the study of Chicago.

Children's References

Campbell, Edna	Our City Chicago	1930	Scribner
Clark, Imogene	Old Days and Old Ways	1928	Crowell
Gordy, W. F.	Leaders in Making American History	1935	Scribner
Hall, Jennie	Story of Chicago	1929	Rand McNally
Johnson, W. H., and others	Chicago	1933	Newson
Johnson, W. H., & Mayer, R. M.	Stories of Chicagoland	1933	Newson
Kane, A., and Mitch, R. I.	The Making of Chicago	1933	Lyons and Carnahan
Nida, Wm. Lewis	Explorers and Pioneers	1934	Macmillan
Strong, Wm. D.	Indian Tribes of the Chicago Region	1926	Field Museum

References for Teacher

Bowen, Louise	Growing Up with a City		Macmillan
Currey, J. S.	Story of Old Fort Dearborn	1912	McClurg
Kirkland, Caroline	Chicago Yesterday	1919	Doubleday
Lewis, L., and Smith, H. J.	Chicago	1929	Harcourt, Brace
Masters, Edgar Lee	The Tale of Chicago	1933	Putnam
Smith, Henry J.	Chicago, a Portrait	1931	Century

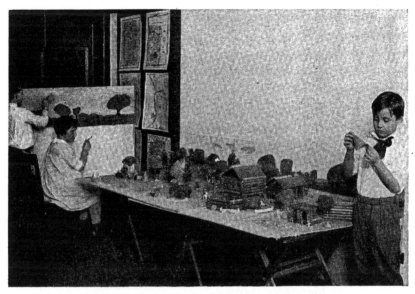

FORT DEARBORN PROTECTS EARLY SETTLERS

B. Through oral discussion.
 1. Discussing of stories and articles read (as a group and individuals), excursions taken, pictures displayed, and talks given by member of the community.
 2. Organizing and giving talks and reports as the result of individual and committee research.
 3. Outlining of subject matter to be used in written reports.
 4. Discussing plans for constructive activities illustrating facts learned.
 5. Discussing ways and means of handling, using and organizing materials, setting goals and standards of work.
C. Through constructive activities.
 1. Constructing individual portfolios for use in collecting and caring for materials related to study of Chicago.
 2. Making of a large blackboard map, to show the coming of the early explorers and settlers and to show the relationship of the site of Chicago to the rest of North America.
 3. Constructing a model of early Chicago: making log cabins, forts, clay animals, ships, people, wagons, trees and landscape.

    4. Planning, arranging and maintaining a news bulletin board for photographs, newspaper articles, kodak pictures, individual creative contributions; as, poems, stories and paintings.

    5. Making and binding of books, both class and individual, for keeping in permanent form the work accomplished.

    6. Organizing and constructing charts and graphs for group and individual reports.

    7. Planning and constructing of motion picture: the explorations in the Chicago area and life in pioneer days.

    8. Making of costumes for the play "From Wigwams to Skyscrapers."

    9. Making some of the stage properties and scenery of the play.

D. Through arithmetic.

    1. Measuring, involving the use of the tables of time, linear measure, surface and liquid measure: in making book covers, objects used in model, charts, maps, in building cabins, in constructing movie, scenery for play, pictures for movies, costumes.

    2. Drawing to scale in making map.

    3. Reading and writing large numbers dealing with population and statistics, real estate values, dates.

    4. Using Roman numerals in outlining chapters or sections for original books.

IV. Social meanings, attitudes, appreciations developing through these experiences.

A keener understanding and appreciation of the following:

A. The work and hardships of the early settlers and explorers.

B. The people who realized the advantage of the site of Chicago.

C. The people who have helped to build the great city of Chicago.

D. Those people in Chicago who have made industrial and artistic contributions to the world.

E. All that is provided by the city for public enjoyment, health and safety: public parks, museums, art institute, schools, roads, sanitation, protection of life and property.

F. The natural beauty of this area.

G. That each child is a citizen of a great community, a great country, and of the world, and that as such, he has his contribution to make.

V. Interpretation and expression of attitudes and appreciations.
  A. Through use of literature for enjoyment and expression of feeling.
    1. Oral reading of some stories of special interest and charm:

Gale, Edwin	Reminiscences of Early Chicago
Hall, Jennie	Story of Chicago

    2. Oral reading of poems:

Longfellow, Henry W.	Hiawatha
Sandburg, Carl	Chicago
Whitman, Walt	Pioneers! O Pioneers!

    3. Oral reading of paragraphs describing some of the beautiful buildings and scenic spots in Chicago.
  B. Through creative composition.
    1. Writing stories to be incorporated in individual histories.
    2. Writing of articles about Chicago for the school newspaper and the yearbook.
    3. Writing letters to parents and absent classmates telling of excursions and other experiences.
    4. Writing descriptions of beautiful places to visit in Chicago.
    5. Composition of epilogue for the movie on Early Chicago History; writing stories describing pictures for the movie.
    6. Group composition of the play, "From Wigwams to Skyscrapers," presented at the end of the year for parents and friends.
  C. Through picture making, design, decoration.
    1. Making of individual and group pictorial maps of early Chicago; and individual map of present day Chicago.
    2. Creating designs for portfolios and book covers.
    3. Drawing illustrations for the history of Chicago.
    4. Painting large pictures showing scenes from early days in Chicago (used in the movie).
    5. Painting landscape background .for model of early Chicago.
    6. Creating posters depicting the evolution of transportation, fire protection, and sanitation in Chicago.
    7. Designing decoration for dodgers, invitations, and programs for the play and the movie.
    8. Designing and making block prints for use in decoration.

      9. Drawing and painting scenery for the play.

D. Through music.

    1. Creating rhythms to old dance tunes such as reels, lancers and quadrilles.

    2. Learning songs to interpolate into a play, featuring the Chicago Fire.

       "Hard Times Comes Again No More"—Stephen Foster
       "Home, Sweet Home"—Payne and Bishop

    3. Learning an old square dance.

    4. Harmonica and rhythm orchestra playing during intermissions of the play.

Source and Reference Books

	Blue Book of Favorite Songs	1928 Hall & McCreary
Hofer, Mari	Popular Folk Games and Dances	1914 A. Flanagan
La Salle, Dorothy	Rhythms and Dances	1926 A. S. Barnes
Robinson, Ethel	School Rhythms	1923 Clayton Summy
Sandburg, Carl	The American Songbag	1927 Harcourt, Brace
Palmer, Winthrop	American Songs for Children	1931 Macmillan

E. Through dramatic activity and social activity, sharing experiences with others.

    1. Spontaneous dramatization in the room and on the playground of scenes from Chicago's history, as:

      a. Marquette and LaSalle on the Mississippi River.

      b. The Chicago Fire.

      c. The Arrival of the Newcomers to Chicago.

      d. Life at Fort Dearborn.

    2. Dramatization of original historical play of Chicago: "From Wigwams to Skyscrapers."

    3. Presenting an original movie at a school assembly.

    4. Giving the play and exhibiting the model of Chicago as a part of a school fair held near the end of the year.

VI. New interests foreshadowing further studies.

A. Desire to study other interesting places in Chicago; such as, industries, the Tribune plant.

B. Interest in present day needs of Chicago.

C. Desire to study the development of other large cities of the United States.

D. Desire to know what Chicago gives to the world and what the world gives to Chicago.

E. Desire to study other sections of the United States and to learn how they were discovered and settled.

Some Essays on Chicago by the Fourth Grade

(Reprinted from the Children's Year Book, the Blue Moon)

TRANSPORTATION IN CHICAGO

The Improvements of Roads in Chicago

After the people of Chicago found out that the wagons could not travel over dirt roads, they put boards over them and that worked very well for a little while, but when the frost went out of the ground the boards rose up, bumpy and uneven. Pretty soon the rains washed them out altogether. Next they tried gravel, but like the board roads, they were washed out by the rains. Next they tried macadam. But soon they had to fix some way of draining the water off. So they dug ditches on either side of the roads so the water would drain off. The ditches were supposed to empty into the river, but they did not go down hill enough for the water to run through them.

Soon the citizens of Chicago decided that they would raise the city of Chicago seven feet so the water would run down hill to the river. There were many men in Chicago who could raise a frame house, but they could not find any one who could raise a brick building. Finally they found a man from New York who could raise a brick building. In this way the process of raising Chicago went on and they did not have any more trouble with their roads for a long time because the water could drain off into the river.

Now we use cement for our roads. In Chicago there are so many people that there aren't enough roads to suit the people, so they have to build in part of the lake. They have one road called the Outer Drive, and they are going to build it along the North Shore in Evanston.

Transportation on Water in Chicago

In Chicago, on water as well as on land, people had different ways of travel. First they had canoes, then flat boats, and then canal boats. The canal boats were drawn by horses. The horses were on the land pulling while the canal boats were on the water. Then there were paddle-wheel boats. They were quite good boats.

In the present day of transportation on water, we use steamboats, both for people and freight. Some boats are larger than others. Some boats carry more than a thousand people. Some people are already using aquaplanes, which are planes used for flying over water and landing on water. They are very expensive now, but when they get less expensive more people will use them in flying over Lake Michigan to and from the Loop.

SANITATION

Water Supply in the Early Days

In the early days of Chicago people drank out of the Chicago river, but they got diseases. They used snow and had clean water to drink then. When that became unsatisfactory, they dug wells, but the marshwater soaked into them.

One man had a bright idea. He dipped up water from the lake and took it in carts to the people. All the people thought this was a good plan, but later more people came and it was too much work and cost too much money. The people chose officers and these officers made laws, and these are the laws:

I. No person could throw a dead carcass of any animal into the river.

II. No person could throw any garbage into the river, streets, or vacant lots.

III. All people must go a mile out of town to dump garbage.

Then they elected a board of health.

They built a hospital for those with diseases, and warned people against poisoned wells. They then wanted city water, so the city built pipes that went into the lake from the pumps. But still that was not so good because fishes and splinters came up the pipes, and dirt came up, too. So they built breakwaters to keep out the dirt and fishes. But splinters still came up the pipes. They had an idea to build iron pipes so splinters did not come in.

There was another question as important as the water question. That was drainage. Chicago was built in a swamp. In spring her streets were swimming. In hot summer they festered with slimy pools. They had an idea. They sloped their streets down to the river and put planks down. They thought their plans had worked, but the flood of 1849 came and it washed all the planks away with it. Then they rebuilt their streets. They had sand from the river and filled in their streets and put planks in again, but this time they sloped their streets into the middle, where a trough took it down to the river.

A Modern Waterworks

We took a trip to a modern waterworks and saw many interesting things there. These are the processes:

First the lake water comes in from a pipe in the lake and then it goes to a large tank where alum is put into it. Alum is a compound that when it settles to the bottom carries a lot of the dirt with it. Then the water goes to the filters. In the filters there are strainers as fine as the finest cloth that take the finest particles of dirt out. Then to make sure it is clean, the men put chlorine in it. Chlorine is a gas that purifies water.

FIRE FIGHTING IN CHICAGO

First Fire Laws

"No stovepipe shall run through a wooden roof unless the roof is covered with tin for six inches around the hole.

"No person shall carry fire through the streets unless it is covered.

"Every person shall have a fire bucket for each stove or fireplace in his house. These buckets, when not in use at a fire, shall be kept in a convenient place. The owner's name shall be painted in white paint on each bucket. In case of a fire, every man shall appear with his bucket or buckets, and shall help put out the fire. Anyone found disobeying these laws shall be fined two dollars."

These are not exactly the words of the first fire laws, but they show us how Chicago has changed. Houses were so little then that men could put fires out with buckets. It would look funny now. There was always the river or a well nearby, so it was not a hard job to get water. But tall grass stretched from cabin to cabin. A spark might burn the whole town.

Fire Fighting in the Early Days

When there was a fire people could not run to a fire box and ring the alarm, but the first one who saw it would run toward it shouting: "Fire! Fire!"

Everyone who heard dropped whatever he was doing, picked up his fire bucket, and went to the fire, shouting also. When they got there they made a line from the house to the nearest well, and while one man dipped up water, the others passed the buckets back and forth (usually they passed the full ones to the fire with one hand and the "empties" to the well with the other hand). After the fire had been put out the owner of the saved house treated them to a supper of oysters, or some such thing.

Some men, who liked excitement, got together and formed the first fire department of Chicago, the "Neptune Bucket Co." They were not paid.

As the city grew, there were more fires so Chicago bought its first fire engine. Men were proud to belong to the company which owned the engine, even though it was only a strong hand pump on wheels. When the church bell rang to sound the alarm, the firemen ran to the engine house (for the firemen did not live in the engine house then), clutched the ropes and pulled the engine out and to the fire. Soon they had several engines, and then started to have contests to see which could shoot the highest stream of water. Once, when there was a big fire, two of the engines were out of order because they had been used too much at one of the contests.

Then they organized the first paid fire department to stay at the engine house all the time and tend to the engines. They put a bell in the dome of the courthouse to ring the alarms. They hired watchmen to stay there all the time.

But yet they did not have the best kind of fire protection. Chicago had a few laws about lumber yards and coal yards in the crowded part of town, and no wooden building down town, but nobody cared for these rules. The city officers did not tell them.

The Chicago Fire

Eighteen hundred seventy-one came and found Chicago a large city. They had three hundred thousand or more people, and nearly sixty thousand buildings. They had a few fireproof buildings, but most of them were brick or stone. The river was crowded and so were the streets. Also they had many parks; and Chicago was only forty years old! But she had forgotten the little things. Here was a wooden house, there, next door, was a beautiful marble building. It was that way all over town.

They had a fair fire department, seventeen steam engines, four hook and ladder trucks, and a river for water supply.

But just the same it was a dry year, with only a few showers. Every day there were forest fires. Then, on Sunday, October 8, a cow upset a lamp in a barn or a man dropped a lighted match in the hay, and Chicago was ablaze.

The fire started at night, on the west side of the river. These people did not obey the fire laws as well as the rest. Their little wooden houses burned like matches. The people did not think to run to the fire boxes. The first one to notify the fire department was the watchman in the courthouse tower, who sent in the wrong alarm. After a mile's run an engine got there, but could do nothing. After a while, the watchman, seeing it spread so fast, sent in the general alarm. The fire drove everything before it and soon crossed the river. The engines also crossed to fight from the south side. It rapidly spread, and burned all Monday and Monday night.

On Tuesday morning a strip nearly four miles long and a mile wide was burned. The best part of the city had been burned—more than seventeen thousand buildings. On Monday and Tuesday mornings it was easy to guess what the headlines of most of the papers of the country said: "Chicago is wiped out, Chicago can never rise again." But we all know very well that with the help of other cities (who gave money) it did rise again.

From Wigwams to Skyscrapers
SYNOPSIS OF OUR PLAY

Act I—Exploration
    Sc. 1—Marquette and Joliet exploring the Mississippi River.
    Sc. 2—LaSalle on the shore of Lake Michigan.
    Sc. 3—Fur trading in Chicago.
Act II—Early settlers.
    Sc. 1—Coming to Chicago.
    Sc. 2—Good times in early days.
Act III—The Chicago fire.
Act IV—A street scene in Chicago of today.

Learning to Choose Healthful Lunches

A Continuing Interest in Fourth Grade

I. **Enriching experiences which aroused and fostered interest and provided background.**
   A. Exploring the cafeteria and the children's dining room.
   B. Feeling the responsibility and privilege of choosing balanced lunches at school.
   C. Studying pictures placed on the bulletin board showing what foods do for the body; also pictures showing right and wrong ways of sitting, standing, eating.
   D. Observing height and weight chart of children in the room, placed on the bulletin board.
   E. Excursions to stores to see how foods are cared for in the markets.
   F. Excursions to the home economics department of the college, to see some of the experiments which the college girls were carrying on.
   G. Looking at and discussing slides and Spencer films, on health topics.
   H. Excursions to the Water Filtering Plant of Evanston.
   I. Excursion to the Bowman Dairy Company.

II. **Problems and questions which led to research.**
   A. Concerning food values.
      1. What constitutes a well-balanced meal?
      2. What foods build strong healthy bodies?
      3. What foods are protective, building, regulating, and energy giving?
      4. How does food become a part of the body?
   B. Concerning everyday foods.
      1. Why is milk a good food? How do we get our milk supply?
      2. Why is it necessary to eat thin-leafed vegetables?
      3. Where do they come from? How can they be prepared?
      4. Where do we get our fruit?
      5. What effect do climate, altitude, soil, have upon the growing of different fruits and vegetables?
      6. What are the most important fruit centers of the world?
      7. Where are some of the important vegetable markets?
      8. What is truck farming? Where do we find truck farming carried on?

9. Where do our meats come from? How do we get meat?
10. How are we supplied with sugar?
11. How is beet sugar made?
12. How is cane sugar made?
13. How do we get maple sugar?
14. Why is it best not to eat too much sweet; as, candy, cakes, puddings?
15. What are the best ways to prepare meats, vegetables, fruits?

C. Concerning exchange of foods.
   1. How does the United States supply us with valuable foods?
   2. What foods does Illinois give to the rest of the country?
   3. What factors influence the price of foods?
   4. How are foods prepared for shipping?

III. Answering questions and solving problems.

A. Through oral discussion.
   1. Discussion of values of choosing properly balanced luncheons.
   2. Discussion of luncheons chosen by individual children and how to improve choice.
   3. Discussion of values of proper eating habits.
   4. Talks on kinds, sources and preparation of foods.
   5. Reports on independent reading carried on by several groups and individuals.
   6. Discussion of charts and posters made by groups.
   7. Reports on experiments carried on by groups and individuals; as, the starch and mold experiment.
   8. Planning of health books and folders that were kept by individual children.
   9. Discussion of pamphlets secured from various fruit and packing companies.

B. Through informational reading.
   1. Reading pamphlets sent by food companies.
   2. Reading books chosen by committee of children as valuable.
   3. Reading to answer questions in tests and checking the individual mastery of subject matter.
   4. Reading as an aid to written stories and reports.
   5. Reading to interpret graphs and charts.
   6. Independent reading to answer questions asked during class discussions.

Books Used by Children

Andress, J. M., and others	Safety Every Day	1939	Ginn
Baker, C. B., and E. D.	The Earth We Live On Unit V	1937	Bobbs-Merrill
Bruner, H. B., and Smith, C. M.	Social Studies, Unit I	1936	Merrill
Burkard, W. E., and others	Health by Doing	1936	Lyons and Carnahan
Camp, R. O.	Story of Markets	1929	Harper
Farquhar, F. F., and others	World Book Encyclopedia	1940	Quarrie
Ford, G. S., and others	Compton's Pictured Encyclopedia	1940	Compton
Fowlkes, J. G., and others	Healthy Living	1936	Winston
Nathan, A. G.	The Farmer Sows His Wheat	1932	Winston
Petersham, Maud and Miska	The Story Book of Foods	1936	Winston

C. Through constructive activities.
1. Arranging exhibit of posters, pamphlets about various topics studied; as, milk, meat, fruits.
2. Arranging and setting up several experiments and demonstrating for the group.
3. Making charts of healthful lunches, breakfasts and dinners.
4. Organizing and arranging large wall chart showing foods belonging to each class.
5. Preserving fruits, drying grapes, making jellies. Making own recipe book of various foods cooked by group.
6. Making charts and slogans of various health rules.
7. Planning, marketing, preparing and serving luncheon two or three times during the year. Preparing certain dishes for luncheon during the year; as, salads, starchy foods. Making cookies for luncheon for mothers. Making cranberry jelly as gift for mothers at Christmas time.
8. Collecting exhibit of fruits from foreign countries; as, pomegranate.
9. Making of picture map showing where our foods are found.
10. Making folder (individual) for collection of interesting pictures, original stories, poems, maps, and pamphlets.
11. Keeping individual records of luncheons chosen and checking food charts.
D. Through the use of arithmetic.
1. Measuring, involving the use of linear and liquid measures.

COOKING STIMULATES WHOLESOME APPETITES

    a. Folio covers, charts, mounts for pictures, lettering.
    b. Ingredients used in buying and cooking projects.
  2. Using the thermometer in cooking.
  . Computing distances that food is brought.
  4. Reading and making simple graphs to show importation of various food products.

IV. Social meanings, attitudes and appreciations developing through these experiences.

    A. Desire to take proper care of the body; as, washing hands before meals, washing teeth, drinking plenty of water.
    B. Satisfaction in being able to choose properly balanced luncheon.
    C. A keener appreciation and understanding of what the right choice of food does for the body.
    D. A willingness to eat and enjoy all sorts of foods.
    E. An understanding of the need for regulating eating habits, and not eating sweets between meals.
    F. An understanding of the requirements for sanitary use and care of rest rooms.

A Picnic Is Enjoyed at the Campus Fireplace

G. Appreciation of plain well-cooked, wholesome food.
H. Appreciation for those whose labor gives us healthful foods.
I. Appreciation for the seasonal changes, and the riches brought by each season.

V. Interpretation and expression of attitudes and appreciations.
 A. Through use of literature: oral reading.

> Johnny Apple Seed—Legend
> The Story of Luther Burbank
> The Dentist—Rose Fyleman
> Joys—Rose Fyleman
> King's Breakfast—A. A. Milne
> Rice Pudding—A. A. Milne

 B. Through creative composition.
  1. Writing reports of farms and ranches where foods are produced.
  2. Writing introduction to fruit books, recipe books and class enterprise book.
  3. Writing invitations to mothers, inviting them to lunch.
  4. Composing and writing health slogans.
 C. Through picture making, design and decoration.
  1. Making designs for health book covers.
  2. Mounting pictures artistically for bulletin board.
  3. Designing and making folios for health pictures and stories.
  4. Making table decorations for luncheons served to mothers at Christmas time and to teachers at Halloween.
  5. Designing and making wrapping paper and cards for wrapping jelly as gifts.
  6. Drawing and painting pictures of fruit.
 D. Through social activity.
  1. The children entertained some of the special teachers and officers of the school at a Halloween luncheon which they had prepared themselves.
  2. At Christmas time they entertained their mothers at a luncheon. Glasses of jelly which they had made themselves were the gifts.
  3. In the spring outdoor lunches were enjoyed at the campus fireplace.

VI. Leads into other fields.
  1. Further study of industries in the United States.
  2. Further study of inventions.

Making a Star Observatory

A Science Enterprise in Fourth Grade

I. **Enriching experiences which aroused and fostered interest and provided a background.**
   A. Previous study of the early explorations, culminating in the discovery of the new world, led to an interest in the earth as a planet.
   B. Pictures pertaining to the solar system were clipped from current magazines and newspapers and placed on the bulletin board.
   C. Pictures of observatories were brought in, such as the Mt. Wilson Observatory and the Yerkes Observatory.
   D. Articles clipped from publications were placed on the bulletin board.
   E. Objects were brought in for exhibition; as, a specimen believed to be a piece of a satellite.
   F. Excursions were made to places of interest:
      1. The Chicago Historical Society in Lincoln Park to see the miniature observatory.
      2. Adler Planetarium where a lecture was given and the heavenly bodies and their location in the heavens were pointed out.
      3. An evening was spent in the open so as to make practical application of the knowledge the group had obtained.
   G. Talks were given the class by the special teacher of science.
   H. Each child chose the one body in the heavens which was of most interest to him and prepared to make an extensive study of it.

II. **Problems and questions were proposed by the class leading to investigation.**
   A. In relation to the different heavenly bodies:
      1. What different kinds of bodies are in the sky?
      2. What is the difference between a planet and a star?
      3. What is a comet and how is it formed?
      4. Why is it that we rarely see a comet?
      5. Are all of the stars really as small as they appear?
      6. How does a star fall from the sky?
      7. What are meteors?
      8. What makes the stars shine and twinkle at night?
      9. What is meant by a constellation of stars?

182

SCHOOL TELESCOPE IS INVESTIGATED

10. How do we measure distance in the sky?
11. Of what is the Milky Way composed?
12. How did the sun get the fire in it?
13. Of what is the moon made?
14. How did all these bodies come into existence?
15. What is an eclipse?
16. What causes the moon to appear to change its shape?
17. Are we able to see all of the stars when we look at the sky on a clear night?

B. In relation to the planets:
1. Are all of the planets the same size?
2. Are any of the other planets inhabited?
3. Why are the sun and the planets called the Solar System?
4. What makes the planets all revolve around the sun?
5. When and by whom was the first planet discovered?
6. Which planet was discovered recently?
7. Which planet is nearest the sun?
8. What is peculiar about the planet Saturn?
9. Of what are the rings around Saturn composed?
10. Why do some planets have more heat than others?
11. Do the planets always remain in the same location?

C. In relation to the earth:
1. How old is the earth?
. How was the earth formed?
. What is the distance of the earth from the sun?
4. If we are so near the sun, why do we not feel the heat more?
5. How long does it take the earth to move around the sun?
6. Why do we have leap year?
7. What makes our seasons?
8. What accounts for the different climates in various sections of our country?
9. What brings about day and night?
10. What is meant by the rotation of the earth on its axis?
11. How long does it take the earth to make a complete rotation on its axis?
12. What is meant by the gravity of the earth?
13. How fast does the earth move?
14. How does gravity keep us from going off into space?

III. **Questions were answered and problems were solved.**
A. Through oral composition.
1. Books read aloud by the teacher and by individuals were discussed.
2. Magazine articles and newspaper clippings brought in by members of the class were discussed.
3. Pictures stimulated interest, and discussion followed which aided in solving problems.
4. Group discussion determined the general organization of the work.
5. Discussion of terms and their meanings aided understanding; as, gravity, axis, light year, constellation.
6. Oral comparisons were made between the different planets.
a. Their distance from the sun.
b. The diameter.
c. Temperature.
d. Length of time it takes each planet to make the revolution around the sun.
e. Length of time it takes each planet to make a complete rotation on its axis.
7. Charts made by individuals were explained.
8. Reports were made of outstanding scientists and their contributions in this field.

9. Observatories where research is being carried on were described.
10. Excursions were planned.
11. Detailed reports were made by individuals on the observations made while on the excursions.
12. Talks given at the planetarium and the observatory were discussed.
13. The group planned an assembly program in which they might share with the school the information they had gained.
14. The group planned a miniature observatory to be used in the assembly.
15. Organization of the topics to be used on the program was determined in discussion.

B. Through factual reading:
1. Group and individual reading of books was carried on to gain information necessary for the solution of the general problems.
2. Articles found in current magazines and newspapers were read.
3. Each child did some independent reading to gain information concerning the special problem which he had chosen.
4. Oral reading was done to report the information found by individuals when carrying on their research.
5. Independent reading was done to answer questions asked during class discussions.
6. Some reading was done to find answers to specific problems in order to prepare the report for the school assembly.
7. Some reading was done in order to reproduce the information on the charts which were to be used with the reports.
8. Reading was required to interpret graphs and charts used in studying the placement of the constellations and the orbits of planets.
9. Reading was done of charts and graphs made by individuals depicting specific information.
10. The children became more skilled in the use of the table of contents and the index.

References for Children and Teacher

Baker, R. H.	When the Stars Come Out	1934 Viking Press
Comstock, Anna B.	Handbook of Nature Study	1939 Comstock
Fontany, Elena	Other Worlds Than This	1930 Follett

Johnson, Gaylord	Stars for Children	1934 Macmillan
Johnson, Gaylord	Sky Movies	1934 Macmillan
Johnson, Gaylord	Star People	1934 Macmillan
Mitton, G. E.	Book of Stars for Young People	1925 Macmillan
Reed, W. M.	Stars for Sam	1931 Harcourt
Washburne, C. W.	Story of Earth and Sky	1933 Appleton
White, W. B.	Seeing Stars	1935 Harter

C. Through constructive activities:

  1. The class carried on these activities in making a miniature observatory.

    a. Constructing the observatory.

    b. Painting the observatory.

    c. Printing the name on the observatory.

    d. Cutting a circular opening for the observatory to make it appear that one was looking through a telescope at the stars.

    e. Installation of the electrical appliance which was to light the charts.

  2. Charts were made by individuals of the following subjects:

    a. The planets.

    b. The relative sizes of the planets.

    c. The relative distance of each planet from the sun.

OBSERVATORY SHOWS MYSTERIES OF THE SKY

    d. Saturn and Saturn's rings.

    e. The earth.

    f. The sun.

    g. The moon.

    h. An eclipse.

    i. The Milky Way.

    j. Comets.

    k. Meteors.

    l. Well-known constellations.

    m. Draco, The Dragon.

    n. The North Star.

3. Enlarged charts were made later, involving these activities.

    a. Enlarging the charts to fit into the observatory.

    b. Choosing the color which would show the designs to best advantage.

    c. Pricking with a large pin on the designs.

4. Posters to advertise the assembly program were constructed.

D. Through arithmetic:

1. Linear measures were used in making the observatory and the charts.

2. The four fundamental processes with integers and fractions were used in drawing the charts.

3. Drawing to scale was done in making the enlargement of the charts.

4. Learning to use the compass was involved in making circles.

5. Reading and writing large numbers was required in making comparisons of the distance of the planets from the sun.

6. Comparing the differences in the diameters of the different bodies in the solar system also involved reading of large numbers.

IV. Social meanings, attitudes and appreciations were developed through these experiences.

A. An understanding and appreciation of:

1. The work done by the astronomers of the past and the present.

2. The knowledge and skill needed by the men who carry on research.

3. The care and accuracy with which observations made must be recorded.

    4. What it means to base opinions upon reliable data.

B. An understanding of:

    1. The many factors which influence the lives of men.

    2. Our location in relation to other bodies in the sky.

V. **New interests foreshadowing future work.**

    A. The children were interested in the weather; as, the temperature of the atmosphere; the clearness and cloudiness of the sky; the direction and speed of the wind; the formation of dew, rain, fog, frost and snow; the warmth or lack of warmth upon the earth.

    B. The origin of the earth, how old the earth is, the changes in the earth's surface, the early vegetation and animal life as revealed in fossils.

How Baby Chicks Are Developed

A Science Experiment in Fourth Grade

I. **Enriching experiences which aroused and fostered interest and provided background.**
  A. The children were interested in the development of life: its origin, period and types of incubation or pregnancy, nourishment of prenatal offspring, methods of furnishing the young with food.
  B. Pictures from current newspapers and magazines pertaining to the development of the baby chick and of a poultry farm were brought in.
  C. Excursion to a poultry farm was arranged.
  D. Newspaper and magazine clippings were posted on the bulletin board.
  E. Enlightening books and pamphlets were collected.
  F. One mother presented the room with an electric incubator, another with five dozen eggs.

II. **Problems and questions which led to research.**
  A. Related to the functioning of the incubator.
    1. What must be the temperature of the incubator?
    2. Why must the temperature remain uniform?
    3. Why must the eggs be kept moist?
    4. Why did the temperature go down when the eggs were placed in the incubator?
    5. What is the value of candling the eggs?
  B. Related to the development of the baby chicken.
    1. What is meant by the fertility of an egg?
    2. How can we tell that an egg is fertile?
    3. What is the white spot on the yolk of the egg?
    4. Of what value are the blood vessels?
    5. What is the source of nourishment for the baby chick?
    6. What makes the eyes of the chick look so large?
    7. How does the baby chick know when it is time to come out of the shell?
    8. How long does it take the chicken to pip his way out of the shell?
    9. Why do not all of the eggs hatch?
    10. What caused one baby chick to be deformed?
  C. Related to the care of the baby chickens.
    1. When should the chick receive its first food?

189

2. What kind of food should be given him?
3. What is a brooder?
4. What temperature is best suited to the new chick?
5. Why is it best not to handle the baby chick?
6. What is the importance of keeping the brooder clean and the water fresh?
D. Related to all forms of life.
  1. Does all life begin in the same way?
  2. Do all babies come from an egg?
  3. How do the different mothers carry their young?
  4. What methods are employed in feeding the young?

III. Answering questions and solving problems.
  A. Through oral composition.
    1. Discussion of experiences on different types of farms. Special emphasis was placed on a chicken farm.
    2. Planning an excursion to a chicken farm.
    3. Discussion of articles read by the teacher and by individuals.
    4. Discussion of newspaper clippings and magazine articles.
    5. Discussion of terms and their meaning; as, fertile, embryo, blood vessels, incubation, etc.

An Incubator Requires Scientific Care

6. Discussion of the procedure to be followed in the use of the incubator.
7. Discussion of diary records to be written by each individual.
8. Organizing and planning material for reports which explained the experiment to visitors.
9. Discussion of plans for constructive activities; as, the making of a candler and a chicken coop.
10. Planning captions and their placement for the motion picture film on the chickens, which was photographed by one of the fathers.

B. Through factual reading.
1. Reading of bulletins sent by the government.
2. Reading of pamphlet which accompanied the incubator.
3. Reading captions under pictures relating to development of a baby chicken.
4. Reading articles found in current magazines and papers.
5. Independent reading to answer questions asked during class discussions.

References for Teacher and Pupil

Comstock, Anna B.	Handbook of Nature Study	1939	Comstock
Farquhar, F. F., and others	World Book Encyclopedia	1940	Quarrie
Ford, A. S., and others	Compton's Pictured Encyclopedia	1940	Compton

C. Through constructive activities.
1. Arranging exhibits of pictures and clippings obtained from magazines and newspapers.
2. Arranging and setting up the preserved models of the baby chicks and demonstrating for the groups from other rooms.
. Making labels for the bottles containing the specimens.
4. Organizing and arranging a large chart for the recording of the temperature of the incubator.
5. Writing diary records.
6. Writing letters to absent classmates telling of the progress and development of the experiment.
7. Writing captions for the motion picture.

D. Through the use of arithmetic.
1. Reading the thermometer in the incubator.
2. Recording the temperature of the thermometer.
3. Counting of the eggs used in the incubator.
4. Keeping record of time required for propagation of the young.

    5. Measurements required for construction of chicken coop and egg candler.

    6. Buying and keeping account of the materials purchased.

IV. Social meanings, attitudes and appreciations probably developed through these experiences.

    A. Scientific attitude toward the origin of life.

    B. Understanding and appreciation of the transformation which takes place in the embryo.

V. Continuing interests.

    A. Much discussion leading to an increased understanding of the development of the human embryo was carried on in the homes and in the school.

    B. Interest indicated further study of the development of both plant and animal life.

Diary Record

Selected from Teacher's and Children's Individual Diaries

Thursday, April 22.

The electric incubator arrived and was set up. Directions were read and incubator started.

Friday, April 23.

The children watched the incubator and regulated the temperature. The incubation process was discussed in detail.

Monday, April 26.

We recorded incubator temperature and found it was running fairly uniform at a temperature of 103 degrees. (It was necessary to keep the temperature near 103 degrees so that the baby chicks would not die.)

Tuesday, April 27.

We recorded the temperature of the incubator and found it continued to run uniformly. The sixty eggs for the incubator arrived. We marked the eggs, putting a red cross on one side so as to know when the eggs had been turned. (Turning the egg twice a day assures a more uniform development of the baby chick.)

Wednesday, April 28.

The five dozen eggs were placed in the incubator. We observed that the temperature of the incubator was lowered because the eggs were cold. By the end of the school day the temperature had risen to 100 degrees. We purchased the solution to preserve the chicken models.

Thursday, April 29. (Second day of incubation)

We checked the temperature of the incubator and found it running 103 degrees. Directions specified the incubator was to remain closed for two days. Therefore, the incubator was not opened.

Friday, April 30. (Third day of incubation)

We recorded the temperature, 103 degrees, and turned the eggs in the incubator. Excursion to the Biology Department of Northwestern University was made to inspect little wax models of the baby chick in the various stages of development. An egg was taken from our incubator, opened, the embryo removed and placed under the microscope. Each child was given the opportunity to observe by means of the microscope the palpitation of the baby chicken's heart. The embryo was placed in the preservative solution and returned to our laboratory. The janitor was asked to check the temperature of the incubator and to turn the eggs during the week end.

Monday, May 3. (Sixth day of incubation)

We opened the second egg and found the baby chick had grown a great deal. It was as big as a small button. Its eyes were big and black. There was a tiny beak and the wings and the feet had begun to grow. We could see the blood vessels around the embryo.

Tuesday, May 4. (Seventh day of incubation)

The third egg was opened. The baby chick was about the size of a penny. The legs and wings had grown and there was a light covering of down on the body.

Wednesday, May 5. (Eighth day of incubation)

The fourth egg was opened. The baby chick's bill had started to develop. The eyes, wings and feet were much larger.

Thursday, May 6. (Ninth day of incubation)

The fifth egg was opened. The eyes of the chick had little white spots on them, indicating the eyelid was growing. The claws had begun to grow. The separation on the beak could be seen.

We candled the eggs. Each child was given an opportunity to candle

an egg. Out of the sixty eggs only seven were found which were not
fertile. Mr. Russell visited the room, and, after the models had been
displayed to him, he remarked that the development of the chicks
seemed somewhat advanced and that in all probability the baby chicks
would hatch before the twenty-first day. We were very much excited.

Friday, May 7. (Tenth day of incubation)

There was no noticeable change in the development of the baby chick
except that it had grown much larger and we could see each part
more clearly.

Monday, May 10. (Thirteenth day of incubation)

For the first time there were signs of life in the baby chick. The body
was covered with down. We could see the ear. His bill was almost
full grown and his claws could be seen much better.

Tuesday, May 11. (Fourteenth day of incubation)

The whole chick was much bigger. There was a great deal more fuzz
on his body. There seemed to be a covering over the eyes. We candled
the eggs and found that only three of the eggs were not fertile. We
were happy, because we knew so many fertile eggs would mean that
many baby chicks would hatch.

Wednesday, May 12. (Fifteenth day of incubation)

When the egg was opened, the baby chick showed real signs of life.
He turned over in the shell and opened his beak several times. There
was a noticeable development in the whole chicken. He was a great
deal larger than the day before. The down was much thicker.

Thursday, May 13. (Sixteenth day of incubation)

When we arrived at school we found that the electric plug which
was attached to the incubator had been disconnected. We thought
surely we would not have any baby chickens.

We took an egg out of the incubator and opened it only to find that
the baby chick was dead. We opened a second egg and this baby
chick moved. We were then assured that the baby chickens had lived
through this accident and that we would have a good hatch.

The baby chick's claws were almost as large as when he came out of
the shell. The feathers were growing. The eyes did not look nearly
so large as they did at first, because the eyelids had developed.

Friday, May 14. (Seventeenth day of incubation)

The feathers were a little thicker, making the chick appear more
plump. The chick moved about such a great deal that we hoped he

might live. He was returned to the incubator. However, he lived only a very short time.

Monday, May 17. (Twentieth day of incubation)

After all of the children had arrived at school we all gathered around the incubator. Everyone was very quiet and we could hear a "Peep-peep." The top was then lifted off and there was one little baby chick in the incubator. He was fluffy and yellow. Several eggs were pipped. We put the top back on the incubator so as to keep the baby chick and the eggs warm.

Before the end of the school day we had three baby chickens. Mr. Russell's prediction had come true.

Tuesday, May 18. (Twenty-first day of incubation)

We could hear a great deal of peeping inside the incubator as we all gathered around to see what was inside. We took the top off. The incubator seemed full of little yellow baby chickens. Some were dry and fluffy; some were partly dry and the feathers clung to their bodies. Some were very wet, while others were just coming from the shell and several eggs were just pipped. During the morning we observed a baby chick emerge from the shell. We saw how he used his beak to cut a ring around the shell. (It takes the baby chicken about four hours to pip this ring.) He then pushed the cap off the shell. About an hour later when we looked in the incubator he was out of the shell. He was all wet and too wabbly to stand on his legs. We had another baby chick! By noon we had twenty-one baby chickens. There remained nine to be hatched. Late in the afternoon we removed these eggs from the incubator as there were no signs that they might hatch. It was necessary to convert the incubator into a brooder, so that the baby chicks would have a comfortable place in which to live. With the hatching of the baby chickens the temperature had gone up. This made it necessary to place them in the brooder which would be cooler and yet would give them the warmth which they needed. We opened the remaining eggs—found in four of the eggs that the baby chicks had died at different stages of their development. The only chicken which showed any signs of life was a little deformed chick which had only one eye and one leg was shorter than the other. He died soon after he was taken from the egg. The remaining eggs were not fertile.

Wednesday, May 19.

We held open house and invited the upper grades in to see the baby chickens and to see the specimens we had preserved. The children explained in detail the experiment. The baby chickens all seemed to thrive upon the care which they were given.

Thursday, May 20.

We held open house again and invited the lower grades in to see the chickens and specimens. An explanation was made by members of the group of the experiment.

Friday, May 21.

All of the baby chickens continued to thrive. We had a motion picture taken of the children and the baby chickens.

All of the twenty-one chicks lived. It had been suggested that the baby chickens be given to a farmer. Children in the school had offered to purchase a chicken. The fourth grade felt they had mothered this brood of chickens. They were reluctant to part with even one baby chick, saying, "We brought them up and took a great deal of trouble to raise them. We want to keep them."

The last day of school each child took home a baby chicken.

UNITS OF EXPERIENCE IN
FIFTH GRADE

A BETTER understanding of the development of our country and the contribution of different sections to this community, has been one attainment desired for the children of the fifth grade. The dependence of one community upon another and the need for coöperation has been emphasized.

One class followed their unit on Chicago in the fourth grade with a study in the fifth grade, of the problem, "What do other sections of the United States contribute to Chicago?" This problem led into a study of the development of industry in the United States; and there was a very thorough review of the changing methods of conducting certain fundamental industries. Corn, lumber, iron and steel, cattle raising, were the industries selected for intensive study. The class was divided for part of this work, and each committee developed a "talkie" on a particular industry.

Another group of children, after completing a study of Chicago, wished to know more about the development of other large cities in the United States. Many large cities were studied on the map, and the reasons for their size were discussed in relation to location and tributary industry. New York, New Orleans, and San Francisco were chosen for intensive study, and much of the history and geography of the United States was found to be involved in the problems that arose concerning the development of these three interesting cities.

Still another group spent their year in fifth grade in an imaginary journey across the United States. They visited the New England States, the Mid-Atlantic States, the South, and the West. Their journey took them to historical shrines, where they learned the story of the section, to scenic spots, and to fields and factories, where they studied the industries.

A delightful enterprise for the summer session has proved to be a study of America's playgrounds. Niagara Falls, Yellowstone Park, the seacoasts of Florida and California, and other resorts and scenic wonders have been studied with enthusiasm. This unit has

A Jig-Saw Puzzle Map Intrigues Its Makers

prepared the children to enjoy more fully their own vacation trips, which usually follow the short summer term in school. It has included not only a study of geographical conditions in scenic regions, but also means of transportation, expenses, routes, and other matters. Posters and pamphlets published by travel bureaus and transportation lines have been among the materials used.

The outlines which follow include a year's study of industries of the United States, and a study, conducted in a different year, on the development of New York City and the Westward Movement. A study of America's playgrounds and a study of water and its uses, both developed in summer sessions, are also included. The outcomes in social meanings and appreciations peculiar to the particular unit have been included with each unit. All of the units have offered opportunities for the practice of certain desirable social attitudes and habits; such as, coöperation with others, readiness to participate in group activities, willingness to accept both group and individual responsibility, consideration for the opinions and possessions of others, independence in carrying out ideas, perseverance in seeing a job finished, conservation of time and materials. The studies have also been accompanied by growth in the powers of expression through creative language, fine and industrial arts, music and dramatization. Outcomes in terms of the specific skills, English and arithmetic, are summarized under Group Records of Progress in Part IV.

What Do Other Sections of the United States Share with Chicago?

A Problem in Fifth Grade Which Introduced a Later Study of Industries

I. **Enriching experiences which aroused or fostered interest and provided background.**
   A. Previous study of Chicago.
   B. Discussion of how the rest of our United States has helped and is helping Chicago.
   C. Excursion to the beach to see different land forms.
   D. Exhibit of physical, product, and resource maps.
   E. Reading of stories and clippings.

II. **Problems and questions which led to research.**
   A. What crops do the different sections of the United States raise that they can share with others?
      1. Considering the surface of the different parts of the United States, what crops would you expect them to raise?
      2. The climate?
      3. The soil?
      4. Considering all three, what crops do they raise?
   B. Which crops are sent to Chicago? What is done with the rest?
   C. What natural resources do we find in different sections of the United States?
   D. Which raw materials are sent to Chicago? What is done with the rest?
   E. What else do the different sections contribute?

III. **Answering questions and solving problems.**
   A. Through factual reading.
      1. Group silent reading to gain information necessary to solve problems.
      2. Independent silent reading to solve problems.
      3. Independent reading for information along lines where interest had been stimulated by the study.
      4. Oral reading to report results of individual research.
      5. Oral and silent reading to interpret globes, graphs, diagrams, maps.

6. Reading to answer tests given to check on understanding of subject matter.

References

Aitchison, A. E. and Uttley, M.	North America by Train and Plane	1937	Bobbs-Merrill
Allen, N. B.	United States	1937	Ginn
Atwood, W. W. & Thomas, H. G.	The Americas	1929	Ginn
Baker, C. B., and E. D.	Making America	1937	Bobbs-Merrill
Barker, E. C.	The Story of Our Nation	1933	Row, Peterson
Dakin, W. S.	Great Rivers of the World	1925	Macmillan
Pitkin, W. B. & Hughes, H. F.	Seeing Our Country	1939	Macmillan
Smith, J. R.	Human Use Geography	1939	Winston

B. Through composition.
  1. Oral composition.
     a. Giving reports as a result of research.
     b. Discussing material read, information brought in, and exhibits.
     c. Discussing plans for working out problems.
  2. Written composition.
     a. Writing labels for product maps.
     b. Labeling and explaining diagrams and drawings.
     c. Writing answers to questions checking comprehension.
C. Through constructive activities.
  1. Making different land forms and physical features in sand at the beach.
  2. Making a physical map of the United States in relief, using a mixture of flour and salt on beaver board.
  3. Making map showing products of different sections being sent to Chicago.
     a. Tracing of map on beaver board.
     b. Painting and shellacking map.
     c. Making and painting clay animals for the map.
     d. Gathering and mounting grains and natural resources.
     e. Making small boat to carry products brought by water.
     f. Labeling trains and trucks used in transporting goods.
     g. Assembling of map.
D. Through the use of arithmetic.
  1. Measuring, using linear table of measure in drawing and constructing maps.
  2. Practicing exercises in proportion to gain skill in drawing maps.
  3. Using four fundamental processes with integers and fractions in drawing and constructing maps.

IV. **Meanings, attitudes, appreciations, developing through these experiences.**
  A. An understanding and appreciation of—
    1. Our natural location.
    2. The wonders of nature in America.
    3. The influence of nature in determining men's activities.
    4. Man's skill in adapting his activities to his natural surroundings.
    5. Abundance of the resources of our United-States.
    6. Extent of our interdependence.
  B. A desire to learn more of our use of natural resources.

V. **New interests foreshadowing further studies.**
  A. Industries in which these products are used.
  B. Life in different regions of the United States.
  C. What Chicago sends to different parts of the United States.

> *Note:* Following this study, the class divided itself into three committees. One committee studied lumber; another group investigated the iron and steel industry; and a third group conducted a unit on stock raising. Outlines of two of these studies follow.

How Does Chicago Obtain and Use Iron?

A Study Conducted by a Committee of the Fifth Grade

I. **Enriching experiences which aroused or fostered interest and provided background.**
  A. Previous studies.
    1. Study of Chicago.
    2. Study of contributions different sections of United States make to Chicago.
  B. Exhibits.
    1. Pictures posted.
    2. Clippings brought in.
  C. Excursions.
    1. Trip to farm to see machinery.

II. **Problems and questions which led to research.**
  A. How does Chicago obtain and use iron?
    1. Where are iron deposits found in the United States? From which deposits does Chicago get iron? Why?
    2. How is iron mined? How is it brought to Chicago?
    3. What process is necessary to change iron into pig iron? How is steel made? What progress has been made in these processes?
    4. Where is coal found in the United States? Where does Chicago get coal for her steel industry?
    . What is coal? How was it formed?
    5. How is coal mined today? How does this differ from the way it was mined long ago?
    7. How is the coal brought to the blast furnace?
    8. What are the products made from iron? How are they made?
    9. What are the products made from steel? How are they made?
    10. What is done with these products?
  B. How shall we show our classmates who are working on other industries how the iron and steel industry is carried on?

III. **Finding answers to questions and problems.**
  A. Through factual reading.
    1. Group reading to gain information necessary to solve problems.

2. Independent reading of material to solve problems.
3. Oral reading to report information found.
4. Independent reading for pleasure following interests stimulated by the study.
5. Silent and oral reading to interpret maps, charts, globes, graphs.
6. Reading to answer tests given to check on information gained.

References

Aitchison, A. E., & Uttley, M.	North America by Train and Plane	1937 Bobbs-Merrill
Allen, N. B.	United States	1937 Ginn
Baker, C. B., and E. D.	Making America	1937 Bobbs-Merrill
Camp, J. M. & Francis, C. B.	Making, Shaping & Treating of Steel	Carnegie Steel Company
Pitkin, W. B. & Hughes, H. F.	Seeing Our Country	1939 Macmillan
Rocheleau, W. F.	Great American Industries Series (Bk. I)	1928 Flanagan
Smith, J. R.	Human Use Geography	1939 Winston

B. Through oral composition.
   1. Organizing and giving talks as a result of individual or group research.
   2. Discussing of material read, information brought in, pictures in exhibits.
   3. Discussing of plans for work and setting up standards to be attained.
   4. Outlining material to be used in stories.
C. Through constructive activities.
   1. Making a motion picture.
      a. Constructing a theater.
      b. Making curtains.
      c. Mounting pictures on cambric.
   2. Making wall hanging of block prints.
      a. Cutting linoleum.
      b. Printing prints on sateen background.
   3. Collecting and arranging an exhibit of different kinds of coal and products of iron.
   4. Planning and constructing posters to advertise motion picture.
D. Through the use of arithmetic.
   1. Measuring in construction of theater, making the curtains, and mounting pictures, using the linear measure.
   2. Measuring in dyeing the curtains, using liquid measure.
   3. Reading and writing large numbers in interpreting

United States production of iron, steel, and commodities made of them.

4. Using four fundamental processes with integers in making the motion picture and theater.

5. Using four fundamental processes with fractions in measuring cloth for curtains and motion picture.

6. Using four fundamental processes with decimals in problems dealing with the production of iron and steel.

7. Using principles of percentage in comparing the production of the United States in comparison with world production of iron and steel.

IV. **Meanings, attitudes, appreciations developing through these experiences.**

A. A recognition and appreciation of the extent of iron ore and coal resources in the United States.

B. An understanding and appreciation of
   1. The marvel of the industrial process.
   2. What miners are doing for us.
   3. The mining possibilities of the United States.

C. A knowledge and appreciation of the change in the life of people brought about by increased production and use of these materials.

D. An expressed desire to help conserve our iron and coal resources.

V. **Interpretation and expression of attitudes and appreciations.**

A. Through literature: oral reading by teacher and pupils of some selections of special charm.

    Guiterman, Arthur—Coal
    Sandburg, Carl—Chicago
    Bryant, William Cullen—Coal

B. Through creative composition.
   1. Writing stories to accompany the pictures in the motion picture program.
   2. Writing stories for the school magazine about the study of industries.

C. Through picture-making, design, decoration.
   1. Painting pictures (18 x 24) with poster paint to show each step in the iron and steel industry, including the part played by coal and the coal industry.
   2. Designing in paper, painting or coloring posters to advertise motion picture.

    3. Making designs of the industry to be used for block prints.

  D. Through social activity in sharing experiences with others. Giving sound motion picture program to classmates and other classes. Original pictures were shown on a hand-made reel, and original talks were given to explain them.

VI. New interests foreshadowing further projects.

  A. Studying other industries.

  B. Making other motion pictures.

How Does Chicago Obtain and Use Lumber?

A Study Carried on by a Committee of the Fifth Grade

I. **Enriching experiences which aroused or fostered interest and provided background.**
   A. Previous studies.
      1. Study of Chicago.
      2. Study of contributions different sections of the United States make to Chicago and to the rest of the world.
   B. Preliminary discussions.
      1. What use is made of products sent to Chicago?
      2. What does she send out?
   C. Trip to farm where branches and cones were gathered.
   D. Spencer films.
      1. Lumbering.
      2. Our Forests and What They Mean to Us.
   E. Exhibits.
      1. Pictures and clippings posted.
      2. Piece of redwood tree brought in.

II. **Problems and questions which led to research.**
   A. How is the lumber industry carried on?
      1. Where are the most important forests in the United States?
      2. What kinds of trees are found in them? How can one tell these different kinds?
      3. How does the amount of forest land to-day compare with that of colonial times?
      4. Why is there less?
      5. How are the forests protected to-day?
      6. How are the trees cut for lumber?
      7. How are they taken to the sawmill?
      8. How are they made into lumber?
      9. Where is this lumber sent and how?
   B. How shall we show the committees on other industries how the lumber industry is carried on?

III. **Finding answers to problems and questions.**
   A. By factual reading.
      1. Independent reading of material to solve problems.

207

2. Independent reading for information along interests stimulated by the study.
3. Group silent reading to gain information necessary to solve problems.
4. Oral reading to report results of individual research.
5. Oral reading of explanations accompanying Spencer film slides.
6. Oral and silent reading to interpret maps, diagrams, globes, graphs.
7. Reading to answer tests given to check on understanding of subject matter.

References

Aitchison, A. E., and Uttley, M.	North America by Train and Plane	1937	Bobbs-Merrill
Allen, N. B.	United States	1937	Ginn
Baker, C. B., and E. D.	Making America	1937	Bobbs-Merrill
Barrows & Parker	United States and Canada	1925	Silver, Burdett
Brigham & McFarlane	Essentials of Geography	1925	American Book
Comstock, A.	Handbook of Nature Study	1939	Comstock
Farquhar, F. F., and others	World Book Encyclopedia	1936	Quarrie
Ford, A. S., and others	Compton's Pictured Encyclopedia	1938	Compton
Patch, E. M.	First Lessons in Nature Study	1932	Macmillan
Smith, J. R.	Human Use Geography	1939	Winston
Trafton, G. H.	Nature Study and Science	1927	Macmillan

B. By language.
  1. Organizing and giving talks as a result of individual or group research.
  2. Discussing material read, information brought in, exhibits, pictures.
  3. Discussing plans for work and setting up standards to be attained.
  4. Outlining material to be used for stories.
C. By constructive activities.
  1. Making of extensive tree exhibit consisting of a tree, bark, lumber, leaves, buds, and cones.
     a. Collecting.
     b. Identifying and labeling.
     c. Arranging.
  2. Building a showcase to use in displaying the exhibit.
  3. Planning, making and binding books of stories, maps, and illustrations.

      4. Making a wall hanging of industry prints.
        a. Cutting designs in linoleum.
        b. Printing on sateen background.
      5. Making maps to show where different trees are found in the United States.
    D. By use of arithmetic.
      1. Measuring.
        a. Using linear measure in construction of books and exhibit case.
        b. Using board measure in working lumber problems.
      2. Reading and writing large numbers in interpreting statistics concerning acreage of forests, production of lumber in the United States.
      3. Counting and using four fundamental processes in determining age of trees by their rings and figuring to place different trees' histories in relation to the history of our country.

IV. Meanings, attitudes, appreciations, developing through these experiences.
    A. An understanding and appreciation of
      1. Our forests.
      2. What those engaged in lumber industry are doing for us.
      3. Our city comforts.
    B. A desire to help protect and conserve our forests.

V. Interpretation and expression of attitudes and appreciations.
    A. By means of creative composition.
      1. Creating stories and verses about trees.
      2. Writing descriptions of the journey from forest to lumberyard, to be placed in lumber books.
      3. Writing items about the study for the school newspaper.
    B. By means of picture-making and design.
      1. Painting large pictures of trees as a part of tree exhibit.
      2. Making illustrations of the steps in the lumber industry to accompany stories in books.
      3. Making sketches of buds, leaves, winter and summer shape, cones, to show others how to identify different trees.
      4. Designing covers for books.
      5. Making designs of the lumber industry for block prints.
    C. By means of social activity.
    Sharing exhibit with classmates.

VI. New interests foreshadowing further units of work.
>   A. Collecting specimens to show summer characteristics of trees.
>   B. Learning uses of forests other than for lumber; as, making of paper.

Enjoying Playgrounds of the United States

An Enterprise in the Fifth Grade Summer Session

I. **Enriching experiences which aroused and fostered interest and provided background for activities.**
   A. Previous studies.
      1. Fifth grade work on industries of the United States.
      2. Fourth grade study of Chicago.
   B. Exhibits.
      1. Large colored posters put out by the railroad companies.
      2. Folders and booklets advertising tours.
      3. Pictures.
   C. Spencer film slide: Yellowstone Park.
   D. Motion pictures.
      1. Dude ranches in New Mexico.
      2. Glacier Park.
   E. Trip to the lake.
   F. Striking bits of description from folders read to children.

II. **Problems and questions which led to research.**
   A. What do people in the United States do for pleasure?
   B. Since traveling seems to be the most important way of spending a vacation, where do people travel in the summer?
   C. Why should they go to these places? What is there interesting on a tour of the Great Lakes? Historical and scenic New England? New York City? Washington, D. C., and vicinity? Philadelphia? The Southern States? Estes Park? California? The Indian Country of the Southwest? Yosemite Park? Salt Lake City? Rainier National Park? Glacier National Park? Yellowstone National Park? Dude Ranches? Wisconsin Lake region?
   D. How might we get some pleasure out of these places this summer while here at school?
      Note: Individual children chose particular places for detailed study.

III. **Finding answers to questions and problems.**
   A. Through factual reading.
      1. Group silent reading to solve problems.
      2. Independent silent reading to solve problems.
      3. Independent reading for information following interests stimulated by the study.

211

4. Oral reading to report information found.
5. Oral and silent reading to interpret maps, diagrams, posters.

References

Aitchison, A. E., and Uttley, M.	North America by Plane and Train	1937	Bobbs-Merrill
Allen, Nellie B.	United States	1937	Ginn
Atwood & Thomas	The Americas, The Earth and Its People	1929	Ginn
Cather, K. D. & Jordon, D. S.	Highlights of Geography —North America	1927	World Book
Halliburton, R.	Book of Marvels	1937	Bobbs-Merrill
Krapp, G. P.	Inland Oceans	1927	Rand McNally
	Pictorial Atlas of the World	1931	Reilly and Lee
	World Atlas	1930	Rand McNally
Smith, J. R.	Human Use Geography	1939	Winston
Retold from St. Nicholas	Stories of the Great Lakes		Century

B. Through language.
   1. Discussing and suggesting plans for work.
   2. Practice in outlining material and organizing information for talks.
   3. Organizing and giving talks as each child conducted the class around the chosen city or park.
   4. Discussing and criticising work done.
C. Through constructive activities.
   1. Marking out on maps suggested places to visit and tours to make.
   2. Making large poster advertisements for the purpose of inducing classmates to visit certain scenic spots on their imaginary trip.
   3. Making models to advertise places.
   4. Making charts to advertise places.
   5. Making class book containing diary of the trip.
D. Through use of arithmetic.
   1. Using four fundamental processes with integers in figuring distances and cost of the trip.
   2. Using linear measure in making advertisements.

IV. **Social meanings, attitudes, appreciations developing through these experiences.**
   A. A knowledge and appreciation of the beauties and wonders of our country.
   B. A knowledge and appreciation of those who make it possible for us to see and enjoy them: travel bureaus; transportation companies; guides.

C. A feeling of gratitude to the national and local govern-
ments, to historical societies and other organizations for
preserving these interesting places, and offering their use
to the public.

D. Some appreciation of the responsibility of those who visit
public playgrounds for their care and protection.

V. Interpretation and expression of attitudes and appreciations.

A. Through literature.
Oral reading of some selections of special interest and
charm.

References

Harper, W. & Hamilton, A. J.	Treasure Trail Series (Far-Away Hills)	1929 Macmillan
Rolfe, M. A.	Our National Parks (Books I and II)	1927 Sanborn
Seymour, F. W.	Indians Today	1926 Sanborn

B. Through creative composition: writing of diary by each
child of one place visited on the trip.

C. Through picture-making.
  1. Sketching of scenes by the lake in pastels.
  2. Painting scenes for advertisements and class diary.
  3. Making posters in colored papers for advertisements.

D. Through dramatic activity.
An imaginary trip to the playgrounds of the United States,
the children taking turns in acting as guide and pointing
out places of interest.

VI. New interests foreshadowing further studies.

A. Playgrounds and interesting places in other countries.

B. Beautiful scenery.

How New York Became Our Greatest City

A Fifth Grade Problem of the First Semester

I. Enriching experiences which aroused and fostered interest and provided background.
   A. Previous studies.
      1. Discovering America.
      2. Study of own community—Chicago.
      3. Vacation exhibit.
   B. Exhibits.
      1. Pictures and clippings on bulletin boards about New York City.
      2. Relics from old New York.
   C. Stories read to the children.
      1. *Peeps at Great Cities—New York*—Hawthorne.
      2. Selections from recent magazines and newspapers.

II. Problems and questions which led to research.
   A. What is New York's early history?
      1. Who discovered it?
      2. Who explored it?
      3. Who first settled there and why did they?
      4. How did the early settlers live?
      5. What was the appearance of New York in the early days?
      6. Who ruled it?
      7. Who were some of the important people in the early history of New York?
   B. Why are cities built?
      1. Why do people live in cities to-day instead of on isolated farms as long ago?
      2. What changes did discoveries and inventions make in power?
      3. What changes in living did changes in power make?
      4. How do we come to have coal? How does it help to build cities?
      5. How do we come to have oil? How does it help?
      6. How does water power help to build cities?
      7. How does iron help to build cities?
   C. How has its geography helped New York to become a great city?
      1. How has its climate helped?
      2. What crops can it get easily?

214

3. What natural resources can it get easily?
4. How has its harbor helped?
5. What advantages does its location have for trade both with the rest of the United States and foreign countries?

D. How have men helped to make New York a great city?
1. How have men aided the growth of New York by improving transportation?
2. How have men solved the sanitation problem for a great city?
3. How have men helped New York by building great schools?
4. How have men helped by building buildings?
5. What has the artist and sculptor done for New York?
6. How has the immigrant helped?
7. How have men helped by building playgrounds, parks and museums?
8. How have publishing companies helped New York?
9. What have men done to make New York a great trading center?
10. What have men done to make New York a great buying center?

Note: Problems A, B and C were worked upon by the group together; in Problem D each child chose one topic to work on and report to the group.

III. Solution of problems.

A. Through factual reading.
1. Reading to find answers to problems (group and individually).
2. Reading for general information along interests stimulated by the study.
3. Reading maps, charts, graphs, globes for information.
4. Reading tests given to check on mastery of subject matter.

Book References

Aitchison, A. E., and Uttley, M.	North America by Plane and Train	1937	Bobbs-Merrill
Allen, N. B.	United States	1937	Ginn
Atwood, W. W., and Thomas, H.	The Americas	1929	Ginn
Chamberlain, J. F.	North America	1927	Macmillan
Farquhar, F. F., and others	World Book Encyclopedia	1936	Quarrie
Ford, A. S., and others	Compton's Pictured Encyclopedia	1938	Compton
Fox, F. C.	How the World Rides	1929	Scribner

Halliburton, R.	Book of Marvels	1937 Bobbs-Merrill
Hawthorne, H.	Peeps at Great Cities	1911 Macmillan
Hotchkiss, C. W.	Representative Cities of the United States	1913 Houghton Mifflin
Irwin, W.	Highlights of Manhattan	1927 Century
Kelty, M. G.	Beginnings of the American People and Nation	1930 Ginn
Pitkin, W. B. & Hughes, H. F.	Seeing Our Country	1939 Macmillan
Rugg, H. O.	Our Country and Our People	1938 Ginn
Webb, V. L., and others	New World Past and Present	1938 Scott

Periodicals

New York Times Picture Section
Fortune Magazine, July, 1939
"New York's World's Fair 1939" (Edited by L' Illustration)

B. Through language.
1. Outlining and giving reports on information found.
2. Discussing problems of work and of subject matter.
3. Setting up standards to be attained.
C. Through constructive activities.
1. Constructing a replica of New Amsterdam.
   a. Cutting houses from wood.
   b. Making trees of sponges.
   c. Making fences of pebbles and clay.
   d. Making ships of clay.
2. Making maps.
   a. Large freehand maps of the harbor for the model.
   b. Maps showing the coal, oil, iron and water power regions of the United States.
   c. Maps of steamship routes to New York.
   d. Maps showing places from which New York gets products.
3. Making a radio for broadcasting stories.
4. Making a table for exhibits.
D. Through the use of arithmetic.
1. Addition of integers.
   Adding different amounts in statistics to get totals.
2. Subtraction.
   Subtracting dates to find how long ago.
3. Double multiplication.
   a. Finding area of plots of ground.
   b. Finding cost of land valued at New York prices.
4. Long division.
   Finding value of one square foot of land in New York when total was given.

5. Reading large numbers in statistics on New York.
6. Fractions.
    a. Expressing parts as a fraction.
    b. Reducing per cents to common fractions in statistics on New York.
    c. Adding common fractions in measuring.
    d. Subtracting common fractions in construction problems.

IV. Social meanings, attitudes, appreciations, developing through these experiences.

    A. An understanding of the beginnings made by the early settlers.

    B. An understanding and appreciation of the marvels that mechanical power has brought about.

    C. Some understanding of the wealth of our country in sources of power.

    D. Some understanding of the wealth of our country in ores and metals.

    E. An appreciation of the values of natural resources and the necessity of conserving them.

    F. An understanding of the important part geographic factors play in determining man's activities.

    G. An appreciation of the contribution made by the immigrant, the artist, the sculptor, the musician, and the engineer.

    H. Knowledge and appreciation of the conveniences to be had in a city made possible by man's use of scientific knowledge.

V. Interpretation and expression of attitudes and appreciations.

    A. Through literature.
    Oral reading by teacher and pupils for pleasure.

Read to children

Allen, N. B.	United States	1925	Ginn
Irving, W.	Rip Van Winkle	1908	Altemus
Irving, W.	Legend of the Sleepy Hollow	1924	Lippincott

Read by the children

Dodge, M. M.	Hans Brinker or the Silver Skates	1903	Century
Hilles, Helen T.	Play Street	1936	Random House
Lewis, W. D. & Rowland, A. L.	Scouting Through	1930	Winston

    B. Through creative composition.
    Writing stories for books on New York.

C. Through picture making, design, decoration.
  1. Making pictures to illustrate the stories written for the New York books.
    a. Crayon drawings.
    b. Diagrams in ink.
    c. Pencil sketches.
    d. Paintings.
  2. Making covers for books.
    a. Cutting designs from poster paper.
    b. Cutting letters from poster paper for titles.
D. Through music.
  1. Discussing and exchanging information and experiences relating to the great musical organizations in New York: ensembles, orchestras, opera, music centers and music schools.
  2. The making and balancing of programs from available piano scores, representing the many fields listed above to be used in appreciation hours.
  3. Singing and listening to old Dutch folk music.

Source Books and Materials

Hamilton, Clarence	Outlines of Music History	Oliver Ditson
Rontgen, Elkin, LeMair	Old Dutch Nursery Rhymes	Augener Ltd.
Davison, Surette	A Book of Songs	E. C. Schirmer
Purcell, Henry	Dido and Aeneas	Oxford Press
Mozart	The Magic Flute	Novello
Schubert	Symphony in B Minor	G. Schirmer
Brahms	Symphony in C Minor	N. Simrock

Current circulars and programs from New York music organizations.

E. Through social activity, sharing experiences with others.
  1. Radio talks for classmates: sharing the stories written with classmates, by reading them behind the scenes as if they were broadcast over the radio.
  2. New York Assembly. Radio idea was used for a New York program for parents and grades four and six.

VI. **New interests foreshadowing further study.**

The children were interested in other large cities of the United States, especially San Francisco and New Orleans.

Fifth Grade Impressions of the City

A City of Steel

A city of steel and of iron and of smoke,
A city of oil and bricks and of coke,
A city of autos and street cars and trains,

A city of boats and of swift airplanes,—
A village of horses and dirt roads is gone,
But a city of skyscrapers stands in the dawn.

Sounds of the City

Autos whiz.
Street cars thump.
Taxis honk.
Huge trucks bump.
Iron wheels screech.
Fast trains boom.
Whistles scream.
Airplanes zoom.
The city knows
These noisy sounds.
They sound all day
When they make their rounds.

The City at Night

Over the city
Night is closing.
Many tired workers
Are quietly dozing.
One by one
Twinkling lights fade away.
The city is sleeping
Until dawns the day.

There is a City

There is a city about which I dream
When the shadows of the evening gleam.
I dream about its marble towers
And about its sweet-scented flowers,
Where its highways are paved with gold,
Where its spires pierce the clouds and hold
In darkened chests a treasure great.
But in this city lies the treasure seeker's fate,
For in these chests of jewels and rich stones
And in this city of sparkling domes
Demons dark and cruel lie,—
The treasure seeker they will defy.

And my dream is not truthless.
With America's treasure, man is ruthless;
So, people, I demand, do not waste
Our country's treasure in greed and haste.

The Broker

The Broker, the Broker,
The Beast of the City,—
Three balls is his sign.
There's money in his line.
Some folks would like to throw him
In the deep and foamy brine.
Isn't it a pity
That the Broker is
The Beast of the City?

How the United States Moved West from New York to San Francisco

A Second Semester's Problem in Fifth Grade

I. Enriching experiences which aroused and fostered interest and provided background.

    A. Previous studies.
        1. Discovering America.
        2. Development of Chicago.
        3. Development of New York including the factors which influence the growth of any city.
    B. Preliminary discussions.
        1. Discussions of other important cities of the United States besides New York.
        2. Discussions which resulted in choice of San Francisco as next city to be studied.
        3. Discussions as to who settled San Francisco led to the conclusion that settling San Francisco involved the settling of our country to Pacific.
        4. Choosing of topic "How the United States moved west from New York to San Francisco" for study.
    C. Exhibits.
        1. Pictures of events in United States history.
        2. Clippings from newspapers and magazines.
        3. Pioneer relics.
    D. Excursions.
        1. To a modern farm in the Northwest territory.
        2. To the Chicago Historical Society to see a replica of a pioneer home, Conestoga wagon, pioneer farm implements, relics of the Civil War.
    E. Spencer film—strips.
        1. Fishing.
        2. Lumbering.
        3. Yellowstone National Park.
        4. Wild animals of North America.
        5. Our forests and what they mean to us.

II. Problems and questions which led into research.

    A. How did the pioneers overcome the first barrier, the Appalachian Mountains, and move into the Northwest territory?
        1. Why had the colonists first settled on the coast?

2. How were these difficulties of mountains and enemies overcome?
3. What advantages did the land west of the mountains offer the settlers?
4. How did the United States open the land west of the mountains for settlement?
5. What routes were used in moving into this territory?
6. By what means did the settlers move into this territory?
7. Who were some of the outstanding people in settling this territory?

B. What has the Northwest territory in the central section of the United States contributed?
1. The climate, soil, and topography of this section are suited to what activities?
2. What natural resources are found here?
3. What are the advantages for trade?

C. How was the frontier pushed to the Pacific coast?
1. How did the United States come to gain the land west of the Mississippi?
2. How did the people find out about this vast new land?
3. How did they get there to settle?
4. What improvements were made in roads?
5. What part did the canals play in the westward movement?
6. Steamboats?
7. Railroads?
8. How could the settlers take care of the vast farms which were now available?
9. Who were the inventors who helped the early pioneers?
10. How did the people live in this new region?
11. What part did the new West take in the government?
12. How did Florida come to be a part of the United States?
13. How did Texas come to be a part of the United States?
14. How did the Oregon territory come to be a part of the United States?
15. What led the people to the Far West?
16. Who were some of the outstanding people in building the West?

D. What is the Far West contributing to-day?
1. The climate, the soil, the topography of the different sections are suited to what activities?
2. What natural resources are found here?
3. How have men used the advantages and overcome the disadvantages?

THE COVERED WAGON SPELLS ADVENTURE

4. How do people differ here from those in other sections?
E. How have all the sections of the United States been brought
more closely together today?

III. Finding answers to questions and problems.

A. Through factual reading.
1. Types of silent reading.
a. Independent reading to solve problems.
b. Independent reading following interests stimulated
by the study.
c. Group reading to gain information necessary to solve
problems.
d. Reading to interpret maps, globes, diagrams.
e. Reading to answer informal objective tests given to
check on understanding of subject matter.
f. Reading suggestions made out by teacher and children
for working out problems.

2. Types of oral reading.
    a. Oral reading to report results of individual research.
    b. Oral reading of explanations accompanying the Spencer film strips.
    c. Oral reading to interpret maps, diagrams, graphs, globes.

References

Adams, J. T.	Epic of America	1933	Little Brown
Allen, N. B.	United States	1937	Ginn
Atwood, M. W. & Thomas, H. G.	The Americas	1930	Ginn
Baker, C. B., and E. D.	Making America	1937	Bobbs-Merrill
Barker, E. C.	The Story of Our Nation	1933	Row Peterson
Burnham, S.	Hero Tales from History	1930	Winston
Farquahar, F. F., and others.	World Book Encyclopedia	1940	Quarrie
Ford, G. S. (Editor)	Compton's Pictured Encyclopedia	1940	Compton
Halliburton, R.	Book of Marvels	1937	Bobbs-Merrill
Kelty, M. G.	Beginnings of American People & Nation	1930	Ginn
Kelty, M. G.	The Growth of American People & Nation	1931	Ginn
Melbo, I. R.	Our America	1937	Bobbs-Merrill
Pitkin, W. B. & Hughes, H. F.	Seeing Our Country	1939	Macmillan
Rugg, H. O.	Our Country and Our People	1938	Ginn
Smith, N. B. and Bayne, S. F.	Frontiers Old and New	1940	Silver, Burdett
Webb, V. L., and others.	New World Past and Present	1938	Scott

B. Through language.
    1. Discussing readings, exhibits, and excursions.
    2. Discussing plans for working out solutions to problems.
    3. Setting up standards to be attained.
    4. Organizing and giving reports as a result of individual research.
    5. Outlining as a group the important events in the Westward Movement.
C. Through constructive activities.
    1. Making individual models of clay or wood illustrating different episodes in Westward Movement.
    2. Making maps showing routes traveled, canals or railroads built, extent of various territories.
    3. Making large charts of 24" by 36" tag board, containing stories, maps, pictures and diagrams.
    4. Making stage properties for the play.

    a. Cutting large covered wagon (6′ x 8′), oxen, trees, bushes, sage brush and fireplace from beaver board and making standards for them.

    b. Making pioneer cradle, stools and guns from lumber.

5. Making costumes for the play.

    a. Cutting dresses by patterns from cambric.

    b. Cutting hunting shirts from cambric to be worn with long khaki trousers.

    c. Cutting sunbonnets.

    d. Making costumes.

D. Through the use of arithmetic.

1. Using linear measure in making charts, stage properties, costumes.

2. Reading and writing large numbers in interpreting statistics on present crop values, distances.

3. Counting money, making change, and keeping accounts in connection with the play.

4. Using the four fundamental processes with integers.

    a. Adding integers in finding crop values in the United States; cost of land.

    b. Subtracting integers in finding how long ago an event took place.

    c. Multiplying to find cost of several acres of land at early values and value today; finding area of plots of ground.

    d. Dividing to find number of acres in a plot of ground.

5. Using the four fundamental processes with fractions.

    a. Adding fractions in finding amount of different colored cambric needed for costumes, amount of beaver board needed for stage properties.

    b. Subtracting fractions in finding amount of cambric left after cutting one costume.

    c. Multiplying fractions to find the cost of the cloth for each costume, the amount needed for several costumes which are alike.

    d. Dividing fractions to find how many costumes can be cut from material on hand.

6. Decimal fractions.

Reading decimal fractions in interpreting statistics.

7. Percentage.

Expressing per cents as common fractions with 100 as the denominator and reducing them to their lowest terms in interpreting statistics.

IV. **Social meanings, attitudes, appreciations developing through these experiences.**

A. Knowledge and appreciation of the hardships endured by the early settlers in surmounting the natural barriers in moving west, and of the hardships endured in making a home and earning a living in a new wild country.

B. Understanding of the important part geographic factors play in determining man's occcupation in the different sections of our country.

C. An appreciation of the vastness of our country.

D. Knowledge of the wealth of the natural resources.

E. Appreciation of the importance of conserving natural resources.

F. Appreciation for the bravery of men who dared to go into a wilderness and build a country.

G. Understanding of the progress made in methods of communication and transportation through man's use of scientific knowledge.

H. Understanding of the progress made in the industries through man's use of scientific knowledge.

I. Appreciation of the ease and luxury of the present-day life compared with that of the early settler.

V. **Interpretation and expression of attitudes and appreciations.**

A. Through creative composition.

1. Writing of the play as an expression of the enjoyment of the dramatic incidents in the westward expansion of the United States.

   a. Writing some scenes for the play as a big group.

   b. Writing some scenes in smaller committees with teachers.

   c. Writing some scenes as committees without teacher help.

   d. Writing some scenes individually.

   e. Writing dodgers to advertise the play.

   f. Writing thank-you notes to those who assisted in giving the play.

   g. Writing thank-you notes for the use of the auditorium.

2. Writing stories or descriptions of activities carried on in different sections to-day.

B. Through literature.

1. Poems read to and by the children:

Austin, Mary	A Pioneer
Braley, Burton	The Pioneers

Bryant, W. C.	The Prairies
Guiterman, Arthur	The Oregon Trail
Guiterman, Arthur	The Tall Men
Lomax, John A.	The MacKenzie Trail
Mac Diarmid	The Call of the Plains
Miller, Joaquin	Pioneers, Pioneers
Miller, Joaquin	The Ship in the Desert

2. Stories from which selections were read orally by the children for pleasure:

Baker, C. B., & E. D.	Making America	1937 Bobbs-Merrill
Bindloos, H.	The Frontiersman	1929 Stokes
Carr, M. J.	Children of the Covered Wagon	1934 Crowell
Coffman, R.	Our America	1930 Dodd
Gabriel, R. H.	Lure of the Frontier	1929 Yale
Grey, K.	Rolling Wheels	1932 Little Brown
Grey, K.	Hills of Gold	1933 Little Brown
Halliburton, R.	Book of Marvels	1937 Bobbs-Merrill
Jackson, H. M.	Nellie's Silver Mine	1924 Little Brown
Lewis, W. D. & Rowland, A. L.	Opening the Great West from "Scouting Through"	1930 Winston
Lewis, W. D. & Rowland, A. L.	Whys and Wherefores	1930 Winston
Smith, N. B. and Bayne, S. F.	Frontiers Old and New	1940 Silver, Burdett
Wilder, L. I.	Little House on the Prairie	1935 Harper
Wilder, L. I.	Little House in the Big Woods	1932 Harper

C. Through picture making, design, decoration.
   1. Making pictures and posters depicting events in the Westward Movement.
   2. Making pictures in paint and crayon to show activities in different sections to-day.
   3. Making block print designs for the programs.

D. Through music.
   1. Singing some of the typical songs of the various sections of the country:

   > Songs of the plains and hills as: "The Dying Cowboy," "Get Along Little Dogies"
   > Kentucky mountain songs and ballads: "The Swapping Song."
   > Southern songs: "Oh Susannah" (Words "California")
   > "My Old Kentucky Home."
   > General: "Quilting Party," "My Darling Nellie Gray."

   2. Playing games such as: "Old Dan Tucker," "Jolly is the Miller."
   3. Learning old dances such as "Virginia Reel."

Source Books

Botsford, F. H.	Folk Songs of Many Peoples	Womans Press
Davison, Surette and Zanzig	A Book of Songs	E. C. Schirmer
Hofer, Mari	Popular Folk Games and Dances	A. Flanagan
La Salle, Dorothy	Rhythms and Dances	A. S. Barnes
Lomax, J. A.	Cowboy Songs—Frontier Ballads	Macmillan
Palmer, Winthrop	American Songs for Children	Macmillan
Sandburg, Carl	The American Songbag	Harcourt, Brace
	The Blue Book of Favorite Songs	Hall & McCreary
	Sociability Songs	Rodeheaver
White and Shackley	The Lonesome Cowboy	G. T. Worth

E. Through dramatic activity.
  1. Giving informal dramatizations of incidents in the Westward Movement.
  2. Giving the finished play, "Pioneer Days."

SYNOPSIS

Act I

Sc. I.—In 1783 Mr. and Mrs. Peter Brinker are living in eastern Pennsylvania with Mr. Brinker's grandfather. The grandfather has a trunk containing relics of New Amsterdam. He tells their stories to his granddaughter-in-law.

Sc. II.—That evening some neighbors, the Tollivers, spend the evening with the Brinkers discussing the recent treaty of peace and their part in the Revolution. Two friends of Boone return from Maryland where they saw him. They persuade the Tollivers and Brinkers to move to Kentucky.

Sc. III.—The Brinkers and Tollivers are packing their wagons to move to Kentucky.

Act II

Sc. I.—In about 1808 the Brinkers are having a party for their grown children in their home near St. Louis. They are very much interested in the Louisiana Territory. During the evening Lewis and Clark come in and tell of their trip.

Sc. II.—One afternoon in 1812 Mrs. Brinker and daughter are sewing in the yard when some people who are on their way to the Oregon territory stop for water. They tell about seeing Fulton's steamboat tried out. They urge the two Brinker boys to go west. The boys, however, have decided to help out in the trouble with England before they go.

Act III

Sc. I.—One evening in 1819 young Dave Tolliver and John Brinker and their families have camped on their way farther west. Dave Tolliver is going to Oregon and John Brinker to western Texas.

Sc. II.—In 1849 a wagon train of forty-niners, among whom is John Brinker, has stopped on the way to California. They meet Kit Carson and discuss the trail. They also discuss the annexation of Texas, the acquisition of Oregon, and the building of railroads.

ACT IV

In 1931 the Brinker descendants in San Francisco are entertaining the descendants of the Brinker who remained in the South after the war of 1812 and the Tolliver descendants from Oregon. The children discover the old Brinker trunk which has come across the country and examine its relics which now also consist of the letters from the South concerning the Civil War and letters from Oregon. The man of the house returns from New York by airplane and the grandmother marvels at the difference in the present day and the old.

VI. New interests foreshadowing further studies.

A. Study of how our country is related to other countries.

B. Study of other countries.

Note: The children were unanimous in their expressions that the above topics should constitute their next piece of work.

Learning to Use and Control Water

Summer School Experiences in Fifth Grade

I. **Enriching experiences which aroused and fostered interest and provided background.**
   A. Members of the class collected rain in open jars.
   B. A collection of water was made about the school.
      1. Drinking fountain in the corridor.
      2. Taps in the science room benches.
      3. Taps in the washroom.
      4. Drinking fountain in the cafeteria.
      5. Dish washing basins in the cafeteria kitchen.
      6. Cubes of ice allowed to melt in glass.
      7. Water dipped from Lake Michigan..
   C. Uses of water were listed.
      1. Relating to health and safety: foods and beverages, cleanliness, refrigeration, recreation, fire protection.
      2. Relating to industry: promotion of plant growth, irrigation, chemicals, machines, plastic arts, navigation.
   D. Members of the class dug into the ground on a dry day until the dirt appeared moist.
   E. A visit was made to the water pumping station in Wilmette.
   F. Inspection was made of a gravity feed water tank in Evanston.
   G. A visit was made to a farm where rain water was collected for washing dishes and cleanliness.
   H. Swimming lessons were given in Lake Michigan, from the Wilmette Beach.
   I. A homemade boat race was held in Lake Michigan.

II. **Problems and questions which led to experiment and investigation.**
   A. The kinds of water.
      1. Why is the rain water collected in the bottle, dirty?
      . Is all the tap water the same?
      . Why should drinking water be purified?
      4. Is it safe to eat ice? What kind of water is ice made from?
      5. Where does the salt come from in salt water?
      6. Is the salt in salt water real salt?
      7. If salt water does not freeze, why do we have icebergs?
   B. Source and testing of water.
      1. When water evaporates, where does it go?

TEMPERATURE OF WATER IS TESTED

2. Can we keep water from evaporating?
3. Does water always evaporate at the same speed?
4. Where does the lake water come from?
5. Why is the ground dry on top and wet underneath?
6. When we pour water into the ground, where does it go?
7. Where does the rain water come from?
8. How do trees give off so much water into the air?
9. Is there more water in the air in a forest than above thinly vegetated land?
10. How does an irrigation system work?

C. Importance and uses of water.
1. Could we live without water?
2. Could plants and animals live without water?
3. Do some plants live in dry regions because they need little water, or do only plants that grow in dry regions need little water?
4. What makes us thirsty? How much water should a person drink?

5. Why do some animals require little water?
6. How does water give us power?
7. When is water an enemy of man?

D. Characteristics of water.
1. How much does water weigh?
2. Why does water make persons feel cool?
3. What is water made of?
4. How can water be purified or distilled?
5. Does water contain life?
6. Are snow, ice, hail, and sleet forms of water? What causes these forms?
7. Why do water drops form on the outside of a cold glass?
8. Why does ice form on the inside of a window in the winter?
9. How can living things live in water?

E. Transportation of water.
1. How does water get into the air?
2. How does water get into the clouds?
3. Why does the water rush out of the taps in different parts of the building?
4. Is water ever transported?
5. What makes waves? tides?
6. How are floods caused?

III. **Finding answers to problems and questions.**

A. Through constructive activities and experiments.
1. Comparing water from different sources.
2. Boiling water and examining the sediment.
3. Melting ice in a tumbler, recording the temperature.
4. Recording temperature of tap water and rain water.
5. The "evaporation" contest.
   Each pupil brings two half-pint milk bottles. Each is filled with water, but one is sealed with a bottle cap and paraffin, and the other is left open. Each child puts his bottles in the same place. Daily record is made of the amount of evaporation.
6. Digging a well on the beach until water is "struck."
7. Floating ice cubes in water. How far into the water do they sink?
8. Construction of faucet water motors in the shop.
9. Building a dam on the beach.
10. Making weight charts of liquids.
    Samples of oil, milk, cream, water, salt water were

brought into the classroom. Equal quantities were weighed and compared.

11. Examination under the microscope of pond water.
12. Observing water form on the outside of a cold glass.
13. Weighing a bowl of water—add a goldfish. Does the weight increase, decrease, or stay the same?
14. Weighing a stone. Tie it to a string. Insert it in water. Re-weigh it.
15. Examining the water pipes in the basement.
16. Blowing an electric fan over a pan of water and recording thermometer variations, if any.
17. Swimming in Lake Michigan. Learning to "float," etc.

B. Through uses of arithmetic.
1. Calculating weight of various quantities of water.
2. "A pint's a pound, the world around" . . . Is this true?
3. Making charts of comparative weights of liquids.
4. Pouring water into jars of unknown capacity to determine volume.
5. Recording temperatures of water containing different amounts of heat.
6. Reading water meters.
7. Calculating water bills.
8. Measuring material for making boats and water motors.
9. Measuring amount of evaporation in the "evaporation" contests.

C. Through factual reading and language.
1. Individual investigations and reports on the following topics:
   a. Drinking fountains.
   b. Irrigation projects.
   c. The Boulder Dam and the Tennessee Valley Dams.
   d. Drainage canals.
   e. City water supply.
   f. How plants use water.
   g. Weather, especially snow, rain, sleet and ice.
   h. Manufacturing ice.
   i. How pumps lift water.
   j. The "water cycle."
   k. How steamboats and locomotives are propelled by water.
   l. How steel boats float.
2. Selected stories read in class relating to water.
3. Making a list of words related to water and its various uses.

4. Collecting pictures in newspapers and other periodicals related to water.

IV. Meanings, attitudes, and appreciations probably developed.
  A. Water is extremely important in our everyday living.
  B. Water can be both friend and enemy of man.
  C. Water is closely related to our health.
  D. Temperature, climate, and other phases of our environment depend somewhat on water.
  E. Water exists in many forms and follows a "water cycle."
  F. Water is power, and the power of water has not yet been fully utilized by man.

V. New interests foreshadowing further classroom experience.
  A. Interest in thermometers.
  B. Interest in fog maps, weather maps, and steamship lanes.
  C. Interest in keeping the proper amount of water in the air we breathe.
  D. Curiosity about the influence of the moon and sun in producing tides, and their relationship to other heavenly bodies.

Pupil References

Andress, J. M., and others	Safe and Healthy Living	1939	Ginn
Baldwin, S. E.	Our Wide, Wide World	1932	Ginn
Beauchamp, W. L., and others	Science Stories (Books 1, 2, and 3)	1936	Scott, Foresman
Beck, G. E.	What Makes the Wheels Go Round	1931	Macmillan
Craig, G. S.	Folkways in Science Series	1933	Ginn
Craig, G. S. and Johnson, G. M.	Our Earth and Its Story	1932	Ginn
Craig, G. S., and others	Learning About Our World	1932	Ginn
Craig, G. S. and Hurley, B. D.	The Earth and Living Things	1932	Ginn
Fowlkes, J. G., and others	Keeping Well	1936	Winston
Fowlkes, J. G., and others	Healthy Bodies	1936	Winston
Fowlkes, J. G., and others	Healthy Growing	1936	Winston
Fowlkes, J. G., and others	Healthy Living	1936	Winston
Fowlkes, J. G., and others	Making Life Healthful	1938	Winston
Fowlkes, J. G., and others	Success Through Health	1938	Winston
Lummis, J. I.	Guide for a Health Program	1929	World Book
Patch, Edith M., and Howe, Harrison E.	Science at Home	1934	Macmillan
Patch, Edith M., and Howe, Harrison E.	Through the Four Seasons	1933	Macmillan
Patch, Edith M., and Howe, Harrison E.	Surprises	1933	Macmillan
Persing, E. C., and others	Elementary Science by Grades	1930	Appleton
Phillips, M. G., and Wright, J. M.	Our Earth and Its Life	1938	D. C. Heath

Phillips, M. G., and Wright, J. M.	Plants and Animals	1938 D. C. Heath
Reed, W. M.	And That's Why	1932 Harcourt
Teeters, W. R., and Heising, C. M.	Early Journeys in Science	1931 Lippincott
Weed, H. T. and Rexford, F. A.	Useful Science	1933 Winston

Teacher's References

Caldwell, O. W., and Curtis, F. D.	Science for Today	1936 Ginn
Clement, A. G., and others	Our Surroundings	1935 Iroquois
Davis, I. C., and Sharpe, R. W.	Science	1936 Holt
Deming, F. R., and Nerden, J. T.	Science in the World of Work	1936 McGraw-Hill
Hessler, J. C.	First Year of Science	1932 Sanborn
Hunter, G. W., and Whitman, W. G.	Problems in General Science	1930 American Book
Lake, C. H., and others	Exploring the World of Science	1934 Silver, Burdett
Pieper, C. J., and Beauchamp, W. L.	Everyday Problems in Science	1933 Scott, Foresman
Powers, S. R., and others	Man's Control of His Environment	1936 Ginn
Regenstein, A. B. and Teeters, W.	Science at Work	1935 Rand McNally
Skilling, W. T.	Tours through the World of Science	1934 McGraw-Hill
Trafton, G. H., and Smith, V. C.	Science in Daily Life	1936 Lippincott
Van Buskirk, E. F. and others	Science of Everyday Life	1936 Houghton

UNITS OF EXPERIENCE IN
SIXTH GRADE

A GROWING interest in the study of the community found expression in one sixth-grade group in a study of community planning, and the construction of a model community. The work was accompanied by much study on the topics of housing, sanitation, recreation, safety, protection, and other vital problems.

Some understanding of the relationship of other countries to our own country and to our own community have been among the attainments desired for the children of the sixth grade. The need and possibility of world coöperation in the present day have been emphasized; and also the importance of a tolerant and understanding attitude. Some classes have got "cues from the news." Current happenings have suggested problems concerning the relationship of a particular country to neighboring countries and to the United States. A desire to understand the current situation has led at times to the study of history, geography, government, and the economic progress of the country under discussion.

Certain periods have sometimes been selected for detailed study. One class made a study of the problem, "What is our heritage from the Middle Ages?" The contribution of medieval Europe in art, architecture, literature, and book-making was studied. The unit was followed by a study of the problem, "What has modern Europe contributed to the United States?" The class investigated the percentage of our population which had been drawn from each country of Europe, the subject of immigration and emigration, and the question of exports and imports.

Other classes have undertaken developmental studies. One group made an extended study of the development of architecture through the ages. Another class chose to study the development of communication in ancient and medieval times. A unit followed on our relations to the modern world, made possible by modern methods of communication and transportation. A World's Fair developed, stimulated by pictures and announcements of the New York Fair and the San Francisco Fair.

It has been customary to give some time especially during the spring and summer terms to the study of natural science. Two different classes have found keen interest in an intensive study of the larger insects of the region. A study of temperature and humidity has proved of value in everyday living. One class found the organization and maintenance of a large aquarium a fascinating problem.

The units outlined here were developed in two or three different years. Outcomes in social meanings and appreciations peculiar to the particular unit have been listed with each unit. All of the units have afforded opportunities for the continued development of certain desirable social habits and attitudes; such as, coöperation with others, respect for the opinions of others, courtesy and consideration, willingness to share ideas and materials, and also such valuable personal habits as thinking a problem through, making sensible and reasonable judgments, carrying on research and using illustrative materials in solving of problems. These units have also been accompanied by growth in the powers of expression through creative language, fine and industrial arts, music and dramatization. Outcomes in the fundamental skills of English and arithmetic have been summarized under Group Records of Progress in Part IV.

Planning a Community

A Study in Sixth Grade

I. **Enriching experiences which aroused interest and provided background.**

    A. Reports by a few children and the teacher concerning visits to small towns in older sections of the United States, where streets were winding and poorly arranged.

    B. Clippings from the local newspaper on poor planning for the future, as illustrated by Fountain Square in Evanston.

    C. Discussion of the merits of a planned community as illustrated by the "World of Tomorrow" at the New York World's Fair.

    D. Pictures from the "World of Tomorrow" at the New York World's Fair.

    E. The children expressed a desire to study in greater detail the functioning of an ideal community.

II. **Problems and questions which led into the investigation.**

    A. Relating to the beginning of cities or towns.

        1. How do most cities begin?

        2. What civic problems might be eliminated if towns were properly planned?

        3. What are the most important aspects of city planning?

        4. What are the most effective ways used for making the average town beautiful?

    B. Concerning an ideal planned community.

        1. What public buildings should be included?

        2. What are the requirements of a modern home today?

        3. What should be the width of the streets and of the sidewalks?

        4. What should be the length of the blocks?

        5. How should the highways be planned? Checkerboard or spider web? Clover leaf crossings?

        6. Should the height of the buildings be regulated?

        7. What are the influences in architecture in public buildings?

        8. What styles should the homes be?

        9. What plans should be made for communication?

       10. Where should railway stations and airports be located?

    C. Concerning the financing of homes.

        1. What is the F.H.A.?

2. What percent will the government loan?

3. How much of your income should go into the building of a home?

4. How much are laborers paid?

5. What is the role of the labor unions in construction?

6. Why should a contractor be employed?

7. What percent does a contractor make when he builds a house?

8. If the laborers charged less, would there be more building and therefore more actual days of work for the laborer?

9. What is a mortgage?

10. What is a building and loan company?

11. What is the basis for determining rent?

12. What is a real-estate company?

13. Can a real-estate company secure a government loan?

D. Concerning the government of a city.

1. Who is the executive?

2. What comprises the judicial department of a town?

3. What body makes the laws in the town?

4. What is meant by commissions?

E. Concerning the protection of life and property.

1. What is property insurance?

2. How does the police department function?

3. How does the fire department afford protection?

F. Relating to provisions made for education and recreation.

1. How is a school financed?

2. Should a man without children pay school taxes?

3. How is a school governed and regulated?

4. What are the benefits of an education?

5. Why are adult education courses offered?

6. Is there a community center in our town?

7. Is the system of parks adequate?

G. Concerning community dependents.

1. What forces cause slum areas?

2. What provisions are made for the blind, deaf, crippled, feeble-minded, orphaned, and those unable to work?

3. Do the social security laws provide a permanent remedy for unemployment?

4. Can any of these dependents be educated to care for themselves?

H. Concerning the safeguarding of industrial life.

1. How do banks and credit aid a community?

2. What is industrial insurance?

LOCAL OFFICERS BECOME TEACHERS

SIXTH GRADERS EVALUATE CITY'S FIRE PROTECTION

3. What is the purpose of labor organizations?
4. How do they benefit employee and employer?
5. What is the W.P.A.?
6. What is the N.L.R.B.?
I. Concerning the safeguarding of the community against traffic accidents.
   1. How can bicycle riders help prevent accidents?
   2. What rules should pedestrians follow?
   3. What are the driving regulations?
   4. What steps have been taken to make Evanston safe?
J. Relating to the cultural side of the community.
   1. What provisions are made to keep the standard of the city theater high?
   2. Is there an adequate library? Is it used?
   3. Does the community center sponsor concerts or art exhibits?
K. Relating to the religious life of the community.
   1. How many churches are there?
   2. Are they attended?
L. Concerning communities of tomorrow.
   1. Why is so little building being carried on?
   2. Are all the needs for homes being filled today?
   3. What will the homes of the future be like?

III. **Answering questions and solving problems.**
  A. Through factual reading.
    1. Reading reference material in order to answer questions.
    2. Studying maps of modern cities.
    3. Reading pamphlets on the subject.
    4. Studying actual blue prints of homes under construction.

References for Pupils

Books

Blough, G. L. and Mc Clure, C. H.	Fundamentals in Citizenship	1939	Laidlaw
Campbell, E. F.	Our City Chicago	1930	Scribner
Carpenter, Frances	Ourselves and Our City	1928	American Book
Farquhar, F. F. and others	World Book Encyclopedia	1940	Quarrie
Floherty, John J.	Make Way for the Mail	1939	Lippincott
Glaser, Samuel	Designs for 60 Small Houses from $2,000–$10,000.	1939	Coward McCann
Holway, H.	The Story of the Water Supply	1939	Harper
Johnson, William	Chicago	1933	Newson
Kreml, F. M.	Public Safety	1937	Bobbs-Merrill
Rogers, Reynolds	Famous American Trains	1934	Grosset and Dunlap
Rugg and Krueger	Communites of Men	1936	Ginn
Shultz, Hazel	Making Homes	1931	Appleton
Wilson, Wilson and Erb	Richer Ways of Living	1938	American Book

Pamphlets

Safe Bicycle Riding	Division of Highways, State of Illinois.
Safe Driving Practice	Division of Highways, State of Illinois.
Safety 'Round the World	American Automobile Association, Safety and Traffic Department, Washington, D. C.
Traffic Safety Rules for Boys and Girls	Division of Highways, State of Illinois.

Magazines

Album of Engines	Model Builders	February, 1940.
Better Homes	Scholastic (Junior)	October 30, 1939.
City Life	Scholastic (Junior)	November 13, 1939.
Frank Lloyd Wright	Architectural Forum	January, 1938.
Homes in the Future	Scholastic (Junior)	October 23, 1939.
New Uses for Glass	Scholastic (Junior)	November 22, 1939.
Warp and Woof	Scholastic (Junior)	December 4, 1939.
Where Accidents Don't Happen	American Magazine	April, 1935.

References for Teacher

Kimball, Fiske	American Architecture	1929	Bobbs-Merrill
Perry, C. A.	Housing for the Machine Age	1939	Russell Sage Foundation

  B. Through constructive activities and experiences.
    1. Making maps of an ideal community.
    2. Building a city to scale.

NEIGHBORHOOD AIRPORT IS APPROVED

3. Laying out plots and acting as real-estate agents.
˙. Interviewing contractors.
. Visiting homes under partial construction.
6. Seeing a motion picture of the building, step by step, of a moderate priced home.
7. Viewing a motion picture about new plastics being created by Dupont for household use.
8. Visit to City Hall and Fire Department.
9. Sponsoring an assembly upon "Safety" with an officer from the local traffic department.
C. Through language.
1. Outlining done by the group.
2. Taking notes upon reference materials read.
3. Giving reports upon findings.
4. Discussion of completed work.
D. Through the use of science and arithmetic.
1. Wiring of each home in the model community for electric lighting.
2. Scale construction of buildings, streets, trees, and street signs.
3. Drawing to scale maps of the planned community.

4. Figuring yearly and weekly wage of laborers.
5. Figuring percentage of loan granted by the government.
6. Estimating percentage of income a man should invest in a home.
7. Estimating income of the contractor.
8. Problems relating to mortgages.
9. Problems relating to rent.
10. Computation of taxes.
11. Computing cost of property insurance.

IV. **Social meanings, attitudes, appreciations developing through these experiences.**
   A. An appreciation of the beauty of our own community, and the effort required to make it so.
   B. Knowledge of zoning and zoning laws.
   C. An appreciation of the need to plan carefully both home and community for efficient and happy *future* living.
   D. A knowledge of various architectural designs in homes and public buildings.
   E. An appreciation of carefully planned highways and their part in the safety of the community.
   F. An attitude of appreciation toward the value of owning a home.
   G. An understanding of the financing of a small home on a modest salary.
   H. An appreciation of the amount of labor, and its cost, needed in home building.
   I. A better understanding of the role of the government in maintaining a city.
   J. An understanding of the paternalism of the Federal Government in granting loans to small home owners.
   K. The Federal Government's role in providing Social Security.
   L. An understanding of the work of the government in aiding community projects.
   M. An understanding of the need of law enforcement in regard to traffic regulation.

V. **New interests foreshadowing further studies.**
   A. Interest in the origin of our Federal Government.
   B. Interest in chemistry which produces so many materials used in housing to-day.

How Architecture Has Developed

A Study in Sixth Grade

I. **Enriching experiences which aroused and fostered interest and provided background for activities.**
   A. Previous studies.
      1. Early explorers of the New World.
      2. Waterways of the United States and their development.
   B. Excursions.
      1. To the Field Museum to see the building and its Egyptian and Roman exhibits.
      2. To the Art Institute to see decorations used in Egyptian and Greek buildings.
      3. To the Deering Library to see the building itself.
      4. To the First Methodist Church of Evanston to see the stained glass windows.
      5. Around the city to note the use of different types of architecture.
   C. Exhibits.
      1. Pictures of famous buildings brought in by children.
      2. Teacher's collection of prints showing famous buildings, stained glass windows, etc.
      3. University prints of famous buildings.
   D. Reading of stories to children:
      Eloise Lownsbery's "The Boy Knight of Rheims."

II. **Problems and questions which led to research.**
   A. Factors influencing the architecture of any country.
      1. How does the location of a country affect its architecture?
      2. What effect does the climate of a country have upon its architecture?
      3. What, if any, effect does the topography of a land have upon its architecture?
      4. May the soil of a country affect its architecture in any way?
      5. How does a country's natural resources affect its architecture?
      6. How might the architecture of a thinly populated country differ from that of a densely populated one?
      7. How might the history of a country affect its architecture?
      8. How might a people's religious ideas affect its architecture?

244

B. Problems considered in connection with each type of architecture studied.
   1. Reasons for particular architecture.
      a. Geography of the country.
         (1) Location.
         (2) Surface and drainage.
         (3) Climate.
         (4) Type of vegetation.
         (5) Population and people.
         (6) Natural resources.
      b. Brief history of the nation.
         (1) Type of government.
         (2) Important events.
         (3) Important people and leaders.
      c. Customs of the people.
      d. Religious ideas of the people.
   2. The architecture.
      a. Characteristics.
      b. Materials used.
      c. Details and decorations.
      d. Symbols.
   3. Famous buildings of this period.
      a. Where built.
      b. Why built.
      c. By whom and when.
      d. Why famous.
   4. Modern adaptations of this type of architecture.
C. Types of architecture studied.
   1. Buildings of primitive people.
   2. Architecture of Egypt (5,000 B.C. to 115 B.C.).
   3. Architecture of Asia: Mesopotamia, Persia, the Orient.
   4. Greek architecture (460 B.C. to 100 B.C.).
   5. Roman architecture (146 A.D. to 365 A.D.).
   6. Early Christian and Basilican architecture.
   7. Byzantine architecture (fourth century A.D. to present time).
   8. Romanesque architecture (fifth to thirteenth century).
   9. Norman architecture.
   10. Gothic architecture (1200 A.D. to 1500 A.D.).
      a. On the continent.
      b. English Gothic.
      c. In Southern Europe.
   11. Architecture of the Renaissance (fifteenth to eighteenth century).

JEAN IS MADE KNIGHT OF THE CATHEDRAL

12. Architecture of the United States (Colonial Period to about 1900).
13. Modern architecture.
14. Architecture of the future.

III. **Solution of problems.**
 A. Through factual reading.
  1. Types of silent reading.
   a. Reading to find answers to problems (individually and in large and small groups).
   b. Reading for information along lines of interest stimulated by the study.
   c. Reading charts, maps, graphs, and globes for information.
    (1) Consulting maps and globes for locations.

(2) Consulting maps on distribution of natural resources, rainfall, ocean currents, ice sheets, population, etc.

(3) Comparing physical maps and uses of each.

(4) Consulting maps for trade routes.

(5) Consulting charts and graphs for pertinent information.

d. Reading plan or guide sheet for study.

e. Reading tests given.

2. Types of oral reading.

a. Reading orally to report information or to prove a point.

b. Reading orally to share information.

References

Atwood, Thomas and Ross, Helen	Nations Beyond the Sea	1930	Ginn
Baker, C. B. and E. D.	Our World and Others	1938	Bobbs-Merrill
Beard, C. A., and Bagley, W. C.	Elementary World History	1932	Macmillan
Beeby, Daniel J.	America's Roots in the Past	1927	Merrill
Brown, Katherine S.	The Young Architects	1929	Harper
Burnham, Smith	Our Beginnings in Europe and America	1930	Winston
Butterfield, Emily H.	The Young People's Story of Architecture.	1933	Dodd, Mead
Farquhar, F. F., editor	World Book Encyclopedia	1936	Quarrie
Ford, A. S., and others	Compton's Pictured Encyclopedia	1938	Compton
Hall, Jennie	Buried Cities	1929	Macmillan
Halliburton, R.	Book of Marvels	1937	Bobbs-Merrill
Halliburton, R.	Second Book of Marvels	1938	Bobbs-Merrill
Hartman, Gertrude	The World We Live In	1935	Macmillan
Hillyer, V. M., and Huey, E. G.	Child's History of Art	1933	Appleton Century
King-Hall, Stephen	A Child's Story of Civilization	1933	Morrow
Knowlton, D. C., and Wheeler, M. A.	Our Past in Western Europe	1933	American Book
Lamprey, L.	All the Ways of Building	1933	Macmillan
Linnell, Gertrude	Behind the Battlements	1936	Macmillan
Naumburg, Elsa H., and others	Skyscraper	1934	John Day
Parker, Cornelia S.	Watching Europe Grow	1930	Liveright
Power, Eileen and Rhoda	Cities and Their Stories	1927	Houghton Mifflin
Smith, J. Russell	Foreign Lands and People	1933	Winston
Verpilleau, E. A.	The Picture Book of Houses	1931	Macmillan
Vollintine, Grace	The American People and Their Old World Ancestors	1930	Ginn
Wells, Margaret E.	How the Present Came from the Past	1932	Macmillan
Whall, C. W.	Stained Glass Work	1931	Pitman Sons
Woodburn, J. A., and Moran, T. F.	Introduction to American History	1930	Longmans

B. Through language.
   1. Discussing problems planned for the purpose of clarifying understanding to those having difficulty.
   2. Making plans for procedure.
   3. Setting up standards to be attained.
   4. Checking on finished work to see if standards were attained.
   5. Evaluating worth of own work with suggestions for bettering the next job.
   6. Discussing skills needing added practice and making provision for this practice, such as:
      a. Outlining.
      b. Note taking.
      c. Punctuation.
      d. Good sentence structure.
      e. Paragraphing.
      f. Writing.
      g. Spelling of important words.
      h. Skills in reading.
      i. Phases of arithmetic.
   7. Learning to spell words commonly needed by the group and by the individual.
C. Through written composition.
   1. Taking notes on information read.
   2. Outlining information for notebooks.
   3. Writing individual and committee reports.
D. Through collecting materials.
   1. Collecting pictures to clarify ideas for notebooks.
   2. Collecting clippings on architecture for notebooks.
   3. Collecting materials for bulletin board.
E. Through constructive activities.
   1. Making maps.
      a. Labeling diagrams of world climatic zones.
      b. Coloring maps to show location of different peoples and countries for notebooks on committee reports.
      c. Making freehand maps to show locations.
      d. Showing on maps the routes for interchange of building materials.
   2. Making title pages for different sections of notebooks.
   3. Making charts and diagrams to clarify points on reports such as blueprints of building plans.
   4. Making models.
      a. Making models in soap of Grecian columns and the Roman coliseum.

        b. Making a cross section of a pyramid in beaver board.
    5. Making properties for a play on the story "The Boy Knight of Rheims."
        a. Making furniture for Master Anton's shop.
        b. Making clay models of objects in the shop.
        c. Making a clay model of Jean's and Marcel's statue.
    6. Making costumes for the play.
        a. Cutting costumes.
        b. Sewing costumes.
        c. Dyeing cloth.
    7. Making posters to advertise the play.
  F. Through the use of arithmetic.
    1. Figuring cost of the play.
    2. Selling tickets for the play.
    3. Keeping accounts.
    4. Settling accounts.

IV. Social meanings, attitudes, and appreciations developing through these experiences.

  A. An understanding of the influence of geographic factors upon the lives of people.

  B. A knowledge of the ways in which people through the ages have met such problems as providing themselves with shelter.

  C. A knowledge of the cultural products which nations of the past have left for later people to enjoy.

  D. An understanding of some of the physical, social and political factors of the world which have influenced the lives of people.

  E. A growing understanding of the interdependence of one section of the world upon another.

  F. An appreciation for the architecture of our modern world and for the work of all those people of the past who have contributed to it.

V. Interpretation and expression of attitudes and appreciations.

  A. Through literature.

    1. All reading together.

        a. "The Boy Knight of Rheims," by Lownsbery.

        b. "Wonder Tales of Architecture," by Lamprey.

        c. "In the Days of the Guild," by Lamprey.

    2. Individual reading of short stories and poems.

  B. Through creative composition.

    1. Writing short stories on architecture.

2. Writing a complete play from the story, "The Boy Knight of Rheims."
C. Through picture making, design, and decoration.
  1. Designing title pages for notebooks.
  2. Making pen and ink illustrations for notebooks.
  3. Making large pencil sketches of famous buildings.
  4. Making street scene in chalk on muslin for back drop in the play.
  5. Making tapestry of chalk on muslin to use in castle scene of play.
  6. Shading strips of cloth to represent pillars in cathedral scene of the play.
  7. Designing costumes.
  8. Painting designs on costumes.
  9. Making sketches of stage settings for the play.
 10. Designing posters to advertise the play.
D. Through clay modeling. Modeling properties to be used in the play.
E. Through music, selected for use in dramatizing "The Boy Knight of Rheims."
  1. "Miserere"—Palestrina. An old Latin chant, McConothy, Beattie, and Morgan, *Music of Many Lands and Peoples,* Silver, Burdett and Company.
  2. "Crusaders' Hymn"—12th Century, Anonymous, Davison, Surette, and Zanzig, *Concord Junior Song and Chorus Book,* E. C. Schirmer Music Company.
  3. "Duke of Marlborough"—Old folk tune, Thomasine McGehee, *My Musical Measure,* Allyn and Bacon.
  4. "Robin M'aime"—Adam De La Halle (1285), *My Musical Measure,* Thomasine McGehee.
  5. "Summer is i-cumen in"—13th Century, Anonymous, Davison, Surette and Zanzig, *A Book of Songs,* E. C. Schirmer Music Company.
F. Through dramatic activities.
  1. Dramatizing scenes from books on architecture for Library Day.
  2. Informal dramatizations of scenes from the book "The Boy Knight of Rheims."
  3. Giving the finished play.

Synopsis of the play

Scene I

At the home of Master Jean d'Orbais, a cathedral builder of France, the family gathers for the feast of St. Anne. To this feast also come Master Anton, a goldsmith, and Marcel and his father. Here plans for Marcel and young Jean d'Orbais are discussed. Marcel is to become an apprentice to Master Jean d'Orbais and young Jean is to enter the shop of Master Anton to learn the trade of the goldsmith in accordance with his grandfather's wishes.

Scene II

Jean d'Orbais' family bring him to Master Anton's shop to begin his work as an apprentice there. Jean soon discovers that Master Anton is a hard master as well as a cheat, but that Colin is his friend.

Scene III

Jean continues his work in Master Anton's shop. He loses his friend Colin as he is summoned to war, but he gains a friend, the Countess. Jean and Marcel decide to model in secret as Jean still finds that his greatest hope is to work some day for the cathedral.

Jean confides to his uncle that his real work is modeling. The masters of the guild come to inspect the shop of Master Anton. Jean is requested to take an order to the Countess.

Scene IV

In returning from the chateau of the Countess, Jean and Marcel have an encounter with robbers but are saved by Jean's father.

Scene V

The masters of the goldsmiths' guild come to his home to question Jean about Master Anton's work. As they have discovered Master Anton's deceit Jean asks to be released from his apprenticeship to work for his father as a cathedral builder.

Scene VI

Jean takes his father and mother to see the statue which he and Marcel have been working on. The Countess brings the bishop there, too. Although Marcel has long ago given up work on the statue, he brings some rough friends there who break the statue.

Jean creeps into the cathedral with his grief over the broken statue and falls asleep. A vision of the first Jean d'Orbais, the great cathedral builder, brings a message to young Jean d'Orbais.

Scene VII

At the chapel of the Countess she makes Jean d'Orbais a knight of his beloved cathedral.

What Is Our Heritage from the Middle Ages?

A Study in Sixth Grade

I. **Enriching experiences which aroused and fostered interest and provided background for activities.**
   A. Our annual Book Fair and book assembly to celebrate National Book Week.
   B. Book displays in libraries and stores visited by individuals and groups.
   C. Reports by two children and a teacher who had visited monasteries, cathedrals, and castles in Europe.
   D. Kodak pictures of cathedrals, castles, and monasteries taken by visitors in Europe.
   E. Recalling stories of knights and castles.
   F. A trip to the Treasure Room of Deering Library to see illuminated manuscripts.
   G. A trip to Newberry Library to see old manuscripts and hear a talk on them.
   H. Picture exhibits of knights, castles, famous buildings of Gothic architecture and old manuscripts of the Middle Ages.
   I. Book, "Gabriel and the Hourbook," by E. Stein, read to children.

II. **Problems and questions which led to research.**
   A. Concerning book-making in the Middle Ages.
      1. Who made the manuscripts before books were printed?
       . Where did the monks live?
         How was the monastery built?
       . Why did the monks make books?
       . What materials and methods were used?
       . What was an illuminated book?
         How did the monks do the other work of the monastery?
      8. How did the monks help preserve peace during the Middle Ages?
      9. When and where was the first printing press invented?
      10. Who invented the first printing press?
      11. How did the first press differ from the modern ones?
      12. How did printed books differ from hand written ones?
      13. Who owned and read the hand-made books? The printed ones?

B. Concerning the feudal organization.
  1. What type of social order developed during the Middle
    Ages when there was no ruler strong enough to keep
    order in the land?
  2. How did the great land owners or feudal lords live?
    a. Why were feudal castles necessary?
    b. How were the castles made?
    c. How were they fortified?
    d. How did men become knights?
    e. What were the duties of a knight?
    f. What amusements did people who lived in castles
      have?
    g. How did these people dress and what did they eat?
    h. What interest did these people have in books?
    i. What stories do we have in our library of life in
      castles?
  3. How did the serfs live?
    a. What were their duties?
    b. What methods of farming did they use?
    c. What were the obligations of the lord to the serf?
    d. What did serfs wear and eat?
    e. What contact did the serf have with learning or books?
C. Concerning rural and urban life.
  1. What part did the towns play in the Middle Ages?
  2. What did the people in the towns do to make a living?
  3. Why were most of the towns of the Middle Ages sur-
    rounded by walls?
  4. What was meant in the Middle Ages by a "free city"?
  5. Why did the people of some towns build great cathe-
    drals?
  6. How did the people build these cathedrals?
  7. How did life in country villages in the Middle Ages
    differ from life in the large cities and towns?
  8. What were the guilds?
  9. Have we any organizations today which compare with
    the guilds?
  10. What stories of cathedrals or life in the towns of the
    Middle Ages have we in our library?
D. Concerning art and literature.
  1. What type of art developed at this time?
  2. Who were the great artists of this period?
  3. What kind of literature was written during this period?
  4. What type of architecture developed?
  5. What are the characteristics of Gothic architecture?

6. In what buildings was this type used?
7. What buildings do we have around us of this type?
8. What were the characteristics of the music of this period?
9. How has the art and literature of the Middle Ages contributed to modern life?

III. Finding answers to problems and questions.
    A. Through factual reading.
        1. Independent silent reading by group to discover answers to questions, followed by reports and discussion.
        2. Reading by individuals along lines in which they were particularly interested.
        3. Oral reading to prove points.

References

Barker, E. C.	Old Europe and Our Nation	1932	Row, Peterson
Beard, W. C. and Bagley, M.	Elementary World History	1932	Macmillan
Butterfield, Emily	The Young People's Story of Architecture	1933	Dodd, Mead
Campbell, Edna F. and others	The Old World Past and Present	1937	Scott, Foresman
Farquhar, F. F., and others	World Book Encyclopedia	1936	Quarrie
Ford, G. S., and others	Compton's Pictured Encyclopedia	1938	Compton
Halliburton, R.	Book of Marvels	1937	Bobbs-Merrill
Hartman, Gertrude	The World We Live In and How It Came to Be	1935	Macmillan·
Hillyer, V. M.	Child's History of the World	1931	Century
Hillyer, V. M. and Huey, E. G.	Child's History of Art	1933	Appleton
King, S. Hall	Child's Story of Civilization	1933	Morrow
McQuire, Edna	Glimpses Into the Long Ago	1937	Macmillan

    B. Through oral discussion.
        1. Reports by individuals on such subjects as old manuscripts, developing printing.
        2. Group discussions about pictures and diagrams, such as that of a monastery, found in books.
        3. Reports on famous English castles.
        4. Reports on famous European cathedrals.
        5. Discussion of costumes and customs of the Middle Ages.
        6. Explanations of individual and group diagrams and pictures presented in connection with reports.
    C. Through constructive activities.
        1. Making models of knights in soap.
        2. Drawing maps showing plans for fortification of a castle.

3. Drawing plan of a village in medieval times.
4. Drawing plan of a monastery of the medieval times.
5. Drawing plans for stage settings to be used in dramatization of "Gabriel and the Hourbook."
6. Making such furniture as a table, a monk's writing table, for play based on "Gabriel and the Hourbook."
7. Making such properties as swords, shields, window frame, and candle holders for the same play.
8. Making costumes for the play.
9. Constructing an hourbook, to be used in the play.
D. Through use of arithmetic.
1. Placing "time" of the Middle Ages.
2. Learning coins used during this period.
3. Finding number of books printed in comparison to handwork done before.
4. Comparing the cost of handmade books and those made by machine.
. Measuring involved in making properties for play.
6. Measuring stage before making scenery for play.
7. Study of proportion in setting and background for play.
8. Measuring involved in making costumes.

IV. **Social meanings, attitudes, appreciations, developing through these experiences.**
A. An understanding and appreciation of the ways of living during the Middle Ages.
B. An appreciation of the customs of chivalry.
C. Knowledge and appreciation of the work which the monks did in preserving classic learning for the world.
D. An appreciation of handmade books and paper.
E. An appreciation of old books.
F. A recognition of the significance of the printing press.
G. A recognition of the importance of modern inventions in connection with printing.
H. Appreciation of the religious painting during this period.
I. Appreciation of work of such artists as Michelangelo, Giotto, and others.
J. Appreciation of the beauty of Gothic architecture.
K. Knowledge and appreciation of the Middle Age period and its contributions to present-day Europe and America.

V. **Interpretation and expression of attitudes and appreciations.**
A. Through silent and oral reading of selected stories and poems.

Alden, R. M.	Knights of the Silver Shield	1906 Bobbs-Merrill
Baker, C. B., and E. D.	Our World and Others	1938 Bobbs-Merrill
Hawthorne, Daniel	The Gauntlet of Dunmore	1937 Macmillan
Lamb, Harold	Crusades	1930 Garden City
Lamprey, L.	In the Days of the Guild	1918 Stokes
Lownsbery, Eloise	Lighting the Torch	1934 Longmans, Green
Lownsbery, Eloise	The Boy Knight of Rheims	1927 Houghton Mifflin
Parker, Beryl and McKee, Paul	Highways and Byways	1938 Houghton Mifflin
Pyle, H.	Men of Iron	1904 Harper
Pyle, H.	Story of King Arthur and His Knights	1903 Scribner
Pyle, H.	Otto of the Silver Hand	1904 Scribner
Stein, E.	Gabriel and the Hour Book	1906 Page
Tappan, E. M.	When Knights Were Bold	1911 Houghton Mifflin

B. Through creative composition.
1. Writing stories on different phases of the work.
2. Writing a diary such as a knight might have written.
3. Writing an imaginary diary of a serf.
4. Writing a letter from son or daughter of a lord to a friend.
5. Creating a play based on story, "Gabriel and the Hour-book."
6. Writing invitations to play.
7. Composing programs to be mimeographed.
8. Composing presentation talk in language of the Middle Ages to use in giving their hourbook to the director of school.

C. Through picture-making, design, decoration.
1. Illustrating material and stories read.
2. Creating designs for shields.
3. Creating designs for costumes.
4. Drawing costumes of knight, squire, page, lady, and other characters of the Middle Ages.
5. Illuminating pages for the hourbook, to be used in the play.
6. Designing a tapestry for a castle scene in the play.
7. Designing a stained glass window for monastery chapel scene of the play.
8. Drawing of feudal castles on a large scale.

D. Through music.
Seeing exhibits of old instruments and old manuscripts provided background and led to the discussion of music notation and the story of the Neumes; and, listening to stories

about the bards, minstrels and minnesingers provided a growing interest and led to the story of Wagner's opera.

1. Listening to selections from "Die Meistersinger"—Wagner.
   Listening to piano arrangements of old country dances.
2. Learning old songs and rounds; such as:
   "Song of the Watch"—English.
   "Sumer is Acumen in"—13th Century.
3. Singing old ballads; such as:
   "Oh, no John!"
   "Strawberry Fair!"
4. Learning old country dances; such as found in:
   "Guild of Play"—Kimmins.
   "Country Dance Book"—Cecil Sharpe.

Source Books and Reference Material

Davison, A. T., and Surette, T. W.	Concord Series, No. 4	1922 E. C. Schirmer
Davison, A. T., and Surette, T. W.	Concord Series, No. 8	1922 E. C. Schirmer
Grove, Sir George	Dictionary of Music and Musicians	1927 Macmillan
Ordway, E. B.	The Opera Book	1917 George Sully
Pratt, W. S.	History of Music	1935 G. Schirmer
Sharpe, Cecil	Country Dance Tunes, Set VIII	Novello
Sharpe, Cecil	Country Dance Book, Part II	Novello

E. Through dramatic activity.

1. Dramatizing scenes from different phases of life in the Middle Ages—castle life, life of monks, and life of a peasant.
2. Giving original play based on the story "Gabriel and the Hourbook." Songs and ballads were used in the play.
3. Giving play for fathers and mothers, and for children of other grades.

VI. New interests foreshadowing further studies.

Interest in modern European countries and recent contributions in the fields of art, literature, music, science, and industry.

Sixth Grade Compositions About Feudal Days

Diary of a Young Serf

Monday, January 16, 1400.

I want to be a knight. I would like to be like Sir John, who saved Lady De Vere's dog, "Fefe." I am ten years old, but I wish I were older. I have been doing very hard work. I get up at four in the morning and go to bed at eleven at night.

The Lord's sister, Lady De Vere, has been keeping me very busy, but now she is asleep and I can write in my diary, which I am very glad to do.

Lady De Vere is an invalid; so I have been doing endless errands to-day and I am glad to get a rest.

This morning I went riding with the lord, which is a great honor.

Tuesday, January 17, 1400.

To-day I groomed the lord's horse and saddled and bridled him. Then the lord went riding.

After that I had to help put down the draw bridge and then pull it up again as some strange people were coming. Everybody was frightened, lest there be war. But Sir Galad made them go away.

Now Lady De Vere is calling me, so I must go.

Letter from a Castle

The following letter is the kind supposed to have been written during the Middle Ages, and is from the daughter of one of the feudal lords to a friend in another castle.

Dear Priscilla:

You have asked me to describe my home, for you have told me about yours.

The castle I live in is square, with a tower at each corner. The wall around the court is twelve feet thick. Of course we have a wall and moat around our castle. My Honorable Father, who is the Lord, just put up a new drawbridge, for he is thinking he will have to fight.

I am glad it is summer now, for it is cool in the castle. In the winter, it is cold, damp and dreary. We plan to have a big feast in the Friendly Room and invite all the serfs if we win this war. We shall build a grand bonfire in the fireplace, so the castle will be warmer.

One of the serfs has a little girl my size that I would like ever so much to play with, and I've heard the watchman in the tower is very jolly. I should like to visit him. I do wish I had someone to play with. It will be even more lonely during the war, for I will not be allowed out of the castle gates.

I hope your life is as nice as mine and better.

Sincerely yours, .
Genevieve

Diary of a Knight During Days of Feudalism

Tuesday, July 11, 1250.

The town is all excited. From the castle the clear blast of the bugle was blowing. The knights soon made ready for war. At dawn we charged the enemy and won our way into town. We tried to get into the castle. Finally another knight and I thought of a way to do it. We divided ourselves into groups and surrounded the castle. Then we took boarding ladders and put them over the moat. We chose the bravest knight to cross the moat first, and then one by one we crossed. We finally took the castle and marched home, arriving at sunset. There was much rejoicing and a great banquet. There was music and dancing, and great fires in the fireplaces.

What Has Modern Europe Contributed
to the United States?

A Study in Sixth Grade

I. **Enriching experiences which aroused and fostered interest and provided background.**
  A. Reports with slides.
     1. Given by one child who had visited Europe.
     2. Given by adults who had visited European countries.
  B. Exhibits.
     1. Pictures and clippings showing changes in transatlantic travel.
     2. Newspaper articles and pictures showing relations between the United States and European countries.
     3. Articles made in European countries.
     4. Pictures of people of European countries.
     5. Pictures and folders showing well-known pleasure resorts of Europe.
     6. Pictures showing sports in different countries.
  C. Slides and motion pictures of Europe as a whole and different sections.
  D. Display of books containing stories and poems from Europe.
  E. Excursions.
     1. To the Evanston Public Library to see models showing life in different countries.
     2. To Art Institute to see European contributions in art, sculpture, and architecture.
  F. Radio reports concerning events in Europe.

II. **Problems and questions which led to research. (The class was divided into committees, each committee preparing a report on a particular country.)**
  A. Topography, climate and location.
     1. What effect does the topography of the land have upon the occupations carried on in each country?
     2. What effect does the climate have upon the occupations and products?
     3. What advantages or disadvantages does the location of each country have upon its development?
  B. Government and people.
     1. What assistance or hindrance has the government of the country been to its development and contribution?

EACH CONTRIBUTES TO WORLD'S FAIR

2. Who are some of the outstanding people in this country today? Why are they famous?

3. What are some of the interesting customs of the people?

C. Industries.

1. What industries are carried on in each country?

2. How is the country especially suited to these?

3. What cities have gained importance from these industries?

4. What products are exported to other countries?

D. Contributions.

1. What distinctive contribution has each country made in folk or modern literature?

2. In art and sculpture?

3. In architecture?

4. In science and invention?

5. In ideas of government?

6. In music?

7. To travelers visiting the country?

8. What are the leading recreational centers?

E. Immigration to the United States.
1. What proportion of our people have come from Europe?
2. From what countries have most of our immigrants come?
3. What contributions have these people made in coming to our country?
4. What are some of the problems their coming has raised?

III. Answering questions and solving problems.
A. Through factual reading.
1. Reading reference material needed to answer questions brought up in class discussions.
2. Studying railroad and steamship folders describing European countries.
3. Map study locating European countries and cities.
4. Map study locating main commercial routes between the United States and Europe.
5. Map study tracing some of the air flights across the Atlantic.
6. Oral reading to answer questions and prove points.

References

Aitchison, A. E.	Europe the Great Trader	1939	Bobbs-Merrill
Atwood, W. and Thomas, H. G.	Nations Beyond the Seas	1938	Ginn
Atwood, W. and Thomas, H. G.	Home Life in Far Away Lands	1933	Ginn
Baker, C. B., and E. D.	Our World and Others	1938	Bobbs-Merrill
Barrows, C. A., and Parker, E. P.	Europe and Asia	1936	Silver, Burdett
Beard, C. A., and Bagley, W. C.	Elementary World History	1932	Macmillan
Bryant, L. M.	Children's Book of Celebrated Buildings	1924	Century
Farquhar, F. F. (Editor)	World Book Encyclopedia	1940	Quarrie
Ford, G. S. (Editor)	Compton's Pictured Encyclopedia	1940	Compton
Halliburton, Richard	Book of Marvels	1937	Bobbs-Merrill
Hillyer, V. M.	A Child's Geography of the World	1929	Century
Hillyer, V. M.	A Child's History of the World	1931	Century
King-Hall, S. M.	A Child's Story of Civilization	1933	Morrow
Leeming, J.	Ships and Cargoes	1926	Doubleday
Lester, K. M.	Great Pictures and Their Stories	1927	Mentzer
Powers, E. and R.	Boys and Girls of History	1936	Macmillan
Powers, E. and R.	More Boys and Girls of History	1936	Macmillan

Smith, J. R.	Human Use Geography	1939 Winston
Vollintine, G.	The American People and	1930 Ginn
	. Their Old World	
	Ancestors	

B. Through discussion.
   1. Study of problems and questions: those relating to separate countries were made by individual children or committees and reports given to the class.
   2. Discussion of picture exhibits.
   3. Discussion of completed work.
   4. Voluntary contributions of material read in magazines and books.
C. Through constructive activities.
   1. Making maps.
      a. Showing commercial routes between the United States and Europe.
      b. Showing recreational centers of Europe.
      c. Showing air flights across the Atlantic.
      d. Showing where artists have lived, inventions have been made, famous buildings are located.
   2. Making graphs.
      a. Showing percentage of various European nationalities in the United States.
      b. Showing exports and imports of different countries.
   3. Making posters.
      a. Advertising recreational centers to the traveler.
      b. Showing customs, costumes and life of people of various countries.
      c. Showing contributions different countries make to others.
   4. Collecting pictures and newspaper stories for notebooks.
   5. Making models.
      a. Showing types of architecture in soap.
      b. Making models of typical scenes from different countries.
D. Through use of arithmetic.
   1. Measuring in making maps.
   2. Measuring in making posters.
   3. Comparing time required to cross Atlantic now with that of years ago.
   4. Computing cost of passage to Europe.
   5. Computing cost of sending cables to Europe.
   6. Making graph showing percentage of various European nationalities in the United States.

7. Making graphs showing leading exports of various countries.

IV. Social meanings, attitudes and appreciations probably developed through these experiences.

A. A certain understanding of the problems of other races and other nationalities.

B. An appreciation of the interdependence of people and nations.

C. An appreciation of the courage displayed by immigrants coming to this country.

D. An understanding of the many adjustments people have to make when living in a foreign country.

E. An understanding of the present-day transatlantic transportation.

F. An appreciation of the daring and courage displayed by aviators crossing the Atlantic.

G. An appreciation of the work of such people as Madame Curie, Pasteur, Marconi, and others.

H. An appreciation of the value in being able to speak French and other languages.

I. An appreciation of the representative music of European countries.

J. Some appreciation of European art, architecture and literature.

V. Interpretation and expression of attitudes and appreciations.

A. Through literature.

1. Folk stories of various countries read or told by members of the class.

2. Stories of some outstanding people as Pasteur, Madame Curie, and others, read or told to the class.

3. Sharing of some modern books about European countries.

4. Enjoyment of some stories about immigrants.

Folk Tales from Europe

Casserley, Anne	Michael of Ireland	1927	Harper
Casserley, Anne	Whins of Knockattan	1928	Harper
Fleming, R. M.	Round the World in Folk Tales	1925	Harcourt
Gask, Lilian	Folk Tales from Many Lands	1929	Crowell
Grimm Brothers	Grimm Fairy Tales	1917	Harper
Mac Donnell, Anne	The Italian Fairy Book	1914	Stokes
Steel, F. A.	English Fairy Tales	1918	Macmillan

Modern Stories of Europe

Aanrud, Hans	Sidsel Longskirt	1935	Winston
Beuret, G.	When I Was a Girl in France	1925	Lothrop
Brann, Esther	Nicolina	1931	Macmillan
Burglon, Nora	Children of the Soil	1933	Doubleday
Byrne, Bess	With Mikko through Finland	1932	McBride
Hertzman, A. M.	When I Was a Girl in Sweden	1926	Lothrop
Quiller-Couch, A.	Roll Call of Honor	1926	Nelson
Seredy, Kate	The Good Master	1935	Viking
Spyri, J.	Heidi	1924	Winston

Books About Immigrants

Antin, Mary	Promised Land	1917	Houghton
Beard, A. E.	Our Foreign-Born Citizens	1922	Crowell
Bercovici, Konrad	Around the World in New York	1924	Century
Bok, E. W.	A Dutch Boy Fifty Years Afterward	1921	Scribner

B. Through creative composition.

1. Writing stories about any contribution any country had made.

2. Writing stories urging friends to see certain places in certain countries.

3. Writing stories of what children found especially interesting in any country.

C. Through picture making and design.

1. Drawing pictures showing costumes and customs of different countries.

2. Making illustrations representing the various recreational centers of Europe.

3. Drawing illustrations on topics of notebooks.

4. Drawing airships and ocean liners to show means of intercourse.

D. Through music.

A little knowledge of the nationality of some of the great composers and their compositions, together with the folk music of European countries, already known to the children, provided a background and a live interest. Singing and hearing folk music gave a source for the discussion and analysis of social and temperamental characteristics of several nations. The similarity of many folk tunes of several nations led to the study of exchange through bards, minstrels and the like.

1. Singing.
    a. Folk songs in unison and in parts such as:

    > German,—Winter Goodbye
    > Bohemian,—Annie, the Miller's Daughter
    > Russian,—The Peddlar—Gloria
    > Italian,—Funiculi, Funicula—Santa Lucia
    > Swedish,—The Locust Tree—Country Dance
    > British,—Londonderry Air—Loch Lomond—Dear Harp
    > —Keel Row

    b. Composed songs:

    > Die Lorelei—Silcher
    > The Smith—Brahms
    > Chorales—Bach
    > The Golden Day Is Dying—Palgren

2. Instrumental music (heard by means of records):
    a. Small forms of the Masters—minuets, sarabands, gigues, bourrées,—

    > Bach, Rameau, Purcell, Scarlatti, Handel and others.

    b. Excerpts from operas:

    > Siegfried—Motives and story from Angela Diller's Book.
    > Nibelung Ring—Motives and story from Berstein.
    > Sigfrido—Wagner—Piano Score—G. Ricordi.
    > Magic Flute—Mozart.

Source and Reference Books

Bernstein, A. M.	The Do-Re-Mi of the Nibelung Ring	1928	Greenberg
Botsford, F.	Folk Songs of Many Peoples	1922	Womans Press
Botsford, F.	Folk Songs of Many Peoples—2	1922	Womans Press
Davison-Surette	One Hundred Forty Folk Songs	1922	Schirmer
Davison-Surette	A Book of Songs	1922	Schirmer
Davison-Surette	Concord Junior Song and Chorus Book	1927	Schirmer
Diller, Angela	Wagner's Siegfried	1931	Schirmer
Grove, Sir George	Dictionary of Music and Musicians	1927	Macmillan
Hamilton, C.	Outlines of Music History	1913	Ditson
Jacques—Dalcroze,	Art and Education	1930	Barnes
Pratt, W. S.	A History of Music	1935	Schirmer
Radcliffe—Whitehead	Folk Songs for Children	1903	Ditson
Scholes, P.	Complete Book of the Great Musicians	1923	Oxford
Surette, T. W.	Music and Life	1917	Houghton Mifflin
Welch, R. D.	Appreciation of Music	1927	Harper

E. Through social activity.

Assemblies were held in which the various committees shared exhibits, reports, literature and music with other committees or other grades.

VI. New interests foreshadowing further studies.

After this survey of European countries the interest spread to other continents. Questions such as the following were raised:

1. What do we get from South Africa?
2. What does Alaska send to the United States?
3. What do the Hawaiian Islands raise?

Behind the News in China and Japan

A Study in Sixth Grade

I. Experiences which aroused interest and provided background.

    A. The undeclared war between China and Japan, which the children had become acquainted with through:

        1. Newspaper and magazine articles.

        2. Pictures of conditions in China and Japan.

        3. Radio news bulletins and news reports.

        4. Newsreels, March of Time, etc.

    B. Motion pictures based on China, such as *The Good Earth,* which some of the children had seen at motion-picture theaters.

    C. Library collection of pictures showing life in the two countries, placed on bulletin board.

    D. Selected films and slides shown at the school.

II. Problems and questions which led to research.

    A. Relating to conditions in modern times. (Question asked by the children.)

        1. Why did Japan send her troops into China?

        2. Where and how does China obtain money and materials?

        3. Where do Japan and China get their airplanes?

        4. How do the other countries feel about the situation?

        5. What can Americans do to help relief in China?

    B. Relating to China. (Questions for study suggested by the children.)

        1. What are some of the customs of the Chinese people?

        2. What kinds of houses do they live in?

        3. What do the people eat?

        4. What are the main rivers and seas of China?

        5. What are the important cities of China and where are they located?

        6. What kind of schools do the Chinese have?

        7. How do the Chinese make a living?

        8. What kind of weather do they have in China?

        9. What kind of religion do they have?

      10. Is the Chinese government like ours?

      11. What is the Great Wall of China?

      12. How old is China? What is its history?

      13. What inventions originated in China?

      14. Do the Chinese do much manufacturing?

15. How large is China? How many people are there in China?

C. Relating to Japan. (Topics for study and discussion suggested by the children.)

1. History of Japan.
2. The Japanese silk industry.
3. Customs, clothes, houses.
4. Physical conditions.
5. Trade and transportation.
6. Japanese cities.
7. Farming in Japan.
8. Size and population of Japan.
9. Expansion of Japan.
10. Religion in Japan.
11. The fishing industry.
12. The mining industry.
13. Manufacturing.
14. The government of Japan.

III. Answering questions and solving problems.

A. Through factual reading.

1. Individual and group research on topics chosen from those above, using the following references:

Atwood & Thomas	Nations beyond the Seas	1938	Ginn
Barrows and Parker	Europe and Asia	1936	Silver, Burdett
Beard and Bagley	Elementary World History	1932	Macmillan
Carpenter, Frances	Our Neighbors Near and Far	1933	American Book
Farquhar, F. F., and others	The World Book Encyclopedia	1936	Quarrie
Ford, A. S., and others	Compton's Pictured Encyclopedia	1938	Compton
Franck, H. A.	China	1935	Owen
Franck, H. A.	The Japanese Empire	1929	Owen
Franck, H. A.	Glimpses of Japan and Formosa	1939	Appleton
Halliburton, R.	Second Book of Marvels	1938	Bobbs-Merrill
Hillyer, V. M.	A Child's Geography of the World	1929	Century
Hillyer, V. M.	A Child's History of the World	1931	Century
Seeger, Elizabeth	The Pageant of Chinese History	1935	Longmans
Smith, J. R.	Foreign Lands and Peoples	1933	Winston
Stull and Hatch	Our World Today	1931	Allyn and Bacon
Whittemore, K. T.	Asia the Great Continent	1937	Bobbs-Merrill

2. Study of the globe—proximity of China and Japan to the United States.

NOTES ARE TAKEN ON RADIO·TRAVEL TALKS

    3. Map study, including scale of miles, key, latitude and longitude, physical and political features.

B. Through language.
    1. Writing stories about the maps and what they tell.
    2. Writing reports on the individual and group topics.
    3. Conducting group discussions with all children participating.
    4. Making oral reports on research topics.
    5. Making oral reports on news broadcasts, newspaper and magazine articles, etc.

C. Through constructive activities.
    1. Coloring and filling in outline maps of China and Japan.
    2. Drawing freehand maps of China.
    3. Making individual maps with original ideas, including such things as pictures of cities and areas.
    4. Making and keeping scrapbooks of newspaper articles, pictures, maps and stories of China and Japan.
    5. Drawing small maps of Japan, then enlarging them to scale by the method of squares.

6. Stenciling and mimeographing small outline maps for each child.

D. Through the use of arithmetic.
1. Using rulers to sixteenths in measurement of distances on maps.
2. Using fractions in figuring out enlargements.
3. Estimating the area of China by multiplying length times width, then correcting for deviations from a true rectangle.
4. Looking up the area of China in books and comparing it with the estimate.
5. Figuring out why different books give different areas.
6. Looking up and comparing the population of China, Japan, the United States and other countries.
7. Using long division to figure out density of population.
8. Figuring the age of China and Japan.

IV. Social meanings, attitudes and appreciations developing through these experiences.

A. A sympathetic understanding and appreciation of the problems of other peoples of the world, which have grown out of historical and geographical factors.
B. A growing appreciation of the interdependence of peoples.
C. An increasing ability to draw conclusions from reliable information—to substitute facts for opinion or hearsay.
D. An increasing ability to read newspapers and magazines more carefully and more critically.
E. A growing interest in world affairs, as evidenced by more listening to news broadcasts, more interest in the front pages of the newspaper, and an eagerness to discuss information gained in this manner.

V. Interpretation and expression of attitudes and appreciations.

A. Through literature.
1. Reading Chinese and Japanese stories and reporting them to the class.
2. Class reading of *He Went With Marco Polo,* by Kent.
3. Listening to a young lady from Korea, who told stories about her country, the children, their costumes, sports, houses, and way of living.
4. Writing stories and making short talks on the more pleasant phases of Japanese and Chinese life.

B. Through picture making and design.
1. Creating designs for borders on maps.

2. Drawing, coloring and painting pictures of Chinese and Japanese scenes to illustrate stories.
3. Designing, cutting and decorating a Chinese wall hanging made of linoleum.
4. Choosing contrasting colors for maps made of colored paper, and arranging the color scheme.

C. Through social activity.
1. Making a trip to Chicago's Chinatown, visiting stores, shops, museums, town hall, and many other interesting places.
2. Eating Chinese food in a Chinese restaurant.
3. Showing and explaining to other children in school some of the souvenirs brought from Chinatown.
4. Holding room assemblies to exchange ideas and information about individual and group activities.

VI. New interests foreshadowing further studies.
A. A desire to study other countries of the world and their relations with each other, especially Russia, Germany, Italy, England and France.
B. A desire on the part of some to continue the study of ancient history which they began in connection with China.
C. A desire to use radio in the classroom wherever possible as a source of information and of interesting material in the field of social studies.

Sharing the Earth with Insects

A Study in Sixth Grade

I. **Enriching experiences which aroused and fostered interest and provided background.**

  A. A Polyphemus moth was found on the playground and brought into the class for study.

  B. A microscope was brought to school by one of the boys.

  C. A new boy entered summer school who had much information to offer and made many contributions.

  D. Many insects were soon brought in for study, including a swallowtail butterfly, monarch butterfly, Cecropia moth, grasshoppers, dragonflies, bees, stag beetles and many others.

  E. Glass cages were brought, so that we might watch and care for the insects.

  F. A collection of mounted butterflies was brought in by a member of the class.

  G. Several walks were taken in the school vicinity and observations made of butterflies, bees and other insects.

II. **Problems and questions which led to experiment and investigation.**

  A. General questions.

    1. What are the different stages in the life of an insect?

    2. What are meant by the terms egg, larva, pupa, chrysalis and cocoon?

    3. What is the best way to catch and care for insects?

    4. What types of insects are helpful to man?

    5. What may be done to protect and foster desirable insects?

  B. Specific questions about the *Monarch Butterfly:*

    1. How is the monarch butterfly distinguished from all others?

    2. Is the flight of the monarch rapid or leisurely?

    3. Are its bright colors an advantage or disadvantage?

    4. Where is the monarch caterpillar found?

    5. What are the colors and markings of the monarch caterpillar?

    6. What does it do when frightened?

    7. How long does it take to mature?

    8. How does it shed its skin?

9. Why is the monarch chrysalis called a "jewel of jade and gold"?
10. Where may the chrysalis be found?
11. How is it attached to the object?
12. How does the chrysalis change in color?
13. After the change to chrysalis how long before the butterfly emerges?
14. Where does the butterfly deposit her eggs?

C. Specific questions about the *Red-legged Grasshopper:*
1. Why is this insect called a grasshopper?
2. Which pair of legs is the longest?
3. Which is the shortest?
4. How does the grasshopper prepare to jump?
5. Why is he so skilful in jumping?
6. How far can he see?
7. How many eyes are there, and where are they situated?
8. How long are the antennae?
9. How does the grasshopper eat?
10. What kind of crops does he destroy?
11. Can the grasshopper fly as well as jump?
12. How many pairs of wings has it?
13. How do they differ in size and use?
14. How does this insect breathe?
15. Where are the ears of the grasshopper located?
16. If the grasshopper is caught, how does it show that it is offended?
17. What becomes of the grasshoppers in winter?
18. Where are the eggs laid?
19. How can you tell a young from a full-grown grasshopper?
20. What enemies does the grasshopper have?
21. Is it useful to the people of any country?

Note: Similar questions were asked about other insects studied.

III. Finding answers to problems and questions.

A. Through constructive activities.
1. Insects were kept in glass cages for study.
2. Some of the specimens were mounted on cards for study.
3. Slides were made according to directions to be used in microscope. Slides were made of different butterfly wings, tibia and claw of grasshopper, leg of bee, and several others.

B. Through use of arithmetic.
   1. Some arithmetic was involved in making the slides according to the directions given.
   2. Enlarged drawings were made, showing insects two or three times their natural size. Drawings were mounted carefully for display.
C. Through language.
   1. Oral reports were given of individual observations.
   2. Class discussions were held concerning facts discovered in observations and in reading.
   3. Written records were kept of each study.
   4. Observations made on walks were kept and recorded by the children.
D. Through factual reading. Books were used to supplement observation.

References

Beard, Dan	American Boy's Book of Bugs, Butterflies & Beetles	1932	Lippincott
Comstock, Anna B.	Handbook of Nature Study	1939	Comstock
Comstock, John H.	An Introduction to Entomology	1936	Comstock
Fabre, J. Henri	Insect Adventures	1927	Dodd, Mead
Farquhar, F. F., and others	World Book Encyclopedia	1936	Quarrie
Ford, A. S., and others	Compton's Pictured Encyclopedia	1938	Compton
Lutz, Frank E.	Fieldbook of Insects	1935	Putnam
Powers, Margaret	The World of Insects	1931	Follett
Weed, Clarence M.	Insect Ways	1930	Appleton

IV. Meanings, attitudes and appreciations probably developed.

A. An attitude of curiosity about insects and their relation to plants and to men.
B. A recognition of the economic value of many insects and their function in nature.
C. An appreciation of the beauty of many insects and the interesting characteristics they display.
D. Understanding and appreciation of the way insects are protected by means of coloring, scent and other gifts.
E. An attitude of respect for the rights of all living things.
F. An eagerness to share experiences and observations.
G. An attitude of respect for those children who had a wide background for the study through previous reading and experience.

V. **Interpretation and expression of attitudes and appreciations.**

A. Through literature.

The children enjoyed reading orally bits from two or three books of special interest:

Bertelli, Luigi   The Prince and His Ants   1910 Holt
Maeterlinck, M.   The Children's Life of   1919 Dodd, Mead
         the Bee

B. Through picture-making.

1. Graphic drawings were made of insects studied.
2. Illustrative blackboard drawings were made by the children.
3. Designs and borders were developed using the monarch and swallowtail butterflies as motifs.

VI. **New interests foreshadowing further studies.**

A keen interest was developed in other phases of nature. Questions were asked about trees, wild flowers and birds, and many children said they were going to continue their reading through the summer. One child who was disappointed because we did not study wild flowers, said she was going to start her study early next spring.

Maintaining an Aquarium

A Continuing Interest in Sixth Grade

I. Enriching experiences.

A. Exhibits.
   1. Those brought by children from home, including fish, tadpoles, snails, turtles.
   2. Those found in the science laboratory of the college.

B. Excursions.
   1. To the canal (not far from the school). The brink was visited and observations made as to the kind of water life which could be found nearby.
   2. To the Fish Hatchery at the Wilmette Harbor.
   3. To the Shedd Aquarium in Chicago.
   4. To the Zoology Laboratory at Northwestern University to observe various aquaria and to make inquiries concerning the making of a balanced aquarium.
   5. To the pet and fish store to buy plants and fish for the school's large aquarium, which had not been in use for a while.

C. Pictures of various types and kinds of fish. (National Geographic, Nature Magazine, and Outdoor America provided many.)

D. Articles posted on the bulletin board, cut from magazines and newspapers.

E. Reports given by various children explaining the preparation of home aquariums.

F. Reading of letters received from various organizations for the care of fish; as, Department of Interior, Washington, D. C.; also the Izaak Walton League. (A list of available films may be had.)

G. Making close observation of the development of animal life in the aquarium after it was set up in the room.

II. Problems and questions.

A. Concerning the aquarium.
   1. Why do people have aquariums?
   2. What is a balanced aquarium? How can we balance our aquarium?
   3. What kind of an aquarium do we wish to set up, tropical, salt water, or an ordinary one?

WATER CREATURES FASCINATE

4. What are the main points to keep in mind in the preparation of an aquarium:—
   a. How much water should be used?
   b. How many fish to a gallon of water?
   c. What creatures can be kept in an aquarium?
   d. How many gallons of water will our aquarium hold?
      How long is it? How wide and how high? How
      many cubic inches in a gallon? How can we measure
      the amount of water?
   e. What kind of plant life do we need and how much?
   f. How should the water be changed and how often?
   g. What is the best location in the room for an aquar-
      ium?
B. Concerning the fish.
   1. What and how and when are fish and other water crea-
      tures fed?
   2. How can sick fish be cared for? What are the symptoms
      of sick fish? What are some of the common diseases of
      fish?
   3. How are fish fitted for living in the water? How do they
      protect themselves?

4. How are baby fish born, and how are they cared for?
5. What are the names and habits of some of the common fish?
6. What kind of water creatures are there, that are not fish?
7. What are some of the queerest fish?
8. How do fish eat, breathe? Can fish hear, feel?
9. What are the names of parts of the fish and the purpose of each part; as, gills, fins, scales?
10. How do snails, tadpoles, differ from fish?
11. Where do various kinds of fish come from? How can fish be brought to a large aquarium (as the Shedd Aquarium in Chicago)?

III. Answering questions and solving problems.

A. Through oral reports and discussions.
1. Discussion of excursions taken to hatcheries, stores and aquariums.
2. Reports and discussions of stories read from books and pamphlets, and films seen both by children and teacher.
3. Discussion of oral and written reports brought in by groups and individual children, on various topics, such as,
   "What kind of plant life do we need?"
   "How many fish can we keep in our aquarium?"
   "How are fish especially fitted for living in the water?"
4. Reports of detailed observations made by individuals, while visiting hatcheries and aquariums, and also while observing life in room aquarium.
5. Discussion of letters received from informational sources; as, State Game and Fish Commissioner, United States Bureau of Fisheries.
6. Appointing committees for care of fish, and other responsibilities.

B. Through informational reading.
1. Reading pamphlets sent by Bureau at Washington, D. C.
2. Reading informational material found in encyclopedias and natural science readers and books.
3. Studying maps to locate the native home of various kinds of fish.
4. Studying diagrams and pictures of anatomy of fish to learn how they are fitted for life in the water.
5. Reading pictures, shown in books, magazines and films, used in explaining fish and plant life.

6. Reading records of experiments performed.
7. Reading directions for the performing of experiments.

Books Used By Children

Burgess, Thornton	The Burgess Sea Shore Book for Children	1929	Little, Brown
Farquhar, F. F., and others	World Book Encyclopedia	1936	Quarrie
Ford, A. S., and others	Compton's Pictured Encyclopedia	1938	Compton
Henderson, D. M.	Children of the Tide	1926	Appleton
Kaempfer, Fred	The Aquarium—Care and Treatment	1930	Kaempfer
Mellen, Ida	The Young Folk's Book of Fishes	1927	Dodd, Mead
Patch, Edith M.	First Lessons in Nature Study	1926	Macmillan
Persing, E. C. & Thiele, C. L.	Elementary Science	1930	Appleton
Smalley, Janet	Do You Know About Fishes?	1936	Morrow
Trafton, Gilbert H.	Nature Study and Science	1930	Macmillan

Books Used By the Teacher

Comstock, Anna B.	Handbook of Nature Study	1939	Comstock
Crowder, William	Dwellers of the Sea and Shore	1923	Macmillan
Curtis, Brian	The Life Story of the Fish	1938	Appleton
Downing, Elliot R.	Our Living World	1928	Longmans, Green
Innes, William T.	Goldfish Varieties and Tropical Aquarium Fishes	1929	Innes

C. Through constructive activities.
   1. Arranging exhibit of pictures collected.
   2. Making diagrams of various kinds and parts of fish, snails, tadpoles.
   3. Making map or diagram of aquarium, placing the castles and plants.
   4. Making of class folder, to keep important pictures, pamphlets for future reference.
   5. Making pictorial map, showing the sources of various fish at the Shedd Aquarium.
D. Through the use of arithmetic.
   1. Measuring size of aquarium, length, width, depth.
   2. Computing cubic inches in the aquarium.
   3. Understanding the terms cubic inches, volume, rectangle.
   4. Computing gallons of water needed for the aquarium.
   5. Estimating the number of fish for amount of water.

6. Estimating the number of plants for number of fish and other creatures.
7. Measuring quarts, gallons.
8. Keeping account of cost of equipping the aquarium.
9. Using thermometer to test temperature of water.
10. Keeping record of time required for propagation of young.

IV. **Social meanings, attitudes, appreciations probably developed through these experiences.**

A. Wholesome attitude and outlook toward reproduction.
B. Appreciation of the conservation of natural resources otherwise exterminated by industry.
C. Understanding of the work done by hatchery to conserve little fish.
D. Some understanding of nature's provision for protection and care of water life.
E. Appreciation of the beauty found in sea life.
F. Gratitude to those who have made such places as the Shedd Aquarium, Field Museum, available for boys and girls.
G. Understanding of the knowledge and skill needed by those who care for fish life.
H. Appreciation of the work of men called scientists, in discovering facts.
I. Appreciation and understanding of the care and accuracy needed in reporting any observation and experiments.
J. Appreciation of the value of close, correct observation of even small details in answering questions accurately.
K. Appreciation of what it means to base opinions on ample reliable data.

V. **Interpretation and expression of attitudes and appreciations.**

A. Through use of literature.
1. Silent and oral reading of some delightful stories from books such as:

Bronson, W. S.	Finger Fins	1930 Macmillan
Butler, Evah	Along the Shore	1930 John Day
Carr, William H.	The Stir of Nature	1930 Oxford Press
Heal, Edith	How the World Began	1930 Thomas Rockwell
Reed, W. M.	The Earth for Sam	1929 Harcourt, Brace

2. Listening to interesting descriptions from magazines: as, National Geographic and Nature Magazine.

B. Through creative composition.
   1. Composing letters to absent class members, telling of balancing the aquarium.
   2. Writing accounts describing the process of balancing the aquarium, excursions taken, and experiments tried.
C. Through picture making, designing and decorating.
   1. Drawing pictures of fish.
   2. Mounting lovely pictures of fish life for individual science books and for the bulletin board.
D. Through social sharing.
   By means of a microphone and amplifier the class broadcasted a program on water life from the science laboratory to the children's assembly.

VI. New interests, foreshadowing other studies.
A. A study of water and what it means to life.
B. A study of various types of plant life in water.
C. A study of the development of plant and animal life upon the earth.

PART III

The Day's Procedure

ARRANGING THE PROGRAM

ALTHOUGH the program provides a time for each type of activity, these various types of activity are not carried on as isolated "subjects," but are usually unified by certain large purposes or goals. Time is allowed for individual creative enterprises and for individual practice in the mastery of certain fundamental skills. Small groups are formed within each room according to individual needs and interests.

The program is flexible and may be altered from month to month or day to day, except that periods devoted to physical needs must remain fairly constant. Both room teachers and special teachers are willing to adjust the schedule to allow time for excursions, sketching trips, cooking enterprises, experiments in science, projection of films and slides, and other enriching experiences.

The school offers a day program for all children enrolled in the second grade and in higher grades. Below second grade, there is a choice of morning session or day session. The day session for younger children is open only to those whose physical and emotional needs and home situation suggest that a day at school is desirable.

The day program for all groups includes a dinner, with careful attention to habits and attitudes in relation to foods. The menu for the younger children is planned by a nutritionist and sent to the parents for each week in advance. Beginning with fourth grade the children learn to choose their own menu under guidance, and a study of foods and food values is included as a part of the program. In the nursery school, kindergarten, and three primary grades, the noon meal is followed by a rest period on cots, with training in relaxation. Sleep and outdoor play constitute the afternoon program for the nursery school and kindergarten children.

A number of special teachers assist in the guidance of children's activities, beginning in the primary grades, but all work in close touch with the room teachers. The teachers of music, art, crafts, and physical education, assist the children and the room teachers of certain grades in carrying on group projects, and they also pro-

vide for creative enterprises and for the development of appreciations and skills in their own fields.

In any school, "progressive" or otherwise, children's interests
beyond the offerings of the curriculum will appear and may provide
some of the most valuable experiences in the child's growth. These
interests or "hobbies" often present an important cue to a child's
character development. Hobbies can, in general, be divided into
four groups, and experience in the Children's School has shown
that children's responses in many experiences are often parallel to
their hobbies.

To desire knowledge and to satisfy a sense of curiosity seem at
least partly responsible for some hobbies that children have pursued
in the Children's School. Extracurricular experiences of this type
usually relate to an unusual interest in books, a desire to know and
identify birds and insects and other natural phenomena, and to
pry and investigate into otherwise unknown fields of the academic
type. Children with such hobbies make extensive use of the library.
Time for free reading in the library must be provided in making
the weekly program.

As the cross section of any community would show, the first
group of hobbies has the smallest number of devotees, and is over-
shadowed by that great group of hobbies of the second type, those
based on the acquisition of things and objects. Illustrations of these
are experiences relating to collecting autographs, pictures or designs
of vehicles, buttons, coins, sometimes butterflies, labels, newspapers,
postmarks, maps, rocks, shells, stamps, streetcar transfers, timetables,
wrappers, and other objects that circulate in various colors, values,
and denominations. All hobbies mentioned and many others have
had outlets in the program of the Children's Schools. Hobby periods
and hobby clubs for children interested in collecting have been
common in the middle grades. Collecting and arranging objects
of insignificant value, has afforded training in organization, and
has sometimes led to collection of more valuable materials later.

The third class of hobbies, those related to the creation or making
of objects, generally involves manual activity. Like the second

Nancy Likes to
Paint

ɔys the
ter

is Lost in
Library

group, experiences in these fields are very popular with children and again provide opportunity for experiences of lasting value. The most common hobbies in this group are building aquaria, block printing, leather work, metal craft, basketry, and other kinds of creative work and constructive activities in the manual arts shops. Some of these kinds of hobbies and interests lend themselves readily to use in group projects or enterprises. Others are pursued individually in the shop, the art room, the science laboratory, and all the classrooms. Knitting and sewing, photography, printing, cooking, instrumental music, experimental work with electricity, radio, chemicals, and similar hobbies, provide additional creative and constructive situations. Photography has become one of the most popular hobbies with young and old alike, and it is this hobby, developed into professionalism, that has given us so many popular picture magazines that are among the most successful periodicals in America today. In the middle and upper grades of the Children's School, camera clubs, sewing clubs, groups in instrumental music, groups in various crafts, and groups interested in scientific experiment and invention, have from time to time been accorded additional periods for work, outside the class program. One or two periods a week have been set aside in certain grades for interest groups of this sort. Play clubs for baseball, badminton, and other sports have been popular after-school activities.

The fourth type of hobby is the one that sometimes must be given the most serious consideration from a standpoint of child development. Hobbies in this class tend to give a cue to an inferiority feeling, worship, or a quest for power where the satisfactions to desires are not readily available. Children in the upper grades who are unduly fond of animals and strongly revel in their superiority over the animal and their ability to make the living creatures "obey" are often wanting in success in other lines of activity. Likewise this is sometimes true with hobbies concerned with hunting and fishing and the collection of miniature objects that in life possess superb power or attraction; as, toy soldiers or implements of war. An overdose of hero worship, evidenced in collecting pictures of persons unusually prominent in present-day activities, is an indication of this psychological background. The scientific care of animals holds

THE CAMERA CLUB DEVELOPES AND ENLARGES PHOTOGRAPHS

interest for many children, but may have a special appeal for the child whose social relationships to others of his own age are not fully satisfying. Camping and hiking, with their opportunities to master and control natural forces, while of value to nearly all boys and girls, may give particular satisfaction to the reserved child who has not achieved the social leadership he craves.

All the types of hobbies and interests described have provided valuable experiences for boys and girls in the Children's School at certain levels of growth. Teachers, however, have at times sought to lead a child who had an all-engrossing individual hobby into some form of social cooperation or sharing that would give equal or greater satisfaction.

A Check List of Fifty Famous Fancies Popular with Boys and Girls

_____Airplanes 1, 2, 3
_____Animals 1, 2, 4
_____Aquaria 3
_____Autographs 2
_____Automobiles 2, 3

_____Art Appreciation 1
_____Basketry 3
_____Birds 1, 4
_____Block Printing 3
_____Boats 1, 2, 3

_____Books 1
_____Buttons 2
_____Camping 4
_____Chemistry 3
_____Coins 2

_____Dogs 1, 4
_____Dolls 2
_____Dressmaking 3
_____Fishing 4
_____Gardening 3

_____Hiking 4
_____Hotel Soap 2
_____Insects 1, 2
_____Knitting 3
_____Labels 2

_____Leather Work 3
_____Metal Work 3
_____Miniature Objects 2, 4
_____Musical Instruments 3
_____Newspapers 2

_____Pets 1, 4
_____Photography 3
_____Playing Cards 2
_____Postmarks 2
_____Printing 3

_____Radio, Wireless, Telephone 3
_____Road Maps 2
_____Rocks 2
_____Shells 2
_____Souvenirs 2

_____Sport and Celebrity
     Photographs 4

_____Stamps 2

_____Streetcar Tranfers 2

_____Timetables 2

_____Trains 2, 3

_____Travel 1

_____Tropical Fish 3

_____Wood Carving 2

_____Woodwork 3

_____Wrappers 2

KEY

1—To Acquire Knowledge or Satisfy Curiosity.
2—Acquisition of Objects and Things.
3—To Create or Make Objects.
4—To Provide Satisfaction for Feeling of Inferiority, Worship, Quest for Power.

PROVISION FOR INTER-CLASS ASSEMBLIES

With social sharing an important goal in the Children's School, assemblies have become longer and more frequent. An informational assembly occurs at nine o'clock on every Tuesday morning, when all groups from first to eighth grade meet to hear the announcements of the Student Cabinet and of the various committees working on festivals and other school activities. Complying with a request from the Student Cabinet for "longer" assemblies, the eighth grade, acting as an assembly committee, has invited each grade to share their plays and their lore with the school. Volunteers for each week have supplied interesting programs. Following are some of the programs that occurred in a single semester.

The eighth grade presented a skit advertising their Supreme Insurance Company, Safe, Sane and Secure! The skit revealed a well-organized stock company, ready to sell insurance on schoolbooks and other belongings to their schoolmates, and eager both to protect their patrons from losses and to pay dividends to stockholders.

A group of the seventh grade presented a humorous and instructive radio skit, telling of their vacation experiences in different parts of the United States. At another time a few skilful artists from the junior high school art class drew original cartoons for the amusement of the school.

The fourth grade prepared an original "movie," called "Explorers and Explorations." Each picture depicted some of the colorful breath-taking adventures of the first men to reach the shores of the new world and to explore this section of the continent. These were explained by the boys and girls as their pictures were shown on a large and ingenious reel of their own making.

The fifth graders, who had been studying the development of transportation in our country, prepared a series of lantern slides for an assembly, showing the vehicles of pioneer days, the first engines and steamboats, and the latest inventions in streamlined trains, trailers, and airplanes.

The sixth grade presented some book riddles during National Book Week. They also presented a skit at another assembly, advertising their newspaper, *The National News.*

The primary children preferred to share their projects with neighboring grades rather than to perform before the school in a large assembly. The first grade circus was given separately for junior kindergarten, senior kindergarten and second grade. Agile ponies showed their ability to stand on a chair, to push a ball, to race, buck, bow, and tell their ages. Ponderous gray elephants proved that they could stand on a ball, catch peanuts, parade, stand on two chairs, and walk with front feet on another elephant's back. Strong men, clowns, dancing ladies and dancing Indians, in appropriate costumes, all did their parts with zest.

The third grade invited the fourth grade and the second grade on separate days to see an exhibit of their science hobbies and to hear the different members of their class explain and demonstrate their collections of butterflies, shells, agates, sea-animals in bottles, and mounted autumn leaves; and demonstrate their experiments with germination of seeds, transpiration of leaves, and water life in an aquarium.

After a trip to the Navy Pier, where they saw boats lowered to the water level, and went through a coast-guard cutter, the second grade constructed a model harbor and invited friends to see it.

In two music assemblies held every week by a primary group and an upper grade group, the children shared with one another their favorite songs, and also their favorite melodies for the instruments which they were learning to play. The senior kindergarten visited one of the primary music assemblies and invited the first and second grades to come in to their rooms and have a sing with them.

The Thanksgiving assembly began with a processional in which all the children of the school carried gifts of fruits and vegetables for the Mary Crane Nursery School at Hull House. The fifth grade with the help of original drawings told of their excursion to Hull House to see the nursery school there.

For two weeks preceding Christmas all assembly periods were used for the creation and preparation of the Christmas festival in which several groups participated. The program included a processional and singing by the younger children, and an original Christmas play written by the seventh and eighth grades, and presented by all the grades from fourth to eighth. A king of merrie old England, in seeking an heir, disguised himself as a beggar, so ran the story, and stood on the street before the cathedral, as groups of children, carollers, soldiers and revelers passed by. His observations disclosed a worthy heir, and the announcement of the one who would be his successor was made at the Christmas feast, following the songs and dances and miracle plays with which the courtiers entertained their king.

PROVISION FOR USE OF COMMUNITY RESOURCES

The Chicago area provides a community rich in resources, which can add inestimably to the vitality and reality of learning experience. All groups in the school spend considerable time, as interests and needs suggest, in observing and utilizing community resources. Many points of interest are within walking distance of the school. School cars, parents' cars, and public conveyances have been used for longer trips. Excursions may occupy a half-hour period, a half-day, or a day; and occasionally an upper grade group has taken an excursion lasting two or three days. The children are helped to learn the regulations of the institution which they visit, and to give cooperation.

An excursion may be the starting point of a new interest; but usually the group goes with a definite purpose: to transact business; to gain needed information; or to enjoy an aesthetic experience. Children of nursery school, kindergarten and primary grades go to the beaches to play; to gardens, greenhouses and parks to see flowers and birds; to the pet store to buy a pet or food for pets; to the market or to a special shop to buy materials for activities; to the post office to mail a package; to a farm to get fruits or vegetables for use at school; to the airport to get facts needed for construction; to the harbor to watch boats of many kinds. A ride to the city on a suburban train brings the children into a large station, where overland trains may be visited. The zoo is often the destination of an eager group.

For middle and upper grades the neighborhood includes the entire Chicago area. Groups of children have enjoyed community recreation with their teachers. Together they have attended intercollegiate football games at the Stadium; concerts of the Chicago Symphony Orchestra at Orchestra Hall; matinees at the Chicago City Opera House; approved motion pictures and plays at local theatres. Among the institutions where they have frequently gone to see exhibits and to get information of various sorts are: the Field Museum of Natural History; the Chicago Academy of Science; the John G. Shedd Aquarium; the Museum of Science and Industry; the Museum of American History; the Art Institute of Chicago. Factories, large department stores, business offices, banks, publishing houses, social settlements, markets, mail-order houses, broadcasting studios, have all been at times the environment of firsthand experience.

The school has prepared for teachers' use an Excursion Guide Book, which gives brief descriptions of centers that have proved valuable for education; notations concerning exhibits, pictures, pamphlets, guides and guidebooks, that may be found at each center; and information concerning advance arrangements and transportation. The office of the Children's School aids teachers in arranging excursions and providing transportation.

The Chicago area provides not only interesting centers for excursions, but excellent libraries, where books and films may be secured by loan. Audio-visual aids and equipment for their use are available in the school library for loan to classrooms, as follows:

55 phonograph records.
Magnovox electric phonograph.
11 reels of 16 mm. films.

Sound motion picture projector.
Silent motion picture projector.
Microphone for use with sound projector.
Portable radio.
Film strip projector.
26 Spencer film strips.
Reflectoscope.
Lantern slide projector.
300 lantern slides.
68 maps.
3,000 miscellaneous pictures.
700 pictures of Visualized Curriculum Series.

The school library also has available lists of films which may be obtained free or for low rental prices from various film libraries in the Chicago Area; and teachers are given aid in selecting and ordering films for classroom use.

The portable phonograph and records are in continual use in connection with music activities; the portable radio is used frequently by middle and upper grades both for music appreciation and for study of current events. Original radio broadcasts by the children have afforded an interesting type of assembly program.

The school encourages children also to take their own pictures of school and community activities, and for this purpose has available a Gráflex camera, a motion-picture camera, and an Elwood enlarging machine.

In many other ways the children share in the life of the community. Parents and other citizens have come to the school upon invitation to talk to the children about school and community problems, or to share with them pictures, films, curios, and tales collected in travel. Frequently upper grade children have had the experience of conferring with school officials, business men, and city officers concerning school and community projects. Occasionally the opportunity has presented itself for the children to serve the neighborhood in some vital way; as, beautifying the school environment, or notifying city authorities of points where warning signs are needed.

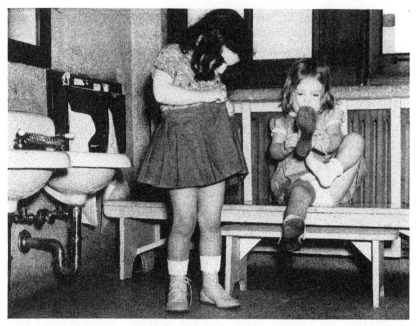

DRESSING IS A BIG TASK

DAILY PROCEDURE IN THE NURSERY SCHOOL

The Nursery School of National College of Education is an integral part of the Children's School. In this respect it belongs to a very small group of nursery schools which hold the same relationship to the rest of an elementary school as any grade within the school. The children upon leaving the Nursery School automatically go into the next level, the Junior Kindergarten, which is approximately the four-year-old group. The teaching staff consists of a trained and experienced director with one full-time assistant. The cooperating members of the school staff are: psychologist, parent education advisor, physician, nurse, speech specialist, nutritionist. A group of advanced students give part-time assistance.

Children are accepted in the school usually in order of application, but preference is given to children and to families where there is special need of the help that the nursery school affords. Some children are in the school on the recommendation of the family physician. A physical examination and psychological tests are required before the child is admitted to the school. The child must be physically in condition to enter into the nursery school activities successfully, and must be normal or superior in mentality. The group, twenty in number, with nearly an even number of boys and girls, ranges in age from two years to four years. Only fifteen are accepted for the day session.

The session varies according to the needs of individual children. Those enrolled for the morning session only, come at eight-thirty and go home at eleven-thirty. Children living at a considerable distance from the school, those whose parents are engaged in study or work, and those who have special needs, are usually enrolled for the full-day session. The afternoon program closes at three o'clock.

The procedure follows. The program is very flexible, except for rest, meals, elimination.

8:30 Arrival by school car, or with the parents.
Medical inspection by school physician. Isolation of doubtful cases. Children admitted to their room after receiving pass from the physician. Toilet period for a few children. Drink of water.
Out-of-door play, if the weather permits. Play on apparatus, boxes, boards, barrels, with Kiddie Kars, wagons, and other wheel stock. Excursions and trips to points of interest in the neighborhood, climbing on logs, picking flowers, playing in the field, . . . Songs, stories, and rhythms are used out-of-doors as freely as indoors when the interest warrants their use.
Play indoors if weather is stormy. Water play, use of all indoor materials such as clay, small toys, hollow blocks, easels and paints. As children come in a few at a time, wraps are removed, with emphasis on creating a desire to help one's self.

10:15 or later. Toilet period for all—a few children at a time—with special emphasis on procedure, and on growth in independence.

10:20 Mid-morning luncheon of fruit juice or tomato juice served to a few at a time, as the children are ready. (Some exceptions are made according to the advice of the physician.) As a rule the children help in the preparation and serving of this mid-morning meal, and in the clearing of tables.
Rest on cots (with blankets if necessary) in a quiet room, lasting from ten to twenty minutes, depending on the needs of the children. The children are divided into a younger and older group at this time, and rest alternates with guided activity. Stories, poems, songs, rhythms and constructive materials are

introduced to the two groups to meet the needs of varying ages. Children are free to join centers according to interests.

11:30 Dismissal of those children enrolled for the morning session only. Toilet period for remainder of group. Thorough grooming for dinner.

11:45 Dinner—served by children. Emphasis is placed on creating a happy atmosphere, which is conducive to good eating habits and attitudes. Dinner is followed by a toilet period, and removal of outer garments.

12:30 Nap on cots, using sheets and blankets in darkened, cool, well-ventilated room. Nap is followed by toilet period, dressing, putting on wraps.

2:30 (or when children are dressed, following nap). Out-of-door play until time to go home.

3:00 Dismissal. Many children use school car. Some go with parents.

DAILY PROCEDURES IN THE JUNIOR KINDERGARTEN

(Very flexible, except for rest, meals, elimination.)

8:30 Arrival of children by school car, or with parents. Medical inspection by school physician. Isolation of doubtful cases. The children are admitted to their room after receiving pass from the physician.

Drink of water.—Children serve themselves from small pitchers and drink from small cups on trays.

Toilet period for those children who need it.

Out-of-door play if the weather is favorable. The children play on apparatus, boxes, boards, barrels, tricycles, wagons, and other wheel toys. Clay, paint and soap bubble materials are taken out for use on warm, sunny days. Excursions to points of interest in the neighborhood, climbing on logs, picking flowers, playing in the field, are common activities. Singing, listening to stories, and simple rhythms are used out-of-doors as freely as indoors when the interest warrants their use.

Sleds and snow shovels are provided in winter time. (On very cold days, children go indoors at 9:30.)

Outdoor toys are put away; five or six children come inside at a time after they have helped put away the toys they were using. Play indoors if weather is stormy. The children may play with water and with all indoor materials such as clay, paints, work bench, puzzles, etc.

10:00 Removal of wraps, with emphasis on creating a desire for independence.

Toilet period for all—a few children at a time—with special em-

phasis on proper procedure, and on growth in independence.
Groups gather as they are ready for fruit juice or tomato juice,
served at little tables.

Free play, including activities in the doll corner, building with
blocks, spontaneous dramatic play. Any creative materials such
as clay, crayons, paint, which may interest the children, are used.

Music. Rhythms are developed from the interests of the group
and may include clapping, skipping, hopping, marching, rolling,
skating, swimming, and many other interpretations. Musical instruments including gongs, bells, sandblocks, and drums are
sometimes used. Songs are correlated with the activities of the
days, seasons, and particular interests of the group.

10:50 Story groups. Two or more teachers establish centers, using picture books, rhymes or simple stories. Story groups alternate with
rest, using adjoining rooms.

Rest on individual cots, with blankets. Morning pupils rest first,
and then put on wraps to go home. Day pupils rest later.

11:25 Dismissal of morning children with parents or by bus.

Toilet period for day children. Hands are washed and hair is
combed, in preparation for dinner.

11:30 Dinner at small tables. The children get their own dinner from
a serving table and replenish their own dishes from little covered
dishes in the center of the small tables. The emphasis is
placed on creating a happy atmosphere, which is conducive to
good eating habits and attitudes.

12:00 Undressing and placing shoes under chairs at side of beds and
clothes on chairs. Children put on sleepers for sleeping.

Sleep on cots with a sheet and blanket, surrounded by individual
screens.

2:00 Dressing. Children learn to take responsibility for themselves.
Toilet period. Putting on outdoor wraps.

2:30 Outdoor play, weather permitting. (Indoor free play or music in
inclement weather.)

3:00 Dismissal of children with parents or in the buses.

DAILY PROCEDURE IN THE SENIOR KINDERGARTEN

(The program is flexible, except for the time for food, elimination and rest, and varies with the seasons and interests of the
day. In general, however, this procedure is followed.)

8:30 Children arrive by school car or with parents. Medical inspection by school physician. Children present the physician's pass
for entrance into their room. Wraps are removed with attention

to skills and orderly habits. Emphasis is placed on a buoyant beginning for the day.

Work period includes caring for pets and plants; following individual and group interests: constructive activities using blocks, wood, clay, crayons, paint, and many other materials; dramatic play.

Conference—bringing to the group interesting activities of the first period, discussion and evaluation of work done, solving problems, planning for the needs of the next day.

9:50 Toilet period. Serving of fruit juice.

Small groups rotate going to the toilet, accompanied by a teacher. Tomato or fruit juice is served informally. Centers are established by the teachers using books, pictures, poems, nature materials and so forth, so that small groups may rotate.

10:20 Music—including singing, rhythmic movement, use of simple instruments, listening to instrumental and vocal music; literature—including stories read and told, creative expression in terms of original verses, stories, relating incidents; excursions in the school building and community; outdoor play; and at times directed handwork. The activities depend on weather, interests, and the needs which have grown out of the earlier activities of the day. Frequently two groups alternate—one going outdoors and one remaining indoors for music, literature, etc.

11:20 Dismissal of children who do not stay for the afternoon session. Preparation of other children for dinner—toilet, washing, combing hair, rest.

11:40 Dinner served to small groups at small tables. Toilet period following dinner, and removal of outer garments.

12:30 Naps—on cots with sheets and blankets in darkened, well ventilated rooms. As children waken they put on shoes and outer garments. Then follows a toilet period, and putting on wraps. Outdoor play until dismissal.

3:00 Dismissal. Many children use school cars; some go home with their parents.

DAILY PROCEDURE IN THE FIRST GRADE

(Flexible, except for certain periods devoted to physical needs.)

8:30 Inspection by school physician—Isolation of doubtful cases. Removal of wraps, with emphasis on proper care of belongings. Care of room plants and pets.

Self-initiated activities, engaged in by individuals or groups, usually in the fields of fine and industrial arts social studies and science. Constructive activities may be preceded or followed by a discussion period for the purpose of planning further activities, evaluating what has been accomplished, or solving problems common to the group.

9:50 Attention to physical needs. Toilet period. Informal serving of fruit juice or tomato juice.

10:10 Reading activities, which may include group composition of stories about some special interest, reading of such stories from charts or booklets made by the children, or reading of interesting stories from "real books." The class is usually divided into small groups for reading, and one group may be engaged in some sort of individual reading activity.

11:00 Music activities, which include listening to folk songs and arts songs, singing, and bodily response to music.
Outdoor play. Activities on the playground include play with apparatus and with toys, such as wagons, sleds, balls; constructive activity and dramatic play with boxes, logs, snow; simple active games.

11:45 Preparation for dinner. Use of toilet rooms.
Dinner at small tables with teachers. The menu is planned by a nutritionist and emphasis is upon desirable attitudes and habits in relation to foods.

12:45 Preparation for naps by placing individual sheets and blankets on cots, and removing shoes.
Rest or nap in cool darkened room. Toilet period following nap.

1:30 Activities adapted to group interests or needs. These may include stories, art work, more reading, choric verse, manuscript writing, or other types of experiences.

2:30 Outdoor play, similar to morning period.

3:00 Dismissal.

DAILY PROCEDURE IN THE SECOND GRADE

(Flexible, except for certain periods devoted to physical needs)

8:30 Inspection by school physician—Isolation of doubtful cases. Care of wraps and belongings; attention to plants and pets.
Art and industrial activities, individual or related to some group interest; as, carrying the mail or developing a harbor.
Discussion period for planning and judging work, reporting on excursions and other related experiences, may precede or follow activity period.

9:50 Reading activities involving use of literary, informational or work-type materials, according to needs and interests of individuals or small groups. Children's library is used by small groups on certain days.

10:20 Toilet period, followed by informal serving of fruit juices.

10:30 Music activities, including music appreciation, singing, and bodily rhythm. Music may provide interpretation or expression for the outstanding interests of the group.

11:00 Arithmetic activities involving either solution of number problems related to group activities, arithmetic games, or practice in mastering certain needed skills. Children often work individually or in small groups.

11:30 Outdoor play, varying with the season: constructive and dramatic play with materials; free play on apparatus, group games.

12:00 Preparation for noon meal. Use of toilet rooms.
Noon meal, with menu planned by nutritionist. Emphasis on desirable habits and attitudes at table.

12:50 Rest on cots in cool, darkened room. (Sheets and blankets provided.) Stories are read aloud by the teacher during part of this period. Rest is followed by a toilet period.

1:40 Written and oral composition related to individual or group interests. Needs for spelling and improved handwriting become evident in written work, and practice is provided.

2:30 Flexible period for nature experiences, excursions, dramatic play, and other activities, suggested by interests of the group.

3:00 Dismissal.

Tentative Weekly Program—Grade Three

Time	Monday	Tuesday	Wednesday	Thursday	Friday
8:30	Individual Activities				
9:00	Social Studies, Science and Handicraft	Assembly	Social Studies, Science and Handicraft		
10:00	Reading Activities (individual or in small groups)				
10:30	Language and Spelling	Music Activities			Language and Spelling
11:00	Games and Play (playground or gymnasium)				
11:30	Art (individual and group)	Language, Spelling and Literature			Art (individual and group)
12:30	Lunch and Rest (menu planned by a nutritionist)				
1:30	Outdoor Play or Free Reading in Library				
2:00	Group Interests and Needs	French Elective or Individual Interests and Needs			Group Interests and Needs
2:30	Individual and Group Work in Arithmetic				
3:00	Dismissal				

Note. Activities such as handicraft, music and art, carried on by special teachers, frequently, though not necessarily, are connected with some enterprise which the group is pursuing. A strong interest in group undertakings is manifested by these specialists and ample opportunity is given to enrich the work through the channels of shop work, music and art.

The program is flexible, and periods are frequently extended to provide for continued interest in a particular field. The teacher is free to arrange for excursions, experiments and other enriching experiences.

Tentative Weekly Program—Grade Four

Time	Monday	Tuesday	Wednesday	Thursday	Friday
8:30	Making Plans for the Day				
9:00	Social Studies and Science	Assembly	Social Studies and Science		
10:00	Shop (Group and Individual Enterprises)	Music Activities			Shop (Group and Individual Enterprises)
10:30		Individual and Group Work in Arithmetic			
11:00	Reading in Groups and Reading Conference				
11:45	Lunch (Menu planned by child as part of the work in hygiene)				
12:30	Language and Spelling	Art (Group and Individual)	Language and Spelling	Art (Group and Individual)	Language and Spelling
1:15	Games, Sports, and Dancing (Playground or Gymnasium)				
2:00	Group Work in Literature or Individual Free Reading in the Library				Music Assembly Game Assembly or Motion-Picture Assembly
2:30	Group Interests and Needs	French Elective or Individual Interests and Needs			
3:00	Dismissal				

Note. The daily program for the fourth grade is a flexible schedule which may be adjusted easily to meet the needs of the group. It is changed from day to day as need arises. Children and teachers together often talk over and plan the work of the day. When longer work periods are required in order to accomplish the purposes of the group, or of individual children, more time is allowed.

While certain scheduled periods are taught by specialists, the teachers in these various fields work closely with the room director and so are informed concerning room activities and interests of major importance. Because of this cooperation there is no definite break or boundary between the many phases of the school work.

Tentative Weekly Program—Grade Five

Time	Monday	Tuesday	Wednesday	Thursday	Friday
8:30	Individual Work Period				
9:00	Social Studies, Science, and English	Assembly	Social Studies, Science and English		
10:15	Language Usage and Spelling				
10:45	Games, Sports, and Dancing (Playground or Gymnasium)				
11:30	Social Arithmetic and Arithmetic Practice				
12:00	Lunch (Menu chosen by children as part of the work in hygiene)				
12:45	Group Interests and Needs	Music Activities			Hobby Clubs (Sewing, Cooking, Camera, etc.)
1:15		French Elective or Individual Needs			
1:45	Group Work in Literature or Individual Free Reading in Library				
2:15	Enterprises in the Shop and Art Room (Group and Individual)				Music Assembly, Game Assembly or Motion-Picture Assembly
3:00	Dismissal				

Note. Due to the fact that our special teachers also teach classes in the college department we schedule a definite time when they are available to work with each group; however, this schedule is most flexible. Groups may exchange periods, or one grade may have more time in the shop, when some activity demands, and another may have more help from the music teacher at that time. On some days the needs and interests may fit the planned schedule; on another day the program may be entirely disregarded while the group spends a whole half day on an excursion, or perhaps working on an assembly program for other groups. The daily and weekly program of activities tends to be determined by, and centered around large group enterprises, with special provision for individual needs and interests.

Tentative Weekly Program—Grade Six

Time	Monday	Tuesday	Wednesday	Thursday	Friday
8:30	Individual Activities				
9:00	Social Studies, Reading and Composition	Assembly	Social Studies, Reading and Composition		
10:15	Social Arithmetic and Arithmetic Practice				
10:45	Games, Sports and Dancing (Playground or Gymnasium)				
11:30	Language Usage and Spelling				
12:00	Lunch (Menu chosen by child as part of the work in hygiene)				
12:45	Science Problems and Hobbies	French Elective or Individual Needs			Science Problems and Hobbies
1:15		Music Activities			
1:45		Group Work in Literature or Individual Free Reading in the Library			
2:15		Enterprises in the Shop and Art Room (Group and Individual)			Music, Game or Motion-Picture Assembly
3:00	Dismissal				

Note. In making the above program attention was given first to the general routine of living. Children arrive at school between 8:30 and 9:00 and leave at 3:00. Lunch for this group comes at 12:00. A long play period is considered essential. Second, attention was given to those things which belong in the school week and which are largely determined by the program of the school as a whole; such as, assemblies and time for activities guided by special teachers in music, art, shop, and French. Third, attention was given to those activities which are common in the program for a sixth grade. Next, and most important of all, attention was given to insuring its flexibility in order to adjust to vital and dynamic interests which arise and which should take precedence over routine. Changes are frequently made, ranging from slight variation to complete deviation, as in the case of excursions. It may be added that we are committed to use any or all offerings whenever they will serve to enhance our studies.

SKETCHES OF VARIOUS DAYS

IN EVALUATING the work of a school or a class, perhaps the most important record is the story of a day, for the day is the child's unit of living. In the modern school it is impossible to choose a typical day for description, since no two days are alike.

The section which follows includes sketches of several days in the pre-school, and one selected from the records of each grade teacher. Growing purposefulness in activities, ability to work and play in larger groups, more sustained interest in a single center, readiness to work for more remote goals, are evident as the children grow older.

Since the nursery school is the newest child in the school family, a brief explanation concerning the organization of the program and the objectives is included here.

Organization of the Nursery School

As the program of the nursery school is carried out day by day, it may be noted that the only set periods which come at regular times each day are those which relate to physical needs such as food, sleep and elimination. The other activities of the day vary according to the needs and interests of the children, as well as weather.

The group is often divided into smaller groups in order to prevent over-stimulation and fatigue which sometimes come with a large group of children. This division allows for following up individual interests by giving opportunities to choose what individual children wish to do or see. Division of the group also makes for growth, as a few who are ready for something more advanced may have it without exposing those in a less mature state. Those verging on four may be ready for some form of handwork, some rhythmic work or an excursion which would be beyond the level of the younger members.

It may be noted that children are not *required* to join social groupings such as a group coming together for songs or stories, or to look at pictures, but they come and go of their own free will. The teacher with the group at the time tries to make the center of interest so interesting that the children will want to come and join in. At various times throughout the year records have been kept which show the span of the children's attention as they join such centers of interest. The records show a gain in some individuals from two to twenty minutes. It has been our aim to keep the nursery school free from organization and routine except as the social development of the children reached a stage where they were ready to come together and do more in groups. It has been our aim also to have as free and homelike an atmosphere as possible and to avoid falling into the category of schools where "children like hothouse plants are forced into premature development," as one of our American educators has expressed it.

While all phases of the school curriculum have their beginnings in the nursery school, we are stressing those beginnings only by giving the children ample opportunity to enjoy the stages of investigation, experimentation and manipulation in their use of materials. Health habits, gain in emotional control and stability, development of desirable attitudes and appreciations along with the development of skill in the use of the body are the main objectives of the nursery school.

Parent education through conferences, parents' meetings, observations in the nursery school, and through mothers' classes are considered of utmost importance in our work with the nursery school child. A specialist in the field of parent education plans the classes for the mothers but is assisted by the nursery school director and other members of the pre-school staff. The director holds the conferences with student teachers who are working in the nursery school, keeps the records of the children, and arranges for the cooperation of specialists on the staff. She is not a detached person, an executive or overseer who acts as an administrator for the nursery school, but she is the head teacher who works closely with the children and students in her group throughout the entire day.

A DAY IN SEPTEMBER
Nursery School

Number enrolled, 20   Chronological Age range, 2-4 to 3-7
Number present, 16   Mental Age range, 2-4 to 4-5

At eight-thirty two children came up the hall, having arrived in one of the school cars. Following them was a student teacher who reminded

PETS ARE FED EACH MORNING

them that a visit to the doctor's office was the first thing to be done upon arrival. One child willingly cooperated with the doctor in the morning inspection of eyes, throat, neck, ears, hands and chest, while the other one, not yet feeling entirely secure and free in the physician's hands, was loath to be inspected. The doctor asked about the child's dog and approached the child in a very friendly, informal way. The inspection given was somewhat superficial, but a step or two in advance over the inspection of this particular child on previous days, the doctor appreciating the need for building up a favorable attitude and confidence before proceeding very far in her work.

After inspection the children went down to the nursery school room where the director was waiting near the door to greet them and help make them feel at home. They put their "tickets" (slips of colored paper given to them to show they had been to the doctor's office) in a basket used for that purpose. The teacher helped them remove their sweaters. In completing the task one child turned his inside out. She assisted in showing the child how to turn the sweater right side out.

She reminded the children that they should look for their "markers" on their own lockers. This they did and having found them they hung up their sweaters and caps. They then went to the toilet room where an assistant teacher was ready to give necessary help. (Care is taken at the beginning of the year to build favorable attitudes and not burden the children with too much stress on procedures and habits all at once. As each child appears ready and interested in carrying on certain procedures leading to definite routines and habits he is encouraged. Caution against fatigue and boredom is necessary if right attitudes are to be formed and right habits happily established.)

Following a toilet period these children returned to the playroom where they were interested in watching and in helping care for the bird, feed the rabbit and the turtles, and change the water on two bouquets. Other children came in about this time, some with their mothers, some having come in the school cars. They too brought their "tickets" from the doctor's office. One child, a very young one with hospital experience and unpleasant associations, was admitted without going to the doctor's office. The mother had been especially conscientious in looking over the child before bringing him. Some of the children went to the toilet immediately, while others after removing their wraps, sought the various play materials and centers of interest. (The director in individual conferences held with the mothers before the opening of school had been given the span and schedule for each child in regard to toilet needs and was meeting individual needs accordingly.)

A free informal play time indoors ensued until about nine ten when most of the group had arrived. All of the children then got ready to go out-of-doors. They went to the playground where they had a happy, free and lively time with wagons, kiddy cars, boards, boxes and jungle-gym, sawhorses, barrels and other flexible and crude equipment. They played house, train, iceman and many other dramatic plays. There was almost no cooperative play, but "each man for himself" was happy and busy in his own interests. Several children trotted back and forth on the walk, ran up and down boards and flitted from one bit of equipment to another, investigating, experimenting, manipulating, learning.

During this time the milkman arrived with his friendly, toothless old horse, "Nig," who had already won the friendship of the children in the few days they had been in the nursery school. Several children had brought apples or sugar from home which they placed on a cement wall which separates the sidewalk from the sloping driveway. The children's heads were on a level with the horse's head, yet they were safely out of danger of the horse's feet—an ideal arrangement for feeding and petting the horse.

An airplane flew by which the children stopped to watch. One of

Logs and Boxes Prevent Unemployment

the teachers spontaneously sang a simple short airplane song. The children looked at her and listened as she sang it over and over again while several children joined in singing it as best they could.

At ten minutes before ten several children went indoors to the lavatory to get ready for the mid-morning luncheon consisting of orange juice. As they finished, having gone to the toilet, washed their hands, and combed their hair, some went to the rug where there was a supply of picture books and where a teacher was enjoying looking at books, too. Four children joined her and together they looked at pictures, talked about them and said Mother Goose rhymes over and over again. Some of the children played with the dolls, while others watched the rabbit in his cage. When all of the children had come in from the playground and were ready for orange juice, the teachers went to the tables which were set with glasses of orange juice and napkins. Each child had a certain place at the table, but some needed help in remembering where they sat. The children took care of their chairs, napkins and glasses when finished. (During the first few days of school the tables were not set, but glasses of orange juice were given to the children in a most informal way, with as little ceremony as possible.)

After this mid-morning luncheon two mothers came and took their children. (These youngsters were of the type easily over-stimulated and were making their adjustment to the nursery school a very gradual one by coming for part of each morning but lengthening the time of their stay each day.) A rest period on cots was the next procedure. This rest time was of about ten minutes duration—just long enough to have the children settle down and get a "feeling" for the atmosphere of a rest period.

Another out-of-door period followed, but this time the group was divided and went to different centers of interest. Some went to the log pile where they climbed and jumped and had a delightful dramatic play time of riding on trains and airplanes. A group of four with a teacher, went down to the canal which adjoins the playground, to throw stones in the water and to watch the sea gulls. Another group went to the school garden where they picked asters and cosmos. As they came walking up the playground bearing their flowers the teacher spontaneously began "One foot up and one foot down. This is the way to London town." Several children joined in the rhythm with her and chanted the rhyme as they walked on up to the door. They took their flowers to the nursery school room and helped arrange them in vases for the luncheon tables.

At eleven o'clock the children who remained for the afternoon session began entering the room in small groups and had a toilet period. They were given ample time to enjoy the process of making ready for the noon meal. Those who present no problems in food and sleep and whose parents desire they stay for the half day only were dismissed at eleven-thirty. As the others finished at the lavatory, they helped set the tables (put on doilies, napkins, silver and cups). Two children helped an assistant teacher put the sheets and blankets on the cots. Several others of their own volition got picture books from the shelf, while some played with dolls. (Paints, sand and other materials that would tend to soil their hands are taboo at this time.)

When luncheon was ready to serve one child asked to ring the chimes to call the children together for luncheon. When all were seated at their places, the teacher at each table asked one child to go to the serving table for the plates. (Small servings were given to several children who were appetite problems. Two of these, however, asked for second helpings.) As each child finished, he placed his napkin beside his plate, pushed his chair under the table and was excused. He then went to the lavatory, and after going through the regular toilet procedure, he removed his outer garments, hung them up, and went to his bed, where he removed his shoes and then got into bed.

As the luncheon was about over, two children were asked to help clear the tables, which they did with a good deal of joy and efficiency. By one o'clock all of the group were ready for their naps. Screens were placed around each bed. Several children needed help in relaxation, but by one thirty-five all but one child was asleep. This child rested for three quarters of an hour and then was allowed to get up and dress. As the others wakened (their naps varied from an hour to an hour and twenty minutes) they went to the lavatory, dressed and got ready to go out-of-doors. When three children were up, a teacher went to the playground, and as each one of the others was ready, he joined the group in out-of-door play. At a few minutes before three several mothers came, to take their children home. Each child was given a note on which was recorded the length of his nap, how much he ate at luncheon, any defecation and any unusual happenings that the teacher wanted the parents to know about (as, emotional upheavals, accidents).

By three o'clock all were dismissed, many of them going home in the school cars, each car having not only the driver but a student teacher in charge of the children.

A DAY IN NOVEMBER

Nursery School

The children, on coming from the doctor's office, removed their coats and hats. After the usual toilet procedure they returned to the

playroom where each one sat at a table, poured a cup of water for himself and drank it. This new phase of procedure had been under way
just a few days. Some children gave evidence of not caring for water
and therefore poured and drank only a small amount. Others poured
a full glass and drank it down heartily. As each finished he put on
his wraps and went to the playground. There the children used the
boards, boxes, kegs, junglegym and wheel stock. Several children asked
for water and paint brushes so they could "paint." A large hollow box
of soft wood with all sides nailed on, served as a very satisfactory
place for driving nails. The children used heavy hammers and large
headed shingle nails. Later on a group of five children went to the other
end of the playground where they had a rollicking time turning somersaults and playing wheelbarrow in the grass. The rabbits were let loose
on the grass and the children had fun watching them eat.

At quarter of ten the children began taking their wheel stock to
the "play house." The group then went indoors for toilet period and
rest. Following this rest time they put on their wraps and went out-
of-doors again. Eight of the children traveled on kiddy cars and in
wagons two short blocks to the neighborhood grocery where they bought
various kinds of vegetables. They carried these unwrapped back to
the school.   (These children were chosen for this experience because
they live in hotels or have servants so that they have little or no contact
with kitchens, cooking, seeing vegetables and groceries in their "raw"
state. The aim was to familiarize them with the common vegetables and
let them handle, feel and play with them.)

While this small group went to the store, the rest of the children
went to see the construction work on the Bahai Temple, a large edifice
two blocks away. They were deeply interested in seeing the great trucks
dump stone and gravel and in observing iron beams hoisted high into
the air. After watching for a half hour and asking many questions
they went back to the school and got ready for dinner.

On their return trip some of the children ran along, playing they
were driving dump trucks. They stopped for a few moments in front
of one of the neighbor's houses to watch and talk to a puppy in the
yard. Two children gave evidence of being somewhat afraid of the
dog and ran up and stood close to a teacher. She expressed a great
liking for the dog, called him and petted him as the children looked on.
(The teacher made a point later of visiting the dog every few days.
She took with her five children, including the two skeptical ones, and
after several visits all were thoroughly enjoying "Scotty.")

The preparation for dinner, serving and the rest of the afternoon
procedure was much the same as described in the record of a "Day in
September."

SOAP BUBBLES ARE ENJOYED ON RAINY DAYS

A DAY IN APRIL

Nursery School

It was a very rainy day. After the children had come in and gone through the usual procedures of morning inspection, toilet and a drink of water, the group was divided, the younger children staying in the nursery school room to play with wagons, kiddy cars and other wheel stock. These children put on sweaters and caps and the windows were opened wide so that they could have the advantage of the outdoor air without being in the rain.

The older children went to the Children's Library where they spent a delightful half hour looking at picture books and telling rhymes. (The teacher used in addition to Mother Goose, some of Dorothy Aldis' poems and some from Tippetts, "I Go A-Traveling.") On their way back from the Library they went into the school gymnasium where ten minutes were spent in running, hopping and galloping, the teacher accompanying their rhythmic expressions with suitable music on the piano.

When they returned to the room the usual lavatory period followed, in preparation for their mid-morning luncheon. Some of the children helped set the tables, and to clear them when finished. After the rest period of fifteen minutes the younger children left the room to go on an excursion about the building. They went to the fountain in the front of the building where they fed and watched the goldfish. From there they went down to the boiler rooms to see the great boilers which heat the building. They were interested in watching the engineer shovel coal and in watching the fire when the doors were opened.

While the younger children were off on this "excursion," the older ones were given their choice of blowing soap bubbles or helping the maid in the kitchen make sandwiches for the luncheon. (Both were familiar experiences.) Three children wanted to make sandwiches, while the other six wanted to blow bubbles. Just before the younger ones returned at eleven o'clock, these older children were asked if they would not like to come together for a story. All but one came, and he preferred to continue making sandwiches. The story used was "The Wee Little Woman" by Elsa Beskow. Following the story the children got ready for the noon meal. The rest of the program for the day was much the same as recorded for "A Day in September."

When the children were up and dressed following their naps, the rain was still streaming down; so clay was put on one table for the children and paper and crayons at another. The children busied themselves with these materials while one teacher moved among them, making suggestions, giving approval or encouragement and genuinely enjoying the activity with them. (On days when there is a damp, penetrating wind or a steady downpour of rain and the weather is such that the children cannot go out, we make a point of having some experience or activity outside of the nursery school room so that the children will not feel so confined to one place.)

THE PONY IS A FAVORITE AT THE FARM

AN OCTOBER DAY IN THE JUNIOR KINDERGARTEN
(following a day at a farm)

Number enrolled, 24	Chronological age range, 3-9 to 4-9
Number present, 21	Mental age range, 3-9 to 5-8

With the approach of Halloween had come the query, "Where shall we get pumpkins to make jack-o'-lanterns?" One of the children said he had seen pumpkins at a farm nearby, and several mothers had agreed to take us in cars.

We had spent a whole morning at the farm; we had seen pumpkins in the fields, beets and carrots buried in dirt trenches, hens and geese strutting across a farm yard, puppies playing in the barn, and a huge pig in a pen. We had participated in farm activities to the extent of sliding down the haystack, patting the horses and climbing on the low branches of the apple tree.

When we returned to school, each child carried a small pumpkin, and the teachers had pumpkins for the room and bags of fresh vegetables for the school pets.

When the children came to school the following day, it was evident that the farm interest was still keen. They entered the room in small groups from the doctor's office, where the daily health inspection takes place. Richard discovered some wooden farm animals in the "help yourself" cupboards, and without a word went to work making block fences, inside which he put the animals. Joan and Bradford joined him, offering to make a barn. Joe and Roy made a truck with blocks and directed Arthur to help load cabbages and drive the truck. Betty painted a picture of some pumpkins, and Jean drew a picture of a teacher sliding down a haystack. Georgiana's drawing was of a guinea pig saying, "Thank you for the lettuce you brought from the farm." Anne and Marian made apples and pumpkins out of clay, and Mary-ellen looked at a picture book of animals. Out of the twenty-one children present, twelve were working on some representation of the farm experience.

At the end of the activity period we all went to see Richard's farm-yard. He explained where each animal lived. Joan showed us how the barn doors opened. Roy drove the vegetable truck and told us he was going to Chicago. We looked at the painting and drawings, wrote stories about them and tacked them on the bulletin board. The clay fruits were put away to dry. Blocks and animals were put away in the cupboards again.

After the toilet period some of the children went to the library to look at picture books; some went to a corridor where posters of dairy farming were on display. On their return to the room, the teacher read "Grandfather's Farm" by Read and Lee.

Mid-morning lunch of orange juice and a short rest period followed. Then the teacher called the children to sit on the rug and said, "Who can sing a song about a pumpkin?" Immediate response from the children showed a wealth of ideas, an eagerness to sing for the group and a willingness to listen to others. These are some of the songs we heard: .

Richard:	Halloween night, Halloween night, We will see some jack-o'-lanterns.
Gene:	I see a pumpkin, I see a pumpkin, I see a pumpkin.
Dick:	Once a man took a pumpkin and put a light in it, and then it was a jack-o'-lantern.
Georgiana:	Halloween, Halloween, Halloween is coming soon.

The words of this last song seemed to fit the tune of a German folk song, "The Chickadee" found on page 75 of Surrette's book, "One Hundred Forty Folk Songs." The teacher sang the first part of the song, using Georgiana's words, and sang "tra-la-la" for the rest of the song. She suggested that the children think of other phrases to sing. Many suggestions were received, and the finished song was sung over and over again:

> Halloween, Halloween,
> Halloween is coming soon.
> Pumpkins bright
> Shine at night
> On the window sill.
> We will go out to the farm,
> We'll buy pumpkins big and small.
> Halloween, Halloween,
> Now it's Halloween!

After singing we all put on wraps. Each one helped himself as much as he could. Outdoors we played on boxes and planks, climbed on the junglegym, or coasted down the driveway in wagons. At dismissal time, some children went home, and the rest came into the room to get ready for dinner. Each child went to the lavatory, washed his hands thoroughly and combed his hair.

Sixteen of us sat down at four tables to a dinner of creamed lamb, baked potato, buttered spinach, raw carrot sandwich, milk and fruit cup. The teacher had put the portions of food on the plates, and each child had carried his own to his place. During the dinner we talked of how we would make jack-o'-lanterns, using the pumpkins we had brought from the farm.

When dinner was over the children went to the room where cots had been set up for the naps. Each cot was provided with a pair of blankets and a sheet. Each child removed his shoes, his suit or dress, and lay on the cot that bore his name. The teachers sat beside several children who needed help in quieting down. Soon every child was asleep.

As each child awoke, he got up, put on his shoes and suit, went to the toilet and dressed for outdoor play. We went to play on the logs, dramatizing boats, with passengers and captains. When the school cars came into the driveway, each child ran to the car that was to take him home. Some children went home with their mothers.

A SNOWY DAY IN JANUARY

Junior Kindergarten

> "It's snowing, it's snowing
> The north wind is blowing."

We heard the children singing in the halls long before they reached the rooms. When they did come in, after they had seen the doctor, their suggestions were curiously alike—"Let's go out right away." So after

SNOW BRINGS JOLLY FUN

the admittance slips had been deposited and everyone had his coat buttoned warmly, we went out.

The playground was deep with white, glittering snow. It was too deep to use sleds, but just right for other activities. Some children scuffed through the snow, tumbling down every few feet. A small group played "Follow the leader," making tracks across a wide stretch of snow. One little girl rolled over and over, occasionally lying flat and watching the snowflakes that were still flying. A little boy started to make a snow man. Others joined him and rolled enough balls to make several snow men. Some of us made and threw snowballs at the trees, or just to see how far we could throw them. Nearly everyone tasted the snow and many brought snowballs into the room "to see what would happen to them."

After having been out for about forty minutes, we brushed and stamped as much snow as possible off ourselves and went into our room. The children talked happily about the good time they had had while they removed their snow suits, galoshes, caps and mittens. The janitor had been asked to lay a fire in the fireplace which the teacher lighted as soon as she came in. The children hung their mittens on the fire screen and stayed to watch the blazing logs.

A toilet period followed; then two of the teachers read stories to groups of us as we sat on the rug near the fire. One read "The Snow-Man" by Kruger and Sondergaard; the other, "The Snowball" in Maud Lindsay's book, "Story Garden for Little Children." We sang all the snow songs we knew, "Jingle Bells," "Little Snowflakes," "It's Snowing," and "The North Wind Does Blow."

Mid-morning luncheon was served to us on the rug, the teachers passing cups of orange juice on trays. Later, the children carried the trays of empty cups to the kitchen. Then they lay on small cots to rest. It was a particularly pleasant rest period, because we could hear the crackling of the logs in the fireplace, and see the shadow of the dancing flames.

After the rest period, the teacher called the children and said, "If you had paper and chalk, what story would you tell?" "About snow falling," "I would tell about snow men," "I can draw snow on the roofs," "I can make tracks in the snow," were some of the replies. Black paper and chalk were quickly placed on the tables and everyone worked on his picture. Some children drew snow men with stick arms and hats; some made children sliding down hills on sleds; others made snowflakes falling on roofs and sidewalks. One little boy made a picture of a boy shoveling in the deep snow. The teachers drew pictures, too, and offered suggestions to children about their work.

As it was snowing too hard to carry pictures home, everyone put his

HOME-MAKING CONSUMES MUCH TIME

in his locker. We had to stop work in time to get some of the children ready to go home in the school cars or with their mothers. The children staying for the afternoon helped to put away chalk and wipe off the tables before getting ready for dinner.

A MORNING IN JUNE

Junior Kindergarten

In the fall a group of children had shown great interest in having parties for the Kindergarten dolls. The children had outlined a house with blocks into which the doll furniture had been moved and in which housekeeping had been set up. The dolls were undressed and put to bed; they were dressed and brought to the table for meals.

This play lasted several days; later in the year it reappeared, and the teacher suggested that dolls might be brought from home to enjoy a school party. The idea was hailed with enthusiastic response. "I'll bring my doll, Mary Anne. She has such pretty clothes." "Oh, I'll bring my baby doll. She likes parties." Some children offered to bring toy dogs, cats, or monkeys.

Certain preparations for the party were made. Some children washed and ironed the doll clothes; others washed and dried all the doll dishes. Another group cut and folded paper napkins.

On the day of the party all the dolls arrived wearing their best dresses and smiles. The toy animals looked all ready to perform tricks and stunts. One of the children said, "Oh, it's too crowded in this room with all the dolls. Let's go out on the lawn." So out we went, carrying dolls, small chairs and tables, and dishes. The dolls were cared for by several children while others went to pick flowers for table decoration. The garden yielded bouquets of pretty pansies and the tables looked very attractive. As soon as each group finished its work of setting tables or arranging flowers, the children went into the building for a toilet period.

When we came out again, we carried pitchers of orange juice and cups. Each child sat on the grass near his doll and poured fruit juice into a cup for himself and into a doll cup for his guest. During lunch the children talked about their dolls, told us their names and how they played with them at home.

Some of the children wanted to give an animal show for us. We all sat on the logs while the toy dogs turned somersaults, the toy monkeys climbed trees and a toy kitten played with a string.

One of the teachers had brought some books for us to read. Among them, "The Katy Kruze Book of Dolls," "The Animal Mother Goose" and in Maud Lindsay's book, "A Story Garden for Little Children," we found a story of "The Lost Doll." We sat under the trees and enjoyed stories and pictures until the school cars came to take the children and dolls home.

A DAY IN DECEMBER

Senior Kindergarten

Number enrolled, 30	Chronological age range, 4-8 to 5-9
Number present, 26	Mental age range, 5-0 to 6-10

The Senior Kindergarten children began to arrive at 8:20. They went to the doctor's office where the daily medical inspection took place, and were given their tickets of admission to the room. The teacher and the student assistants were on hand to greet the children, making such suggestive comments as "You're just in time to help feed the rabbits"— "I'm sure you can manage your galoshes yourself, but I'll be glad to help you if you really need help with your leggings"—"Did you find something at home for the headlight of your engine?"—"I have the paint ready for your book ends." . . . The children came in, a few at a time, until nine o'clock, when twenty-six had arrived. Each child had his own hooks for his wraps, and his own shelf for unfinished work and sundry treasures, labelled with his full name in manuscript writing.

After the wraps were removed and hung up, the children began to work in varying degrees of rapidity. Some got out their materials with decided definiteness of purpose, while others wandered about the room, chatting with the teachers, the children, to the pets (two birds, fish, turtles, white mice), watching others paint, work with clay, wood or blocks, assisting with folding and cutting napkins, watering plants, buttoning smocks for their neighbors, commenting upon and asking questions about the work of others. By 9:10 all but three children had settled into some sort of purposeful activity.

"We need some more icicles for Santa Claus' house," said the teacher to one of the children. "Dunder and Blitzen have broken their stalls. Those big corner blocks will probably hold them together better than the way they were built before. Try them, and see if they are stronger," she said to another, and to the third, "Jane and Marie are at home with colds today. Let's wrap up some of our jelly (made in October) and when you go home you can stop at their houses and leave the jelly at their doors. Of course you will not go in where some one has a cold."

Some of the group had built a large structure with the set of Fox Blox the day before, which they called "Santa Claus' house." They had made a mailbox, and on it had placed a sign which read "Santa Claus" (a carry-over from a previous house-play, where the children who live in apartments had used names on their mailboxes). In the house was an upturned soap box, a telephone (made from a scrap of broom handle, a few pieces of wood, and a buttonmold with pencilled numbers for a dial), many sheets of manila paper, and several pencils—all of which constituted Santa Claus' desk and materials. There were three chairs in the house in addition to Santa Claus' chair. Outside the house were some crude partitions known as the reindeer's stalls. A great deal of dramatic play went on, in and about these structures, interspersed with work upon them.

By 9:45 nearly all of the children had joined the play, some pretending to hang up their stockings and go to sleep, while others were Santa Claus, reindeer, or helpers. Some scribbled make-believe notes which they stuffed into Santa Claus' mailbox, and then registered real concern if he were not prompt about jotting down the messages, on his book. Finally the number of children involved in the play made it unwieldy for them to manage happily alone.

"Let's have all these reindeer go back to their stalls to be fed," said the teacher. "Here, Dasher, is a place for you . . . and one for Dancer . . . and for Prancer," and so on, until about a third of the children were in the "barn." "And here, helper, is a pail of water for these little animals—they must be very thirsty." "Now all of the children are going to bed," said one child. "Hang up your stockings securely," said the teacher, "and when every one is sound asleep, perhaps the reindeer will come prancing over your roof-tops." "I think it's almost midnight, Santa Claus! You had better be on your way!"

With such suggestions from teacher and children, the play was kept moving—interchanging characters, incorporating every one into the fun. "Reindeer have antlers. We should have antlers. Antlers are horns that stick up like this," said David, stretching his arms above his head and spreading out his fingers. Forthwith many of the children adopted his suggestion. "If we make a lot of noise they'll hear us," said Betsy. "You're right," agreed the teacher. "Anyway, reindeer have small feet," suggested someone else. "Small feet that move very swiftly," was the answer.

Gradually all of the other children finished their work, or arrived at a point where it could be stopped for the day. Materials were put away, and all joined in the Santa Claus play. As the fleet reindeer circled about the room, the teacher began to supplement the activity with piano music (Jingle Bells), thereby adding to the activity, and also defining a span of time so that it did not continue too long. (The free-activity, or work period, had dovetailed into a period of dramatic and rhythmic play.)

After all had had fun and satisfaction it was suggested that they sit together on the big rug, and that one of the student teachers be asked to tell "The Night Before Christmas." "I know what 'miniature' means; it means 'little.' " . . . "Yes, and that's the story that says 'St. Nicholas' instead of 'Santa Claus.' " . . . "And I know what 'Dunder and Blitzen' means. That's German for 'Thunder and Lightning' " . . . remarked the children. Then the teacher began, " 'Twas the Night Before Christmas," with the children joining in, where they knew the lines. After they had finished telling the story, the teacher showed the pictures, while the children pointed out various details of interest, and repeated occasional sentences or phrases in the story such as "He was chubby and plump, a right jolly old elf," when they came to that picture.

After the pictures had been shown, the teacher said, "It is ten o'clock now. The big hand is straight up, on twelve, and the little hand is on" . . . "Ten," chorused the children. . . . "Time to get ready for our mid-morning luncheon." . . . Then, "Let's have Miss X. . .'s children go down the hall to the toilet room." And when this group had separated from the rest, "Now Miss Y. . .'s children may set the tables, and my children please step over to the desk. There are several errands to be done." As the first children came back from the toilet-rooms, the others went, while small tasks were given those who had returned first, such as placing chairs at the tables and straightening the doll corner, until all were ready.

Then the teachers sat down at the various tables, remarking "Luncheon is all ready now," and the children went to their places, too. Some were called by name. (The method of getting the groups together at this time is quite casual. Sometimes the children are seated first. Two or three will sit and chat, or sing, or tell rhymes, while waiting for the rest. Each child has a specified table at which to sit. They all understand that no one begins to pour until all are seated, and rarely need reminding.) Then followed such exclamations as—"O boy, we have tomato juice this morning." . . . "When are we going to have grapefruit juice again? I like that!" Someone started to pour the tomato juice while the teacher commented, "Bob always passes the pitcher so that the next person can take hold of the handle." . . . "June, you haven't spilled a drop. When you first came, you had much trouble about tipping your cup, but you never do that anymore. I believe you're getting bigger!" When everyone was served the children began drinking. The teacher finished first, and with great ceremony asked, "Will you please excuse me? I have finished." All but one child did likewise. One child from each table gathered the cups and pitcher on the tray (the children rotate the responsibility of clearing the tables), discarded the napkins and doilies, and took the tray to the kitchenette, which is in one corner of the room.

In the meantime the teacher had lighted a row of red candles along the top of the piano. Someone started to sing, "Christmas time is coming soon." A teacher caught the tune, and played it on the piano. All gathered around and joined in the song, some standing, some sitting, and some pretending to dance around an imaginary tree. This was repeated several times. Then the teacher seated herself beside the piano, with a number of the children's products (of the activity period) in her lap.

"Annette has made a book about the story called 'The Little Fir Tree.' If you will all sit down on the rug, everyone can see it. Annette, tell the children what this printing on the cover says." (It was "The Little Fir Tree, Picture Book" on two lines.) "Annette wanted to number her pages and had trouble in remembering how some of the numbers looked. So this is what she did. She just started with number one on the clock, and counted down to the number she wanted." Then the teacher asked the child to demonstrate how she had found four, seven, three. "Well, let's see these pictures! Here are the giant fir trees with their great branches. And down here beside them is that *little* fir tree. And on page two, you can see the men coming into the forest in their one-horse open sleigh. Jingle Bells . . . Jingle Bells," and all sang the song through twice. They went on through the book, the child explaining some of the pictures, the children making suggestions about how the city streets should look, and so on. When they came to the last page showing the decorated tree, they sang, "O Christmas Tree" (German folk tune). "We haven't had 'Away in a Manger,'" said Jimmy, and without further ado he started it.

After the songs were over, the teacher said, "I have some other things here that you will want to see. This is the engine that Larry is making for his little brother. It's a good engine, isn't it—smokestack, bell, cab? But Larry can't make the wheels stay on. Perhaps someone can help him with his problem. Jack, can you think of a better way to fasten these wheels on? . . ." There were a number of new discoveries in method, as well as problems, which were discussed in the group. Suggestions and comments were made which gave many of the children a spur for proceeding on the coming day, and interested many in the work of others. (Such a conference period often follows the initial work period.)

Following this discussion the teacher placed the names (on cards) of seven children, in a rack, who were to accompany a student to the gymnasium for play. (Often all of the children go, but at times the group is divided in order to give special help to one-legged skippers, and to children whose coordination is below average generally.) While these children were gone, the remainder of the group started getting their wraps on. (And winter in Evanston means the whole category of outer wearing apparel.) With a divided group, the teachers were able to stress self-help, encouraging a child here, helping another there, and commending others. As soon as four were completely clad, a student teacher started for the playground with them so that they were not kept waiting. (The policy is "first ready, first out.") As others finished dressing, the teacher sent them down to join their playmates, and she brought up the rear with the last contingent.

While this preparation for out-of-door play was going on, the children who had gone to the gymnasium raced around the room a number of times, with evident enjoyment in the freedom of space there. Then a large pad was placed in the center of the room, and the teacher suggested, "Let's have some donkeys over here. All these donkeys place their front hoofs on this pad, and kick as hard and as high as you can, with your hind hoofs." (According to Richardson's "The Pre-School Child and His Posture.") They also played crab, elephant, duck (from the same series), and then tried hopping about the room, first on one foot, and then on the other. After playing in the gymnasium, the children all went to get washed, in leisurely fashion, and then returned to their room, which was now empty, to get ready for out-of-door play, too.

The out-of-door play was quite varied in nature. Some of the children climbed on logs and jumped off, while others climbed up and played airplane. A few ran 'round and 'round in the bushes, some pushed packing boxes together and got inside and played "bear." Two sleds were pressed into service. Both teachers participated in the play, moving about from group to group. After about fifteen or twenty minutes the teacher raised her hand. (The signal for the group to get together.) Those who were very intent on their play were told "Miss _____ has her hand up." One child did not come. In a chorus the children shouted, "Let's play Black Tom"—(the favorite game). "All right," said the teacher. "Who shall we have for Black Tom"—"You," was the answer, so the teacher was Black Tom. Just as the game was well under way the one dissenting child came to join the game. "I'm sorry," said the teacher, "but you did not obey the signal. Please stay outside the fence." (There is an enclosure—a disused tennis court—within the playground, which is usually used for games.) . . . After the group had played Black Tom three times, it was 11:30. The school cars had arrived to take the children home. One group of children went inside with one teacher to get ready for luncheon; a second group went to the front corridor with another teacher, to meet their mothers; and the third group went home in the school car with a student.

(The afternoon session is similar to that of the Junior Kindergarten, described on Page 319.)

A DAY IN MARCH

First Grade

Number enrolled: 25
Number present: 23

With a skip and a hop down the hall, and a joyous entrance into the first grade room came a pair of twins. A "ticket" from the examining physician was in one hand. A flashlight was in the other.

"Good morning, Miss _____! Lookie," said Jane, "I can be an usher in our movie." "And I," said Billy, "can be the one to make the pictures move. Daddy let us bring his flashlight!"

More soberly, but still in an enthusiastic mood came Nanette. This time it was a pattern for an usher's cap, which she had made at home. And so they came—some with "material" contributions; some with good news about home events; some with interesting comments on observations made on the way to school.

A word of explanation concerning the orienting experiences that initiated this movie interest, will help the reader to understand the record.

One day a member of the group brought in a unique shadow picture that he had made at home. Silhouettes of objects had been cut of black paper—a house, a tree, some flowers, a kite, and a child. They had been pasted very loosely on light-weight white paper. When the child moved a flashlight behind the picture in a darkened room, the trees swayed and twisted in the wind. The flowers nodded their heads. The child ran, his arms tugged at the string, and the kite dipped and rose at sudden intervals.

As might easily be imagined, there was an immediate response, and twenty-five six-year-olds wanted to do likewise. The outcome was a unanimous desire to have a movie. Experiments in cutting and pasting were made, and the plan finally developed into A Story Movie with the selection of The Three Bears, The Three Little Pigs, and Little Sambo as the stories to be depicted. A decision was also made to select some verses to portray.

It had been decided to invite the kindergarten to come to the theatre and to see the movie. In order that the guests might better appreciate the humor and the plot it was thought a good plan to read the stories dramatically, before the pictures were shown.

The theatre building, housing the screen and equipment necessary for the performance, had been built the day before of large floor blocks. It was a good-sized structure, seven feet long and three feet high. The center screen section was two feet, five inches wide.

This day in March, materials were already about the rooms as the children entered, to stimulate good habits of purposefulness in using the self-directed period. Nanette immediately got to work on her usher caps, and five or six children, attracted by her pattern, worked with her. The open space for the screen had been measured by two children who arrived early and they, with the help of a teacher, were soon busily engaged in measuring some dark red sateen for a curtain. One half of the curtain had been cut and a child was hemming it. At the other end of the same group of tables several children were cutting animals, freehand, from some gold paper. These were to be pasted on the curtain for decoration, in accordance with a plan previously made.

Some children were engaged in activities unrelated to the group interest. A few were looking at books in the room library, and others were drawing and writing at the blackboard. The playing of the chimes culminated this activity. The children cleared away materials, swept the floor and put the room in order. When each child had done all he could to help, he came to join the group on the rug.

The main theme of the following discussion was the wording and planning of an invitation to extend to the kindergarten. Various suggestions were given, as: Come to our movie; We hope you will come to see our movie; We want you to see our movie. The teacher suggested that sometimes invitations were sent in rhyme, like a little song.

She then asked if anyone had a suggestion. Many attempts were made and the two following really took shape.

Will you come! Will you come!
On the run! On the run!
To see our movie! To see our movie!
It will be fun! It will be fun!

The Three Bears
You will see.
Come to the Movie
And sit with me.

This last idea made an immediate appeal. The last lines seemed to come more or less as an accident. But the idea of sending an individual invitation and having an individual guest pleased the children. It was to be sent as a letter.

After a little stretch, reading numbers from the board and taking a corresponding number of jumps, hops and stoops, the children were ready to go to work on the next unit of their plans.

To make possible greater individual help, and to allow each child to develop as closely as possible at his maximum rate, the children were divided into three major groups. The classes were named for individuals in each group. The name of the class was changed frequently, and the children were shifted from group to group as a need was felt. This was done not only to recognize accelerations or retardations, but to eliminate any feeling of inferiority or superiority among the individuals or groups. Different books and materials were used in each case to make it impossible or at least difficult to check up on the other class.

Theodore's class set to work immediately to learn to write on the blackboard part of the message that had been planned. They worked in the smaller room of the first grade unit.

Allan's class got their primers to review the story of Little Sambo, and to organize it into various scenes to be cut for posters.

James' class found materials to use in cutting silhouettes. These were mounted on unprinted newspaper. Each scene from the story of The Three Bears was to be mounted on a separate sheet. The scenes had been selected the day before with the help of their books.

Having worked for about twenty minutes, the children that had been writing arranged their chairs for a reading time. They tried out for the various parts in The Three Little Pigs, to see which ones could more closely imitate the tone of voice and the mannerisms of each character.

Allan's class felt that they had their ideas for the various posters of Little Sambo well in mind, and they were ready to attack the cutting and arranging of characters and properties, with vim.

James' class used the blackboard to practice writing the titles of the

RHYTHM INSTRUMENTS ADD TO JOY IN MUSIC

three stories, since these would be needed in making programs, and also in writing the invitations.

As the groups finished their work, opportunity was given for them to go to the lavatories. Tomato juice was served from a buffet table informally, as they returned. A center was established for choric verse, which the children joined a few at a time after they had finished drinking the juice.

A great deal had been accomplished, much effort had been expended during the last hour, and the children were ready and eager to go to the floor below for music. The children's music interest lately was in a rhythm orchestra. The teacher had the rhythm sticks ready, and the children, after greeting her, found places about the room. Different meters were tapped while the children were seated. Then they tried to see if they could walk and tap the meter with the sticks. Bells and tambourines were used to find the strong beat in each measure. All the children took part. Songs about animals were sung and dramatized; also miscellaneous songs were selected by the children.

The children returned to their classroom after music to put on wraps for an outdoor play period. About thirty minutes were spent out-of-doors in vigorous play. There was play on the junglegym, the turning bars, the teeter, the balance boards and the jumping board. Some children entered into dramatic play with big packing boxes and boards, and on a big pile of logs. Other children played games; as, stoop tag and the hen and her chickens.

Following play time came preparation for dinner. After the noon meal and the rest period were over, the children tried out some of the movie posters they had made in the morning. One group had been promised a trip to the library to look through Mother Goose and other books for suitable verses to use for motion pictures. The other two groups had a most joyous, in fact hilarious time, enjoying for the first time the funny gyrations of their characters.

In addition to a good time, very valuable suggestions were given for pasting down parts that moved too much, and loosening arms, legs, ears, or parts of objects when more movement would give greater charm or fun. Objects pasted here and there with a little puff in the middle cast good shadows.

We also discovered that by moving the flashlight in various ways, quite different results were given. Moving the light up and down gave a getting up and stooping down effect. Moving the light back and forth quickly gave a shivering effect, required each time Sambo was approached by a tiger. Moving the light in a circular fashion gave a running reaction, again much required in these stories.

Three o'clock came much too soon this day, but we had more days of fun and preparation ahead of us and therefore our good-byes were as happy as usual.

AN OCTOBER DAY

Second Grade

Number enrolled: 22
Number present: 20

Eight-fifteen and the first school car had arrived. Several children came bounding into the room bearing their tickets which showed they had passed the daily inspection at the doctor's office. "Um! How's the jelly? It sure smells good." They were at once attracted to the two large bags of grapes and apples which had been dripping during the night. The children had had an excursion to the country on the previous day and had experienced a glorious time washing and preparing the fruit for cooking.

After inspecting the bags, and commenting on the "lots of juice," one child cared for the bird, another fed the mice, while another fed and chatted with Polynesia, a much beloved parrot that is frequently loaned to the school. As other children came in, they too inspected the bags and fruit juice, and then set to work on the construction of small mail trucks, mail boats, a post office made of apple boxes, and some small doll furniture. Some went on to designing covers for the stamp books they were making, while others pasted stamps, brought from home, in their books. A donation of Japanese stamps for everyone from our little Japanese girl, caused great enthusiasm. Others used clay or painted at the easels.

At the close of the work period, a conference followed. Usually the needs and accomplishments of the morning's work is the basis for discussion, but this morning, the jelly making was the chief concern. Several children had brought recipes for grape jelly, and the simplest one had been made into a chart and was ready for use. The recipe was consulted and discussed. The next step was to measure the juice. The group donned their smocks and gathered in a circle about the tables, while the children took turns measuring the juice with a standard cup. On the day before, they had discussed measuring cups, pints, and quarts. The recipe called for one cup of sugar to one cup of juice; so after finding out how much juice there was, an equal amount of sugar was measured. Two of the group put the juice on an electric grill in the room. The hands on a picnic plate clock were set so that the time needed for cooking could be figured.

A discussion of the need for sterilizing the glasses followed. Some children filled a dish pan with water, while others washed the glasses and placed them in the pan to sterilize. Others went to the lavatory to prepare for mid-morning lunch of fruit juice and crackers. This was served in the usual informal style of helping oneself as each returned to the classroom.

When finished with juice, each took out his reading rack and reader. Each child selected the book he wished to read or had been reading previously. Those who wanted to begin new books, chose them from the room bookshelves and took them to the teacher for approval. In this way guidance was given in selecting books that were suitable to the ability of the individual. The books available represented a wide range in degree of difficulty with a wealth of easy material so that each child might be able to travel at his own pace without discouragement of competition. There was also a wide variety of material to choose from, so that individual tastes in reading content might be satisfied. A tagboard filing card for each child served as a record of the books read. The teacher noted books completed on this card. If a book proved too difficult and the child turned to another volume, the number of pages read was recorded. The teacher also made occasional notes on reading habits and abilities. This period lasted for a half-hour, as the teacher moved about, listening to an individual read, or enjoying some humorous bit, or helping some pupils attack and sound out new words. Toward the end of the reading time, a few of the children asked if they might read to other children; so there were several groups of twos reading to each other.

A half-hour of outdoor activity followed with lively play on the log pile, or in self-organized ball games, while some had great fun raking and piling leaves, then jumping in them. With outdoor play over and wraps removed, the cry arose, "How's the jelly? What do we do now?" The group assembled and three children were asked to add the sugar to the juice. Others removed the glasses from the boiling water by using tongs, and placed them on trays ready for the jelly. While the juice and sugar cooked, three game centers were suggested by the teacher. Some children played India; others played a number game using dominoes as the combinations to be added; and the third group used real coins. In this group one child who was advanced in under-standing of arithmetic gave each child a problem in imaginary purchas-ing and then asked him to select and add the coins needed. The teacher interrupted the games for a few minutes to show the children that the juice was ready to be removed. A discussion of how to test had taken place the day before. Time on the real clock in the room was noted, and by looking at the make-believe clock, they could figure out how much time it had taken to cook the jelly. Now that the juice was ready, each child left his game long enough to fill three glasses as the teacher care-fully supervised the process. One glass was for the child, another for his mother, and the third to be left at school for children who might be ill and absent during the winter. "I'm going to get sick often!" was the laughing remark of several.

With the juice safely poured into the glasses, games ended, and a clean-up committee was appointed for washing the cooking utensils. This was done by the children in the diet kitchen. The others went to the lavatories to get ready for dinner. After hand washing and combing of hair was completed they returned to the room for a few minutes of poetry. Those who had been at work in the kitchen soon joined the others and made ready for luncheon, too. At twelve-thirty the group went to the children's dining room where the main meal of the day was served. Hearty appetites and lively conversation were much in evidence. The meal was served in as homelike style as possible, and social visiting and good spirit prevailed. When all were finished, the children returned to their room where cots had been set up by the janitor. The shades were drawn. Each child got his own sheet and blanket from his com-partment in the cupboard, made his bed, removed shoes and settled down for a half-hour. After this time of quiet and relaxation, the teacher read several chapters in the beloved "Story of Dr. Doolittle."

The teacher asked individual children to get up by writing on the board such suggestions as "Mike, you may put on your shoes," or "Lois, please get up now." When all were ready, with sheets and blankets put back in the cupboard, and cots folded and stacked in the corridor, the children gathered for a brief discussion about what more they needed to do to the jelly. Plans were made for the next morning for the melting of the paraffin and covering the jelly. The question of what paraffin is made of and why it is put on jelly, entered into their conversation. One child mentioned that it was "too bad John was absent for he had missed the fun of helping make the jelly," but another suggested we could take a glass to him and also write letters telling him how we made our jelly. With eagerness on the part of most of the children, they set to work writing simple letters to John. One child addressed a large envelope, and when finished, each put his letter in the envelope. Teddy volunteered to mail the letters on his way home. Armin went to the school office to purchase the necessary stamps to carry John's letter.

The remaining half hour was spent on the playground, most of the children engaging in self-organized dramatic play about the pirates on "Dr. Doolittle's" ship. The junglegym served as the sea-worthy craft. Others played on the seesaw or watched younger brothers or sisters at play in the nursery school sand box. Two-fifty found the school cars pulling into the driveway. The children assembled at the gate to await the arrival of their particular car and to leave for home after a happy day of learning, experiencing and living together.

A TUESDAY IN MAY

Third Grade

Number enrolled: 25
Number present: 24

Upon coming into the room this May morning the children went at once to their committee groups to participate in their particular work toward completing plans for the Third Grade Fair which was to be held the following morning at ten thirty. These committee groups were the classes as they were divided for reading, and each group was working on a different interest. One group had planted seeds and bulbs and was preparing potted plants for sale. Another group had made puppets and a stage and was going to give an original nature play they had worked out. The other group, with the help of all the children, had studied rather intensively about maple syrup and maple sugar. After having corresponded with two firms in Vermont, they had bought maple sugar cakes and maple syrup, had made booklets telling about the maple sugar, and had made recipes to sell. So this morning there were many plans to complete and a great deal of work to do.

At nine o'clock the children all went to their music class. The music room was on the first floor and a teacher went with them. Interest was held in the work of the day and the discussion continued as they walked along. Spring songs were used, and the music period was a happy time.

When the group came back to the room again, the children working on the puppets had some finishing work to do with them. One puppet needed an apron made and another needed the hair sewed on. There were seven working in this group. Some added new ideas to the complicated strings that worked the puppets.

The group arranging the garden sale had their flowers pretty well ready. Two boys finished the planting, and the rest cooperated with those getting the booklets put together. The stories for the booklets had been composed by the children, stencils had been cut by the teacher, and all the children had helped with the mimeographing. The covers had been designed in art class, and the children had cut the stencil and run the covers off on bright colored paper, using the mimeograph. This morning the pages of the booklets had to be put together. Each part was put in a separate pile, and the children went to work. It required skill to get the pages in order, for they discovered they had not numbered the pages, and so it was necessary to read parts of the stories. The matter of punching the holes for the brads required so much strength that the engineer, who came into the room at that time, assisted. There were fifteen children working. The books were almost finished in the thirty minutes.

Most of the group went to the home economics laboratory on the third floor, at ten o'clock. There the children took turns pouring the maple syrup into half-pint, pint, and quart containers. They took turns also in putting on the covers. There was discussion as they worked about the prices that should be charged for the syrup, and they decided that a quart should sell for less than two pints, if they were sold separately, because it was less trouble to prepare a quart. When the syrup was poured, two girls washed the funnels and cleared away the tables, leaving the jars of syrup in neat rows. Three boys carried the empty tin cans and boxes to the basement. The rest of the group went back to the room and finished some work in their arithmetic workbooks. One little girl worked alone with a teacher, using the cards for reviewing subtraction facts.

At ten-thirty all the children went out on the playground. The entire play period was used in making definite plans for the arrangement of booths for the sale. The group that was going to give the puppet show measured the space and set the stakes for the tent which was to be placed in the back part of the fair grounds. The children decided to place the booths selling the maple syrup products and the plants at the outside of the fair grounds. At the close of the outdoor period the pupils went to the lavatories, washed their hands, and afterward drank tomato juice in their room.

During the spelling period, which followed, a review of the following words was made: leaves, flowers, syrup, expensive, puppets. These new words were studied: buckets, boil, sounds, amount. The teacher wrote each new word on the board. After the word has been discussed as to syllables and sounds, she erased the word and the children wrote it on their papers. Then the teacher wrote the word on the board again for comparison with the word the children had written. The review words were spelled orally by the children and written in the same way. At the close of the study period, the children found their spelling books, and the teacher dictated the words.

During the period set aside for social studies, the group working on the puppet show moved the little stage into the art room, which was next to the third grade room, and went with their teacher to have a last rehearsal. The group that had worked out the flower and garden booth finished a story they were reading from "Peter and Polly in Spring," which told about the process of taking the maple sap from the trees. The other reading class read from the booklets they had helped make. Each child chose the story he wished and read orally.

At twelve o'clock the chairs and all materials were put back into place, and all of the children except three went to the toilet room and got ready for lunch. These three girls who did not stay at school for the luncheon went outside to play while they waited for the school car to take them home.

The noon meal was served in the children's dining-room, second and third grades sharing the room from twelve to twelve-thirty. The children sat in small groups of six or eight, with teachers at some of the tables. The dining-room had been newly furnished by the Parents' Council with early American tables and chairs; and the children were very eager to add drapes, pottery and pictures. The earnings from the Third Grade Fair were to be used for this purpose. Part of the conversation at the table concerned the size of possible earnings at the Fair, and how far the money would go in securing the materials desired.

When the children in the dining-room had finished their lunch, they went back to their room to get the individual bags containing their sheets and blankets. Then they went to one of the first grade rooms which had been aired, the shades lowered, and cots set up for rest.

At one-thirty the children engaged in individual activities. Several had spelling corrections to make. A few children went to the library. Some read books there, and three checked books out to take home. Two girls and two boys went with a teacher to finish painting a booth in the manual training room. Two girls made some price tags.

The whole group went outside to play at one-fifty. They played together—"Fox and Chickens" and "Three Deep." A teacher played in the games and the pupils were very energetic and played hard. As they came in every child took a drink at the fountain.

The French teacher came to the room for the French lesson at two-twenty. After the close of the lesson there was a short discussion with the room director as to the time the "Fair" products and materials would have to be carried outside the following morning. Children volunteered to help with the work they thought they could do best, and a few last reminders were given from one to another to make sure that everything would be taken care of when the sale began. The children then hurried outside to the school cars.

A MORNING IN NOVEMBER

Fourth Grade

Number enrolled: 20
Number present: 19

As the boys and girls came into the room, they went about selecting their lunch from the menu on the blackboard. One food was selected from each group, thereby assuring a balanced meal. This routine had become so habitual that it required none of the teacher's time. As soon as the pieces of paper on which they had written their menu were turned over to the child who was checking them, the boys and girls felt free to do what interested them most. A few chose to read; others worked on drawings begun the day before; some looked at the animal map which the class had been making; more than half were chatting in a pleasant tone to each other or to the teacher.

At nine o'clock the teacher sat down at the large table in the center of the room, around which the children's tables were arranged.

"It is time for our news reports, boys and girls. Let's put all other work aside."

Without hurrying, the children became attentive and several hands were raised. Thornton was chosen to speak.

"Yesterday afternoon I went with Mother and Dad to see Mrs. Smith. There were several kinds of stuffed animals in this house. Some of them had been killed by Mr. Smith; others had been given to him."

"What kinds were they?"

This and many other questions followed. Then a boy told of similar animals he had seen at the museum. Another child had read in the paper that the Giant Baby Panda which had died earlier in the year could now be seen in the same museum. The Student Cabinet representative, Nancy, was then called upon to report the previous day's meeting. Among other things she said that she had volunteered for the fourth grade to explain their animal map in assembly, and that if the class wanted to do it the next assembly date could be theirs. At first the others were not enthusiastic, but when it was explained that the program would be only a report of the work they had done, the responsibility was accepted very seriously.

"Our time is going by very rapidly. Don't you think it would be well to hear from the groups who read stories yesterday?" suggested the teacher. "Will you need to have short group meetings first to remind yourselves of your plans?"

Groups two and three went to their leaders and began discussing their plans; group one looked over their stories. Within three minutes all worth-while discussion seemed to have been completed; and the teacher asked which group would like to report first. Group three was chosen first as the teacher knew they had a fine report and needed the encouragement of an eager audience. Although the four boys who made up the group were slow readers, they told in a very interesting way two short stories their leader had chosen. After the report they asked if there were any questions.

"Did the book tell about any other animals in the far North?"

"Do the walruses eat seals, too?"

"What does forage mean?"

When these were answered, the group leader asked if there were any comments.

"It would have been better if John hadn't leaned against the board all the time."

"Sometimes it is hard to hear what Pat says."

"I thought the last story was very well told."

There was generous agreement to this comment and a member of the class suggested that it was good enough to be told in assembly. When asked if the members of the group would like to tell the story in assembly, they were quite willing.

In a similar way groups one and two reported. The teacher then asked the group if there were unfinished plans that should be provided for during the morning. The class responded with the comment that the map needed more animals on it and should have some names on it. The class then decided to cut letters that could be placed on the map, marking all the oceans and continents. Several children agreed to help get the map ready. One child suggested making some small animals for a table display, like the Japanese paper animals that were to be seen in the display case in the hall. The teacher suggested they take that idea to the art teacher in the afternoon. One of the group leaders asked to choose another animal story for his group to read. The other group leaders thought they had better do the same. So while the leaders went about finding the stories, the teacher and the remainder of the group began the work on the map. Some cut out animals, others tried to find "new" animals to put on those continents that the class felt needed more. A few worked out the size of letters that would look well on the map and began cutting them.

A few minutes before ten all the work was put away in order for the group to go down to the music room. When asked what they would prefer doing during the period the music teacher was with them, the children asked to dramatize airplanes. The imagination that this and succeeding rhythms took was very enjoyable to the group. Finally the music teacher asked them if they knew a song she had prepared to sing for them. It was a new song about animals of the forest. They immediately asked to learn it.

Fruit juice was waiting for the group when they returned to their room. After the music hour, three days a week, the children had become accustomed to studying words. Sixteen new words from the Newlon-Hanna list were presented for discussion and analysis. When asked if there were words the class wanted to add, one boy suggested some animal names that interested him. A member of the group who was cutting out letters thought all should learn to spell the names of the oceans and continents. It was decided to add the continents to this week's list and the oceans to the following week's work.

The time from ten fifty to eleven thirty was set aside for reading. For several days the questions arising in the conference time had been answered at the reading time through group research. As the group leaders had already selected stories, they were asked to put the names of the books and the page numbers of the stories on the board. Then each child read the story selected for his group, the teacher moving among them to help as was needed. As the group finished reading, each one assembled in a corner of the room to discuss the story and plan a report, or perhaps to read it aloud. The reports were to be made at the next day's conference period.

At eleven-thirty the boys and girls went outside for forty-five minutes of play under supervision of the playground director. At twelve fifteen the children came in to wash hands and get ready for lunch. They were all looking forward to the period with the art teacher which was to follow lunch.

A MORNING IN THE SUMMER SESSION

Fifth Grade

Number enrolled: 24
Number present: 24

As the fifth grade children came in one morning in summer school, several got out their science scrapbooks to work on them. Each had made his own cover design and was working it out in his own individual manner. Some were using chalk or crayon and others were cutting their cover designs out of paper. Several needed help from the art teacher, so took their materials into the art room to work.

Other children arrived with collections of leaves to be used in various ways in their scrapbooks. Some children asked the teacher for help in getting leaves ready for pressing. Others put their leaves into containers of water to keep them fresh until a later date when they would make blueprints or splatter prints of them for their scrapbooks.

Still other children arrived with travel booklets or maps and either showed them to classmates or started getting information from them related to their work in social studies on interesting spots in America. Two children brought insects which they were interested in studying. The teacher and several children found material in the bookcase on the various subjects desired. A few went to the library to find additional material.

At nine twenty the children all put away their individual jobs to work together in choric verse. Children first chose review poems in which they could show the rhythm with some physical activity. They walked to such verses as "Hannibal crossed the Alps," "The Grand Old Duke of York," and "We be the king's men." They pulled imaginary bell ropes to "The little white chapel is ringing its bell," and did an Indian step to "Beat on the buckskins."

As the class had enjoyed one Jonathan Bing poem very much, the teacher presented a new one she had found. After the teacher had read the poem she asked who the different speakers were in the story. Then the children were asked to listen again to what each said. The third time the poem was given children volunteered to take the parts of the soldier, the archbishop, and Jonathan Bing. After the poem had been read several times with different children taking individual parts, the class was closed.

Next the children turned to their jobs in social studies. Each child had been reading and writing stories about interesting spots of America. From the first week of the session they had been interested in showing their mothers what they had been doing. It happened that several of their mothers were themselves students in the summer session of the college. Several ways had been suggested such as individual books about the places chosen, a dramatization of an imaginary trip around America, or a scene in a travel bureau. Some objections had been raised to all the suggestions.

Today the teacher introduced their problem by asking them if they could think of any other place where people talked a good deal about vacations besides in a travel bureau. One child immediately suggested the Union Station. The teacher asked if they could work out a dramatization in the Union Station which would tell about interesting summer playgrounds in America. All began enthusiastically suggesting how it could be done.

Out of the discussion plans were evolved for a scene in the Union Station. A trainman would call a train from the East, and the people who had taken trips to eastern points would come in from the train. Some would be talking to one another about points they had visited, and some would talk to the people who met them. Then other people would come in to buy tickets west. These people would be talking to their friends who came with them about the proposed trips. After tickets were bought the western train would be called and all would go out. The children who had studied spots in the South were to meet those coming in, bring friends to the train, or take the parts of the ticket agent, and the person at the information desk. Before the class closed, a list was made of the characters each would take, how they would dress, and what topics they would discuss. Then the class went down to the music room for rhythms.

As soon as the children were seated on the floor near the piano, choices were given for the first part of the period. Walking to music with full, precise Dalcroze arm movements to indicate the meter was the first activity. Changing the accent and the movement one measure after the music had changed proved to be challenging and afforded fun. The group was then divided into three, four, or five parts as indicated by the meter used and each group assigned a definite pulse on which to step; as, group one stepped on the first or accented pulse, group two stepped on the second beat, and so on. The suggestion was then given that instead of stepping the pulse of the meter, each group should improvise a rhythmic pattern of its own which it would step to an assigned phrase while hearing the given pattern of the music played. This required strenuous concentration and effort but the children worked at it until each group had succeeded. They enjoyed this activity. They now agreed that they were ready for some quieter enterprise. The last part of the period was given over to rhythmic pantomiming and dramatization of familiar songs.

On the way back from rhythms the children were given a few minutes

SUMMER SCHOOL BRINGS WATER PLAY

to go to the lavatory and to get a drink of water. When they returned to the room, they got ready for their arithmetic work.

The day before someone had asked how much farther from Chicago it was to San Francisco than to New York, and they had discovered how they could figure distances from the large wall map. A child explained the scale of miles and another had found from the map that the scale was 45 miles to the inch. There had followed a discussion of how to use the scale of miles.

Today the teacher gave each child a paper on which were the names of ten pairs of cities followed by blanks for writing the distances between them in inches and in miles. Individual children came to the map, measured the distance between different cities, and gave the information to the group. Distances were taken to the nearest inch. Then the group spent a half-hour in working out individually the actual distance between the cities.

When the half-hour was over, all work was laid aside in the room. Instead of going to the playground for games, plans had been made to go to the nearby beach for swimming. Children dressed at school and then walked to the beach. At the beach the boys and girls were divided into three groups. Some swam, several waded, and others played games on the beach. After forty-five minutes of fun the children walked back to the building to dress before going home for the day.

A WEDNESDAY IN APRIL

Sixth Grade

Number enrolled: 22
Number present: 22

"Today is the day we pour!" "Let's get ready now!" "Did the plaster of Paris come?"

Such were the remarks of some sixth graders as they came into the room. This was the event to which the group had been looking forward for days. At the back of the room five boys were somewhat proudly surveying a huge diorama of Switzerland. This was their work and their idea, and now the time had come to put on the finishing touches.

Two boys interested in the study of electricity had brought their electric trains to school sometime before, and had run them in the back of the room. The class had been studying present-day living in Europe, and one group was preparing a report on Switzerland. One of the boys suggested that they construct a Swiss scene and make it alive by running the trains through mountain passes and a tunnel. This idea was eagerly seized upon by the other boy, and they invited three of their friends to help them out.

For three weeks the boys had worked together, drawing plans, building a table, elevating and banking the track so that the train would stay on the curves, building the mountains out of wadded newspapers, figuring out the size and shape of the tunnel, and making sure that the trains would run. Some of the boys wanted to start pouring right away, but it was agreed to wait until 12:45 when the art teacher could help them, as the group had not used plaster of Paris before and wanted to do it right.

Then the children settled down to the problem of choosing their menu for lunch. This activity is a regular part of the hygiene program in the middle grades. The children chose a meat or meat substitute, vegetable, salad, bread and butter, dessert and milk. Those who did not care for meat or salad were allowed to choose an extra vegetable. It was the turn of a boy to act as secretary, and he recorded the choices and took the menu slip down to the dietician.

The first period was scheduled for arithmetic and was set aside for individual work. Most of the children worked in their workbooks, each on a different aspect of fractions or decimals. They had started out in two groups and now had twenty-two, each individual progressing at his own rate of speed. From time to time there was a small group at the board with a teacher discussing some difficulties and problems common to all of them. Then they would return to their seats as they felt that their difficulties were smoothed out, and continue to work under their own direction.

Near the end of the period the teacher asked each one in turn what he had learned. Many had learned small details and one or two had been successful in overcoming a hitherto major difficulty. Individual plans and suggestions for the next work period were made jointly by children and teacher.

A teacher came in at that moment for the English activities, and was greeted with smiles and expressions of joy, for today was set aside for work on their newspaper, *The National News* (described in a separate record at the end of this sketch). Some children had already put away their arithmetic and were writing original poems or completing news assignments. Others, after a short conference with a teacher, took pads and pencils and started out on their rounds of the classrooms in search of news and other material for the newspaper. A few who had finished their written work were discussing the arrangement of the paper and the illustrations. The period went so quickly that it was past time to go outside before the children noticed it.

At ten-fifteen the group split, the girls dressing in gym suits and sandals for dancing, the boys putting on sports clothing for outside play. On Mondays and Wednesdays the girls of the fifth and sixth grades enjoyed dancing together, while the boys of those grades had supervised activities on the playground. Today the dancing class was particularly concerned with developing graceful and rhythmical form in walking, running, and leaping. The girls asked at the end if they could do their Russian dance, which they executed very skillfully.

The boys, meanwhile, had organized into two teams, had chosen their captains, and were engaging in a game of softball under the supervision of the director of physical education. One boy recovering from an operation and another with a heart ailment were acting as officials. The director frequently, and especially when mistakes were made, gave

BOYS DEVELOP SKILL IN BASEBALL

suggestions and instructions that would improve the individual skill and technique and also the teamwork in the game. The game ended in a close score of 8 to 9. Judging from their remarks the boys seemed to be well satisfied with their efforts and were looking forward to Thursday when both girls and boys would engage in such activities as softball, soccer, kickball and others. On Tuesdays, Thursdays and Fridays, boys and girls played together.

The social studies period at eleven o'clock was one of great activity. Some were making maps of European countries, others were reading to find answers to key questions, or outlining material for reports. Near the close of the period the boys at the back of the room carefully covered up the train tracks and other vulnerable portions of the Swiss scene so that they would not be smeared with plaster of Paris. A number of newspapers were brought up from the basement and spread around the table to keep the floor clean. At last everything was in readiness and all washed up for lunch.

Two children had previously set the tables in the children's dining room and were waiting for the others as they came down. The boys and girls formed in line at the cafeteria counter and took their lunch on trays to the dining room next door. There was an informal seating arrangement in groups of six or eight at a table, divided today into two tables of girls and two of boys. Most of the children were hungry and some went back for second servings of vegetables and milk.

After lunch there was a ten-minute free period when the children could direct themselves. Some of them wandered around the building looking at posters and displays in other rooms. Others dressed and went outside to watch the Junior High School boys play soccer. The only restriction was that this was to be a quiet period with no violent activity.

At 12:45 the art teacher came in to help with the plaster of Paris. Two large pans were borrowed from the cafeteria, water and plaster of Paris were mixed and the fun began. The boys thought that it was better than making mud pies. They soon found out, however, that the material was much more difficult and had to be handled quickly or it would become hard. Those who did not pour were working in the art room drawing pictures and making clay figures, but one by one they drifted in to watch the activity. Before long most of the class was helping. Even so, it was two o'clock before the work was finished—time to go to the library.

Three of the boys volunteered to stay down and clean up while the others went to the library. Some continued to read books which they had previously chosen; others were guided in the selection of books by librarian and teacher; and still others went at once to the magazine rack to find *Popular Science, The American Boy,* and other favorite magazines. After such an active day a quiet library period was enjoyed by all.

SIXTH GRADE PUBLISHES A NEWSPAPER

As there was no play club after school today, the children went home, some in the school buses, some in private cars, and others in public conveyances, to share with families and playmates the experiences of the day.

THE NATIONAL NEWS

On certain mornings throughout the year the halls and bulletin boards of the school displayed large, colorful posters bearing such reminders as, "Get Your Copy! Four cents." These gay posters had been made by the fifth and sixth grade children in their art classes to advertise their newspaper, *The National News*. This paper, published several times a year, was the work of the fifth and sixth grade classes in English. It was a typewritten copy of from five to eight sheets, mimeographed, arranged, and stapled by the children.

In the beginning the classes listed all of the topics likely to be found in a good school newspaper. For suggestions they referred to *My Weekly Reader, Young America*, local newspapers, and publications from other schools. After a long list had been made, each child chose the topic in which he was most interested as his particular responsibility.

The compiled list included the following suggestions. All, of course, were not included in each issue, and in some numbers certain topics were given special emphasis.

World news	Holiday customs
Excursions	French stories (from the French classes)
Sports	Interviews with teachers and children
Room activities	Unusual facts
Book reviews	Inquiring reporter's questions
Movie news	Recipes
Cartoons	"How to keep well" column
Illustrations	School calendar for the month
Maps	Student Cabinet news
Assemblies	All school activities, such as festivals
Personal news	Customs in other lands as, "A Swedish Dinner"
Riddles	Individual experiences, such as "Fun on Skis" or
Jokes	"Our House Boat"
Puzzles	Advertisements
Origin of holidays	

Being reporters and visiting the various classrooms with pads and pencils in search of news, appealed to several. Interviewing teachers and children who had returned from vacation trips or who had had unusual experiences, was an opportunity for others. Reporters with a "nose for news" conducted the column containing personal items. Inquiring reporters besieged teachers and children alike with such questions as "What do you want most for Christmas?" "What is your favorite sport?" "Where would you like to spend your summer vacation?"

A variety of interests, however, allowed for tasks appealing to all. The artists in the group took over the work of designing the heading and providing the illustrations. It was found that small illustrations in keeping with the content or season of the year, added life and interest to the page. The art teacher gave help and suggestions as needed.

A few articles of world interest appeared in each issue. The sixth grade, interested in current world affairs, made many fine contributions. Occasionally these were accompanied by illuminating maps and diagrams. Many members of the group considered this type of article very important, and were always on the alert for items of interest.

Others centered their interests in the school world about them, and made a real effort to be "up to the minute" on what was going on in all grades as well as plans made for the future. It was found that "future events" make real news. Excursions, a maple syrup sale, a garden sale, the May Festival, activities of the Student Cabinet, the sixth grade play, *Waggery Town*, graduation plans, and many similar activities were to be found on every hand.

While *The National News* was sponsored by two grades, it attempted, in a general way, to represent the school and to appeal to children of all ages. It was soon learned that "names make news," and that a really successful issue of the paper should contain names of some children in all grades. Such columns as the personal news, news flashes, future ambitions of our National classmates, and new friends at National, added many names.

Another effort made to catch the interest of all ages was to ask the readers to participate actively by doing such things as draw pictures or write the last line to a jingle. Occasionally readers were asked to connect dots to make a picture, write the answer to a riddle, work a puzzle, or write the name of a person described.

In every group are to be found a few "class poets." Several verses were printed in every issue of the paper, and at times there was a full poetry page. Some of the contributions appear below.

February

February is a month of frost and slush,
Birthdays coming in a rush!
Washington, Lincoln and others great,
Almost a birthday for every date!
And then comes Valentine's day, too,
When Valentine greetings are sent to
  you.
But I will not be the one to sigh,
When this famous month goes rolling by,
For then Sweet Spring is on its way—
We can expect it any day!

J. K.

April

It's been raining, raining all day long,
The birds have stopped their little song,
Now it's clearing up, I think—
The sky is turning a bluish pink.

J. D.

Spring House Cleanin'

Mother's spring house cleanin'
And puttin' things away
  And I can't find my baseball
Or anythin' today.

She put away my pencils
And she put away my bat
  'Cause mother's spring house cleanin';
I can't even find my hat!

In boxes big and small
She put everythin' away
  And things are in a turmoil
'Cause it's spring house cleanin' day.

M. H.

Sports held first place in the interest of many, particularly the boys. All games and athletic events were covered by energetic reporters. Book and movie reviews were very popular with the girls. Good books and motion pictures were recommended. Cartoons, individual experiences, holiday customs, and unusual facts were contributed in great numbers. With the school newspaper as an incentive, the children read more widely and became more discriminating in recognizing topics of real interest. At the suggestion of one child several short animal stories written in French were included.

All contributions were discussed and commented on by the class. All of the material offered could not be used and so selections had to be made by the group. This work called for judgment made on the basis of interest, style, originality, and good English. After the material was chosen and typed time was devoted to the arrangement. Here something was learned about the "make-up" of a newspaper, such as the location of outstanding articles, correct groupings, and the place of illustrations.

The fact that *The National News* sold for four cents a copy added great stimulus to the venture. Each time two business managers were elected, one from each grade. These two leaders were to check on all expenses and profits and were elected to their offices because of their ability in arithmetic. Even so, they were given the help of the class, for the business end of the project provided work for the entire group.

All paper and stencils used were bought from the school store. A bill was received giving the exact amount purchased. This expense, of course, had to be subtracted from the profits. With cost in mind, the children estimated the number of papers which should be sold so that a fair profit might be netted. To add to the profits, advertising space was sold, according to the prices listed below.

IT PAYS TO ADVERTISE
ADVERTISE IN THE NATIONAL
NEWS

Prices for advertising

For ⅛ of page 7c
For ¼ of page 13c
For ⅜ of page 20c
For ½ of page 26c
For full page 50c

National News 4c a copy
For particulars speak to any member of
the sixth grade.

Space was sold to the "Supreme Insurance Company" operated by the eighth grade, to the faculty committee in charge of the Clare Tree Major Plays to advertise their productions, to the College girls advertising different activities, and to committees in charge of various sales.

After all materials were paid for and a receipt sent to the class, the remaining money was deposited in the school bank. With each issue this amount increased and was drawn on from time to time to fulfill a sudden and worthy desire on the part of the class.

PART IV

Group Records of Progress in a Few Important Skills

RECORDING PROGRESS IN TERMS
OF SPECIFIC SKILLS

THE school does not advocate the integration of all activities in large group enterprises or "units of work." Many incidental activities and short-lived interests have great value both for individuals and groups. Fields like music, art, and literature afford vast opportunities for pleasure and enrichment of experience outside the particular studies which the group may have chosen to make. Skills like arithmetic, reading, and spelling require some systematic practice in addition to the experience afforded in practical activities.

Group records of progress are included in Part IV of this volume for English, including composition and spelling, for reading, and for arithmetic. Such records have been made in the senior kindergarten and grades one to six. Part V describes individual records of progress which are kept at all levels.

The group records of progress beginning in senior kindergarten follow a form that has been used in courses of study for other schools. They list books and materials and types of activities for children of varying abilities in each grade, and also include some probable outcomes in information, attitudes, appreciations, habits and skills. In making the record for each skill, as arithmetic, teachers have summarized all the practical experience that children have gained in that skill through their various units of experience. In addition to the summary of activities carried on in group projects, the record for each skill also includes incidental activities growing out of children's spontaneous interests, and reference to systematic practice and testing wherever this has been carried on. The records were made first in parallel column form, and later for convenience in printing and reading were recast in outline form.

Such records will change from year to year as better materials become available, and investigation and experiment suggest improved procedures. They will also reflect particular interests of each new group of children.

355

DEVELOPMENT OF READING READINESS IN THE KINDERGARTEN

AN OUTSTANDING growth in language power should be one significant outcome of the kindergarten activities. Through spontaneous informal conversation about interesting experiences, through guided discussions related to children's projects, through dramatic play, through literature and creative composition, the kindergarten offers numberless opportunities for growth of vocabulary and power of expression. It is largely through this expanding understanding and use of language that the kindergarten prepares for reading and for the composition work of the elementary school.

Much of the content of children's early reading material centers about nature, home and community life. The kindergarten builds readiness for reading by providing experiences in these areas. Various pets are raised and observed. Plants bud and blossom under the children's care. Playing in the woods, by the lake and in the spacious outdoor playground during the different seasons of the year gives contacts with birds, elements, and growing plants.

The community in which the school is located is rich in opportunities for visits to harbors, lighthouse, airports, fire stations, electric and steam trains, stores, and other centers. The school is well equipped with materials for use in dramatic play. Thus, through firsthand experiencing, dramatic play, discussion, and through use of picture books and story books which are read to the children, concepts are developed which make it possible for them to interpret clearly and with rich association the material they will find later in books.

Occasionally, a few children who have high mental ages and previous experience in nursery school and junior kindergarten show a spontaneous interest and a high degree of readiness for reading. This interest is fostered and guided.

References on Reading Readiness

Betts, E. A. Prevention and Correction of Reading Difficulties, pages 18-26. 1936, Row Peterson.

Harrison, Lucile. Reading Readiness. 1936, Houghton Mifflin.

Hildreth, Gertrude. Learning the Three R's, Chapter V. 1936, Educational Publishers, Inc.

Lane, Robert. The Progressive Elementary School, Chapter V. 1938, Houghton Mifflin.

McKee, Paul. Reading and Literature in the Elementary School, pages 99-100. 1934, Houghton Mifflin.

Reed, Mary E. An Investigation of Practices in First Grade Admission and Promotion. 1927, Bureau of Publications, Teachers College, Columbia University.

Smith, Nila B., and others. Reading—A Tool for Learning. 1938, Association for Childhood Education.

Witty, Paul, and Kopel, David. Reading and the Educative Process. 1939, Ginn.

Language and Literature Experience in the Senior Kindergarten

A ACTIVITIES

I. Oral composition—individual.

A. Morning greetings.

As each child enters the room in the morning one of the teachers is always available to greet him and to make him feel that she is glad to see him. Very often this opportunity leads the child into telling of something that has happened at home—father gone on a trip, the purchase of a new car, or some trivial bit of information, such as, "We had strawberries on our corn flakes this morning." This contact enables the shy child to feel more free and to express himself more readily than he would if he were asked to participate in the conversation of a group of children.

B. Judging work.

In group discussions many children contribute in making suggestions or constructive criticisms of one another's work guided by questions, such as, "Why should John's boat be made pointed on the front?" "How can Julia make moccasins that will stay on her feet?" If interest is high, there is little need for stimulating verbal expression, but it takes artistic guidance on the part of the teacher to lead the conversation along worth-while channels and to give individuals opportunity that will make for individual growth.

C. Making plans.

The children gain freedom in language ability by being allowed to assist in the making of plans; such as planning for a trip to a farm, to the airport or the museum; planning for the making of cookies, or for giving a movie before another group.

D. Discussing common experiences.

Frequently the discussion of stories used in the group, of films the group has seen, or other experiences they have had together furnishes stimulus for worth-while language contributions.

E. Relating anecdotes.

The luncheon period with its informality and air of sociability brings forth the relating of personal anecdotes and humorous stories.

F. Dramatic play.

Dramatic play, rich in mood, and largely spontaneous, offers unlimited possibility in expressing of ideas, in creating of dialogue, and in the building up of vocabulary. Children will often use words or expressions not characteristic of their daily use of language, which they have heard in stories and which become their own when they relive the incidents and characters in dramatic play.

G. Creative composition of stories and verse.

Mood or experience may lead the child into creative expression of an original story, or bit of verse, or song.

II. **Oral composition—group.**

A. Correspondence.

At times occasions arise when the children feel the need of sending invitations for some affair. The group may compose an invitation to the first grade to see the baby guinea pigs which have just arrived or to the mothers asking them to attend a party planned for them.

If information is needed (such as, "On what day of the week may we visit the lighthouse?" or "Where can we get some pictures of planes?"), the children cooperate in dictating a letter which will bring the desired answer.

B. Group expression in story composition.

Following an experience which has been common to the group and which has made a deep impression on the children, the group may create together a story, a poem or a song.

III. **Language interests leading to beginning reading.**

A. Interest in names.

The kindergarten child soon begins to feel the need of learning to write his own name in order to label his drawings, woodwork and other belongings. Whenever he wants to write his name the teacher does it for him in manuscript writing on the blackboard or on a sheet of paper, and he watches her do it. In this way he is seeing the movements and forms in the process so that he may learn to form the letters correctly. When children are left to copy words, many poor habits arise because they have no imagery for procedure. The child uses crayons to write his name. The interest in learning to do this often carries over into writing his name on the blackboard. Nearly all of the children learn to recognize their own names and the names of their friends.

STORIES AND PICTURES PROVIDE STIMULUS FOR CONVERSATION

B. Need for labels.

As the year goes on, many types of labels prove necessary, such as the name of a boat, a train, or a store built of blocks. "To Mother" on a Christmas card or Valentine, "The Senior Kindergarten Movie," "Cookie Sale," are typical examples of the need for labels. The teacher writes these and they naturally serve as a basis for beginning reading.

C. Reminders and news notes.

Many situations arise where reading comes in naturally. As a reminder, the teacher may write out notes to be taken home; such as, "Wear rubbers to-morrow," "Bring recipe for jelly." From time to time sentences about interesting things that are going to happen, are put on the bulletin board; such as, "Thursday we go to the airport," "Bill will be six Tuesday." These notes are discussed and form a center of interest for reading.

D. Records of experiences.

As the year goes on some mature children who show especial interest, are exposed to more reading material and are given opportunity to evolve very simple stories following a common experience, such as:

"We had fun at the airport.
We saw the planes in the sky.
We saw the planes on the ground.
There were planes in the hangar.
I wish I could fly."

These little stories are often printed on charts, and are "read" by the children with great delight. Their reading, however, is chiefly by sentences. There is no formal drill in word recognition, but a few words and phrases of especial interest and importance are learned. No attempt is made to secure independent reading of new material.

B. Points on Which the Teacher Must Be Constantly Alert.

She must be an example in the linguistic development of her children by:

I. Using good diction.
II. Enunciating distinctly.
III. Using correct grammatical form.
IV. Having fluent speech.
V. Using well-modulated tones.
VI. Being sensitive to child's speech difficulties and helping him as intelligently as possible to overcome these.
VII. Helping child in every way to develop emotional stability and confidence so that he may gain in freedom of expression.

C. Books and Materials Used

I. All books and materials used form a basis for oral composition with the kindergarten child. Because of his inability to read, much of the information needed to carry on activities must come through the language contributions of the teachers and the parents.
II. Pictures relating to group interests, to children's individual experiences, and those to be enjoyed for their beauty only, are often incentives to language expression.
III. Excursions of all kinds and the objects seen lead to an abundance of conversation. The inhibited type of child not given to free verbal expression often forgets himself and becomes quite talkative when on an excursion.
IV. Things brought from home, nature materials, things the

children make, letters, postal cards, all furnish valuable stimulus for conversation at the kindergarten level.

V. Stories read or told to the children furnish much stimulus for conversation and creative effort in original stories or poetry. Some of the favorite stories which have been used and have been most conducive to discussion or have stimulated creative effort on the part of the children are from the following collections:

Aldis, Dorothy	Here, There & Everywhere	1928	Minton Balch
Aldis, Dorothy	Everything & Anything	1927	Minton Balch
Clark, Margery	Poppy Seed Cakes	1924	Doubleday
Fyleman, Rose	Fairies & Chimneys	1920	Doubleday
Milne, A. A.	When We Were Very Young	1924	Dutton
Tippett, James S.	I Live in a City	1929	Harper
Tippett, James S.	I Spend a Summer	1930	Harper
Tippett, James S.	I Go a-Traveling	1929	Harper
Thomsen, Gudrun Thorne	East o' the Moon and West o' the Sun	1912	Row Peterson

Some other books which are included in the kindergarten library are as follows:

Association for Childhood Education	Told under the Green Umbrella	1930	Macmillan
Association for Childhood Education	Sung under the Silver Umbrella	1935	Macmillan
Association for Childhood Education	Told under the Blue Umbrella	1937	Macmillan
Association for Childhood Education	Told under the Magic Umbrella	1939	Macmillan
Bannerman, H.	Story of Little Black Sambo	1903	Stokes
Barlow, Ruth C.	Fun at Happy Acres	1935	Crowell
Beskow, E.	Pelle's New Suit	1930	Platt & Munk
Brock, E. L.	The Greedy Goat	1931	Knopf
Brooke, L. L.	Johnny Crow's Garden	1929	Warne
Flack, M.	Angus and the Ducks	1930	Doubleday
Gág, Wanda	Snippy and Snappy	1931	Coward-McCann
Heward, C.	The Twins and Tibiffa	1923	Macrae
Kunhardt, D.	Little Ones	1935	Viking
Lathrop, D.	Who Goes There?	1935	Macmillan
Lee, E. & Reed, H.	Social Science Readers	1928	Scribner
Martin, C. M.	At the Farm	1930	Scribner

D. Probable Outcomes

I. Related to oral composition.

A. Poise and fluency in verbal expression, gained through the social opportunities offered.

    B. Ability to participate in making plans which will be for the good of the group.

    C. Readiness to accept criticism which will be of help, and to give suggestions to others in the spirit of helpfulness.

    D. Respect for the opinion of others and some independence in expressing his own opinion.

    E. Enjoyment of conversation with others.

    F. An appreciation for language as a means of interchange of ideas.

    G. Some ability to express mood through language in the form of stories, verses or dramatic interpretation.

II. Related to literature and reading.

    A. Some appreciation of beauty and rhythm in language.

    B. Appreciation of literary stories and verses on child's plane of experience.

    C. Appreciation of written forms as something necessary to attain.

    D. Feeling of need for reading, which becomes a meaningful medium through which individuals can interpret and express.

PROVISION FOR LANGUAGE
PROGRESS IN THE ELEMENTARY
GRADES

THE mastery of oral and written composition, writing and spelling in all of the six elementary grades is motivated by the children's activities. Opportunities for all forms of oral and written composition are continual, and as these are used, needs for practice work in handwriting, spelling and language usage become apparent. In first grade, handwriting and spelling have been subordinated to composition, and practice has been provided as specific needs have arisen. Beginning in second grade, some systematic practice in spelling has been included. Words have been selected both from composition needs and from standard lists. Beginning in fourth grade, systematic practice in language usage has been found desirable.

Since the children read and use in many ways their own compositions, reading is closely related to the development of language. It is impossible to separate the records for reading and language without involving some repetition. For all English activities, the class is often divided into small groups, and materials and procedure are adapted to meet the needs of the group.

A special teacher of speech visits each grade in the school during a conversation period, and selects the few who need speech reeducation. After a study has been made of each child's needs, individuals and small groups meet with the speech teacher until the difficulty has disappeared. The children enjoy this work, and sometimes ask to continue it after the need has been met.

In the intermediate grades those children who are considerably above standard in English attainments are excused from practice work, and frequently bear heavier responsibilities in social activities.

In the outlines which follow, outcomes tend to be cumulative from year to year. Effort is made in each grade to maintain desirable attitudes and appreciations, habits and skills, developed in preceding grades.

ENGLISH IN FIRST GRADE

Language and Writing

A. ACTIVITIES

(The oral English is spontaneous, and may occur at any time during the school day, as the opportunity or need arises.)

I. Activities related to personal experiences outside of school.
   A. Oral individual reports of week-end or daily excursions.
   B. Oral individual reports of home interests.
   C. Relating stories about members of the family.
   D. Relating experiences and retelling stories of plays, home movies, dramatizations.
   E. Retelling bits of news about airplanes, boats, famous people, community activities.

II. Activities related to good health and citizenship.
   A. Oral formation of necessary rules. (Occasionally written for charts, signs.)
   B. Oral discussion of need for safety and care in crossing streets, playing in the water, playing on the playground.
   C. Voting to elect representative leaders for activities: oral discussion of qualities needed.
   D. Oral discussion of relative value of foods, stressing those desirable and beneficial.
   E. Oral discussion of value of sleep and advisable hours for retiring and arising.
   F. Discussion of proper types of clothing for varying temperatures and weathers.
   G. Discussion of worth-while activities on the playground—conduct on the playground.

III. Activities related to group enterprises.
   (General interests and types of activities listed here. See records of units of experience for details and specific activities.)
   A. Oral.
      1. Purposing and planning activities.
      2. Deciding by discussion which activity or method to use.
      3. Intelligent solving of problems in construction, block building, measuring, in balance and artistic arrangement, by group discussion.

4. Critical evaluation and judgment of the worth of an activity, idea, art production or art form.
5. Finding ways and means of carrying ideas to completion.
6. Seeking information from each other and giving information to each other.
7. Organizing ideas for individual pictures or posters or for a frieze.
8. Composing of letters by individuals and the group.

B. Written.
1. Writing on the blackboard the number of votes in an election, number of articles made for a project.
2. Writing numbers on stamps, house numbers, price tags and lists.
3. Making signs for buildings, vehicles of transportation, departments in stores or post offices.
4. Labeling exhibits of curios, materials. (Phrase units encouraged.)
5. Writing simple letters to mail to friends; as,

> Dear Mother:
>   I like school.
>   I like to read.
>   Patsy

> Dear John David:
>   We are having a fine time at school. We made a rhyme. I will tell it to you:
> "Squirrel, squirrel, scamper up the tree,
> And throw the little nuts down to me."
>   We have a squirrel. Miss Baker found him in her bedroom and she brought him to school. We named him Little Mitchell. He climbs all over us and eats nuts.
>   I wish that you would come back to school.
>   Waring

6. Invitations to parents or friends to see an exhibit or dramatization or to attend a party.

IV. Activities related to nature.

A. Oral.
1. Telling anecdotes, stories, about pets.
2. Planning for care of room pets.
3. Relating personal experiences with nature.
4. Individual creating of verses about pets, elements, seasons, birds, insects, flowers.
5. Group work in creative verse making; as,

> O Butterfly! O Butterfly!
> You come in the Spring.

You dance upon the flowers.
You are a pretty thing.

Little bird! Little bird!
Where do you go?
I go to the South
Where the warm winds blow.

The clouds are white,
The sky is blue.
We will go skating to-day
With you.

6. Group and individual work in creating songs, words, tunes.
7. Group composing of stories about pets, related to experience reading; as,

The Gray Squirrel

My squirrel can eat nuts.
He can hop and climb trees.
He ran out to find nuts.
He climbed a big, big tree.
There were so many branches that he was lost.
It began to get dark.
Gray Squirrel began to cry.

A bluebird came to him.
He said, "Why do you cry, Gray Squirrel?"
The squirrel said, "I cry because I can't find my way home."
"I will help you. Follow me," said the bluebird.
Gray Squirrel was glad to get home again.

Baby's Surprise

Molly was a little baby.
She was only two years old.
She lived on a farm.
There were little ducks and chickens on the farm.

Baby went to get eggs.
She saw no eggs.
She looked and looked,
But she could see no eggs.

One day she went to look for eggs.
She saw no eggs,
But she saw little baby chickens.

B. Written.
1. Learning to write names of the pets in the room.
2. Writing simple stories of two or three sentences.

V. Activities related to reading and the use of the library.

A. Oral.
1. Discussing ways and means of keeping books clean and in good condition.

    2. Discussion of values of holding books correctly.

    3. Group discussion of subtle points in a story.

    4. Asking and answering questions.

    5. Telling of personal experiences similar to those in the story.

    6. Retelling story read, or the part read the preceding day.

B. Written.

    1. Writing on the blackboard the page numbers for daily reading.

    2. Writing "yes" and "no" answers to silent reading tests.

    3. Writing names of characters in solving work-type problems.

VI. Activities related to the lunch period.

A. Telling anecdotes and comparing experiences. Much of the discussion related to personal experiences, nature, good health and citizenship takes place at this time.

B. Conversation about beauty in color schemes, pottery, arrangement of tables.

C. Telling of riddles and conundrums.

D. Composing original riddles and conundrums.

E. Playing guessing games as, "I see something blue," or "My father owns a grocery store and in it he sells something that begins with s."

B. Procedure in Learning to Write and Spell

I. Group or individual composition of material to be used for signs, letters, or other purposes; blackboard reading of material which is to be written later.

II. Study of words needed.

A. Each word is taken separately.

B. The teacher pronounces slowly and simultaneously writes word on the blackboard three or four times. Manuscript ("print writing") is used.

C. The child is given opportunity to pronounce the word as the teacher writes it on the blackboard.

III. Practice in writing on the blackboard.

A. The child goes to the blackboard and practices pronouncing and simultaneously writing the word.

B. After some experimentation by the child specific suggestions are given for improving technique and the practice continues with increasing skill.

C. When separate words are learned, phrases from the composition, as, Dear Mother, I like, will go, may be practiced to gain knowledge of spacing.

D. For the beginning stages a teacher may:
   1. Teach only one or two letters at a time . . . adding each time to the first part, a new letter. (example: D—Da—Dad—Daddy)
   2. Later if the word is long or difficult, teach it in syllables, as Val-en-tine.

IV. Practice in writing on paper.
   A. Very little writing is done on paper, as blackboard writing encourages freedom and large writing. Paper is introduced only when the writing is to be used for some specific purpose, as an invitation or holiday greeting.
   B. Words or simple phrases are practiced separately. It is often advisable to build a word by letters as suggested above, as it is a problem to adjust size and proportion to paper.
   C. Then whole sentences may be practiced, with attention to spacing.

C. Materials Used

I. These materials are used for written work.
   A. The blackboard.
   B. Soft, dustless chalk.
   C. Soft blackboard erasers.
   D. Soft, large practice pencils, with blunt point.
   E. Ruled practice paper: wide ruling.
   F. Soft pencil erasers.
   G. Plain envelopes for mailing letters.

II. These materials are used in connection with spelling.
   A. Spelling list made by teacher.
   Lists of words needed in practical application are made. Words are stressed that child will need repeatedly in written composition.
   B. Spelling notebooks.
   A list is kept by the children of the words they have learned.

D. Probable Outcomes

I. Information, attitudes, appreciations.
   A. Related to oral conversation and composition.
   1. Interest, alertness, and joy in conversation.

2. A growing feeling of confidence in addressing a small group.
. A willingness to share experiences.
4. Alertness toward evaluating ideas, good form in expression, and a happy response to constructive suggestions for improving own work.
5. Growing respect for ideas and opinions of others and a willingness to wait turns to express child's own opinion.
6. A growing willingness to condense and organize material and a willingness to consume a minimum amount of time in addressing the group.
7. Some understanding of simple sentence structure and a desire to use complete sentences.
8. A willingness to use well-modulated tone that can be easily heard.
9. A willingness to use a pleasant tone rather than use a loud, harsh tone.
10. A desire to use expressive language with a minimum amount of slang.

B. Related to written composition.
1. An interest in learning to write and spell.
2. An eagerness to improve his technique.
3. A feeling of joy and satisfaction in completing some undertaking in handwriting.
4. Some understanding of the use and function of letters and letter writing.

II. Habits and skills.

A. Related to oral composition.
1. Gradual elimination of nervous habits and the development of poise in speaking before a small group.
2. Growth in ability to speak distinctly, slowly and in a tone that is easily understood.
3. Growth in ability to hold to the topic of conversation.
4. The ability to wait turns.
5. Some ability in original thinking in planning or problem solving.
6. Some ability to retell incidents or short stories with correct sequence of events.
7. Growth in ability to be a courteous listener.
8. The ability to compose a friendly letter of two or three short sentences.
9. Growth in ability to use simple, complete sentences,

correct tense, and a vocabulary that will make fluent speech possible.

10. The ability to recognize rhyming words, and for many the ability to compose simple two to four line verses.

B. Related to written composition.

1. The ability to write legibly with chalk or large soft pencil.

2. The ability to use large arm movement while at the blackboard and relaxed movement when writing on paper.

3. Ability to form all commonly used letters accurately and with correct movements.

4. Some degree of skill in obtaining correct proportion of various letters.

5. The use of capitals at the beginning of a sentence and for names.

6. The use of periods and question marks at the ends of sentences.

7. Ability to spell and write from thirty to sixty simple words used in practical situations during the year. The number of words depends on the readiness of the child or the group for this type of work.

English in Second Grade

Language, Writing and Spelling

A. ACTIVITIES

(The oral English is spontaneous, and may occur at any time during the school day, as the need or opportunity arises.)

I. **Activities related to incidental experiences.**
   A. Discussion of nature material brought in, obtaining as much information as possible.
   B. Reports on experiments and observations of nature material.
   C. Written reports of the results of nature experiments and observations.
   D. Discussion and explanation of pictures and toys brought in, sometimes composition of original stories about pictures.
   E. Making own book of experiences, and writing stories about the pictures, as "The Funny Book," "Dolly's Book."
   F. Retelling anecdotes and humorous stories at the lunch table.
   G. Making original riddles and taking part in guessing games.
   H. Writing of verses and songs, expressing appreciations.

Buoys

Rocking! Rocking! Rocking
Tired from being pushed by the waves—
Lonely too, for no ships have passed
For many days.
Ding-dong! Ding-dong!
Ringing and telling the boats
That there is danger.

Group composition.

Milkweeds

Some people
When they are in their boats
See milkweeds growing
Along the shore.
Fly! Fly!
The seeds with their silk
Fly through the air
Like a plane in slow motion
And then they float down
Like a parachute.

Group composition.

372

LANGUAGE AND ART JOIN HANDS IN CREATING AN ORIGINAL PLAY

II. Activities related to group enterprises.
   A. Offering suggestions in forming purposes and plans.
   B. Offering constructive criticism of work of group, as to best color to use, durability of material, fitness for the purpose.
   C. Composing group and individual stories for different projects; as, captions for movies, book of stories of animals.
   D. Making plans for excursions; oral discussions on what to look for, standards of conduct.
   E. Relating orally experiences and observations of excursions.
   F. Writing individual stories on excursions.

III. Activities related to health and good citizenship.
   A. Group discussion of activities on playground.
   B. Forming of rules in both organized and informal play.
   C. Discussion in forming necessary school rules to make for better citizenship; constructive criticism and suggestions arising from such needs.
   D. Keeping a careful record of each child's weight and height, leading to discussion on how to obtain correct weight and posture.
   E. Informal talks concerning healthful foods, hygienic habits. (Often held at lunch time.)

IV. Activities related to reading.

    A. Discussion of stories read individually or by the group.

    B. Group discussion of current topics brought in for bulletin board.

    C. Forming library rules and discussing use of library cards.

    D. Discussing various library readings and activities.

    E. Writing answers to comprehension checks on reading.

V. Activities related to correspondence and communication.

    A. Composing and writing group and individual letters to parents and absent children.

    B. Writing "Thank you" notes for gifts, parties, favors.

    C. Composing and writing invitations, programs, notices, for school plays and entertainments.

    D. Composing and writing messages for greeting and gift cards: Christmas, Easter, Mother's Day, Valentine's Day, birthdays.

B. Procedure

I. Procedure in writing.

    A. Continuing with manuscript writing.

    B. Thirty minute period a week in improving technique of writing: watching the teacher make the correct form; studying the form carefully; then writing without the copy; noting improvement.

    C. Stress laid on writing of complete sentence and correct use of capitals, periods and question marks.

    D. Stress placed on use of margins in writing letters and stories.

II. Procedure in spelling.

    A. Lists prepared of words needed in written composition.

    B. Method:

        1. Words to be studied are first presented in a sentence.

        2. Individual child pronounces and spells word orally as teacher writes word on board.

        3. Closes eyes and spells word before writing.

        4. Writes word on board or paper without copy; rewrites to improve form or correct errors.

        5. Often pronounces word slowly and simultaneously writes it.

        6. Places word in individual spelling book.

7. Uses word as further need arises in written work.
8. Reviews spelling of word until certainly learned.
C. Words taken from children's interests and needs.
D. Some additional words taught from standard lists.
E. Much practice in spelling by analogy, writing phonetic lists of similar words.

III. Use of tests and scales.

A. Handwriting compared with scale; scale placed on bulletin board for study.
B. Spelling tests given near the end of each semester by psychologist.

C. Books and Materials Used

I. Materials for written composition.

A. Wide ruled composition paper.
B. Soft lead pencils, with blunt point.
C. Narrower lined paper for numbers.
D. Large envelopes for mailing letters.

II. Spelling lists.

A. Words coming from group projects and individual needs.
B. Standard spelling list (used for checking): Horn's List of 300 words most likely to be used in children's writing during the first three years.
C. Individual spelling books for words often needed.

III. Standard tests:

Metropolitan Achievement Test. World Book Company.
Morrison-McCall Spelling Test. World Book Company.
New Standard Achievement Test. World Book Company.

Note: Forms are selected which have not been used for over a year.

IV. Writing scale.

Conard, Edith N. Manuscript Writing Standards. Bureau of Publications, Teachers College, Columbia University.

D. Probable Outcomes

I. Information, attitudes, appreciations.

A. Readiness to participate in purposing and planning group activities.

B. Willingness to give and accept constructive criticism for the improving of work.

C. Respect for the opinions of others and an independence in own thinking and manner of expression.

D. Understanding the need of expressing oneself clearly, concisely and in an interesting manner.

E. Realizing the need for gaining the interest of an audience when telling stories, riddles, anecdotes, by knowing well what one is going to say.

F. Understanding the importance of a pleasing and well-pitched voice so that one can be heard easily.

G. Some appreciation of the beauty of language and a desire to use it well in speaking and writing.

H. Appreciation of beautiful and legible handwriting and a desire to improve own handwriting.

I. Desire to enlarge spelling vocabulary and to be accurate in spelling words.

II. Habits and skills.

A. Growing ability to speak before a group with poise, to speak distinctly, to participate in group planning and constructive criticism.

B. Growing ability to tell stories, anecdotes, in an interesting manner.

C. Ability to compose letters or compositions independently, of six to eight sentences in length (many compose two sheets and more).

D. Ability to write with a smaller pencil with some degree of legibility and uniformity.

E. Greater neatness and more artistic appearance in all written work.

F. Ability to leave margins in written work; to use capital letters for sentence beginning, proper names, days of week and special days; period or question mark at the end of a sentence.

G. Mastery of words commonly needed in own compositions; mastery of selected words from standard spelling lists.

English in Third Grade

Language, Writing and Spelling

A. Activities and Procedure

I. Oral and written composition.

A. Related to personal experiences and current events.
1. Oral reports and sometimes written stories about trips taken during the year to farms, forest preserves, lake; travel of greater distance, as trips to Florida, California.
2. Oral discussions about current events posted on bulletin board and reported from home reading.
3. Writing verses and songs expressing appreciations.

Birds and Flowers

Spring is here and I am glad.
'Cause I hear the birds calling
And see the leaves falling
And see the flowers growing
And hear the wind blowing.

The lilac bush is budding,
The birds are on the wing.
The flowers are slowly opening,
Now, we know it is Spring.

Spring is in the air,
Gardens, gardens everywhere,
Boys and girls in the Kindergarten
Working all morning in their spring garden.
—Reprinted from the Children's Magazine.

The Pumpkin

I found a yellow pumpkin
Growing in a field,
And I asked the yellow pumpkin
What he would like to do.
And much to my surprise, he said,
He would like to go to school.
So I asked the yellow pumpkin
If he would be good,
And much to my surprise
He said, he would.
So I told the yellow pumpkin
I would tell him what to do.
He must smile at the children
And keep every rule.
So I and my Daddy fixed up his smile
So he could go to school for awhile.
—Reprinted from the Children's Year Book,
"The Blue Moon"

377

B. Related to health and good citizenship.
1. Discussion of food, toilet habits, rest habits, drinking water and milk, as these points arise in the daily routine.
2. Discussions about standing, sitting and walking well.
3. Discussions pertaining to school property and the right way to care for one's self in the corridors, library, dining-room.
4. Discussion of points that make good citizenship in the community; regard for one's own safety and the safety and welfare of others; conduct on the street and in public buildings (often arising in connection with walks and excursions).
5. Choosing responsible leaders for group activities and committees, discussion of qualities needed.
6. Comparisons made of different officers and working groups in our school and their duties.
7. Discussion of characters in stories; such traits as kindness, bravery, jealousy and helpfulness.
8. Composition of rules for games and for use of playground.
9. Group composition and presentation of a puppet show, illustrating school and home courtesies.

C. Related to group enterprises.
1. Oral reports on reference readings.
2. Oral suggestions made in purposing and planning group work; as play, maple sugar sale.
3. Discussion of pictures, slides and motion pictures used; questions asked leading to further research.
4. Outlining plays, class working together.
5. Spontaneous conversation in dramatization.
6. Oral discussions in planning costumes and properties for plays.
7. Reports on experiments with seeds, flowers, plants, and observations of water creatures.
8. Reports following excursions on points observed.
9. Constructive criticism offered on all group work, during execution and after completion.
10. Making books recording interesting facts learned and discoveries made: composing and writing individual stories for books on topics of individual or group interest.

D. Related to use of library and books.
1. Discussion of use of encyclopedias, dictionaries, magazines, large globe, and other library materials.

PUPPETS SHOW SCHOOL COURTESIES

  2. Sharing with one another material found in library through book reports and stories.

 E. Related to correspondence.

  1. Writing letters to the group when away on a trip.

  2. Writing informational letters to absent children.

  3. Writing to children in other schools.

  . Writing letters of inquiry to business firms.

  . Writing notes thanking people for help and gifts.

  6. Writing invitations to mothers and to other grades to attend functions.

  7. Writing greeting cards for special days: Easter, Mother's Day; writing notes or cards to accompany gifts and donations.

  8. Oral discussions about letters written and letters received.

II. Practice in improving manuscript writing.

 A. Studying handwriting scales posted for a short time in room.

 B. Comparing writing of individual children with scale; with samples from other rooms and from other children in room.

 C. Noting weakness and working for improvement in size, uniformity, spacing of words, evenness of margins, neatness and beauty of finished page.

D. Watching the teacher's movements in writing and correcting wrong habits in forming letters; practicing single letters, words and phrases from compositions.

E. Noting progress; practicing with pen after a certain degree of proficiency with pencil has been attained.

III. Procedure in learning to spell.

A. Lists made of words needed in compositions.
B. Practice activities.
  1. New words are used in oral sentences to make clear the meaning.
  2. Children watch as word is written on the blackboard by the teacher.
  3. The word is pronounced slowly, and the parts or syllables noted; attention is called to peculiarities; line may be drawn under the difficult or familiar part of the word.
  4. Children pronounce the word, spell it softly. Some children learn more accurately by pronouncing the word slowly while simultaneously writing the word quickly, emphasizing the visual imagery.
  5. Children close eyes and spell silently.
  6. Then the word is written without a copy, and later compared with the correct form. Study is continued if needed.
  7. Often the word is written in a sentence or used immediately in written composition.
  8. Words are reviewed as frequently as needed.
C. Lists made from children's compositions are checked on standard lists and other words from the standard lists are introduced.

IV. Use of tests.

A. Frequent informal tests are given by the teacher, to determine what review work is needed; what words from standard lists are already mastered.
B. Standard tests are given by the psychologist at the end of each semester. Progress chart for each child is made and studied to determine where special help is needed.

B. Books and Materials Used

I. Materials used in written work.

    A. Paper.

        1. Wide spaced paper for composition work.

        2. Manila tag board for making posters.

        3. Large envelopes for mailing letters.

        4. Unruled white construction paper for making greeting cards, valentines.

        5. Colored construction paper and poster paper to use in making covers of books, programs, posters.

    B. Soft lead pencils.

    C. Fountain pens.

    D. Manila folders to hold compositions and other written materials.

II. Spelling materials.

    A. Lists made from words used in letters, written stories, poems, and a few from reading.

    B. Published lists used for checking only.

        Newlon. J. H. and Hanna, P. R. 1935. The Newlon-Hanna Speller. Houghton Mifflin.

        Horn's List of 300 words most likely to be used in children's writing during the first three years.

    C. Mimeographed lists of words causing special difficulty to group.

    D. Individual filing boxes for children's own list of words needed.

III. Standard spelling tests.

    Morrison-McCall Spelling Test. World Book Company.

    New Stanford Achievement Test. World Book Company.

    Metropolitan Achievement Test. World Book Company.

    Note:—Forms are selected which have not been used for a year or more.

IV. Writing scale.

    Conard. Edith N. Conard Manuscript Writing Standards. Bureau of Publications, Teachers College, Columbia University.

C. Probable Outcomes

I. Information, attitudes and appreciations.

    A. Readiness to take part in purposing and planning class activities.

    B. Growing willingness to give and receive suggestions for improved work.

    C. Increasing respect for opinions of others, and regard for approval and disapproval of others.

    D. Realization of need for expressing one's self clearly.

    E. Beginning of a desire for clever and unusual forms of expression.

    F. Growing desire to compose stories, and friendly letters that will inform and amuse the reader.

    G. Growing desire to attain a clear, pleasing speaking voice, with distinct pronunciation.

    H. Appreciation of good handwriting of others, and a desire to improve in writing.

    I. Growing desire to make written work artistic as well as legible and neat.

    J. Growing desire to enlarge the vocabulary, both oral and written.

II. Habits and skills.

    A. More ease when relating experiences to the group or talking to adults; greater poise and better voice control.

    B. More ability to tell a story well, orally or in writing, giving incidents as experienced.

    C. Ability to compose an interesting letter, two or more pages in length.

    D. Some facility in composing original verses, songs and riddles.

    E. An enlarged vocabulary and a growing ability for individual forms of expression.

    F. A growth in eliminating slang, undesirable colloquialisms and gross errors in speech and written composition.

    G. Improvement in form and legibility of handwriting; ability to use a fountain pen the latter part of the year.

    H. Ability to use correct form in writing friendly letters with superscription, salutation, complimentary close.

    I. Habit of using capital letters for proper names, days of week and month, town, street, and state; also beginning of sentence or exclamation.

    J. Habit of using period at end of sentence and after abbreviations. Correct use also of question mark, exclamation point, hyphen and apostrophe for possession.

    K. More independence in all written work and fewer errors.

    L. Mastery of spelling words most used in the grade.

    M. Mastery of all selected words from a recognized spelling list.

English in Fourth Grade

Language, Writing and Spelling

A. ACTIVITIES AND PROCEDURE

I. Activities related to personal experiences.

A. Oral.
1. Reports on events in the home and community during the week end.
2. Reports on vacation experiences: Summer, Thanksgiving, Christmas, Spring, and other holidays.
3. Telling jokes and humorous stories at lunch time.
4. Discussing the local weather conditions.

B. Written.
1. Outlining, organizing reports to be given.
2. Writing captions for booklets, charts of vacation.
3. Writing letters to absent friends, telling of interesting events at school.
4. Keeping personal account books of allowances.
5. Writing talks, poems, stories relating to vacation experiences.
6. Writing poems and rhymes expressing feelings about nature and other experiences.

Hiding

Hiding is a lot of fun,
You have to duck around,
And sit very still in the hiding place
Until you are found.

And while the person hunting you,
Goes looking round and round,
It's very hard to sit still,
Until you are found.

April

April has come at last,
All of the winter has past,
The buds are all out,
And the flowers are about,
Because April has come at last.

April has come at last,
All the winter has past,
When I go to sleep at night,
It is still very light,
Because April has come at last.

383

My Pony

As down the street I rode my pony
The flowers nodded their heads at me.
I saw my little playmate Tony
As gay as gay could be.
I waved to him, he waved to me,
As down the path I trotted.
A bird was singing in a tree.
Over the hill the cows were dotted.
Then I turned my pony's head.
I was headed for home.
Away, away and away we sped.

Upon That Lonely Shore

The middle of a lonely night
Upon a lonely shore
The lonely wind blew
Upon the lonely four.
Father, Mother, Sister, Brother,
On that lonely shore.
The lighthouse, the lighthouse
That sheltered the lonely four,
The lighthouse, the lighthouse
Upon that lonely shore.
—Reprinted from the Children's Magazine.

II. Activities related to citizenship and good health.

A. Oral.

1. Reports and discussion of Student Cabinet projects.
2. Discussing needs of the group, relative to setting standards for the use of the halls, the toilet rooms, dining room, auditorium, library.
3. Planning a rating chart for individual behavior.
4. Discussing methods used in choosing officers for any organization.
5. Listing desirable qualities for certain officers.
6. Discussing the value of making right choice of food for lunches.
7. Discussing the height and weight charts relative to individual needs.
8. Discussing the hygienic care of the body—posture, light, desks, chairs, handling and using books.
9. Discussing happenings of the day, local and national, or current events.

B. Written.

1. Organizing and making good citizenship chart, captions and individual rating chart.
2. Writing notices for committee meetings.
3. Writing notices of various projects sponsored by the Student Cabinet.

DRAMA DEVELOPS LANGUAGE POWERS

4. Writing ballots in voting.
5. Posting list of nominees for office.
6. Writing and posting examples of healthful lunches as guides in choosing menu.
7. Writing and composing health slogans.
8. Keeping records of lunches and comparing with chart showing well-balanced meals.

III. Activities related to group enterprises.
    A. Oral.
        1. Organizing and giving talks, or reports, as a result of individual and group research.
        2. Discussing experiences and information brought in from making inquiry or reading.
        3. Discussing excursions taken—before going and upon return.
        4. Discussing movies and slides used in the class room.
        5. Discussing working problems and means of solving.

6. Setting up of standards of workmanship for various phases of the work.
7. Discussing and giving constructive criticism of finished work.
8. Discussing the problems related to the cooking and serving of special luncheons.
9. Giving group and individual reports upon assigned topics.
10. Giving dramatizations, dialogues, shadow plays.
11. Discussing the contents of the Class Diary—judging the best story, poem, anecdote to be included in the diary.
12. Giving announcements and reports of progress of various committees engaged in research problems.
13. Giving explanations of various experiments carried on.

B. Written.
1. Outlining material for both talks and written stories.
2. Taking notes from reference materials read.
3. Keeping records of progress in work.
4. Writing stories, poems, of explorations and discoveries, colonial days, and other topics.
5. Writing stories for books, talkies, plays, dialogues.
6. Writing labels and captions for maps, charts, paintings, experiments.
7. Writing notices to advertise various enterprises, as Jelly Sale, April Magazine.
8. Making booklet of cooking recipes used in cooking projects.
9. Making calendar of historical events.
10. Writing announcements and bulletin notices for other rooms about interesting exhibits.
11. Writing money orders, checks, receipts.

IV. Activities related to reading and the library.

A. Oral.
1. Discussing books and stories read.
2. Sharing interesting parts of books with others.
3. Telling stories read for the enjoyment of others.
4. Reporting good points of books, in order to recommend them to others.
5. Dramatizing sections of books—impersonating certain characters in books.
6. Organizing and planning book activities; as, Book Days, Day with Certain Authors.

7. Discussing the use of the files, reference books, in the library.
8. Discussing answers to check tests given upon selected books read by the group, or books read to the children by the teacher.

B. Written.
1. Filling in the form (mimeographed) of books read by the pupils.
2. Writing advertisements for books.
3. Making book file for individual book reports of books read.

V. Correspondence—personal and business.

A. Oral.
1. Discussing when to write letters, how to write various kinds of letters, to whom to write.
2. Discussing letters received as result of correspondence.

B. Written.
1. Notes, letters asking for privileges, to College authorities.
2. Notes thanking both groups and individuals for kindnesses or aid.
3. Notes of apology when needed.
4. Invitations for several room enterprises.
5. Business letters to firms requesting material.
6. Notes accompanying money donations for various purposes.

VI. School publications.

A. Oral.
1. Planning the organization needed for the publishing of a magazine.
2. Discussing the financing, the staff and their duties.
3. Planning the means of advertising.
4. Discussing how to secure interesting material for publication.
5. Discussing how to set the standards for materials published.
6. Discussing the mechanical problems, as binding and printing.

B. Written.
Writing interesting and worth-while selections for the publication.

VII. Practice in language usage.

A. Class discussion of points of correct usage.
B. Practice in work books.
C. Practice on mimeographed materials to help maintain skill and for review.
D. Correcting own compositions with teacher's guidance.
E. Working in pairs, correcting work.

VIII. Practice in manuscript handwriting.

A. Using charcoal for large letter forms; using broad-edged pens for large letter forms; practicing with chalk at the blackboard; writing with pencils and with fountain pens.
B. Practice on letter forms and phrases for legibility, beauty and speed. (Marjory Wise—Manuscript Writing Technique, used as a guide.)
C. Samples of writing kept in individual folders for each child, improvement in legibility and speed noted; often scored and discussed.

IX. Practice in spelling.

A. Words needed in written work.
  1. Words are checked by children and teacher.
  2. Tests in context are given on words needed by ⅓ of the group. These are rechecked from time to time and rating sheets or graphs are kept by each child noting his improvement.
  3. A class list or dictionary is kept, made available for children who need help.
B. Words from spelling list.
  1. Discussion of words in list, sentence work and blackboard practice.
  2. Pretest on list.
  3. Study words needed or missed on pretest.
  4. Study words missed on second test and review previous words.
  5. Sentences involving words in new list and review list. Individual checking on words.

X. Taking of standardized tests and improvised tests made by the teacher.

Graphs of improvement are made by the children and teacher and by the psychologist.

B. Books and Materials

I. **Materials used in written work.**
 A. Kinds of notebooks.
  1. Composition notebooks (10 x 8).
  2. Loose leaf notebooks (12 x 10).
  3. Folders (tag board 9 x 12) for filing work sheets.
 B. Kinds of paper.
  1. Lined paper (8½ x 11) (7 x 8½).
  2. Manila tag.
  3. Regular construction paper.
  4. Regular poster paper.
  5. Mechanical drawing paper.
  6. Unlined paper (pads 8½ x 11 and 6 x 9).
 C. Kinds of pencils.
  1. Charcoal for large writing of letter forms.
  2. Medium soft lead pencils.
 D. Pen and ink.
  1. Broad-edged pen sets.
  2. India ink for broad-edged pens.
  3. Fountain pen.
  4. Fountain pen ink.
 E. Envelopes.
  1. For business purposes:
   School envelopes (large and small).
   Plain 3⅜ x 6½.
  2. For notes or friendly letters:
   Plain (small and medium).
   Hand-made ones to match paper.

II. **Work-type materials. (Used by individuals as needed.)**
Guitteau, W. B. Constructive English Exercises. 1936, Johnson Publishing Company.
Hatfield, W. W., and Lewes, E. E. Practice Activities in English. 1936, American
 Book Company.
Thorndike-Century Junior Dictionary. 1935, Scott Foresman.

III. **Spelling materials.**
 A. Standard lists:
Breed, F. S., and Seale, E. C. My Work Book. 1937, Lyons and Carnahan.
Newlon, J. H., and Hanna, P. Newlon-Hanna Speller. 1935, Houghton Mifflin.
 B. Class compiles list of words needed.
 C. Individual compiled list of words needed.
 D. Spelling notebooks.
  1. Large notebook (10 x 11)—for dictation work, sentence
   building and vocabulary study.

2. Small (6 x 4)—for child's own list of words needing special drill from standardized lists and class lists.
3. Medium (8 x 10)—for child's own dictionary containing lists of words needed by the individual child for original composition work, and for lists of correct expressions and new words and phrases.

IV. Standardized tests.

Morrison-McCall Spelling Test. World Book Company.
New Stanford Achievement Test. World Book Company.
Progressive Achievement Test. California Test Bureau.

V. Writing scales.

A. Manuscript scale.

Conard, Edith N. Conard Manuscript Writing Scale—Pen Form. Bureau of Publications, Teachers College, Columbia.

B. Cursive writing.

Ayres, Leonard P. Measuring Scale for Handwriting. Department of Education, Russell Sage Foundation.

C. Probable Outcomes

I. Appreciations and attitudes.

A. An interest in developing the ability to enunciate clearly with a pleasant voice.
B. An appreciation of distinct and correct speech of others and a sincere effort to overcome one's own speech faults.
C. Realization that natural tone of voice in oral composition is quite as essential as an interesting subject.
D. A readiness to participate in purposing and planning group enterprises.
E. Willingness to give and receive constructive criticism for improving work along factual and artistic lines.
F. An appreciation of beauty of language forms and a desire to use them artistically and effectively.
G. An appreciation of beautiful and legible handwriting and a desire to improve own handwriting, as to legibility, form and rate.
H. An understanding of the need for accuracy in spelling and a desire for enlarging the spelling vocabulary.
I. An understanding of the value of language in business and a desire to use it correctly and effectively.
J. Greater confidence and satisfaction in talking and writing.

II. **Habits and skills.**
    A. Language.
        1. Growing ability to speak briefly and in an interesting way from an outline.
        2. Growing ability to use a good quality of tone, enunciate clearly and pronounce correctly.
        3. An increasing skill in the choice and use of new words.
        4. Growing ability to think and speak clearly and honestly.
        5. Growing ability to think and speak well on one's feet.
        6. Growth in mastery of conversational style without the excessive use of run-on sentences introduced by *and, but* and *so,* and the overuse of incomplete expressions.
        7. A noticeable growth in vocabulary, especially with reference to use of more expressive words.
        8. Some facility in using the dictionary for word meanings.
        9. Growing effectiveness in the use of the paragraph through better beginning and ending sentences and through the introduction of interesting details.
      10. Increasing skill in writing a brief composition which has unity, sequence, climax; margin, title; capitals in proper places; correct punctuation and spelling.
      11. Increasing skill in writing short stories and articles with attention to paragraphing, sentence formation and development of the story.
      12. The ability to write a friendly letter one paragraph long, with attention to correct form.
      13. The ability to write a note of thanks, apology, invitation, with attention to correct form.
      14. The ability to write a simple business letter, ordering supplies, seeking information, or making a request.
      15. More skill in phrasing titles that are brief, attractive and keep the point of the story or article in suspense.
      16. Ability to address cards, envelopes, letters, packages, properly for mailing.
      17. Growing skill in recognizing and correcting one's own errors.
      18. The habit of reading all written work for the purpose of self correction; and of looking over the first draft for a better selection of vocabulary, possible errors and general improvement.
    B. Form.
        1. Continued accuracy in the use of forms introduced in preceding grades:

    a. Capitals for months of year, days of week, holidays, beginning of line of verse, etc.

    b. Apostrophe in contractions and possessive forms.

    c. Abbreviations of days, months, measurements, some states.

    d. Exclamation point, quotation marks, question mark, period and comma.

  2. Skill in use of single verbs and subjects, plural verbs and subjects.

C. Handwriting.

  1. The ability to reproduce accurately, manuscript to manuscript, print to manuscript, script to manuscript, blackboard to paper, books to paper.

  2. Ability to write legibly with pencil and fountain pen.

  3. Growing ability to do uniform and artistic lettering and writing.

D. Spelling.

  1. Continued gain in technique in studying spelling.

  2. Continued growth of spelling conscience, indicated by fewer mistakes in papers.

  3. Ability to use a dictionary for help in spelling words.

English in Fifth Grade

Language, Writing and Spelling

I. Activities relating to personal experiences.
  A. Oral.
    1. Reports on interesting events of the week-end, evening, or morning before school.
    2. Discussion of neighborhood happenings common to several.
    3. Reports on vacation experiences.
    4. Telling anecdotes or humorous experiences for pleasure.
  B. Written.
    1. Outlining talks to be given.
    2. Writing reports or stories of vacation experiences.
    3. Writing stories or poems to express personal experiences or feelings.

Maps

I think that a map's a silly thing,
A few colors, some lines, a dot and a ring,
Showing mountains and cities, perhaps a fall,
Something great and something small.

Dogdom

He will always be there when you come home,
He will greet you with a rapturous bark.
He will kiss your hand when it has no food to offer.
He will stay with you in times of sorrow and pain.
He alone remains when all others have deserted you.
He loves you from birth until death.
While other animals turn traitor on you he is still your friend.
From the tiny Yorkshire terrier to the great St. Bernard
The dog is always your best friend.

II. Activities relating to citizenship and health.
  A. Oral.
    1. Discussions of happenings of the day, both local and national.
    2. Deciding on desirable standards of good citizenship and how attained.
    3. Discussions of how to improve individual records of weight kept by school nurse.
    4. Discussions of food problems arising from choosing own lunches.

    5. Discussions of how to make environment conducive to good health.
  B. Written.
    1. Writing captions for good citizenship or health posters.
    2. Drawing up constitutions for good citizenship organizations.
    3. Posting resolutions for room reminders.
    4. Writing individual menu from room menu.

III. Activities related to group enterprises.
  A. Oral.
    1. Organizing and giving reports or talks as a result of individual research.
    2. Discussing exhibits, information brought in, readings.
    3. Discussing work problems and making plans for solution.
    4. Setting up standards of work to be attained.
    5. Discussing and criticizing work finished.
    6. Discussing excursions both before and after going.
  B. Written.
    1. Outlining material for both talks and written stories or reports.
    2. Taking notes.
    3. Writing stories for books, plays, talkies.
    4. Writing labels for diagrams, maps, charts.
    5. Writing answers to questions checking comprehension of subject matter covered.
    6. Writing notices to advertise talkies, plays.
    7. Writing notices of projects for school newspaper.
    8. Writing poems or verses.

IV. Activities related to reading and use of the library.
  A. Oral.
    1. Discussing books or stories read.
    2. Sharing interesting bits from books read by telling them.
    3. Telling stories read for the enjoyment of others.
    4. Reporting good points of certain books for the purpose of advertising them to others.
    5. Formulating and discussing book projects such as Book Clubs, Book Days, and Book Assemblies.
  B. Written.
    1. Filling in mimeographed book report blanks of books read.
    2. Writing advertisements for books read which were thought especially good.

A RADIO BROADCAST IS PRESENTED

V. Activities relating to room procedure.
   A. Oral.
      1. Discussion of problems arising on the playground, in the halls, dining room or classroom.
      2. Discussion of plans for daily or weekly program.
      3. Parliamentary procedure in making and passing motions, voting on questions, and electing officers or representatives.
      4. Discussions of care of room and equipment.
   B. Written.
      1. Writing notices of results of games, articles lost, coming events, for bulletin board.
      2. Writing committee notes and reports.
      3. Writing lists of officers and committees.

VI. Correspondence on personal and business relationships.
   A. Oral.
      1. Discussions of where letters are necessary.
      2. Discussion of the questions, to whom to write and what to write.

    3. Reports of committees or representatives on results of correspondence.

    4. Oral reports or requests made to other rooms asking co-operation on certain projects.

  B. Written.

    1. Composing business letters for information.

    2. Composing letters to accompany money donated for any purpose from class earnings.

    3. Writing informal notes of invitation to exhibits, talkies, dramatizations.

    4. Writing notes to school authorities, asking privileges.

    5. Writing notes of thanks for kindnesses shown and aid given.

    6. Sending notes of apology where privileges have been abused.

    7. Sending notes to other rooms asking for cooperation and accepting invitations.

VII. School publications. (See *National News,* page 348.)

  A. Oral.

    1. Discussion of what would interest others.

    2. Discussion of how to make items interesting.

  B. Written.

    1. Writing items for newspaper.

    2. Writing contributions for the magazine.

VIII. Practice in language usage.

  A. Class discussion of points in correct usage.

  B. Practice in work book on needs arising in class.

  C. Taking mimeographed exercises for maintenance and review.

  D. Taking tests to see if minimum essentials are mastered or to see if further practice is necessary.

IX. Procedure in improving handwriting.

  A. Manuscript.

    1. Making large letter forms in charcoal on paper lined for height.

    2. Practice for manipulation of broad-edged pen.

    3. Practice on letter forms, words, and phrases for legibility and speed.

  B. Cursive or script.

    1. All children in fifth grade learn to read script.

2. Those who desire learn to write script.
    a. Comparison of script letter forms with manuscript letter forms in words and phrases.
    b. Watching words and phrases being written.
    c. Watching letter forms being made.
    d. Practicing on letter forms in words and phrases on the blackboard under supervision.
    e. Writing in script with pencil and then with ink on paper.

C. Progress in writing.
  1. Keeping samples of writing to note improvement.
  2. Having samples of writing scored.
  3. Comparison of results with handwriting scales.

X. Procedure in learning to spell.

A. Words needed in written work.
  1. Keeping list of words asked for in small notebook.
  2. Check by another pupil or teacher on common words needed by child.
  3. Making class list by pupils and teacher of words needed by several.

B. Words from spelling lists.
  1. Program.
    a. Pretest on new words.
    b. Study words missed.
    c. Test on new and review.
    d. Study words missed on last test.
    e. Test in content.
    f. Individual check on words missed in content.
  2. Method.
    a. Studying according to plan in Newlon-Hanna Speller.
    b. Pairing children for checking.
    c. Keeping record of each individual child by teacher of all words missed.
    d. Keeping record by each pupil of all words he missed.
    e. Keeping composite list by teacher of words causing difficulty.
    f. Using large composition book for spelling book.

C. Review words.
  1. Individual check on all words.
  2. Reviewing each week words missed previous weeks.

XI. Use of standardized tests.
  A. By psychology department.
    1. For group placement.
    2. For location of spelling difficulties.
    3. For check on attainment.
  B. By teacher.
    ·1. For locating difficulties.
    2. For check on learning and teaching.

B. Books and Materials Used

I. Written work.
  A. Kinds of paper used.
    1. Lined ink paper (8½ x 11).
    2. Manila tag board.
    3. Construction paper (9 x 12)—(12 x 18).
    4. Poster paper (9 x 12)—(12 x 18).
    5. Mechanical drawing paper.
    6. Note pads.
  B. Kinds of pencils.
    1. Charcoal for large writing of letter forms.
    2. Medium soft lead pencils.
  C. Kinds of pen and ink.
    1. Broad-edged pens, sets of round-hand pens.
    2. India ink for broad-edged pens.
    3. Fountain pen.
    4. Fountain pen ink.
  D. Composition notebooks.
    Folders (tag board 9 x 12) for filing work.

II. Work-type material. (Used by individuals as needed.)

Guitteau, Wm. B. Constructive English Exercises. 1936, Johnson Publishing Company.
Hatfield, Lewis, Sheldon. Practice Activities in English. 1936, American Book Company.
Kibbe and others. Handbook of English. 1939, Scott Foresman.
Thorndike-Century Junior Dictionary. 1935, Scott Foresman.
Winston Simplified Dictionary. 1939, Winston Publishing Company.

III. Spelling materials.
  A. Standard list:

Newlon, J. H., and Hanna, P. Newlon-Hanna Speller. 1935, Houghton Mifflin.

  B. Individual lists and class lists compiled by teachers and children.
  C. Notebooks: Composition books.

IV. Handwriting scales.

A. Manuscript writing.

Conard, Edith N. Conard Manuscript Writing Standards. Bureau of Publications, Teachers College, Columbia.

B. Script writing.

Ayres, Leonard P. Measuring Scale for Handwriting. Department of Education, Russell Sage Foundation.

V. Standardized tests in spelling and language.

Metropolitan Achievement Test. World Book Company.
Morrison-McCall Spelling Test. World Book Company.
New Stanford Achievement Test. World Book Company.
Progressive Achievement Test. California Test Bureau.

C. Probable Outcomes

I. Information, attitudes and appreciations.

A. Willingness to give constructive suggestions for improving own and others' work.
B. Willingness to receive criticism on own work.
C. Readiness to participate in purposing group enterprises.
D. Willingness to accept a share in the responsibility of planning group enterprises.
E. Respect)for the opinions of others.
F. Independence in expressing own opinion.
G. Understanding of need for clear, concise statements in making reports.
H. Appreciation for the need of order in telling stories.
I. A desire to use correct English.
J. A desire to improve own handwriting.
K. An appreciation for beautiful and legible handwriting.
L. A desire to enlarge spelling vocabulary.
M. An understanding of the need for the ability to spell.
N. An understanding of the need for the ability to speak concisely and distinctly before a group.
O. An understanding of the need for the ability to write legibly with a fair degree of speed.

II. Habits and skills.

A. In oral composition.
1. Ability to organize and outline talks and reports.
2. More skill in speaking before a group clearly and distinctly.
3. Increased poise in speaking before a group.

4. More skill in expressing oneself concisely.
5. Ability to tell a story or anecdote in an interesting way.
6. Ability to criticise constructively both own work and others' work.
7. Increased ability to accept and profit by criticism.
8. Increased ability to think a problem through.
9. Increased ability to follow a problem in a class discussion.
10. Ability to follow an outline in giving a talk.

B. In letter writing and composition writing.
1. Ability to write a business letter using correct form.
2. Ability to write a friendly letter in an interesting way.
3. Ability to write informal notes of invitation or thanks.
4. Ability to make a simple outline of material to be used in a composition.
5. Ability to write a composition of some length following an outline and paragraphing material.
6. Ability to take notes.

C. In handwriting.
1. Ability to write either in manuscript or script with pen and ink, working toward a higher standard on a writing scale.

D. In mechanics of written composition.
1. Ability to use with increasing accuracy the following marks of punctuation: period, question mark, exclamation point, comma, quotation mark, and the apostrophe.
2. Ability to use capital letters correctly in all uses.
3. Ability to arrange written work on paper allowing for margins.
4. Increased skill in writing good sentences.
5. Increased skill in writing a paragraph containing good topic sentences.

E. In language usage.
1. More skill in using correctly such words as learn, teach, lie, lay, rise, raise, set, sit, their, there, to, too, two.
2. More skill in using verb forms correctly.
3. More skill in pronouncing words correctly.
4. More skill in avoiding the use of double negatives.
5. Increased skill in using different words rather than overworking a few.

F. In spelling.
1. Ability to spell words needed in written work.
2. Ability to spell selected words from standard lists.
3. Ability to use dictionary as an aid in spelling.

English in Sixth Grade

Language, Writing and Spelling

A. Activities and Procedure

I. Activities relating to personal experiences.
A. Oral.
1. Reports of vacation experiences.
2. Reports on interesting week-end experiences.
3. Interesting observations which have been made.
4. Reports on outside activities (often given during lunch hour).

B. Written.
1. Writing reports or diaries of vacation experiences.
2. Outlining reports to be given.
3. Writing stories and verses of personal experiences.

March Wind

If you should ask the raw March wind
   where he was going and why,
   he might answer this:
I must awaken the flowers,
And blow the clouds away,
And hurry to waken the earth for the Spring,
And the birds must be told to come back on the wing.

A Poem

A poem that does not rhyme
Is just a lovely thought,
Of rivers, fields, mountains, streams,
Of winter, fall, summer, spring,
And oh! of everything.
     —Reprinted from the Children's Magazine.

II. Activities relating to citizenship and health.
A. Oral.
1. Discussions as to standards of good citizenship in school and as a member of the community.
2. Reports on events of present day interest.
3. Discussions as to food values and combinations.

B. Written.
1. Writing rules for good citizenship.
2. Choosing and writing lunch menu from cafeteria menu sent to the room.

III. **Activities related to group studies in social studies and science.**
    A. Oral.
        1. Discussing problems and possibilities in a unit of experience.
        2. Giving of reports by individual children.
        3. Discussing pictures, original illustrations, and exhibits.
        4. Discussing completed work.
        5. Planning any dramatization or program as a summary to unit.
    B. Written.
        1. Outlining material before writing or giving to class orally.
        2. Writing stories for booklet or chart.
        3. Writing answers to questions checking mastery of subject matter.
        4. Taking notes in good form.
        5. Writing notices to advertise play.
        6. Writing original poems.
        7. Writing an imaginary diary which might be a record of the period studied.

IV. **Activities relating to reading and use of library.**
    A. Oral.
        1. Telling stories read, for pleasure of the class.
        2. Recommending interesting books to the class.
        3. Describing parts of favorite books brought from the home library.
        4. Making plans for Book Week.
        5. Discussing material in different magazines enjoyed.
        6. Discussing different types of material found in library.
        7. Discussing ways of finding material quickly.
        8. Examining parts of a book, as title page and table of contents, and discussing value of each.
        9. Discussion of new words.
    B. Written.
        1. Writing recommendations for books.
        2. Placing book reports on mimeographed blank.
        3. Making book puzzles.
        4. Writing short descriptions of books, letting class supply title.

V. **Letter writing.**
    A. Oral.
        1. Discussion as to types of letters.

CHILDREN SHARE VACATION TRIPS

    2. Discussion as to correct form for business and friendly letters.
    3. Discussion as to content.
  B. Written.
    1. Writing thank you letters.
    2. Writing letters to children who have moved away.
    3. Writing notes to other rooms.
    4. Writing notes to school authorities asking privileges.
    5. Composing letters to imaginary people, as book characters.

VI. Activities relating to room procedure.
  A. Oral.
    1. Making plans for any group activity.
    2. Discussion of any room problem.
    3. Electing officers or representatives.
  B. Written.
    1. Writing notices for bulletin board.
    2. Writing lists of officers or committees.

VII. Publishing school newspaper. (See *National News,* page 348.)
  A. Oral.
    1. Discussion as to types of material to use.
    2. Discussion as to value of a striking title, interesting opening sentence, and good closing sentence.
    3. Examination and discussion of magazines and newspapers published by other schools.
    4. Discussion as to number of magazines to print, the price, expenses, and method of selling.
  B. Written.
    1. Writing articles, stories and poems for the magazine.
    2. Outline made by group for organizing the material.

VIII. Practice in language usage.
  A. Class discussion of points in usage.
  B. Exercises on points discussed in class.

IX. Procedure in improving handwriting.
  A. Manuscript.
    1. Charcoal used in making large letter forms.
    2. Practice with broad-edged pens.
    3. Practice on letters, words and sentences, working for uniformity and speed.
  B. Script. (Those who wish may learn and use script.)
    1. Study of letter forms as they are made.
    2. Practice on letter forms and words at blackboard.
    3. Attention given to height of letters, slant, finishing strokes, and to comfortable position when writing.
    4. Writing in script with pencils.
    5. Writing in script with pen.
  C. Progress in writing.
    1. A portfolio is kept throughout the year containing samples of work.
    2. Comparison is made with writing scales.

X. Procedure in learning to spell.
  A. Words needed in written work.
    1. Class list made by group of words needed in various subjects.
    2. List made of errors frequently found in written work.
  B. Words taken from spelling lists.

C. Plan for teaching.
  1. General procedure.
    a. Test all pupils on the new words in the week's assignment.
    b. Supervise pupil's individual study of words missed.
    c. Test all pupils on the new and review words.
    d. Individual study of the words missed.
    e. Test all pupils on the new and review words.
  2. Method.
    a. Say the word.
    b. Use in a sentence.
    c. Say the letters to yourself.
    d. Write the word and say the letters to yourself as you write.
    e. Draw a line under difficult part.
    f. Write the word without looking.
    g. Check to see if you are right.
D. Review words.
  1. Review constantly words missed before.
  2. Individual check on words.

XI. **Use of standardized tests.**
  A. For checking growth in spelling and language ability.
  B. For discovering difficulties common to all.
  C. For discovering individual difficulties.
  D. For grouping in the room.

B. Books and Materials Used

I. **Materials for written work.**
  A. Kinds of paper used for making books, letters and posters.
    1. Lined ink paper (8½ x 11).
    2. Construction paper (9 x 12)—(12 x 18).
    3. Manila tag board.
    4. Note pads (5½ x 8½).
    5. Envelopes and stationery for letter-writing.
  B. Kinds of pencils.
    1. Charcoal.
    2. Medium soft lead pencils.
  C. Kinds of pen and ink.
    1. Round hand pens.
    2. India ink to use with broad-edged pens.
    3. Fountain pens.

4. Fountain pen ink.

D. Portfolio (9 x 12) for filing work.

II. Work-type materials. (Used by individuals as needed.)

Guitteau, Wm. B. Constructive English Exercises. 1936, Johnson Publishing Company.

Hatfield and others. Practice Exercises in English. 1936, American Book Company.

Kibbe and others. Handbook of English for Boys and Girls. 1939, Scott Foresman.

Thorndike-Century Junior Dictionary. 1935, Scott Foresman.

Winston Simplified Dictionary. 1939, Winston Publishing Company.

III. Spelling materials.

A. Standard lists.

Newlon, J. H., and Hanna, P. R. Newlon-Hanna Speller. 1935, Houghton Mifflin.

B. Individual spelling lists and class lists from subject matter and needs.

C. Notebooks.

1. Composition book (6¾ x 8¼).

2. Graph paper for records.

IV. Standardized tests in language and spelling.

Metropolitan Achievement Test. World Book Company.

Morrison-McCall Spelling Test. World Book Company.

New Stanford Achievement Tests. World Book Company.

Progressive Achievement Test. California Test Bureau.

V. Handwriting scales.

A. Manuscript writing.

Conard, Edith N. Conard Manuscript Writing Standards. Bureau of Publications, Teachers College.

B. Script writing.

Ayres, Leonard P. Measuring Scale for Handwriting. Department of Education, Russell Sage Foundation.

C. Probable Outcomes

I. Information, attitudes and appreciations.

A. A readiness to take part in any class activity.

B. A willingness to give and accept criticism, which at this stage should be more discriminating; a critical attitude toward our work.

C. Respect for the opinions of others.

D. Understanding of need for written articles that are unified, planned, and unmarred by misspelled words or other technical errors.

E. Desire to develop greater ability in securing interest through details.

F. Desire to continue vocabulary development.

G. An appreciation of oral work which is given distinctly, concisely and with poise.

H. A desire to speak before a group with increasing attention to definite subject, logical order, and well-chosen words.

I. An appreciation of clear, legible, and beautiful handwriting.

J. A desire to improve own handwriting.

K. Eagerness to enlarge spelling vocabulary.

L. A desire for accuracy in spelling words.

II. Habits and skills.

A. Oral composition.
1. Growth in organizing reports from various types of material.
2. Increased ability to follow outline or notes.
3. Increased ability to speak distinctly and with poise.
4. Ability to participate helpfully in group discussions.
5. Increased ability to give constructive criticism.
6. Development of critical attitude toward own work,
7. Growth in ability to choose interesting and worth-while materials for class reports.

B. Written composition.
1. Ability to write a friendly letter with attention to correct form.
2. Growth in making content of friendly letter interesting.
3. Ability to write a business letter, with attention to correct form.
4. Growth in making content of a business letter courteous and concise.
5. Ability to outline and organize material read, as well as original material.
6. Ability to write a composition of one page or more in acceptable composition form.
7. Increased accuracy in proofreading and correcting own written work.

C. Handwriting.
1. Ability to write legibly and neatly with pencil, fountain pen or broad-edged pen.

2. Ability to use either script or manuscript, working toward a higher standard on a writing scale.

D. Mechanics of composition.
1. Ability to use acceptable composition form, allowing for margins, and leaving one space between title and first sentence.
2. Ability to paragraph consistently.
3. Increased ability to write good opening and closing sentences.
4. Ability to use capitals correctly in all cases.
5. Ability to use the following marks of punctuation consistently as needed: period, comma, exclamation mark, question mark, quotation marks, apostrophe, semicolon, colon.

E. Language usage.
1. A continuing habit of using correctly, words which have been studied in the previous grades; as, *there* and *their; to, two* and *too.*
2. Progress in eliminating such expressions as *this here one.*
3. Progress in eliminating the use of double negatives.
4. Habit of enunciating all syllables correctly.
5. Addition of many new words to the vocabulary, with special attention to definite picture words and phrases.
6. Some acquaintance with common and proper nouns, pronouns, verb forms, adjectives, adverbs, conjunctions, interjections.

F. Spelling.
1. Ability to spell words needed in the writing vocabulary.
2. Ability to spell words selected from standard lists for the grade.
3. Habit of using dictionary to find correct and preferred spelling.
4. Growth in the ability to eliminate careless spelling errors.

PROVISIONS FOR READING PROGRESS IN THE ELEMENTARY GRADES

BECAUSE the children in this school come from a community where books and magazines are much used, interest in reading is very early developed. The nursery school and the kindergartens afford many pre-reading experiences through the use of literature and creative language. The preparatory reading experiences of the senior kindergarten are described on page 358. A mental age of six or over has been found necessary for the rapid attainment of independence in reading; and undesirable attitudes and habits have been the result of expecting progress in reading before the child was ready. As a rule children have remained in the senior kindergarten until a mental age of six or over has been reached. In the case of a child who attains a mental age of six and a half or seven before he is six chronologically, the physical development, social adjustment and emotional stability are considered carefully, and he is allowed to join a reading group only after approval has been given by the teacher, parents, school physician and psychologist.

Reading at all levels is closely related to the activity program. A great deal of the reading material is composed by the teacher and the children, in response to interests and needs arising in connection with the children's experiences. As the children progress in reading power, books are used continually to extend their experiences and to throw light on their problems.

So great has been the eagerness for contact with real books, and so keen has been the desire to learn to read that it has been thought appropriate to set aside definite reading periods each day beginning in first grade. No one method and no one set of books or work books has been used as basal. Methods and reading materials in all grades have been chosen to meet the capacities and interests of individuals and particular groups.

As a rule, the children are grouped for reading according to ability. Each child is placed in a group or given individual guidance following a study of his individual capacities and needs. With the least mature group it has been found especially desirable to provide materials and books that have not been previously used by the more advanced groups in the room. By this means the teachers have been able to eliminate any feeling of discouragement or inferiority that might otherwise prevail among the less capable children.

Promotions from one grade to another are made on the basis of social adjustment and readiness for participation in the activities of the next group. The teacher in each grade continues ability grouping when found desirable, and provides reading materials that meet the capacities of different groups and individuals.

Because many children find joy in independent reading, and do much free reading at home and in the school library, individual differences in reading ability tend to increase, and the need for group practice tends to diminish.

In the outlines that follow, outcomes tend to be cumulative. Effort is made in each grade to maintain desirable attitudes and appreciations, habits and skills, developed in preceding years.

Reading Activities in First Grade

An outline based on records for one year

A. Activities

I. Reading activities related to group experiences. (Material composed by children and teachers.)

    A. From bulletin boards: reading signs, captions under pictures, posters, personal or group notes from the teacher and from each other, as:

> Dear John,
> Will you water the plants to-day?
>   Miss Brown.

    B. From blackboard and charts.

        1. Reading directions or suggestions for activities, reading to follow plans made previously by the group, filling supplies from lists of materials, reading names of committees.

> In our baskets we will put
>   a pair of scissors
>   one jar of paste
>   one lead pencil
>   one box of crayolas

> To-day we will finish the furniture.
> John will finish a chair.
> Peter will finish a chair.
> Nancy will finish the table.
> Patsy will put the design on the bookcase.
> Jo will sandpaper the cupboard.

        2. Reading records of excursions, records of room activities, stories about pets, toys, nature materials.

    C. From booklets.

    Reading from booklets made by the children, stories of group interests and creative individual stories and songs.

    D. From correspondence or communications.

        1. Reading letters, invitations sent from another room or child; as,

> Dear First Grade:
>   The farm is ready.
>   Will you come to see it?
>   Second Grade.

        2. Reading advertising posters and dodgers; as,

> All aboard for a sailing party!
> Be on deck Saturday at 9:00 A.M.
> Station WMAQ.
> Stories and songs about boats.

II. Guided reading from books.

(Pre-primers, primers, and first readers are chosen for groups, for their special interest appeal or because of their adaptation to the needs of the children. Usually different material is selected for each group.)

A. Activities related to the care and use of the child's own book.
   1. Reading from the blackboard suggestions for care of book.
   2. Reading names from the bookplates.
   3. Reading page numbers.
   4. Learning to find stories from the titles rather than pictures alone.
   5. Learning to know and read the names of the various primers and first readers.

B. Individual study.
   1. To find the solution of a problem in the plot.
   2. To prepare for dramatic oral reading.
   3. To select a story to be used for a specific purpose.

C. Oral reading.
   1. To share enjoyment with the group.
   2. For fuller understanding.
   3. To read the dialogue in parts.

III. Enjoyment of the libraries.

A. The room library.
   1. With teacher reading or telling stories.
      a. Listening to stories told or read.
      b. Listening to and learning beautiful poems.
   2. With the child reading.
      a. Free choice of books to read during self-directed or library periods.
      b. Free choice of books to take home to read to the family.
      c. Audience reading to a group or retelling stories found during free reading.

B. The school library.
   1. Referring to school library when room library is lacking in material wanted.
   2. Referring to library for stories, pictures, books related to group interests.
   3. Seeking additional easy reading material to take home.

IT IS FUN TO READ

IV. **Individual use of work-type materials.**

(These materials emphasize careful discrimination and comprehension. They are related to experience reading or selected to correlate with book reading.)

A. Drawing picture to illustrate sentence stories or phrases written by the teacher.

B. Cutting up stories into sentence or phrase units and putting the story puzzle together.

C. Finding the word or phrase to fit the picture in mimeographed material.

D. Framing like words in a column or list.

E. Finding the correct word or phrase to finish the sentence in multiple choice type of exercises.

B. Procedure or General Method

I. **Beginning reading related to the child's experiences.**

A. Child's name, names of pets, are used as an approach to reading.

B. Material composed by children with teacher's help is used as an approach. This material must have:

1. Interesting content.
2. Literary quality, rhythm, lilting repetition, colorful words and phrases.
3. Simple vocabulary.
4. Short sentences.
5. Short units or groups of sentences.
6. Much repetition in the story.
7. Much repetition from story to story.

C. The plan for the first lessons follows:

1. This material is presented on the blackboard, or it may be printed on a chart.
2. Children read the unit as a whole.
3. Teacher suggests content through skillful suggestions and questions.
4. Teacher runs pointer under sentences, to establish correct habit of eye movement; to help the child get the correlation between the spoken and written symbols.
5. The children find separate sentences.
6. The children find short phrases containing interesting words.
7. Eventually some practice is given to fix important and interesting words.

II. Pre-primer reading.

A. The procedure is similar except that material is taken from the book rather than from the children's immediate experiences.

B. When experience reading has been done from charts and the blackboard, for six weeks or more, reading may be done directly from the book without the intermediate presentation on the blackboard or chart.

C. Phrase and word cards are found valuable if the child can compare words and phrases on the card with those in the book, and thus make the transfer.

D. Word cards are especially valuable in beginning reading when used for rapid phrase and sentence building.

III. Advanced book reading.

A. Individual study. (The study is quiet, but may not be entirely "silent.")

1. A thought unit is selected for individual study, short or longer, depending on the ability of the group and the difficulty of the selection.

2. Emphasis is put on comprehension, and study is directed by:

a. Questions related to the content.

b. Problems to solve.

c. Looking for a humorous part.

d. Looking for a kind or gracious deed or idea.

e. Looking for the solution to plot.

B. Oral reading.

1. In first grade oral reading usually follows individual study to develop fluency.

2. Child's motive for oral reading may be:

a. To help the class see the picture.

b. To understand the story better.

c. To share the story with another class or room.

d. To read the story in parts to enjoy the dialogue.

e. To prepare for a dramatization.

C. Discussion. A discussion is often desirable:

1. To clear up meanings.

2. To select favorite characters.

3. To select kind, gracious characters or deeds.

4. To select characters and outline scenes for dramatization.

D. Study of new and difficult words.

1. They may be used in oral discussion before the study

and written on the blackboard to point out characteristics.

2. They may be discovered through the content if good concise suggestions as to content are given before reading.
3. The sounds of the letters are emphasized when two or more words are found which begin with the same sound. Bringing this similarity to the child's consciousness soon helps him to learn independently the function of the letter sounds.
4. Differences in words, as *clock* and *lock, took* and *look, spin* and *in*, as well as the similarity, are noted.
5. Like endings or beginnings as in *father* and *mother, began* and *before*, are noted.

IV. The testing program.

Standardized tests are given at the end of the year, by a psychologist.

1. Results are used as a basis for recommendations for summer reading.
2. Results are used as a basis for guiding in the next grade.

C. Books and Materials Used

I. Materials used for experience reading.

A. Chart and bulletin board.
1. Manila tag board—36 x 24.
2. India ink.
3. Broad-edged pens for manuscript writing—sizes 1, 2, 3, 4, 5.
4. Magazine illustrations.
5. Colored mounting paper.
6. Show card color.
7. Crayolas.

B. Blackboard.
1. White and colored chalk.
2. Pointers and erasers.

C. Booklets.
1. Manila drawing paper (12 x 18).
2. Colored mounting paper.
3. Art materials for illustrations.
   a. Colored poster paper.
   b. Show card color.
   c. Crayolas.
4. Typewriting paper—(heavy quality, for story material).

5. Sight-saving typewriter.
6. Machine for mimeographing.
7. Brads and raffia for binding books.

II. **Graded readers.** (Pre-primers, primers, and first readers are selected according to the interests and abilities of small groups.)

Baker and Reed	Curriculum Readers	1938	Bobbs-Merrill
Baker and Baker	Bobbs-Merrill Readers	1939	Bobbs-Merrill
Baker and Baker	True Story Series	1938	Bobbs-Merrill
Elson and Gray	Elson Basic Readers	1936	Scott Foresman
Gates, A. I., and others	New Work-Play Books	1939	Macmillan
Hahn and Harris	Child Development Readers	1935	Houghton Mifflin
Hildreth, G., and others	Easy Growth in Reading	1940	Winston
Hill and Martin	Real Life Readers	1930	Scribners
O'Donnell and Carey	Alice and Jerry Books	1936	Row Peterson
Smith, Nila B.	Unit Activity Series	1935	Silver Burdett
Storm, Grace E.	Guidance in Reading	1936	Lyons and Carnahan

III. **Library equipment.**

A. Room library equipment.
   1. Reading table and chairs.
   2. Low bookshelves.
B. Picture books and story books for teacher to read to children; as,

Clark, Mary. E.	Poppy Seed Cakes	1924	Doubleday
Ets, Marie	Mr. Penny	1935	Viking
Flack, Marjorie	Restless Robin	1937	Houghton
Flack, Marjorie	William and His Kitten	1938	Houghton
Gag, Wanda	Millions of Cats	1928	Coward-McCann
Heyward, D.	Country Bunny	1939	Houghton
Hill, H. & Maxwell, V.	Charlie & His Puppy Bingo	1923	Macmillan
Hogan, Inez	Little Black & White Lamb	1927	Macrae
Hogan, Inez	The White Kitten & the Blue Plate	1930	Macmillan
Kunhardt, D.	Little Ones	1935	Viking
Lathrop, D.	Who Goes There?	1935	Macmillan
Leaf, Munro	Ferdinand	1936	Viking
Lida	Little French Farm	1939	Harper
Lida	Fluff	1937	Harper
Lida	Plouf	1936	Harper
Lofting, Hugh	Story of Mrs. Tubbs	1923	Stokes
Milne, A. A.	When We Were Very Young	1924	Dutton
Orton, Helen F.	Little Lost Pigs	1925	Stokes
Orton, Helen F.	The Twin Lambs	1931	Stokes
Tippett, J. S.	The Singing Farmer	1927	World Book
Tippett, J. S.	I Go a-Traveling	1929	Harper
Youmans, E.	Skitter Cat	1925	Bobbs-Merrill

C. Easy books for individual children to read; as,

Bannerman, H.	Little Black Sambo	1923	Stokes
Bannerman, H.	Sambo and the Twins	1936	Stokes
Lincoln School	Picture Scripts	1935	Edward Sterne
Read, H. S.	Social Science Readers	1928	Scribner
Sondergaard, A. & Krueger, L.	Ten Little Reading Books	1931	Gazette Press
Szalatney, R. D.	Cock and the Hen	1925	Harper
Troxell, E.	Pammy and His Friends	1928	Scribner
Wright, L. E.	The Magic Boat	1927	Ginn

D. Additional material available in school library: picture file, many story books and informational books.

IV. Practice materials.

A. Word and phrase cards (accompanying charts, pre-primer and first primer).

B. Published work books (accompanying some primers and first readers chosen for individual or group use).

C. Mimeographed materials composed by teacher, related to experience reading.

V. Standardized tests.

Oral Reading Check Tests. William S. Gray. Public School Publishing Company.
Primary Metropolitan Test. World Book Company.

D. Probable Outcomes

I. Information.

A. Related to the function and the purpose of reading. An understanding of the uses of reading in:
1. Record keeping.
2. Following directions.
3. Correspondence and advertisement.
4. Gaining information.
5. Recreation.

B. Related to book construction.
1. The beginning of an understanding of bookbinding, printing, illustration.
2. An understanding of the terms: author, artist, printer.
3. Some understanding of the organization of a book: cover, frontispiece, table of contents, story, title.

C. Related to types and use of literature.
1. Some knowledge of various types of literature: stories, verses, riddles, jokes.
2. An idea of the differing functions of books, letters, magazines, newspapers.

D. Related to library.
   1. The knowledge of a library as a book center.
   2. A little idea of the personnel of a library.
   3. An idea of appropriate behavior in the library.

II. Attitudes and appreciations.
   A. Related to learning to read.
      1. Joy and interest in learning to read.
      2. Appreciation of the value of knowing how to read.
      3. A willingness to enter into all types of reading activities.
      4. An appreciation of the need of careful, conscientious reading.
   B. Related to the use and ownership of books.
      1. A desire to own good books.
      2. A childlike appreciation of the beauty of illustrations and binding.
      3. Some appreciation of the value of books.
      4. A willingness to exercise care and thought in handling books.
      5. A willingness to share books and stories with others.
   C. Related to the library.
      1. Joy in browsing in the library.
      2. A willingness to cooperate with library requirements.

III. Habits and skills.
   A. Related to the use and care of books.
      1. The ability to use books with a minimum amount of wear and tear.
      2. The habit of using a bag, or wrapping a book if it is to be taken home in inclement weather.
      3. The beginnings of an established habit of sitting correctly, holding book correctly, and sitting under correct lighting conditions when reading.
      4. The ability to find stories by page numbers.
      5. For many, the ability to find stories in the table of contents.
   B. Related to the use of the library.
      1. A partially established habit of using the library for help on problems.
      2. The habit of quiet manner and conduct in the library.
   C. Related to mastery of technique.
      1. In group reading.
         a. The ability to concentrate and work purposefully during the reading periods.

     b. The ability to listen attentively to others read.

     c. By the end of the first semester the habit of keeping the place accurately while others read, in a group.

2. For individual reading.

     a. The ability to get the thought when reading individually from any easy book.

     b. The ability to read orally with a considerable degree of accuracy.

     c. The ability to read fluently from simple primers or first readers.

     d. The ability to read orally with sufficient dramatic interpretation to hold the interest of a small group.

     e. The ability to follow simple directions within a vocabulary of primer difficulty.

     f. The ability to distinguish between words with like endings but different consonant beginnings, as *book* and *took*.

     g. The ability to name several words beginning with the common consonants, or consonant combinations.

     h. A growing independence in pronouncing simple phonetic words of three or four letters.

     i. The habit of attacking new words through the content.

     j. The beginning of an ability to solve new words through recognition of small words or word parts within the new words.

Reading in Second Grade

An outline based on records for one year

A. ACTIVITIES

I. **Reading activities related to group experiences.** (Material composed by children and teachers.)
  A. From the bulletin board.
    1. Reading of the room duties.
    2. Reading names on the weekly calendar for care of the room.

> June 1—Monday—Billy, Katharine
> June 2—Tuesday—Amos, Fred

    3. Reading notices, posters and the like sent in from other rooms.
  B. From blackboard and chart.
    1. Reading directions or suggestions for activities.
      a. Definite plans made for following day.
      b. Suggestions for each child of his duty or responsibility toward unit of work; as,

> Leonore will paint the barn.
> Tom will care for the grass.

      c. Recipes, as when making crab-apple jelly.
      d. Names and duties of different committees.
      e. Rules to improve conduct in school and on playground.
    2. Reading original poems, records of excursions, stories of room activities, records of nature experiments.
      a. Original poems stimulated by the seasons, weather, group experiences.
      b. Story of our trip to the farm, "What we learned at the farm," composed by the group. Other farm stories written individually.
      c. Nature experiments and results of experiments; as,

> What we did:
>   We planted peas and beans.
>   We kept one box in the dark.
>   We kept the other box in the sunlight.
> What we discovered:
>   Peas and beans grown in the dark are white.
>   Plants grown in the sunlight are green.
>   Sunlight makes the color in nature.

C. From booklets (made by children containing records or stories of group interests); as,
    1. My Pottery Book—containing original records of
        a. Trip to the Haeger Pottery.
        b. How liquid clay is made.
        c. How we made our molds.
    2. My Farm Book—containing original stories of trip to the farm and different farm activities.
    3. Nature Books—containing original poems and stories, blueprints with the name of each flower and leaf under the print.
    4. Miscellaneous books made by individual children, containing pictures and stories; as,
        a. The Funny Book.
        b. My Doll Book.
        c. My Family.
D. From correspondence or communications.
    1. Reading letters, invitations, sent from other rooms.
    2. Reading messages sent from the office concerning school car, playground and other school activities.
    3. Reading posters and dodgers sent around to the rooms.
        a. Radio program announcements.
        b. Announcements of sales, programs, plays, at the school.
    4. Reading school newspaper and magazine, especially first and second grade contributions.

II. **Guided reading from books. (Readers are chosen for individuals and groups according to the special interest and ability of the child or the group. Grade labels are disregarded.)**
    A. Activities related to the care and use of child's own book.
        1. General browsing through a new book.
        2. Careful making of name plate for book.
        3. Learning to find a story through the table of contents and page number.
        4. Practicing the correct way to turn pages in a book, care for the cover and binding.
    B. Silent reading.
        1. To read for the plot and enjoyment of the story.
        2. To be better prepared for oral reading.
        3. To select story for some special activity.
        4. To gain desired information.
    C. Oral reading.
        1. To enjoy the story with the group.

GETTING ACQUAINTED WITH THE LIBRARY

2. To read clearly and distinctly so that the group will enjoy the story.
3. To read dialogue in parts.
4. To prepare for dramatization.
5. To make clear, points not understood.

III. Free reading.
    A. Use of room library.
        1. Listening to teacher read or tell stories.
        2. Choosing books for free reading at school.
        3. Choosing books to take home.
        4. Reading to a group, story of own selection from library.
    B. Use of school library for material not found in room library.
        1. For informational purposes, as material on farm activities.
        2. For pictures in picture file.
        3. For variety of story and picture books.

IV. **Individual use of work-type material emphasizing careful comprehension.**
  A. Using mimeographed material made by the teacher for books containing no tests: yes and no tests, completion, multiple choice.
  B. Using workbooks published to accompany some readers in use.
    1. Careful check-up by child and teacher on each page before proceeding to the next page.
    2. Developing independence, by referring to the book for help rather than to the teacher.

B. Procedure for Guided Reading

I. **Presentation of new material. (Teacher attempts to stimulate an interest in the story through discussions, pictures, and other materials. Often questions are formulated to guide the study.)**

II. **Individual study.**
  A. Books are selected according to interests and abilities of individuals or small groups.
  B. Children read short story or chapter individually without interruption.
  C. As children ask for unknown words, teacher tells word and then underscores word in her book, or places it on an individual list.
  D. Check-up is made on comprehension through:
    1. Questions related to content, either oral or written.
    2. Solving riddles and problems.
    3. Looking for the high points of interest in the story.

III. **Oral reading of literary selections.**
  A. Oral reading may follow individual study of the story:
    1. To form the basis for oral discussion.
    2. To help group understand the story better.
    3. To help group relive the story: see the pictures, hear the sounds, feel the emotions.
    4. To share a story which one child has studied, and the others have not heard.
  B. Emphasis is placed on reading so that the audience will understand and be interested:
    1. Knowing material well before reading.
    2. Speaking in a clear distinct tone of voice.
    3. Interpreting the story in an individual way.

IV. Word mastery in connection with book reading (presented at a separate time from the reading period).
  A. Words are taken from list obtained in preceding reading lesson.
  B. Words are written on board (preferably not in a column but at random) and studied one at a time for similarity to known words, noting beginnings and endings and emphasizing sounds of letters and combinations. Meanings are stressed.

V. Testing program.
  Standardized tests are given at end of each semester by psychologist. Results are used:
    1. As a basis for grouping within the class.
    2. As a basis for recommendations for summer reading.
    3. As a basis for selecting those who need individual help.

C. BOOKS AND MATERIALS USED

I. Related to experience reading.
  A. Chart and bulletin board.
    1. Manila tag board—cut in sizes for writing stories, experiments, announcements.
    2. India ink.
    3. Round head pens for manuscript writing.
  B. Blackboard.
    1. White dustless chalk.
    2. Pointer and erasers.
  C. Booklet making.
    1. Manila drawing paper (12 x 18).
    2. Colored mounting paper.
    3. Materials for illustration.
      a. Poster paper—colored.
      b. Magazine pictures.
      c. Crayolas and water colors.
    4. Writing paper for story material (wide-lined composition paper).
    5. Brads and raffia for binding books.

II. Primers and readers (selected according to the interests and ability of the group or the individual).

Baker and Reed	Curriculum Readers	1938 Bobbs-Merrill
Baker and Baker	Bobbs-Merrill Readers	1939 Bobbs-Merrill
Baker and Baker	True Story Series	1938 Bobbs-Merrill

Cutright, P. and others	Democracy Readers	1940 Macmillan
Dopp, K. E., and others	Happy Road to Reading	1935 Rand, McNally
Elson and Gray	Elson Basic Readers	1936 Scott Foresman
English and Alexander	Happy Hour Readers	1935 Johnson
Gates, A. I., and others	New Work-Play Books	1939 Macmillan
Hahn and Harris	Child Development Readers	1935 Houghton Mifflin
Hildreth, G., and others	Easy Growth in Reading	1940 Winston
Hill and Martin	Real Life Readers	1930 Scribner
O'Donnell and Carey	Alice and Jerry Books	1936 Row Peterson
Smith, Nila B.	Unit Activity Series	1935 Silver Burdett
Storm, Grace E.	Guidance in Reading	1936 Lyons and Carnahan

III. Library equipment.

    A. Room library equipment.

        1. Low bookshelves.

        2. Reading table and chairs.

        3. Library card file.

        4. Bookrests.

    B. Books to read to children; as,

Armer, L. A.	Forest Pool	1938 Longmans
Bennett, Richard	Shawneen and the Gander	1937 Doubleday
Cobb, B.	Clematis	1927 Putnam
Milne, A. A.	Now We Are Six	1928 Dutton
MonVel, de—M. B.	Susanna's Auction	1927 Macmillan
Phillips, E. C.	Little Friend Lydia	1920 Houghton Mifflin
Verdey, E.	About Ellie at Sandacre	1925 Dutton
Wells, R.	Coco, the Goat	1929 Doubleday
Wells, R.	Peppi, the Duck	1927 Doubleday
Whitney, E.	Tyke-y, His Book and His Mark	1925 Macmillan
Youmans, E.	Great Adventures of Jack, Jock and Funny	1938 Bobbs-Merrill

    C. Easy material for individual children to read; as,

Beskow, Elsa	Aunt Green, Aunt Brown, Aunt Lavender	1929 Harper
Beskow, Elsa	Olle's Ski Trip	1929 Harper
Beskow, Elsa	Pelle's New Suit	1930 Harper
Flack, Marjorie	Walter, the Lazy Mouse	1937 Doubleday
Flack, Marjorie	Willy Nilly	1936 Macmillan
Gág, Wanda	The A B C Bunny	1933 Coward-McCann
Gág, Wanda	Snippy and Snappy	1928 Coward-McCann
Gay, Zhenya	Sakimura	1937 Viking
Hill, H. & Maxwell, V.	Charlie and His Kitty Topsy	1927 Macmillan
Hill, H. & Maxwell, V.	Charlie and His Puppy Bingo	1927 Macmillan
Lee, E. & Read, H.	Social Science Readers	1928 Scribner

LeFevre, F.	The Cock, the Mouse and the Little Red Hen	1920 Jacobs
LeFevre, F.	The Little Gray Goose	1925 Jacobs
Lincoln School	Picture Scripts	1935 Edward Sterne
Lindman, Maj.	Snipp, Snapp, Snurr and the Buttered Bread	1934 Whitman
Lofting, Hugh	Noisy Nora	1929 Stokes
Lofting, Hugh	Story of Mrs. Tubbs	1923 Stokes
Newberry, Clare	Barkis	1938 Harper
Newberry, Clare	Mittens	1936 Harper
Orton, Helen F.	Bobby of Cloverfield Farm	1922 Stokes
Orton, Helen F.	Little Lost Pigs	1925 Stokes
Orton, Helen F.	Prancing Pat	1927 Stokes
Orton, Helen F.	Prince and Rover of Cloverfield Farm	1921 Stokes
Tippett, James	I Go a-Traveling	1929 Harper
Tippett, James	I Live in a City	1929 Harper
Tippett, James	The Singing Farmer	1927 Harper

D. Additional material available in school library: picture file, many story books, dictionary, large globe.

IV. **Practice materials.**

    A. Published workbooks, accompanying some readers chosen for individual or group use.

    B. Mimeographed comprehension checks made by teacher to accompany books without tests.

V. **Tests.**

    A. Informal tests, given from time to time.

        1. Oral reading—chart kept recording the number and kind of errors made by each child, in mispronunciation, substitution, insertion, words unknown, omission.

        2. Silent reading—same type of chart as used in oral reading, recording words child asks for when reading silently.

    B. Standardized tests.

    Metropolitan Achievement Test. World Book Company.
    New Stanford Achievement Test. World Book Company.

D. Probable Outcomes

I. **Information.**

    A. Related to the function and purpose of reading: fuller realization of the uses of reading in record keeping, outlining plans, following directions, correspondence, advertisement, gaining information, recreation.

    B. Related to book construction.

        1. A fuller understanding of bookbinding, printing, engraving, work of author, artist and printer.

  2. Better understanding of organization of a book: cover, frontispiece, table of contents, chapters.

  3. Some understanding of the construction of a newspaper and magazine.

 C. Related to types of literature.

  1. A clearer knowledge of various types of literature: stories, factual articles, prose, poetry, riddles, jokes, songs.

  2. A better idea of the differing functions of books, letters, magazines, newspapers, posters, dodgers.

 D. Related to library.

  1. The knowledge of library as source of getting information through maps, pictures, magazines, encyclopedias, globe.

  2. The knowledge of library as a place to enjoy books of all types.

  3. An understanding of the personnel of a library.

  4. Knowledge concerning the function of a library card; the taking out and returning of books.

  5. Understanding of appropriate behavior in the library.

  6. Beginning of knowledge of where to find books wanted in the library.

II. Attitudes and appreciations.

 A. Related to learning to read.

  1. Added interest and joy in learning to read because of desire to gain knowledge about certain things.

  2. Deeper appreciation of the value of knowing how to read.

   a. Satisfaction in solving problems through reading.

   b. Joy in being able to read to others.

   c. Joy derived from being able to read interesting stories and poems for own pleasure.

  3. Feeling of need for all types of reading activities.

   a. Reading for pleasure.

   b. Reading for information.

   c. Reading to give to others.

   d. Reading carefully to follow directions.

  4. Confidence in ability to read with increasing independence.

 B. Related to the use and ownership of books.

  1. Stronger desire to own good books as child realizes how much book world can give.

  2. A fuller appreciation of the beauty of books as shown through printing, illustrations, bindings.

3. Better appreciation of the value of books and willingness to exercise more care in the handling of books.
4. Willingness to share books and stories as home library increases.
C. Related to the library.
  1. Added joy in browsing in the library.
  2. Continued willingness to cooperate with library rules and regulations.
    a. In taking out books.
    b. In care and use of library books.
    c. In responsibility in returning books.

III. Habits and skills.
A. Related to the use and care of books.
  1. Ability to use a book with very little wear and tear, not marking in the books, folding the leaves, bending cover back.
  2. Ability to mark the place correctly in a book if needed.
  3. Continued habit of sitting correctly, holding the book correctly and in right lighting conditions when reading, at the same time enjoying a natural relaxed freedom.
  4. Ability to find a story by the page number and through the table of contents.
  5. The habit of caring for a book taken home from school.
    a. Protecting from the weather when needed.
    b. Not leaving on playground or in the school car.
    c. Treating book carefully at home.
    d. Seeing that book is brought back.
B. Related to the use of the library.
  1. Beginning of a habit of using library.
  2. Habit of quiet manner and conduct in the library.
  3. Effort toward being responsible for returning books within the time limit, and without a reminder.
  4. Ability to take books out and return books independently with the help of the librarian and not the room teacher.
C. Related to the mastery of technique.
  1. Well-established habit of concentration and purposeful work through the reading period.
  2. Increased ability in getting the thought when reading individually.
  3. Certain degree of ability in retelling or discussing the story read.
  4. Considerable accuracy and independence in taking com-

prehension tests, and answering comprehension questions.

5. Ability to read orally with a marked degree of accuracy.
6. The ability to read orally fluently and with sufficient dramatic interpretation to hold the interest of the group.
7. Habit of listening courteously to others read.
8. The ability to keep the place in group reading.
9. The ability to read material used in the group independently and quite fluently.
10. The ability to follow somewhat simple directions within the child's reading vocabulary.
11. The ability to note differences and likenesses in beginnings and endings of words.
12. The ability to attack many new words phonetically, pronouncing them as wholes.
13. A growing ability to recognize new words through the context.

Reading in Third Grade

An outline based on records for one year

A. Activities

I. Reading activities related to group experiences. (Materials composed by children and teachers.)

  A. From the bulletin board.

    1. Reading notices from other rooms and from the school office.

    2. Reading changes of program and special invitations to programs and assemblies.

  B. From the blackboard.

    1. Reading suggestions for work before regular school day begins; as,

      Finish number work.

      Correct spelling.

      Mount pictures.

    2. Reading daily plans made by the group; as,

      Bill and Andrew will work on the Mexican house.

      Loraine and Edith will paint scenery.

    3. Reading directions for committees working on specific projects.

  C. From children's papers and notebooks.

    1. Reading poems composed by groups and individuals; records of trips taken during vacations; stories written about animals and pets; stories telling of excursions, as to Field Museum and Shedd Aquarium.

  D. From booklets containing original work of children; as,

    1. Book of Poems.

      Vacation Poems.

      Halloween Poems.

      Winter Poems.

      Rainy Day Poems.

    2. Individual books made by children according to particular interests; as,

      My Trip to the Aquarium.

      A Trip to the Country.

      Gathering Seeds in Autumn.

      My Book of Flowers.

  E. From correspondence.

    1. Invitations from other rooms.

    2. Dodgers sent to the room from other rooms.

3. Letters from business firms of whom questions had been asked.
4. Letters from children who were absent from school for several days at a time.

F. From school newspapers and magazines.

II. Guided reading from books. (Readers are chosen for individuals and groups according to ability and different interests. Grade labels are disregarded.)

A. Activities related to the care and use of child's own book.
1. Using the table of contents to find selections.
2. Practicing the correct way to turn pages in a book, care for cover and binding.
3. Practicing correct way to open a new book.

B. Silent reading.
1. To enjoy an interesting story.
2. To select story for some special activity.
3. To find outcome of story.
4. To gain specific information.

C. Oral reading.
1. To take part in a dramatic reading of the story.
2. To help the group to enjoy the humor or beauty of the selection.
3. To prove points that were not clear.
4. To provide the basis for a group discussion.
5. To share a story which one child has enjoyed and the others have not heard.

III. Free reading.

A. Use of room library.
1. Choosing books to read alone.
2. Selecting books for home reading.
3. Selecting material to read to the group.

B. Use of school library.
1. Enjoying library period by looking at books on shelves.
2. Using school library for material not in room library: information about topics of study; pictures and magazines; large globe; variety of story books.

IV. Individual use of work-type material, emphasizing comprehension.

A. Using booklets accompanying some sets of readers; checking up after each test to be sure work is correct.
B. Using independent work-type books to gain certain needed skills.

B. Procedure for Guided Reading

I. Presentation of new material. (Teacher stimulates interest in the story through discussions, pictures, or objects. Questions to guide study may be formulated.)

II. Silent study.
  A. Children read entire story silently, if story is not too long.
  B. Teacher underlines unknown words in her book as children ask for them; makes list of words found difficult.
  C. Check-up is made on comprehension through questions and discussions.

III. Oral reading of literary selections.
  Oral reading often follows silent study of story, with emphasis on these points:
  A. Reading so that audience will enjoy story, hear the sounds, see the pictures, understand the meaning.
  B. Knowing the material before reading.
  C. Speaking clearly in a pleasing tone.

IV. Word study in connection with book reading (presented as needs suggest).
  A. Words are presented from lists made in preceding lessons.
  B. Words are written on board, alone or in phrases, meaning explained, similarity to familiar words noted.

V. Testing.
  Standardized tests are given at the end of each semester by psychologist and results are used:
  A. As a basis for grouping within the class.
  B. As a basis for selecting those who need special help.
  C. As a basis for recommendations for home reading.

C. Books and Materials Used

I. Graded readers (chosen according to the interests and ability of the individual or the group).

Baker and Reed	Curriculum Readers	1938 Bobbs-Merrill
Baker and Baker	Bobbs-Merrill Readers	1939 Bobbs-Merrill
Baker and Baker	True Story Series	1938 Bobbs-Merrill
Cutright, P. and others	Democracy Readers	1940 Macmillan
Dopp, K. E., and others	Happy Road to Reading	1935 Rand-McNally
Elson and Gray	Elson Basic Readers	1936 Scott Foresman

English and Alexander	Happy Hour Readers	1935	Johnson
Gates, A. I., and others	New Work-Play Books	1939	Macmillan
Hahn and Harris	Child Development Readers	1935	Houghton Mifflin
Hildreth, G., and others	Easy Growth in Reading	1940	Winston
Hill and Martin	Real Life Readers	1930	Scribners
Huber. M.B., and others	Wonder-Story Books	1938	Row, Peterson
O'Donnell and Carey	Alice and Jerry Books	1936	Row, Peterson
Smith, Nila B.	Unit Activity Series	1935	Silver-Burdett
Storm, Grace E.	Guidance in Reading	1936	Lyons and Carnahan

II. Room Library.

  A. Equipment.
  1. Low bookshelves.
  2. Reading table and chairs.
  3. Library file cards.
  4. Bookrests.

B. Books read to the children; as,

Bemelmans, Ludwig	Castle Number Nine	1937	Viking
Bemelmans, Ludwig	Golden Basket	1936	Viking
Cobb, B. B. & E.	Clematis	1927	Putnam
Collodi, C.	Pinocchio	1923	Winston
Morley, M. W.	Little Mitchell	1904	McClurg
Sterne, E. G.	White Swallow	1927	Duffield

C. Books read by individual children; as,

Adams, S. W.	Five Little Friends	1922	Macmillan
Batchelder, M.	Peggy Stories	1924	Scribners
Bianco, M. W.	Poor Cecco	1925	Doran
Bianco, M. W.	The Velvet Rabbit	1927	Doran
Brock, E. L.	Little Fat Gretchen	1934	Knopf
Burgess, T. W.	Old Mother West Wind	1910	Little Brown
Burnett, F.	Little Lord Fauntleroy	1914	Scribner
Colum, P.	The Peep Show Man	1929	Macmillan
Coolidge, F. C.	Little Ugly Face	1925	Macmillan
Dalgliesh, Alice	American Travels	1933	Macmillan
Grahame, K.	The Wind in the Willows	1908	Scribners
Hill, Helen & Maxwell V.	Little Tonino	1928	Macmillan
Horne, R. H.	The Good Natured Bear	1930	Macmillan
Hulbert, W. D.	Forest Neighbors	1915	Row Peterson
Hunt, C. W.	Peggy's Playhouse	1924	Houghton Mifflin
Hunt, C. W.	About Harriet	1916	Houghton Mifflin
Hyams, L.	The Dog Who Looked Around	1939	Bobbs-Merrill
Lang, A.	Cinderella	1926	Longmans Green
Lathrop, Dorothy	Bouncing Betsy	1936	Macmillan
Lathrop, Dorothy	Hide and Go Seek	1938	Macmillan
Lida	Spiky, the Hedgehog	1938	Harper
Lindman, Maj	Snipp, Snapp, Snurr and the Big Surprise	1937	Whitman

Milne, A. A.	Now We Are Six	1927 Dutton
Morrow, E.	The Painted Pig	1930 Knopf
Mulock, D. M.	Adventures of a Brownie	1924 Harper
Orton, H. F.	Little Lost Pigs	1930 Stokes
Phillips, E. C.	Little Friend Lydia	1920 Houghton Mifflin
Phillips, E. C.	Wee Ann	1919 Houghton Mifflin
Phillips, E. C.	The Pop-Over Family	1927 Houghton Mifflin
Reno, E. W.	The Pup Called Cinderella	1939 Bobbs-Merrill
Simon, B., & Michelle, M.	Peg and Pete See New York	1939 Bobbs-Merrill
Wells, R.	Coco the Goat	1929 Doubleday
Wells, R.	Peppi the Duck	1927 Doubleday

Note: Books related to units of work are included with units of work and are not repeated here.

III. **Additional material available in the school library: picture files, large globe, large dictionary, encyclopedias, many easy books suitable for independent reading, magazines.**

IV. **Practice materials.**

A. Published work-type materials, accompanying some readers, selected for group use.

B. Mimeographed comprehension checks made by teacher to accompany some stories not followed by tests.

V. **Tests.**

A. Informal test records kept by teacher.

1. Oral reading chart kept with errors of each child.

2. Silent reading chart kept of words asked for in independent reading.

B. Standardized tests.

Metropolitan Achievement Test. World Book Company.
New Stanford Achievement Test. World Book Company.

D. Probable Outcomes

I. **Information.**

A. Related to the function and purposes of reading: fuller realization of needs for reading to follow directions, to carry on correspondence, to gain information and pleasure.

B. Related to book construction.

1. Better understanding of processes involved in making a book, work of author, artist, printer, binder.

2. Better understanding of organization of book into cover, table of contents, frontispiece, chapters, index.

C. Related to types of literature.
1. Better understanding of different types of literature: fables, fairy stories, poetry, jokes, factual reading, humorous stories.
2. A better idea of functions of books, magazines, letters, posters.
D. Related to library.
1. Fuller knowledge of the library as a source of information: encyclopedias, dictionary, reference books.
2. Fuller knowledge of library as a place to read books for pleasure.
3. Fuller knowledge of effective use of library.

II. Attitudes and appreciations.

A. Related to reading.
1. Added interest and pleasure in learning to find out things alone.
2. Increased appreciation of value of knowing how to read.
3. Satisfaction in solving own problems through reading alone.
4. Joy in reading to others and in reading for own pleasure.
5. Feeling of need for various kinds of reading skills; painstaking reading to follow directions or master facts; thoughtful reading to solve problems; rapid reading for pleasure; fluent reading to give pleasure to others.
B. Related to the use and ownership of books.
1. Increased desire to own good books.
2. Appreciation of the beauty of books, in binding, illustration, arrangement.
3. More of an idea of value of books.
4. Increased willingness to share books with others.
C. Related to library.
1. Increased interest in going to library alone and in cooperating with librarians in regulations of library, for taking out books, for care and use of books, and for returning books on time.
2. Interest in starting a home library.

III. Habits and skills.

A. Related to the use and care of books.
1. Ability to use books carefully with as little wear and tear as possible.
2. Improvement in posture while reading.

3. Ability to find the story by using the page number in table of contents.
4. Better habits in caring for books taken home from school: protecting from weather; not losing books on campus or in school car; bringing book back on time.

B. Related to the use of the library.
   1. Increased skill in using the library.
   2. Good self control in the library; ability to consider a group.

C. Related to mastery to technique.
   1. Continued habits of concentration and purposeful work in reading.
   2. More skill in reading to solve problems.
   3. Increased ability at getting thought when reading silently.
   4. Ability to follow directions accurately.
   5. Independence in taking comprehension tests.
   6. Increased ability to retell a story read, and to report orally on factual material acquired through reading.
   7. Improved ability to read orally so that others can understand and enjoy what is read.
   8. Increased ability to read orally, smoothly, accurately and in a pleasing tone.
   9. Development of speed in silent reading and fluency in oral reading.
   10. Continued habit of listening courteously while others read.
   11. Increased ability in attacking new words in parts, and in recognizing common word beginnings and word endings; increased ability in pronouncing new words by comparison with words previously learned.

Reading in Fourth Grade

I. **Reading of material composed by teacher and children.**

A. Related to personal experiences.
1. Stories describing vacation experiences.
2. Stories of interesting happenings at home.
3. Original conundrums, riddles and puzzles.
4. Personal account books and diaries.
B. Related to group interests.
1. Signs, posters, maps, charts, pictures, graphs, pertaining to vacation, Halloween, Valentine's Day, Christmas, and other interests.
2. Captions for movies, titles of books, pictures.
3. Stories written about various aspects of problems under study, as, "How We Get Oranges for Breakfast," "How to Feed Baby Chicks."
4. Lists of books prepared for use as reference material on various problems.
5. Various cooking recipes.
6. Group and individual diaries kept of experiments performed.
7. Directions given on blackboard for conduct and plans for excursions taken, as excursion to fire department in study of Chicago.
8. Class records and stories from bulletin board.
9. Bills, receipts and financial reports related to selling enterprises.
10. Original poems and stories, included in school newspaper and magazine.
11. Orders made out for supplies needed for various activities.
12. Records of achievement both of group and individual.
13. Correspondence with other rooms, firms, school authorities; personal letters; announcements, advertisements and programs.
14. Scenes of original plays.
15. Reports giving facts found in answer to questions and problems.
16. Lists of spelling words formulated by the group, growing out of needs.
17. Lists of materials available or needed.

438

THE LIBRARY LEADS TO NEW ADVENTURE

C. Related to citizenship and health.
 1. Charts for height and weight.
 2. Original health slogans and rhymes.
 3. Original stories for health play, given by the group.
 4. Original menus, composed for parties.
 5. Charts, records, graphs, pertaining to habit. formation, rules for self-control.
 6. Committee reports and recommendations pertaining to right use of halls, toilet, playground, school equipment.
D. Related to room procedure.
 1. Program for the day; plans for the week; plans for large units of work.
 2. Notices posted by individuals (teacher and children) pertaining to room activities, committee meetings, use of materials.

II. Library activities.
A. Organizing and using the room library.
 1. Reading plans for organization of room library.
 2. Reading book lists chosen to be included in room library.

3. Scanning individual and class lists of books read.
4. Reading selections from favorite books, brought from home, placed in room library.
5. Reading book reports written by teachers and children.
6. Listening to interesting poems, stories, articles read by the teacher, individual children and groups of children.
B. Learning to use the school library.
  1. Learning to know the position of groups of books, as reference, fiction, science.
  2. Understanding and using the card catalogue and picture file.
  3. Understanding and using the globe, encyclopedias, large dictionary and other reference material.
  4. Using individual cards for drawing out books, with proper procedure.
  5. Learning best methods of finding materials effectively.
  6. Learning the habits necessary for effective use, as low voices, placing books upon shelves in right order.
C. Enjoying the school library.
  1. Finding books of interest and sharing with others.
  2. Sharing beautiful pictures, new books and magazines.
  3. Dramatization of stories read.
  4. Reading poetry and memorizing parts liked best.
D. Caring for books.
  1. Learning value and care of books.
    a. Discussing the process of making books, their history and development.
    b. Looking at pictures, movie of a book in the making.
    c. Discussing the value of books, cost of making. Comparative prices.
    d. Discussing the proper treatment of new books, as opening the book, using a marker, inserting a bookplate.
    e. Making bookplates and markers for books.
    f. Making of book ends and book standards for displaying books.
  2. Learning to use books.
    a. Maintaining hygienic habits of reading, as correct posture both standing and sitting; proper way of holding book, for turning pages and securing light.
    b. Reading charts as reminders of above points.
    c. Discussing and learning to use title page, preface, table of contents, chapter headings, index, notes, references, appendix and illustrative materials.

d. Using the dictionary for the purpose of arriving at pronunciation of new words independently.

III. Guided reading activities for appreciation and skills (from books).
  A. Silent reading.
    1. Reading to answer questions related to social studies, natural and general science.
    2. Reading to follow directions:
      a. Making various objects.
      b. Cooking experiments.
      c. Arithmetic problems.
      d. Playing games.
      e. Following daily program.
    3. Reading to reproduce ideas and information through graphic and plastic materials, as pictorial tables, puppet show, time chart of historical events.
    4. Reading to verify conclusions, by citing authorities.
    5. Reading to judge values.
      a. To find favorite stanza or paragraph.
      b. To find most beautiful descriptive scenes, the best character sketches, well-chosen words and phrases.
      c. To get general impression to see if material is usable for certain definite work.
    6. Organizing and outlining material by listing main points.
    7. Selecting the central thought of a story, or a paragraph.
    8. Reading to note important details.
    9. Interpreting maps, graphs, charts.
    10. Reading and discussing new words, helping to build a more comprehensive vocabulary.
    11. Reading and discussing selections for the purpose of visualizing details.
  B. Oral reading.
    1. Giving informal programs of stories and poems by the Book Club.
    2. Giving dramatizations of poems, stories.
    3. Sharing selections from favorite authors and poets.
    4. Reading worth-while sections from magazines, newspapers and books, related to various class discussions in social studies, natural and general science.
    5. Sharing humorous stories and conundrums at birthday parties and on festival days.
    6. Reading to support judgment and to prove points in discussions.
    7. Reading certain parts to discuss the answers to questions

proposed by the children or the teacher.

8. Reading poems for enjoyment; dialogues and monologues for interpretation.
9. Sharing interesting, exciting, dramatic and humorous passages.
10. Reading in relay: children working in small group prepare to read a selection to another group, the purpose being pleasure and not to have any break in the story.
11. Group to group reading: children in small groups, each group having a different book, read the story to another group.
12. Reading to select stories and poems for room programs.
13. Reading to advertise books to other children.
14. Reading to understand the story better.

IV. Use of work-type material (as needed by groups and individuals).
   A. Teacher made.
   1. Practice to build vocabulary, as selecting words from content to use in original sentences.
   2. Underlining word that means the same.
   3. Underlining word that has opposite meaning.
   4. Underlining phrase which best gives thought of paragraph read.
   5. Using checks on comprehension of reading: true-false; completion tests; multiple choice.
   6. Using three-minute tests to check rate of reading.
   7. Using objective tests on social studies, natural and general science.
   8. Keeping individual and class score sheets.
   9. Practice in finding reference to topics on certain pages.
   10. Practice in using the index as an aid in finding references to questions and problems.
   B. Printed material.
   Using practice exercises and tests as individual needs suggest.

V. Use of standardized tests.
   A. To determine standard of accomplishment for individuals and the group.
   B. To form basis for organizing groups within the room.
   C. To help in diagnosing difficulties of both group and individuals.
   D. To provide basis for remedial help in a group and for individuals.

B. Books and Materials Used

I. **Library equipment in the room.**
   - A. Furniture and equipment.
     1. Reading tables and chairs.
     2. Bookcases, book ends, bookrests.
     3. Maps, globes, puzzle maps.
     4. Stamps for marking dates.
     5. Rack for placing books advertised by groups and individual.
     6. Bulletin board for posting library notices, newspaper clippings, pictures.
     7. Museum table (made by group) upon which to place completed books and posters.
   - B. Accessories.
     1. List of books suitable for fourth grade reading.
     2. Mimeographed copies of book report forms, including:
        Name of child.
        Name of book.
        Author.
        Date completed.
        List of important characters.
        The best points about the book.
     3. File for pictures used in social studies.
     4. File for pamphlets dealing with natural and general science and social studies.
     5. Card file, with cards containing comprehension questions, concerning certain books, dealing with specific topics.

II. **Books for individual reading; as:**

Atkinson, Agnes A.	Skinny the Gray Fox	1936	Viking Press
Carroll, L.	Alice in Wonderland	1920	Macmillan
Chrismas, A. B.	Shen of the Sea	1925	Dutton
Coatsworth, E. J.	Away Goes Sally	1934	Macmillan
Davis, LaVinia	The Keys to the City	1936	Scribner
DeAngeli, M.	Copper-Toed Boots	1938	Doubleday
DeAngeli, M.	Petite Suzanne	1937	Doubleday
Dyott, George M.	Nip and Tuck	1935	Viking Press
Ekerle, I.	Through the Harbor	1938	Bobbs-Merrill
Emerson, Caroline	Father's Big Improvements	1936	Stokes
Field, Rachel	Hitty, Her First Hundred Years	1930	Macmillan
Ghosh, P. S.	The Wonders of the Jungle	1915	Heath
Kipling, Rudyard	Just So Stories	1920	Doubleday
Leetch, D. L.	Annetje and Her Family	1928	Lothrop

Leetch, D. L.	Tommy Tucker	1925 Lothrop
Mukerji, D. G.	Kari, the Elephant	1927 Dutton
Muloch, Dinah	The Little Lame Prince	1918 Lippincott
Muloch, Dinah	Adventures of a Brownie	1918 Lippincott
Ratzesberger, Anna	Camel Bells	1936 Whitman
Reed, W. M.	The Earth for Sam	1930 Harcourt Brace
Reed, W. M.	The Stars for Sam	1931 Harcourt Brace
Thompson, A. T.	The Birch and the Star	1910 Row Peterson
Walker, J. L.	How They Carried Mail	1930 Sears
Wiggin, K. D.	The Birds' Christmas Carol	1916 Houghton Mifflin
Wilder, Laura I.	Farmer Boy	1933 Harper
Wynne, A.	For Days and Days	1919 Stokes
Youmans, Eleanor	The Forest Road	1939 Bobbs-Merrill

III. Books for reading groups (used according to interests and abilities of the groups, disregarding grade labels).

Baker and Baker	The Earth We Live On	1937 Bobbs-Merrill
Baker and Baker	Bobbs-Merrill Readers	1939 Bobbs-Merrill
Cutright, P., and others	Democracy Readers	1940 Macmillan
Eichel, C. G. and others	Treasure Chest of Literature	1935 Houghton Mifflin
Elson and Gray	Elson Basic Readers	1936 Scott Foresman
Gates and Ayer	Work-Play Books	1932 Macmillan
Hahn, Julia L., and others	Child Development Readers	1938 Houghton, Mifflin
Lewis and Rowland	New Silent Readers	1931 Winston
Smith and Bayne	Distant Doorways	1940 Silver Burdett
Smith, E. E., and others	Adventures in Reading	1931 Doubleday
Wright, Wendell W., and others	Modern World Readers	1934 Johnson
Yoakum, G. A., and others	Reading to Learn	1935 Macmillan
Thorndike-Century	Junior Dictionary	1935 Scott Foresman

IV. Periodicals.

1. National Geographic (for pictures).
2. Nature Magazine.
3. Popular Mechanics.
4. My Weekly Reader.
5. Story Parade.

V. Practice materials.

A. Work-type printed material, accompanying some readers chosen for group or individual use.
B. Teacher made material.
   1. Sets of vocabulary cards, using words needed by children.
   2. Mimeographed material—involving:
      a. Material to test comprehension (true-false, completion, multiple choice).

b. Material assisting children to do research in phases of natural and general science and social studies.

VI. Standardized tests.

New Stanford Achievement Test   World Book Company
Progressive Achievement Test   California Test Bureau

C. PROBABLE OUTCOMES

I. Outcomes in information.

A. A growing knowledge of how books, newspapers, periodicals, have developed.

B. A better knowledge of the work of the author, artist, printer, binder.

C. Some background for judging the mechanical make-up of the book; as, the cover, title page, contents, type, paper.

D. A growing knowledge of books as sources of information and pleasure.

E. A growing knowledge of kinds of books and their uses; as encyclopedias, dictionaries, readers' guide, atlas.

F. An increasing knowledge of the origin, function and use of the library:

1. Proper procedure in drawing out books.
2. The library as an index to the best books to read.
3. How libraries get books—source of money and gifts.
4. The work of the various officers in the library.

G. An increased understanding of the cost of books and their value.

H. A growing knowledge of authors and something of their life and works.

I. A better understanding of how to use books in solving problems.

J. A better understanding of the hygienic way of using books, holding book for proper light, posture of body when reading.

K. Some knowledge of best means of making progress in reading.

L. Some knowledge of best habits of study.

II. Outcomes in attitudes and appreciations.

A. An appreciation of the beauty of descriptive words and phrases.

B. A growing appreciation of good literature and the charm of certain characters and incidents described in classic books.

C. A growing capacity for securing enjoyment from the use and ownership of books.
D. A developing love and appreciation for good books.
E. An enjoyment in hearing stories read and an appreciation of the need for courtesy on the part of the listener or audience.
F. A growing joy in selecting and preparing a story to read to others.
G. A willingness to use books as a source for information.
H. A growing pride in the school library.
I. An increasing desire to cooperate with others to build a better library.
J. An increasing responsibility in the care and use of library books, and a willingness to handle books carefully.
K. An appreciation and growing desire to improve the quality of voice, to secure clear enunciation and correct pronunciation in reading.
L. A growing appreciation of the value of different kinds of reading skills, as:
   1. Reading to follow directions.
   2. Reading to find details.
   3. Reading to predict outcomes.
   4. Reading to solve problems, answer questions.
M. An increasing willingness to practice necessary skills in order to insure growth and overcome wasteful habits.

III. **Outcomes in habits and skills.**
   A. Progress in eliminating undesirable habits; as, head and lip movement, repetition.
   B. Increasing ability to master new and unfamiliar words, by
      1. Fitting word into the context.
      2. Picking out phonetic elements.
      3. Using dictionary.
   C. More ability to make effective use of table of contents, word lists, chapter and marginal headings.
   D. More ability to read with a definite purpose, to judge, organize, during the process of reading.
   E. A growing ability to scan books to judge their worth or merit.
   F. A beginning of ability to skim over material quickly and to get the gist of it.
   G. A beginning of ability to take notes on material read.
   H. A beginning of ability to organize material in terms of problem or purpose and to locate information for such, involv-

ing the use. of reference books and readers' guides.

I. A beginning of ability to collect and arrange isolated material found in different sources dealing with the same problem.

J. A beginning of ability to find main topics and details under these topics, in a selection.

K. An increased ability to read accurately and fluently both silently and orally.

L. An improvement in the ability to read orally with a well-modulated voice and with poise.

M. Progress in power to hold the interest of a group in oral reading.

Reading in Fifth Grade

I. **Reading of material composed by teacher and children relating to group interests.**

A. Reading bulletin board (blackboard also used for some notices).

1. Directions or suggestions for work, excursions, play activities.
2. Names on committees.
3. Lists of materials available for certain projects.
4. Class records in spelling, arithmetic, and other work.
5. Signs and notices from other rooms and school office.
6. Financial reports from activities; other committee reports.
7. Class weight and height chart.
8. Class lists of spelling words needed.
9. Room menu.
10. Daily or weekly program.

B. Reading finished pieces of work in social studies.

1. Finished stories and poems.
2. Finished books.
3. Stories for talkies.
4. Parts in plays written.
5. Graphs, charts, posters, diagrams, and maps made by children to show information gained.
6. Titles or captions of pictures.
7. Diaries written on vacation trips.
8. Reports gained through reference material.

C. Reading correspondence.

1. Letters, invitations, and notices written to share with classmates and for criticism.
2. Invitations, letters, and notices from other rooms.
3. Correspondence from school office and outside firms.
4. Letters received from absent classmates.

D. Reading school publications.

1. Articles submitted for use in school publications.
2. School newspaper and magazine.

E. Reading individual records.

1. Individual progress charts.
2. Individual records of jobs finished and jobs yet to do.

FIRST AID TO LIBRARIANS

II. Caring for and using books.

   A. Caring for books.
      1. Continuing respectful handling of books.
      2. Preparing new books for use, by careful opening and marking for identification.
      3. Discussing points to remember in care of book.
      4. Proper marking of place when leaving story.
      5. Making book ends and book markers.
   B. Continuing good reading habits.
      1. Practicing proper posture when reading, both standing and sitting.
      2. Continuing proper holding of book with reference to distance from eyes, convenience for turning pages, and proper lighting.
   C. Using books effectively.
      1. Finding pages quickly.
      2. Using table of contents, index, title page, maps and pictures to the best advantage.

III. Library activities.
   A. Enjoying room library with teacher.
      1. Listening to teacher read books, read or tell favorite poem or story.
      2. Reading aloud favorite story, poem, or portion from book.
      3. Reading pictures together.
      4. Memorizing favorite poems.
      5. Bringing favorite book from home for room library.
   B. Use of school library.
      1. Learning plan of library and location of books, such as:
         a. Location of reference material.
         b. Location of historical material.
      2. Learning how to find different material related to group interest, by use of readers' guide, encyclopedias, book lists.
      3. Learning how to take books from the library by a new. system.
      4. Continuing to use the library so that all concerned may enjoy it; as, using low voices, no unnecessary talking, replacing books correctly.
      5. Enjoying new books and magazines.

IV. Independent individual reading for pleasure and information.
   A. Advertising good books to induce others to read.
      1. Reading aloud portions of the book, stopping so that other children will want to go on and read the book.
      2. Dramatizing bits from a book.
      3. Placing the book itself on display.
      4. Posting report of book read.
      5. Making poster advertisements of books enjoyed.
   B. Keeping records of books read.
      1. Filling in mimeographed blanks for books read, stating title, author, date read, opinion of book, and a sentence or two as to its content.
      2. Keeping records in individual folders of books read.
   C. Organizing a Book Club (a spontaneous activity).
      1. Forming club of those people who wish to do extensive home reading.
      2. Making wall poster for club members.
      3. Keeping a classified list of books in different fields read by each member.
   D. Guiding individual reading (activities carried on with help of teacher and librarian).

1. Checking on book report as to whether book is listed in Children's Catalogue.
2. Posting list of good books for children to choose from.
3. Posting advertisements of good books for boys and for girls, such as lists of pirate stories, school stories, animal stories.
4. Discussing why care should be used in selecting books.
5. Discussing what constitutes a good book.

E. Using books of informational type to solve problems.
1. Looking up material on topics in social studies.
2. Reading material found on problems to classmates.
3. Collecting books for committees on specific topics.
4. Making simple bibliographies for social studies topics.

V. Group reading activities for skills and appreciations (from books chosen according to group interests and needs).

A. Silent.
1. Reading for main idea of the story after an introduction of one or two motivating questions by teacher.
2. Reading for specific information such as answers to questions.
3. Reading selection quickly and carefully to be followed by a comprehension test.
4. Reading for main idea of paragraph for the purpose of outlining or retelling.
. Reading to find topic sentence in a paragraph.
6. Learning to skim through material for information sought.
7. Reading to note new and interesting words.
8. Discussing new words met for the purpose of building a vocabulary.
9. Reading to dramatize.
10. Reading directions for playing games, making objects, following suggestions for work.
11. Reading to note details.
12. Reading arithmetic problems.
13. Using dictionary as aid.

B. Oral.
1. Giving informal story and poem programs by one group for another.
2. Reading parts of stories enjoyed, such as humorous bits to group.
3. Reading to prove point in discussion.
4. Reading portions to answer question.

     5. Reading poems for enjoyment of pictures, rhythm, rhyme.

     6. Reading to enjoy dialogue.

     7. Reading to understand the story better.

VI. **Use of work-type material (as needed by groups and individuals).**

  A. Teacher made.

    1. Using exercises to build vocabulary, such as:

      a. Using words from content in original sentences.

      b. Taking multiple choice test on words, such as:

        Underline the words that mean the same:

          large   small   big   wide   hard

    2. Using checks on comprehension after reading; as, true-false tests, multiple choice tests, and completion tests.

    3. Using work sheets on topics in social studies to be filled in as information is found.

    4. Using work sheets on finding material, as finding pages where certain topics will be discussed in a given book.

    5. Taking three-minute reading tests, checking on words read per minute and comprehension.

    6. Taking objective tests on material in the social studies.

  B. Printed material.

    Using work-type readers or workbooks accompanying readers selected for individual or group use.

VII. **Use of tests.**

  A. By teacher—giving informal objective tests to check on skills worked for.

  B. By psychologist—giving standardized tests as basis for grouping, for remedial work, and for summer reading.

B. Books and Materials Used

I. **Library equipment in room.**

  A. Furnishings.

    1. Bookcase.

    2. Library table (30 x 50) and four chairs.

    3. Book ends (made by children).

    4. File for library cards (made by children).

    5. Bookrests.

  B. Materials.

    1. Tagboard folders (9 x 12) for each child's book reports.

    2. Mimeographed blanks for reports on books.

II. Books for group study. Selections are made according to needs and interests of groups, without regard to grade labels.

Baker and Baker	Making America	1937	Bobbs-Merrill
Baker and Baker	Bobbs-Merrill Readers	1939	Bobbs-Merrill
Cutright, P., and others	Democracy Readers	1940	Macmillan
Eichel, C. G., and others	Treasure Chest of Literature	1935	Houghton Mifflin
Elson and Gray	Elson Basic Readers	1936	Scott Foresman
Gates and Ayer	Work-Play Books	1932	Macmillan
Hahn, Julia L., and others	Child Development Readers	1938	Houghton Mifflin
Lewis and Rowland	New Silent Readers	1931	Winston
Smith and Bayne	Frontiers Old and New	1940	Silver Burdett
Smith, E. E., and others	Adventures in Reading	1931	Doubleday
Wright, Wendell W., and others	Modern World Readers	1934	Johnson
Yoakum, G. A., and others	Reading to Learn	1935	Macmillan
Thorndike-Century Junior Dictionary		1935	Scott Foresman
Winston Simplified Dictionary for Schools		1939	Winston

III. Room library.

A. A few such books as:

Alcott, Louisa M.	Jack and Jill	1928	Little Brown
Carr, Mary J.	Children of the Covered Wagon	1934	Crowell
Colum, P.	Arabian Nights	1923	Macmillan
Eggleston, E.	Hoosier School Master	1928	Macmillan
Enright, Elizabeth	Thimble Summer	1938	Farrar
Field, Eugene	Poems of Childhood	1925	Scribner
Fox, F. C.	How the World Rides	1929	Scribner
Fox, Frances M.	Flowers and Their Travels	1936	Bobbs-Merrill
Grey, Katherine	Rolling Wheels	1932	Little Brown
Grey, Katherine	Hills of Gold	1933	Little Brown
Grinnell, G. B.	Jack Among the Indians	1900	Stokes
Grinnell, G. B.	Jack in the Rockies	1904	Stokes
Hader, B. & D.	Spunky	1932	Macmillan
Halliburton, R.	Book of Marvels	1937	Bobbs-Merrill
Hawthorne, N.	Wonder Book	1910	Houghton Mifflin
Hilles, Helen T.	Play Street	1936	Random House
Kipling, Rudyard	Jungle Book	1916	Doubleday
Knox, Rose B.	The Boys and' Sally Down on a Plantation	1930	Doubleday
Lear, Edward	Nonsense Book	1925	Little Brown
Lee, Melicent H.	Pablo and Petra	1934	Crowell
Lee, Melicent H.	Children of Banana Land	1936	Crowell
Melbo, Irving R.	Our America	1937	Bobbs-Merrill
Patch, Edith M.	First Lessons in Nature Study	1926	Macmillan
Phillips, E. C.	Gay Madelon	1931	Houghton Mifflin
Riley, James W.	Little Orphan Annie and other Childhood Poems	1931	Bobbs-Merrill
Sidney, M.	Five Little Peppers	1909	Lothrop
Simon, Charlie M.	Teeny Gay	1936	Dutton
Simon, Charlie M.	Lost Corner	1936	Dutton

Simonds, Tom A.	A Boy with Edison	1931 Doubleday
Spyri, Johanna	Heidi	1927 Ginn
Stevenson, B. E.	The Home Book of Verse for Young Folks	1922 Henry Holt
Thomas, M. L.	Carlos	1938 Bobbs-Merrill
Thomson, J. E.	Aviation Stories	1929 Longmans Green
Weil, Ann	The Silver Fawn	1939 Bobbs-Merrill
White, S. E.	The Magic Forest	1928 Macmillan
Wilder, Laura I.	Little House in the Big Woods	1932 Harper
Wilder, Laura I.	Little House on the Prairie	1935 Harper

B. Maps.
  1. One political map of the United States.
  2. One physical map of the United States.
  3. One blackboard outline map of the United States.
C. Pictures.
  1. Four permanent framed French prints of village, forest, lake and harbor.
  2. Picture file containing photographs and prints related to seasonal material, industries, history of the United States, miscellaneous topics.
D. Periodicals.
  1. National Geographic (for pictures).
  2. Nature Magazine.
  3. Popular Science.
  4. My Weekly Reader.
  5. Story Parade.

IV. Practice material.
  A. Publishers' material.
  Workbooks accompanying some readers chosen for group or individual use.
  B. Teacher-made material.
    1. Informal objective tests, to test comprehension.
    2. Informal vocabulary drills.
    3. Work sheets to guide reading.

V. Standardized tests. A choice is made of the following:

Metropolitan Achievement Test	World Book Company
New Stanford Achievement Test	World Book Company
Progressive Achievement Test	California Test Bureau

C. Probable Outcomes

I. Information.
  A. A better knowledge of how books and magazines are made.

B. More knowledge of particular authors, artists, publishers, and their contribution.

C. A better understanding of how to use books to solve problems.

D. Added information concerning the kinds of books, such as encyclopedias, history, fiction, science, poetry, drama.

E. A better understanding of what constitutes a good book.

F. A better understanding of how to select a book to read.

G. A fuller understanding of where and how to find material in the library.

H. More knowledge of the work of the librarian, how books are accessioned, checked out, catalogued.

I. A better knowledge of the purposes for which reading is used.

II. Attitudes and appreciations.

A. Growing joy in using books.

B. More appreciation of the beauty of illustrations, binding, decoration.

C. More appreciation for fine quality of paper in a book, readability of print, wide margins, artistic arrangement.

D. Growing delight in reading stories which are well written.

E. Beginning of appreciation for definite qualities in style of writing, such as choice of words, humor, rhythm, forceful repetition.

F. Better appreciation for informational value of books.

G. Better appreciation for books as a means of solving our everyday problems.

H. Growing respect for the value of books, especially of superior editions.

I. Growing pride and pleasure in ownership of books.

J. Continued willingness to handle books correctly.

K. Appreciation for skill in different kinds of reading, such as ability to read carefully in following directions, ability to read rapidly to get the story.

L. Growing pride in the school library.

M. A desire to cooperate with others to build a better library.

N. A growing responsibility in using library books.

O. A desire and willingness to share pleasure found in books with others.

P. A growing willingness to find information to help solve group problems.

Q. A willingness to help others find information.

III. Habits and skills.

A. Continued habit of handling books so as to preserve them in good condition.

B. Continued habit of handling books correctly and hygienically with reference to light, eyes, posture.

C. Development in ability to find books needed or desired in the library.

D. Development in skill in finding topics desired in reference material, as in encyclopedias.

E. Continued habit of listening courteously and attentively while others read.

F. Progress in elimination of faulty habits of reading such as repetition, omissions, insertions, faulty eye-movements.

G. Growth in ability to skim through material for most important facts or material relevant to some problem which is being solved.

H. Development in ability to select gist of a paragraph.

I. Beginning of ability to select gist of a story and put down in proper sequence in an outine.

J. Growth in ability to take a few simple notes from reading.

K. Growth in ability to note details in reading.

L. Ability to read and carry out directions within known vocabulary.

M. Ability to read orally from books used in the group, so that others can comprehend.

N. Growth in ability to interpret so that others can enjoy the story.

O. Ability to read silently and get the thought independently from books used in the group.

P. Growth in ability to recognize new words from context, from phonetic elements, or resemblance to familiar words.

Q. Development in skill in using the dictionary as an aid in reading.

Reading in Sixth Grade

A. Activities and Procedure

I. **Reading of material composed by teacher and children relating to group interests.**

   A. Reading notices from bulletin board or blackboard.
     1. Daily program.
     2. Room menu.
     3. Notices and posters announcing activities in other rooms.
     4. Weight charts.
     5. Reports from committees, such as final reports on sale of magazine.
     6. Results of playground activities.
     7. Arithmetic reasoning problems from blackboard.
     8. Directions as to excursions, assemblies, and other group projects.
     9. Notices of materials needed in special classes such as music and art.
    10. Maps, diagrams and graphs.
   B. Reading correspondence.
     1. Letters received from former and absent members of the group.
     2. Invitations and notes received from other rooms.
     3. Letters of various types which have been written as class work.
   C. Reading completed work.
     1. Completed books made by individuals.
     2. Original stories and poems.
     3. Diaries or reports of vacation trips.
     4. Reports prepared for social studies, science or current events.
     5. Parts written for play.
     6. Maps, charts and diagrams made by children.
   D. Reading school magazine.
     1. Articles which have been written for magazine.
     2. Titles of articles to be used (with organization of material in mind).
     3. Completed magazine.
   E. Reading individual records.
     1. Book charts which show each child's record.
     2. Contracts giving suggestions as to amounts of work to be accomplished in a given period of time.

FACTS FROM READING ARE USED IN WRITING AND ART

II. Library.
    A. Enjoying room library with teacher.
        1. Reading pictures together.
        2. Reading or telling favorite story or poem.
        3. Hearing teacher read or tell favorite stories and poems.
        4. Bringing favorite books from home to be shared with the class.
        5. Planning exhibits of books for library table, such as different collections of poetry and science books.
    B. Use of school library.
        1. Learning arrangement of library, so as to find reference material and pictures easily.
        2. Using reference material, encyclopedias, atlas, in an efficient way.
        3. Checking books from the library and keeping rules governing book loans.
        4. Observing rules of quiet in library which make for efficient use.

III. Caring for and using own books.

    A. Caring for books.

        1. Treating a book as a valued possession, to be handled with respect.

        2. Using correct way of marking place in book.

        3. Making book ends and bookcases in manual training for home and school use.

        4. Discussing ways of making an occasional note or comment in own book.

        5. Discussing individual bookplates and manner of marking books for identification.

    B. Handling of books.

        1. Continuing correct position when reading.

        2. Discussing the convenient and comfortable ways for holding book, with reference to light, distance from eyes, and rapid turning of pages.

        3. Using title page, preface, table of contents, index, chapter headings, topic headings, maps, pictures, in an effective way.

IV. Independent individual reading for pleasure and information.

    A. Guiding individual reading (with help of teacher and librarian).

        1. Posting lists of good books suitable to read.

        2. Exhibiting suitable books.

        3. Occasionally bringing in magazine reviews of good books, such as the prize books of the year.

        4. Occasionally reading what children in other schools have written concerning certain books.

    B. Keeping records of reading.

        1. Filling in mimeographed blank, for some book read, giving title, author, date, main characters, a few sentences about story, opinion of book, and opinion as to reading difficulty.

        2. Writing name of book and author on wall chart, which makes a permanent record for the term.

    C. Pleasure reading.

        1. Reading aloud from a favorite book which the child wishes to recommend to the class.

        2. Telling briefly parts of books to arouse interest of class.

        3. Giving a few sentences describing book, letting class give title.

        4. Reading book reports children have written.

     5. Dramatizing portions of story.
D. Reading to gain help in solving problems.
    1. Reading reference material in social studies.
    2. Reading charts and graphs, such as those showing exports from various countries.
    3. Reading and interpreting maps for such information as rainfall, physical features, population.
    4. Reading pictures relating to social studies and science.
    5. Reading factual material of general interest to class.
    6. Collecting books for room use, which have to do with subject under discussion.
    7. Listing helpful books connected with any unit.
    8. Discussing parts of book, and their value in finding material quickly.

V. Group reading from book (chosen for probable appeal to group and for adaptation to ability of group, without regard to grade labels).
A. Silent reading.
    1. To interpret statistical materials, such as tables, maps, graphs.
    2. To follow printed or written directions with accuracy, as recipes.
    3. To visualize described details through reading.
    4. To "skim" reading material in search of statements bearing upon problem; to scan paragraph headings, index page, table of contents.
    5. To select the central thought of a paragraph.
    6. To select details in order to outline material.
    7. To collect, organize, and interpret data presented in books.
    8. To determine relative importance of different facts.
    9. To determine whether statements are based on facts or opinions.
   10. For specific answers to questions.
   11. In order to prepare for some type of comprehension test.
   12. In order to prepare for dramatization.
B. Oral reading.
    1. To answer questions.
    2. To verify opinions and statements.
    3. To check accuracy of previous reading.
    4. To learn dramatic or dialogue parts in preparation for a play.
    5. To interpret character parts in a narrative.

6. To enjoy poetry, interpreting the mood, the story through the voice.
7. For purpose of sharing that which has been enjoyed with others.
8. To interpret maps, charts, graphs.

VI. **Use of work-type material (when needed by groups or individuals). Exercises made by teacher and pupils.**
   A. Using guide sheets in social studies, giving questions, directions and suggestions.
   B. Checking comprehension of reading by true-false tests, completion sentences, multiple choice tests, writing answers to mimeographed questions.
   C. Practicing exercises to build vocabulary, such as:
      1. Finding as many synonyms as possible for given words.
      2. Rearranging lists of words so that synonyms will be opposite one another.
      3. Making individual lists of difficult words found in reading.
      4. Using set of mimeographed sentences such as the following:

      His very manner was hostile— (unfriendly, gracious, timid).
      Underline the word in parenthesis that means about the same as the word underlined in the sentence.

      5. Underlining well-chosen words and phrases in paragraphs.
   D. Preparing maps and diagrams interpreting quantitative facts.
   E. Occasional use of outlines giving main headings, with children filling in sub-topics.
   F. Taking three-minute reading tests checking on comprehension and number of words read per minute.

VII. **Check tests.**
   A. Given by teacher. Informal objective tests to check reading ability, used as a basis for choosing books and material.
   B. Given by psychologist. Standardized tests used as basis for summer reading, remedial work, and for grouping.

B. Books and Materials Used

I. **Library equipment in room.**
   A. Furniture.
      1. Bookcase.

  2. Library table and chairs; bookrests.

  3. Book ends, made by children in woodwork class.

  4. File for library cards.

 B. Materials.

  1. Library loan cards.

  2. Mimeographed forms for book reports.

II. Books for group study, used according to interests and abilities of groups; as,

Baker and Baker	Our World and Others	1938	Bobbs-Merrill
Baker and Baker	Bobbs-Merrill Readers	1939	Bobbs-Merrill
Cutright, P., and others	Democracy Readers	1940	Macmillan
Eichel, C. G., and others	Treasure Chest of Literature	1935	Houghton Mifflin
Elson and Gray	Elson Basic Readers	1936	Scott Foresman
Gates and Ayer	Work-Play Books	1932	Macmillan
Hahn, Julia L., and others	Child Development Readers	1938	Houghton Mifflin
Lewis and Rowland	New Silent Readers	1931	Winston
Smith and Bayne	On the Long Road	1940	Silver Burdett
Wright, Wendell W., and others	Modern World Readers	1934	Johnson
Yoakum, G. A., and others	Reading to Learn	1935	Macmillan
Thorndike-Century Junior Dictionary		1935	Scott Foresman
Winston Simplified Dictionary for Schools		1939	Winston

III. Room Library.

 A. Books for individual use; as,

Baldwin, J.	The Story of Roland	1930	Scribner
Beard, D. C.	American Boys' Book of Bugs, Butterflies and Beetles	1932	Lippincott
Brann, Esther	Nicolina	1931	Macmillan
Burgess, T. W.	Burgess Bird Book	1919	Little Brown
Burglon, Nora	Children of the Soil	1932	Doubleday
Byrne, Bess S.	With Mikko through Finland	1932	McBride
Church, A. J.	Iliad for Boys and Girls	1924	Macmillan
Church, A. J.	Odyssey for Boys and Girls	1925	Macmillan
Halliburton, R.	Book of Marvels	1937	Bobbs-Merrill
Halliburton, R.	Second Book of Marvels	1938	Bobbs-Merrill
Hillyer, V. M.	A Child's Geography of the World	1929	Century
Hillyer, V. M.	A Child's History of the World	1924	Century
Kingsley, C.	Greek Heroes	1928	Macmillan
Lamprey, Louise	In the Days of the Guild	1918	Stokes
Lamprey, Louise	Masters of the Guild	1920	Stokes
McMurray, F. I.	Pathways of Our Presidents	1939	Bobbs-Merrill
Pyle, H.	King Arthur and His Knights	1903	Scribner

Pyle, H.	Merry Adventures of Robin Hood	1883 Scribner
Reed, W. M.	Stars for Sam	1931 Harcourt, Brace
Seredy, Kate	The Good Master	1935 Viking Press
Stein, Evaleen	Gabriel and the Hour Book	1906 Page
Untermeyer, L.	This Singing World	1923 Harcourt
Van Loon, H. W.	Story of Mankind	1926 Liveright
Walker, Joseph	How They Carried the Mail	1930 Dodd Mead
Washburne, C. & H.	Story of Earth and Sky	1937 Appleton
Yeager, Dorr	Bob Flame, Ranger	1934 Dodd Mead

B. Periodicals such as the following:
   1. National Geographic (for pictures).
   2. Nature Magazine.
   3. Popular Mechanics.
   4. Story Parade.
C. Maps.
   1. One political map of Europe.
   2. One political map of Asia.
   3. One map of the world.
D. Pictures.
   1. Four framed French prints—series on the four continents.
   2. Picture file including science material, pictures pertaining to ancient civilization, pictures to be used for special days.

IV. **Practice materials.**
   A. Guide sheets to guide factual reading.
   B. Mimeographed checks to test comprehension.

V. **Standardized tests, selected from the following list:**

Metropolitan Achievement Test	World Book Company
New Stanford Achievement Test	World Book Company
Progressive Achievement Test	California Test Bureau

C. Probable Outcomes

I. **Information.**
   A. A better knowledge of well-known authors, artists, publishers, of juvenile books.
   B. A thorough knowledge of the parts of a book, such as title page, preface, table of contents, index, chapter and paragraph headings, glossary, bibliography.
   C. An understanding of how to use this information for finding material quickly.

D. A thorough knowledge of kinds of books, such as dictionary, encyclopedias, atlas, history, science, fiction, poetry, drama.
E. A knowledge of the cost of books; different editions of the same.
F. A knowledge of the purposes for which reading is used; as advertising, communication, recreation, problem solving, general information, specific directions.
G. Detailed information concerning favorite authors.
H. A knowledge as to the arrangement and plan of the school library and the public library; the duties of the librarian; the card catalogue; how books are checked from the library; how the library is supported.
I. A knowledge of various magazines and types of information each contains.
J. A better understanding of the information gained through reading charts, graphs, maps, diagrams.

II. Attitudes and appreciations.

A. A keen appreciation of books with beautifully colored illustrations, fine bindings, artistic printing and decoration.
B. A continued willingness to handle all books properly.
C. A better appreciation of style; of such qualities as humor, repetition, rhythm, apt phrasing.
D. An appreciation of the vivid imagery, simple direct expression, and musical word selection found in poetry.
E. An appreciation of the informational value of books.
F. Readiness to refer to books for solution of problems.
G. An appreciation of cost and value of books.
H. An appreciation of the value of a private library.
I. An appreciation of different kinds of reading; as,
    1. Rapid reading for pleasure and general information.
    2. Careful reading for details.
    3. Exact reading for following directions.
    4. Thoughtful reading for problem solving.
J. An appreciation of and pride in school library.
K. Pleasure in cooperating with others in building school library.
L. Willingness to share books for pleasure of the group and to bring information to group.
M. Attitude of responsibility in using library books.

III. Habits and skills.

A. Continued habit of handling and treating all books with respect.

B. Continued habit of handling all books correctly and hygienically with reference to light, eyes, posture.

C. Greater skill in using library; finding books quickly.

D. Greater skill in using bibliographies, encyclopedias, table of contents, index, reader's guide.

E. Continued habit of being an attentive member of the audience while others read.

F. Continued growth in building a reading vocabulary.

G. Growth in ability to read maps, charts, pictures, graphs.

H. Growth in ability to follow printed directions with accuracy.

I. Development of ability to visualize described details.

J. A growth in the ability to locate data.

K. Ability to "skim" reading material effectively.

L. Ability to select central thought with supporting details.

M. Growing ability to distinguish between main heading and subheads and to tabulate such in outline form.

N. Growing ability to judge the soundness and general worth of statements.

O. Growth in ability to determine the relative importance of different facts.

P. Growing ability to read with critical attitude.

Q. Ability to read orally from books used in the grade, so that others can comprehend and enjoy what is read.

R. Ability to read silently and get thought from books used in the grade.

S. Ability to reproduce material read in a concrete way through dramatization and oral reports.

T. Ability to see likenesses and differences in words, to discriminate between words that look much alike, and to recognize new words from their similarity to words previously learned.

U. Ability to use glossary and dictionary.

DEVELOPMENT OF NUMBER CONCEPTS IN THE KINDERGARTEN

IN THE use of number the kindergarten does not formulate definite lists of skills to be mastered, but seeks merely to utilize opportunities as they arise for building number concepts and developing a number sense. The record which follows includes the experiences of a single year, and some of these opportunities may not recur. However, the activities of the senior kindergarten each year afford many situations where interest in number is stimulated. The ability to count accurately and to recognize objects in groups has been found fundamental to rapid progress in arithmetic; and the kindergarten may well supplement the home and community in providing practical experiences of this sort.

Number Experience in Senior Kindergarten

A. ACTIVITIES

I. Activities related to the kindergarten program.
   A. Serving of luncheon.
      Children placed a certain number of napkins and the same number of glasses on each table. Some children were given a tray full of glasses and were asked to place them on tables, then come back and tell the director how many glasses were on his tray. For many children this number has run up to eighteen or twenty. Chairs about the tables were counted in order that the number would correspond to the places set.
   B. Toilet procedure.
      The children were asked to use one towel only. They were requested to push the liquid soap container only three times so as not to waste soap. There was counting of number of toilet facilities, and counting of children to determine how many children must wait.
   C. Passing out of constructive materials.
      As need arose the children counted papers, crayons and other materials.
   D. Use of the calendar.
      With the beginning of the New Year an interest arose in

466

calendars. A large calendar for the room was introduced and the guinea pigs' birthday was recorded. This stimulated an interest in the birthdays of the children. When a child had memorized when his birthday came, he was shown on the calendar which was his month. He then counted up until he came to the date of his birth, and if he could write his name to mark the day, he did so. If not, it was written for him. The teachers commented on children's ages, and comparison was made of ages.

E. Use of the clock.

With a number interest has come many questions about numbers on a clock face and how a person can tell time. The use of the hours was our starting point. We counted the minute marks and have timed ourselves in doing certain activities, as replacing of materials "in five minutes," or while the big hand moves from one number to the next. Drawing of clock faces on the blackboard and counting out the time on these has been of decided help and interest. An hour glass was shown to the children, and a discussion as to its use followed. There was great interest in its operation.

F. Use of the index in books, and numbers on page.

The teachers have made a point of using the index in story and song books, and of commenting on the page numbers.

II. Activities related to group interests.

A. Use of thermometer in connection with study of temperature.

This interest arose when the group was engaged in playing boat. The detecting of icebergs was discussed, and while "play" thermometers were made at first, many children wanted to go on into a consideration of a real thermometer. A large one was secured and the temperature indoors was recorded, and later the temperature out-of-doors was noted. Many children followed this interest for a period of five weeks, each day recording the findings. Children ruled off a chart, for days of the week and for temperature indoors and out-of-doors. The teacher recorded the days of the week and the date. Children recorded temperature. The children found that water placed in a shallow pan on the window sill would freeze if the temperature was below 32°.

B. Measuring of wood used for various articles made by children.

Use of inches came first and a need for counting up

inches on the ruler. This led to a discussion of the foot rule. The children soon fell into the habit of counting up the inches on their pieces of wood. This was true of a group of about seven who showed an early interest in anything that involved numbers. These children found that it took twelve one-inch spaces to fill out the ruler and that the ruler was called a foot. By marking the ruler off on a yard rule, with crayon, they found that three lengths of the ruler was as much as the length of the yard stick. This was only of passing interest, however.

C. Counting of money in connection with Book Fair conducted by parents.

Children brought pocketbooks containing money in all denominations, and also checks to pay for books. A brief explanation of what a check is and what it stands for, was given to the group.

D. Cooking experiences.

The children made candy for their fathers at Christmas time. They also enjoyed the making of applesauce, of jelly and of cookies. These activities involved simple counting and measuring. Actual measuring of ingredients helped children to gain some sense of quantity. They found in pouring out the jelly that the measuring cup held more than one jelly glass could hold.

E. Voting.

Voting on questions that arose in connection with the work; such as, what story to have, what activity to pursue next, name for new dolls, has led to counting and abiding by the results.

F. Making numbers.

The children made numbers for engines, license plates for cars, etc.

B. Books and Materials Used

I. Materials used in daily program.

A. Glasses, napkins, chairs to count, used at the lunch period.

B. Towels, soap container, facilities for toilet procedure.

C. Paper, crayons, scissors, paste jars, and other supplies.

D. Calendar with numbers 1½ inches high, with each number ruled off in a square, so that there was little confusion in reading numbers.

E. Clock face supplied by Ideal School Supply Company, Chicago, Illinois; the room clock with Arabic numbers; hour-

glass and three-minute sandglasses; pictures of sundials.
F. Song books and story books, with pages numbered.

II. Materials used in units of work.

A. A large thermometer, compliments of "The Chicago Daily News." The numbers on this were almost an inch high with spaces over an eighth of an inch marking off the degrees.
B. A foot ruler with inches clearly marked. Later a yardstick was introduced.
C. Pennies, nickels, dimes, half dollars, dollar bills and checks.

C. PROBABLE OUTCOMES

I. Related to kindergarten program.

A. Number consciousness increased through practical application at the luncheon period. Children felt need for knowing how many places were to be set, so that no one would have to go without orange juice.
B. Felt need for being economical in use of lavatory materials so that there would be a supply of towels and soap. Appreciation that selfishness on part of some would deprive others of material.
C. Skill in counting developed through passing of materials for the group. Felt need for being able to count.
D. A knowledge gained as to the purpose of calendars. Ability to recognize figures, and to name them in sequence.
E. Ability to tell time even to the minute gained by several children. Favorable attitude in learning to tell time. A feeling for time or time sense by using time for one activity and then finding there was no time left to do certain other things. Knowledge concerning the hour glass and its use.
F. Some idea of how one finds a desirable place in a book, gained by seeing the teacher use index and page numbers.

II. Related to group interests.

A. Information as to how a thermometer operates, and how temperature is recorded. Knowledge that the thermometer acts as a means of telling whether or not the weather is cold. Skill (attained by many) in reading the thermometer.
B. Knowledge of linear measure gained to some degree. Felt need for some means of measurement in order to have accuracy in woodwork.
C. Knowledge of various coins, pennies, nickels, dimes, quarters, half dollars, and dollar bills: number of pennies to

make a nickel and dime. Some idea as to the value and use of checks. Some understanding of the value of money.

D. Knowledge that to have cooking successful there must be accuracy and directions must be followed.

E. Knowledge of which numbers are larger than others, gained by counting votes. Some understanding of the fact that the majority rules, and that the social thing to do is conform happily to the wishes of the majority.

PROVISION FOR ARITHMETIC PROGRESS IN THE ELEMENTARY GRADES

THE objective in the teaching of arithmetic has been to use arithmetic continually and naturally in school enterprises, wherever the need for it appears, thereby developing knowledge and appreciation of its importance in life situations, and at the same time to provide for the systematic mastery of the skills which are deemed necessary by those who have studied the subject scientifically. No attempt is made to subordinate the teaching of arithmetic to an activity program, or to force arithmetic practice into social activities where it does not belong. However, numerous practical problems involving arithmetic arise in every grade, and these often provide direct motivation for practice exercises.

In the first grade, no definite period is set aside for number experience, but opportunities for developing a number sense and for mastering certain fundamental concepts are utilized wherever they occur. Beginning in second grade, time is provided each day for the mastery of skills in computation, and for the discussion and solution of the number problems of the group. Much of the practical work, however, can not wait for a time schedule, and arithmetic experience is afforded in connection with many other activities. In mastery of fundamental processes, the newer grade placement is followed, which postpones certain complicated processes until greater readiness has been developed.

As in the case of reading, the children are often grouped for arithmetic according to capacities and needs; and methods and materials are selected to fit the capacities and provide for the normal development of individuals and groups. Individual practice materials carefully made or selected for each child, have been found most desirable in developing independence, in overcoming weaknesses, and in building specific skills.

In the outlines that follow, outcomes tend to be cumulative from grade to grade. Each year effort is made to maintain desirable attitudes and appreciations, habits and skills, developed in preceding years.

Number Experience in First Grade

A Summary Based on Records for One Year

A. ACTIVITIES

I. Activities related to room procedure.
  A. Counting and learning to see number of objects in a group.
  1. Taking attendance in small groups.
  2. Grouping children for committees, reading classes, songs, rhythm work, playground activities.
  3. Voting occasionally on debated questions and counting to determine majority.
  4. Setting small tables for lunch periods and for parties, counting out articles needed for each table.
  5. Arranging chairs and distributing materials for group work, counting number needed for group.
  B. Measuring, weighing.
  1. Dividing blackboard for writing and drawing.
  2. Measuring for various art and industrial enterprises.
  3. Getting measured and weighed in doctor's office at regular intervals.
  C. Learning to make and recognize figures.
  1. Numbering pages in original booklets.
  2. Recognizing pages in primers and readers.
  D. Using and understanding time.
  1. Using clock as a guide in daily program.
  2. Using days and months in planning events; recognizing dates of special days.
  3. Recognizing dates of children's birthdays and their ages.

II. Activities related to group enterprises.
  (For fuller account see Units of Experience in First Grade)
  A. Playing post office.
  1. Depositing $5.00 in first grade bank for use in playing post office; pennies for letters; nickels for packages.
  2. Counting to find number of stamps needed to mail letters. Writing withdrawal slip for amount of money needed from bank.
  3. Counting money to see what was income in post office for day.
  4. Counting money in bank each day to be sure none has been lost.

BUYING IS ENTHUSIASTIC AT PLAY TIME

    5. Weighing packages when children wish to mail little gifts made from clay and wood.

    6. Writing house numbers in sending letters.

B. Playing store.

    1. Depositing $5.00 in first grade bank, in pennies, nickels and dimes, for playing store.

    2. Pricing; estimating proportionate value of article; writing price tags; writing price lists.

    3. Buying and selling; drawing amount needed from bank to make purchases; computing to give customer total cost of articles chosen.

    4. Paying cashier.

C. Planning a picture-story movie.

    1. Outlining program—number and sequence of pictures.

D. Making cookies for valentine gift.

    1. Reading figures in recipe.

    2. Measuring with teaspoon, tablespoon, cup; using pint and quart containers.

E. Playing with children's toys and games.

    1. Balls and bean bags: used for counting and easy addition.

2. Lotto: used for recognizing figures.
3. Dominoes: used for recognizing objects in groups.

III. **Practice in reading and writing figures and other skills, as need arises and children show readiness.**

B. Books and Materials Used

I. **Materials for practical experience with numbers.**
   A. Materials used in counting:
      1. Children (counting for attendance and grouping).
      2. Handwork materials, books, pencils.
      3. Articles used at lunch: tables, chairs, doilies, glasses.
   B. Materials used in measuring.
      1. Rulers (in woodwork, sewing).
      2. Yardstick (in building, dividing blackboard, making garden).
      3. Nails (in measuring various sizes).
      4. Teaspoons, tablespoons, cups, pint and quart bottles (in cooking enterprises).
      5. Clock and calendar (in planning time).
   C. Materials used in weighing.
      1. Scales (pound for weighing packages, children, dolls).
      2. Scales (ounce for weighing letters in play post office).
   D. Materials used in handling money.
      1. Pennies, nickels, dimes.
      2. Cash box, cash register.
   E. Children's own toys and games.
      1. Dolls.
      2. Balls.
      3. Bean bags.
      4. Games like lotto and dominoes.

II. **Informal individual checks.**
   (Involving counting, recognizing objects in groups, reading and writing figures, given from time to time to find out how mature each child is in dealing with concrete number).

C. Probable Outcomes

I. **Information.**
   A. Recognition of many practical uses for accurate counting.
   B. Recognition of several instruments for measuring and weighing and their value.
   C. Recognition of many uses for reading and writing figures.

D. Recognition of some divisions of time and their importance.
E. Introduction to use of money.
   1. Use of money in buying and selling.
   2. Recognition and value of penny, nickel, dime, dollar.
F. Beginnings of information about banking.
   1. Reasons why one may draw money from the bank.
   2. Method of withdrawing funds.
   3. Protection of money in banks.
   4. Officers and workers in banks.
G. Some information about postage.
   1. Reason for paying postage.
   2. Variety of postage rates: regular, special, air mail, registered mail, parcel post.
H. Some information about keeping store.
   1. Duties and responsibilities of storekeeper.
   2. Comparative cost of articles.

II. Attitudes and appreciations.

A. Appreciation of need for accuracy in counting and measuring, and in reading and writing figures.
B. Beginning of appreciation of value of money and a desire to use money wisely for daily needs and for pleasure.
C. Beginning of an appreciation of just remuneration for service.
D. Respect and care for others' money.
E. Beginnings of an appreciation of good proportion in planning buildings, and other constructions.

III. Skills.

A. Counting objects accurately by 1, 2, 5, 10 to 100.
B. Recognition of groups of 2, 3, 4, 5, 6 articles.
C. Recognition of figures to 100; much higher for many.
D. Ability to write figures to 20; to 100 and over for many.
E. Mastery of a few easy addition and subtraction facts by all children; mastery of further addition and subtraction facts by those more ready.

IV. Comprehension of terms and ability to think through these terms.

A. Inch, foot, yard, pound, ounce, scales.
B. Hour, minute, day, week, month, year, date.
C. Penny, nickel, dime, dollar.
D. Cash, cash box, cash register, bill, check, balance.
E. Cashier, clerk, salesperson, customer.
F. Vault, safe, bank.

Number Experience in Second Grade

A Summary Based on Records for One Year

A. ACTIVITIES

I. **Activities related to room procedure.**
  A. Use of ruler and yardstick.
    1. In many art and industrial enterprises.
    2. In measuring seats and desks to fit the child.
  B. Watching weight and height chart made by the nurse, introducing pounds and feet.
  C. Watching temperature of room; noting differences in degrees inside and outside; testing thermometer in refrigerator.
  D. Testing the dryness of the room with the hygrometer.
  E. Telling time in order to plan and follow the day's program.
  F. Celebrating birthdays and special days (stressing dates and ages; using calendar).

II. **Activities related to group enterprises.**
  A. Conducting gift shop and garden market.
    1. Listing number of articles to be sold.
    2. Estimating how many articles are needed and quantity each child can produce.
    3. Pricing different articles.
    4. Printing price signs.
    5. Acting as a cashier.
    6. Drawing money out of room bank for change.
    7. Handling and making change with real money.
  B. Spending money earned.
    1. Committee was chosen to go to town to buy a flag.
    2. Committee charged flag to school account.
    3. School sent bill to second grade.
  C. Baking cookies for party.
    1. Buying the material for cookies.
      a. Finding how much sugar, butter, eggs, milk is needed if the recipe is trebled.
      b. Purchasing supplies and counting of change.
    2. Interpreting recipe.
      Use of measuring cup, teaspoon and tablespoon, scales, clock.
  D. Making crab-apple jelly in connection with a study of fall

fruits. (Further experience in interpreting recipe and measuring accurately.)
  E. Handling money in connection with other school enterprises.
    1. Buying books at Book Fair.
    2. Paying carfare on excursions.
  F. Counting and measuring in connection with group projects. Many needs for counting and measuring and for use of number facts arose in connection with the study of farm and garden. (See Units of Experience in the Second Grade.)

III. Number games.
  A. Playing games brought by the children; as, dominoes, marbles, tenpins.
  B. Playing outdoor games, involving grouping of children and keeping score.

IV. Explanation and demonstration of new processes.
  A. Presentation of most addition and subtraction facts, and a few multiplication and division facts in concrete situations.
  B. Placing numbers under each other in straight columns when adding or subtracting.
  C. Making and placing the addition and subtraction signs correctly.
  D. Learning to begin on the right side to add or subtract, and to begin at top and add down. Learning different ways to write addition and subtraction exercises.

V. Practice activities.
  A. Practicing on blackboard new processes just demonstrated.
  B. Using mimeographed sheets of new processes.
  C. Using work type books as needed.
  D. Using number cards for both individual needs and in a group, but never for competitive purposes.
  E. Scoring and keeping records of individual achievement.

B. Books and Materials Used

I. Materials for practical experiences with numbers.
  A. Ruler and yardstick.
  B. Clock with Roman numerals.
  C. Calendar.
  D. Thermostat.
  E. Hygrometer (brought in to test humidity of room).

    F. Measuring devices for cooking: measuring cup, tablespoon, teaspoon, quart and pint measures, recipes.

    G. Money and related materials.

        1. Pennies, nickels, dimes, quarters, half dollars, paper dollars.

        2. Bank book, withdrawal slips, deposit slips, bills, receipts, checks.

II. Number games.

    A. The Jolly Bobbers.

    B. Dominoes.

    C. Marbles.

    D. Tenpins.

III. Practice material.

    A. Mimeographed material relating to children's number experiences.

    B. Some practice cards in addition and subtraction facts (both for group and individual use).

IV. Arithmetic tests.

(So far have not found satisfactory standard of measuring arithmetic ability in Second Grade until end of year. Informal arithmetic tests have been devised by the teacher to be used during the year.)

New Stanford Achievement Test—Primary	World Book Company
Metropolitan Achievement Test—Primary	World Book Company

C. Probable Outcomes

I. Information.

    A. Use of money in buying and selling.

    B. Recognition of all the coins and paper money.

    C. Manner of buying and selling in different enterprises.

    D. Use and need of banks.

    E. Necessity of being a quick, accurate thinker when handling money.

    F. Comparison of prices.

        1. Why a standard price.

        2. When prices are fair.

    G. Better understanding of value of books, pictures, pottery and other articles.

    H. Necessity of accurate measurement in cooking, art enterprises and other fields.

II. **Growth of attitudes and appreciations.**
  A. Wise and careful judgment in buying and selling.
  B. Desire to be reliable when handling money.
  C. Appreciation that responsibility in handling money involves:
      1. Keeping accurate records.
      2. Making correct change.
      3. Being fair in your prices.
  D. Respecting others' money as well as your own.
  E. Realizing values of money; and that earning money demands conscientious thinking and hard work.
  F. Appreciation of importance of numbers in care of health; and of duties of school nurse, janitor and engineer.
  G. Desire to use time to best advantage.
  H. Appreciation of fairness in playing games.

III. **Skills in computation.**
  A. Notation and numeration.
      1. Counting accurately by 1, 2, 3, 5 and 10, as needs arise.
      2. Reading numbers in hundreds and thousands, as needs arise.
      3. Reading Roman numerals to XII.
      4. Writing numbers to 500 and above, as occasion demands.
      5. Writing dollars and cents in decimal form.
  B. Addition and subtraction.
      1. Mastery of most addition facts, both in column form and equation form.
      2. Ability to add two and three addends of two figures each (no carrying).
      3. Mastery of subtraction facts corresponding to addition facts, in column form and in equation form.
      4. Ability to subtract with two and three figures in the minuend and in the subtrahend (no carrying).
      5. Ability to check answers.
  C. Multiplication and division.
      1. Ability to multiply by 2 and by 3 and 5 as needs arise in practical situations.
      2. Ability to handle the simplest fractions in practical problems: $\frac{1}{2}$, $\frac{1}{4}$.
  D. Problems.
      1. Ability to solve one-step problems based on child's needs and experiences, involving addition and subtraction facts and simple units of measure.
      2. Ability to compose original problems.

IV. Comprehension of terms
   A. Addition, add, plus, equals, sum.
   B. Subtraction, subtract, minus, less, least, left, remainder.
   C. Multiplication, multiply, times.
   D. Fraction, divide, half, third, fourth.
   E. Price, buy, sell, lend, borrow, charge, pay, pay back, owe.
   F. Bank, check, receipt, bill, withdrawal slip, deposit slip, balance.
   G. Time, minute, hour, half-hour, quarter-hour, day, week, month, year.
   H. Length, inch, half-inch, foot, yard.
   I. Liquid, pint, quart, gallon.
   J. Weight, pound, half-pound, ounce, dozen, half-dozen.
   K. Money, penny, nickel, dime, quarter, half dollar, dollar, five dollar bill.
   L. Shape, square, rectangle, circle.

Arithmetic in Third Grade

An Outline Based on Records for One Year

A. ACTIVITIES

I. **Activities related to room procedure.**
  A. Recording number present and number absent.
  B. Preparing record of absences for school nurse; preparing record of number to be present at noon meal for dietitian.
  C. Planning use of time for outdoor and indoor periods.
  D. Planning time for certain group enterprises and setting dates for special events.
  E. Estimating number of books and other supplies needed for small groups and for room; ordering supplies from school supply store.
  F. Measuring desks and chairs, then .measuring children for correct adjustment.
  G. Studying height and weight chart prepared with the help of the school nurse and noting individual gains.
  H. Much measuring in art and woodwork.
  I. Beginning of interpretation of maps and globes; determining distances as related to time of travel.

II. **Activities related to group enterprises.**
  A. Planting bulbs.
    1. Estimating number of bulbs needed for different areas.
    . Computing cost of bulbs.
    . Computing cost of painting flowerpots.
    4. Computing amount of dirt needed for filling flowerpots and cost.
    5. Purchase of soil from the florist—wise selection of suitable bulbs.
    6. Recording time required for flowers to bloom.
    7. Recording number of days flowers will last.
  B. Churning.
    1. Measuring cream to be used and decision of size of churn to use for the amount of cream.
    2. Ascertaining proportion of cream that became butter according to the amount of buttermilk.
    3. Measuring of small amount of salt used.
  C. Making cheese.
    1. Measuring milk to be used.
    2. Draining milk and measuring part not used.

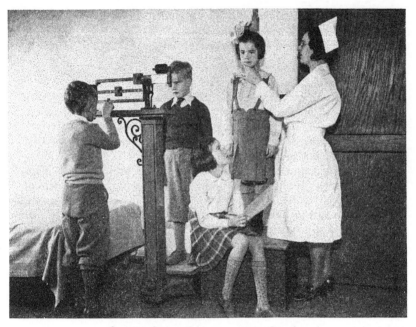

SCALES SHOW SATISFACTORY GAINS

3. Measuring cream used to season cheese.
D. Presenting plays.
   1. Measuring accurately the parts for buildings to be used in dramatization.
   2. Measuring materials for costumes for plays; computing the number of yards of cloth needed.
E. Conducting orange juice booth during school fair.
   1. Counting change to be used.
   2. Measuring orange juice for glasses.
   3. Finding cost when several glasses of orange juice were bought at one time.
   4. Giving change back to customers.
   5. Counting money made after booth was closed each time.
   6. Finding the amount cleared after estimating the cost of ingredients.
F. Selling maple sugar and maple syrup.
   1. Importing maple sugar and maple syrup from a farm in Vermont.
   2. Taking orders in advance from parents and members of the staff.

3. Ordering amount needed.
4. Fixing price in relation to cost of supply and cost of transportation, so as to assure a profit.
5. Delivering orders and collecting money.
6. Paying bills and determining amount earned.
7. Presenting the amount earned to fund for buying drapes for the children's dining room.

III. **Spontaneous interests—Questions which led to discussion and investigation:**
   A. How far does a photographer have to be from a volcano when he photographs it?
   B. How long would it take to walk the distance into a mine?
   C. How did people first tell time?
   D. How long until clocks were made?
   E. What makes banks "break"?
   F. What is interest?
   G. Why are checks used?
   H. Why do people pay taxes?
   I. What is income tax?

IV. **Activities related to play.**
   A. Counting by twos for "Three-Deep."
   B. Counting by threes for "Squirrel in a Tree."
   C. Dividing even sides for "Kick Ball."
   D. Counting by fives for "Hide and Seek."

V. **Explanation of new processes.**
   A. Usually from board, demonstrations given; sometimes directions with pupils following in arithmetic books or work books.
   B. Attention called to new parts of processes.
   C. Much emphasis upon signs and terms and upon the correct way of writing column numbers.

VI. **Practice activities and records.**
   A. Use of mimeographed sheets adapted to ability of groups, followed by individual sheets when needed.
   B. Writing on board: practice in column writing and in writing new forms like dollars, cents, decimal signs.
   C. Use of work books with definite goals for small groups.
   D. Use of individual cards, for individual practice on facts not yet mastered.
   E. Keeping of graph records showing daily progress by child.

VII. Uses of tests.

Tests given by psychologist near the end of each semester. Graph report on tests shown to child—weaknesses noted and plans made for improvement.

B. Books and Materials· Used

I. Materials for practical experience with numbers.

A. Materials for measuring: foot rules, yardstick, scales, measuring cups, measuring spoons, pint and quart bottles.
B. Coins, bills, checks.
C. Clock, calendar.
D. Thermometer.
E. Maps, globes, geography games.
F. Balls and other materials used on the playground.
G. Art and manual training materials.
H. Natural science and social studies materials.

II. Practice materials.

A. Drill cards for mastery of number facts, arranged according to difficulty.
B. Mimeographed sheets of abstract work for practice.
C. Mimeographed sheets of reasoning problems.
D. Individual cards for children who have difficulty with particular number facts.
E. Individual workbooks (used as needed).

III. Workbooks used for reference and review.

Brueckner, L. J., and others. New Curriculum Workbooks 1936, Winston
Upton, C. B. Adventures in Arithmetic 1938 Upton

IV. Tests.

Metropolitan Achievement Test World Book Company
New Stanford Achievement Test World Book Company

C. Probable Outcomes

I. Information.

A. Better knowledge of value and use of money in buying and selling projects.
B. Proper use of order slips when materials are ordered from supply room.
C. Recognition of need for a bill and receipt when articles are paid for.
D. Additional uses of scales in weighing and measuring and use of ruler and yardstick in making definite measurements.

E. Fuller understanding of thermometer and telling time, using seconds on watch.

F. Ideas of heights of buildings in number of stories, and sizes of rooms according to feet.

G. Meaning and use of calendar.

II. Attitudes and appreciations.

A. Realization of need for responsible bankers and clerks.

B. Appreciation of necessity of exact balance in keeping accounts.

C. Importance of buying within means and of careful selection.

D. Appreciation of need for careful measurement in cooking and in various art and industrial enterprises.

E. Appreciation that accuracy is needed for all positions, especially where money is involved.

F. Greater sense of value of time and need of careful planning for wise use of time.

III. Habits and skills.

A. Notation and numeration.
1. Reading and writing large numbers of common interest —into the thousands.
2. Reading and writing of Roman numerals to XX.
3. Writing of dollars and cents in decimal form, signed.
4. Using equation form for all processes.

B. Addition and subtraction.
1. Progress toward automatic response to 100 addition facts and of sums needed in column addition and in multiplication.
2. Ability to add single columns involving 5 or 6 addends; two and three figure numbers with 4 or 5 addends.
3. Ability to add with addends of unequal length.
4. Progress toward automatic response to 100 subtraction facts.
5. Ability to subtract, using minuend and subtrahend of 2, 3, 4 and 5 figures involving carrying.
6. Ability to check answers.

C. Multiplication and division.
1. Progress toward automatic response to 100 multiplication facts.
2. Ability to multiply with two and three figures in the multiplicand and one in the multiplier, and by 10 and 100.

3. An introduction to division (using long division form), as needed in class problems.
4. Ability to deal with fractions in concrete situations, corresponding to multiplication and division facts mastered; as, 1/2, 1/4, 1/3.
5. Ability to check all work.

D. Measurement.
　1. Ability to use common facts of units of measure, as needed.
　　a. Length—inches, foot, yard.
　　b. Liquid—pints, quarts, gallon.
　　c. Weight—ounces, pound.
　　d. Time—second, minutes, hour, day, week, month, year.
　2. Ability to compute distances around areas.

E. Problems.
　1. Ability to solve one-step problems and some two-step problems from local environment and schoolroom needs, involving units of measurement and dollars and cents.
　2. Ability to think through imaginary problems.
　3. Ability to create original problems.

IV. Comprehension of terms.
A. Addition, add, plus, sum, check, column.
B. Subtraction, subtract, minus, difference, remainder.
C. Multiplication, multiply, times, product.
D. Division, divisor, divide, quotient, fraction.
E. Meanings and abbreviations for units of measure; as, in., ft., yd., pt., qt., gal., etc.

Arithmetic in Fourth Grade

A. ACTIVITIES

I. Activities related to room procedure.
 A. School program.
  1. Planning daily program and carrying it out.
  2. Deciding on time required for large units of work.
  3. Allotting time for various types of activities.
  4. Completing work within a given time.
 B. Menu making.
  1. Choosing a balanced menu for a given price.
  2. Keeping records of lunches, comparing them with chart which showed well-balanced meals.
  3. Keeping records of amount of fruit juice and milk needed for mid-morning lunch.
  4. Computing cost of fruit juice and milk by the week and by the year for individual children and for the group.
  5. Organizing and arranging the room and supplies for birthday parties held at lunch time.
  6. Marketing for special luncheons, as Halloween.
 C. Passing and collecting materials.
  1. Counting number of articles needed for classes; as paper, pencils, books, pens.
  2. Choosing number of children to serve on committees for care and distribution of materials.
  3. Marking off spaces in cupboards for various sizes of paper.
 D. Providing and caring for equipment.
  1. Ordering supplies needed; as, paper, pens, paste, and computing the cost.
  2. Computing the cost of framing pictures for the room.
  3. Mastering the combination on locks for individual lockers.
  4. Measuring and making of files for work-type papers in manual training.
  5. Measuring and making garden box for window.
  6. Measuring and making a museum table for exhibits.
 E. Health in the room.
  1. Keeping record of height and weight of individual children.
  2. Measuring desks and chairs for proper seating.
  3. Making graphs, showing gains in weight.
  4. Keeping record of room temperature.

5. Keeping record of glasses of water drunk during the day (during the food unit study).
6. In use of lavatory materials, allotting the number of paper towels and amount of soap necessary for each child. Computing the cost of towels for our grade, if each child uses three in one day.
7. Measuring the distance in holding reading material from the eyes.

II. Activities related to play.

A. Measuring high and broad jumps in contest games.
B. Keeping score in ball games.
C. Measuring wood needed for hurdles on the playground.
D. Measuring and marking off diagrams for playing games, as baseball.
E. Finding sizes of soft-soled shoes needed for gymnasium.

III. Activities related to the library and its uses.

A. Learning to use file and index in library, reading numbers. Learning to find reference material in World Book, Pageant of America, Compton's Encyclopedia, using index volume, chapter headings, both Roman and Arabic.
B. Subtracting to find number of days left to keep a book out, computing dates ahead to find when books are due. Paying fines for over-due books.

IV. Activities related to social studies.

A. Drawing, measuring to scale, using $\frac{1}{4}$, $\frac{1}{2}$, $\frac{1}{8}$ inches in making large world map used in tracing early discoveries; time charts which showed relationship of past and present time.
B. Drawing and measuring in making health charts, health folders, book covers; preparing topical outlines.
C. Computing and measuring mileage on maps in reviewing trips taken during vacation and in learning the miles various explorers traveled.
D. Telling time, using calendars, clocks, sundial, and sun markers. Understanding relationship of past, present, future, century, month, year, day; relationship of day and night, seasons, using longitude and latitude in a simple manner. Computing time with reference to how many years ago events took place, how old would certain prominent people be, were they living now.
E. Discussion of taxes: how taxes are collected; what they are used for at present.

BALANCING PRICES AND VITAMINS

F. Discussion of how money was first invented, what the Indians and early pioneers used in trading; as, wampum, furs.
G. Measuring, using the dry and liquid measure pints, quarts, gallons, pecks, also pounds, dozens, when buying food for Christmas and Halloween luncheons prepared by the children; also when making cookies and jelly as gifts for mothers.
H. Computing the cost of food, total and per person, computing the amount needed for the group. Measuring the ingredients for various recipes, involving fractional parts; as, $\frac{1}{4}$, $\frac{1}{2}$, $\frac{1}{8}$.
   Keeping accounts of these activities.
I. Keeping accounts, finding cost and profit made in editing and selling the April number of the school magazine.
J. Frequent use of the four fundamental processes in solving problems related to all units of learning. (See outlines of units of experience.)

V. **Activities related to explanation and demonstration of new processes.**
   A. Actual measuring of an acre of land on school grounds to

find how big it really is. Measuring a mile on the speed-ometer on the automobile (a school bus activity).

B. Using units of measurement: as, a quart bottle and gallon bottle; scales with ounce weights; clocks with minute and second hands.

C. Picture making in developing understanding of terms: division and multiplication, fractional parts; elements con-tained in problems.

D. Cutting cardboard, paper, apples, to illustrate fractional parts.

E. Outlining steps of procedure in problem solving and in difficult computation exercises.

VI. **Activities related to practice material.**

A. Taking timed tests on the four fundamental processes (ad-dition, subtraction, multiplication and division).

B. Keeping records and graphs of both group and individual progress on timed tests and work book tests.

C. Using individual, self-corrective practice cards for improv-ing accuracy and speed in four fundamental processes.

D. Using individual cards, containing special exercises needed by groups and individuals, at the blackboard.

E. Using workbooks for drill as needed in activities.

VII. **Activities related to arithmetic books.**

A. Using books for further practice in problem solving and in mastering fundamental facts.

B. Using books for review tests and diagnostic purposes. Us-ing books for the introduction and explanation of new processes.

C. Using books as reference material for tables of measurement.

D. Using books as source material by advanced children within the group.

VIII. **Activities related to use of diagnostic tests and remedial work (carried on by teacher with aid of psychologist).**

A. Giving of standardized achievement tests to ascertain the ability of the group as a whole and individually at the be-ginning of the year, and also before beginning any new work unit.

B. Organizing groups and materials for special practice periods, according to information gained from tests given.

C. Giving of oral tests to aid in diagnosing work habits and mental procedure of individual children.

D. Planning and preparing practice material for group and individual use.
1. Practice cards for use at blackboard.
2. Mimeographed sheets.

B. Books and Materials Used

I. **Materials for practical experiences with number.**
A. Foot rule, yardstick, tape measure.
B. Hourglass, clock.
C. Scales, quart, pint, gallon bottles.
D. Peck, bushel measures.
E. Art and handwork materials.
F. Manual training materials.
G. Playground, natural science and social studies materials.
H. Room equipment and supplies.
I. Money, checks, account books.
J. Geography games, maps, globes.

II. **Work type and supplementary materials.**
A. Mimeographed materials related to group units or interests.
B. Mimeographed materials consisting of abstract work for practice; as:
    100 addition facts
    100 subtraction facts
    100 multiplication facts
    90 division facts
C. Mimeographed materials consisting of reasoning problems.
1. Those related to needs of group.
2. Those of graded difficulty for children having special needs.
D. Individual work books.

Brueckner, L. J., and others	New Curriculum Workbooks	1936 Winston

E. Individual work sheets of facts and problems to overcome difficulties shown in diagnostic tests.
F. Individual number cards for drill on facts of four fundamental processes.
G. Individual number cards for blackboard work, to build accuracy and speed in computation.

III. **Arithmetic books for reference and review.**

Brueckner, L. J., and others	New Curriculum Arithmetics	1936 Winston
Knight, F. B., and others	Study Arithmetics	1935 Scott Foresman

IV. **Standardized tests.**

    A. Given by teacher.

    Standardized tests from work books.

    B. Given by psychologists.

Metropolitan Achievement Test	World Book Company
New Stanford Achievement Test	World Book Company
Progressive Achievement Test	California Test Bureau

C. Probable Outcomes

I. **Informational values.**

    A. Some knowledge of the development of methods of telling time and of measures used in telling time.

    B. Knowledge of relative prices of food and the keeping of household accounts.

    C. Knowledge of how retail and wholesale business is carried on.

    D. A better understanding of cost and preparation of food, menu making in relation to body building.

    E. Knowledge of cost and methods of shipping fruits and other perishable foods to the United States.

    F. Knowledge of how prices of foods are influenced by supply and demand.

    G. Information about how liquids and dry materials are measured and weighed.

    H. Knowledge of how to read both the room thermometer and the physician's thermometer.

    I. Knowledge of how mileage is computed on land and sea.

    J. Knowledge of how accounts are kept, correct form for bills and receipts.

    K. A beginning of an understanding of value and use of graphs.

    L. Knowledge of cost of making books, and what discount means.

    M. Information concerning the development of the Arabic and Roman number systems.

    N. Information about dates in history with reference to present-day developments.

    O. Information concerning bartering, trading and present monetary system used in the United States, including banks, checks, accounts (checking and savings), loans, etc.

II. **Social values.**

    A. Appreciation of reasons for budgeting time and using it wisely.

B. A better appreciation of value of money and its wise use.
C. An appreciation of need for careful estimating and ordering supplies.
D. An appreciation of need for careful and thoughtful planning ahead for any work; as in measuring for booklets, charts.
E. Desire to care for the library equipment and to learn to use it correctly; as, return of books on date due, prompt payment of fines.
F. An appreciation and desire to build habits of accuracy, speed, neatness in achieving results in the four fundamental processes with integers.
G. An appreciation of the fact that guessing is dangerous.
H. An appreciation that the ability to handle numbers with facility is an asset and a necessity in every day affairs.
I. An appreciation of the mathematical skill involved in the building of a boat, a clock, the electric lamp and other inventions.
J. An appreciation of the cost and value of school supplies.
K. A desire to pay bills promptly.
L. A willingness to spend money for the good of others.
M. A desire to be fair in fixing prices and to make honest profits.

III. Computational skills.

A. Ability in reading and writing.
  1. Reading and writing Arabic numbers to 100,000.
  2. Reading and writing Roman numerals one to twenty, tens to 100, 500, 1000.
  3. Forming concepts of large numbers.
  4. Reading and writing dollars and cents.
B. Abilities developed in fundamental processes.
  1. Addition of integers.
    a. 100 addition facts.
    b. Adding by endings to 39.
    c. Column addition, with 1, 2, 3 and 4 figures and 5 or 6 addends.
    d. Combinations needed for column addition; additional combinations as needed for multiplication.
  2. Subtraction of integers.
    a. 100 subtraction facts.
    b. Subtraction facts as needed for division.
    c. Subtraction, carrying, 1, 2, 3 places.

    3. Multiplication of integers.
        a. 100 multiplication facts.
        b. Multiplicands 2, 3, 4, 5 figures involving carrying with 1 figure multiplier, and with 2 and 3 figures.
    4. Division of integers.
        a. 90 division facts.
        b. Division using one-figure divisors and long division form; dividends of 2, 3, 4 figures with and without remainders.
  C. Growing ability to use common units involved in measures of length, time, liquid, dry, weight, money, temperature.
  D. Growing concepts of meaning of fractional parts, skill in reading fractions, writing fractions, adding and subtracting simple like fractions.
  E. Ability to solve one and two-step problems using all above skills.
    1. Problems involving school and out-of-school needs.
    2. Original problems of the group and individual.

IV. Comprehension of terms.
  A. Familiarity with the following list of terms used in the four fundamental processes:
    Addition: sum, total, column, add, signs (+ and =).
    Subtraction: subtract, difference, remainder, sign (−).
    Multiplication: multiplier, multiplicand, product, sign (x).
    Division: divide, dividend, divisor, quotient, sign (÷).
  B. Terms used in tables of measurements: pints, quarts, gallons, pecks, bushels, inches, feet, yard, mile, acre, pound, ounce, dozen.
  C. General terms: charge, checks, due, discount, depth, amount, increase, height, average, degree, length, per, buying, profit, loss, retail, wholesale, degree.

Note: Children above average in ability should master the above attainments in a shorter time, and also develop ability to solve more difficult practical problems. Differences in ability are provided for mainly on the time basis.

Arithmetic in Fifth Grade

A. ACTIVITIES

I. Activities connected with room procedure.
A. The program.
1. Deciding on time needed for big pieces of work and for excursions.
2. Planning the daily program.
   a. Deciding on jobs for the day and allotting time needed for each.
   b. Setting time for each.
3. Carrying out program planned.
   a. Telling time.
   b. Individuals figuring how much time is left to finish work or get ready for next class.

B. Making out menu and conducting lunch period.
1. Making out balanced menu from price list to amount to exactly the sum allowed in annual fees paid by parents.
2. Buying extra food for parties and special luncheons.

C. Taking care of health of room group.
1. Adjusting chairs and desks to fit by measuring.
2. Reading thermometer.
3. Weighing and measuring height every two months.
4. Comparing records to see if overweight or underweight.

D. Conducting supply store for the school.
1. Making inventories of supplies on hand.
2. Estimating extra supplies needed.
3. Ordering fresh supplies; as, paper, pencils, crayolas, erasers, clips.
4. Making sales and keeping accounts.

E. Taking attendance.

F. Mastering combinations on lockers.

II. Activities growing out of spontaneous interests.
A. Finding volume of air in the room and amount for each person.
B. Finding averages.
1. On tests.
2. On self-reliance scores.

III. Activities relating to play.
A. Choosing equal number on sides.
B. Adding and comparing scores.
C. Laying off diagrams and fields for different games.

495

STUDY OF TEMPERATURE AND HUMIDITY AFFORDS PROBLEMS

IV. Activities related to social studies.

A. Reading large numbers in statistics on value of natural resources of the United States, crop production of the United States, value of the industrial production, changes in urban and rural population, value of imports and exports.

B. Writing large numbers for charts, books, committee reports, and for stories for talkies on industries.

C. Reading and writing Roman numerals as chapter headings in books.

D. Measuring.

1. Using inch, foot, yard, and rod in laying out acre of ground to get an idea of its size, in constructing a theater for motion pictures, buying cloth for curtains and for foundation for pictures, measuring pictures, making books on industries.

2. Using liquid, dry, and avoirdupois measure in dyeing material for theater curtains.

E. Handling United States money in charging admission to talkies, buying books for library with money earned.

F. Keeping account of money earned and money spent in giving the motion pictures and the play.

G. Adding integers to get total amount earned, expenses incurred, money spent for books.

H. Subtracting integers to find out how long ago events happened, time between events, how much money cleared, costs after discount.

I. Multiplying integers to find areas of pieces of land, and to find cost at urban and rural prices.

J. Dividing to find price per acre when price on total is given, amount of discount where discount is expressed as a fractional part, etc.

K. Enlarging concepts in fractions such as expressing fractional parts, reducing large fractions, in statistics on part of world's resources found in the United States.

L. Adding fractions in finding part United States plays in world production, figuring materials needed in construction, etc.

M. Subtracting fractions in comparing values of United States with certain other countries; figuring amount of material left in construction or amount more needed.

N. Multiplying fractions in estimating amount of cloth needed for mounting pictures when measurement of one picture has been found.

O. Dividing fractions in estimating number of pictures which can be mounted on material on hand.

P. Building concept of percentage by expressing per cents as hundredths and reducing as they are met in statistics and discounts on books.

Q. Drawing to scale in constructing map to show what each section of United States contributes to Chicago and the rest of the world.

V. Activities for explanation and demonstration.

A. Drawing diagrams.

1. Drawing diagrams on the blackboard for explaining steps in four fundamental processes with integers and fractions, as:

$$\tfrac{1}{2} \text{ of } \tfrac{1}{2} = \tfrac{1}{4}$$
$$\tfrac{1}{2} \times \tfrac{1}{2} = \tfrac{1}{4}$$

2. Laying out diagrams on floor or playground to show

$$1 \text{ sq. ft.} = 144 \text{ sq. in.}$$
$$1 \text{ sq. yd.} = 9 \text{ sq. ft.}$$

B. Outling steps on the blackboard.
1. Outlining steps from old to new process for children to draw own conclusions as to how to solve new types of problems.
2. Outlining steps for children to use as guides in new process, that correct habits of procedure may be formed.
C. Drawing pictures to clarify points.
D. Cutting apples to illustrate fractional parts.
E. Cutting cardboard and paper figures to explain steps in fractions.
F. Using different units of measure to explain their equivalents in other units.

VI. **Use of practice materials.**
A. Taking time tests on fact sheets and keeping individual records of progress.
B. Using work book for drill on class needs arising in social studies or other group activities.
C. Keeping individual records by pupil to show his own progress.
D. Taking curriculum test once a month to check progress.

VII. **Use of books.**
A. Using books for additional drill on points needed.
B. Using books for review.
C. Referring to books for explanation of new processes.
D. Using books for reference for tables of measure.
E. Using books for their diagnostic tests.

VIII. **Use of diagnostic tests (conducted by teacher with help of psychologist).**
A. Group.
1. Using diagnostic tests with a new group to find where teaching should begin.
2. Using diagnostic tests during teaching a process to see if certain pupils need to be taught all steps.
3. Using diagnostic tests after teaching to see if some individuals may require further teaching.
B. Individual.
Giving oral diagnostic tests to pupils having difficulty, to discover mental processes used.

IX. **Remedial work (conducted by teacher with advice of psychologist).**
A. Division of class into smaller groups according to needs.

B. Group work.
1. Allowing superior children time for additional creative activities by excusing them from much drill.
2. Planning practice work for those who need it.
   a. Mimeographed work sheets.
   b. Keyed cards for blackboard drill.
   c. Teacher-made cards on work causing difficulty.
C. Individual.
1. Individual drill with fact cards both by self and with teacher.
2. Use of individual work sheets on steps giving difficulty.
3. Oral work with teacher going through process correctly and child going through process correctly.
4. Graphs to show progress.

B. Books and Materials Used

I. Materials for practical experiences with number.
A. Measures—foot rule with sixteenth inch graduation, yardstick, 50 foot tape, pint, quart, gallon, scales, peck, and bushel.
B. Materials.
1. Lumber and material in manual training.
2. Ground included in school campus.
3. Equipment in the room such as desks, chairs, clock, pencils.
4. Art and handwork material.
5. Social and natural science material.
C. Games.
1. Soccer balls.
2. Baseballs and bats.

II. Work type and supplementary material.
A. Mimeographed sheets.
1. 100 facts in addition, subtraction, multiplication, and 90 in division graded according to difficulty.
2. Practice sheets of more difficult steps in four fundamental processes with integers and fractions for group needs.
3. Sheets of practical problems from interests and needs of the group.
B. Workbooks.

Brueckner, L. J. & others	New Curriculum Workbooks	1936 Winston

C. Supplementary material.
  1. Individual number cards for drill on facts in the funda-
     mental processes.
  2. Individual cards made by teacher containing steps of
     processes needing drill by certain pupils.
  3. Printed keyed cards for self-correction in fundamental
     processes.
  4. Individual work sheets to overcome difficulties.

III. Arithmetic books for reference and review.

| Brueckner, L. J. & others | New Curriculum Arithmetics | 1936 Winston |
| Knight, F. B., and others | Study Arithmetics | 1935 Scott Foresman |

IV. Standardized tests.

Metropolitan Achievement Test	World Book Company
New Stanford Achievement Test	World Book Company
Progressive Achievement Test	California Test Bureau.

C. PROBABLE OUTCOMES

I. Informational outcomes.
  A. Related to measurement.
    1. How to find area or surface of rectangles.
    2. How to measure length using common units of linear
       measure.
    3. How to find perimeter of rectangles.
    4. How to draw simple maps to scale.
    5. How to use scale of miles on maps.
    6. How to construct simple graphs.
    7. How to measure dry materials, dry goods, weight.
  B. Related to the social studies.
    1. A knowledge of land values.
       a. In early days of United States.
       b. In both rural and urban localities today.
    2. A knowledge of how land is measured.
    3. A knowledge of taxes, how levied, and purpose.
    4. Information about dates in history.
    5. Information about the size of the United States and
       various sections of it.
    6. Value of crops in the United States.
    7. Value of exports and imports of the United States.
    8. Part the United States plays in world production.
    9. Population of the United States both urban and rural.
   10. Changing population of the United States.

11. Cost of wars.
12. Extent and value of the natural resources of the United States.
13. Change in volume and time required in the industrial output brought about by change from hand to mechanical power.

C. Related to the use of money.
1. Reasons for discounts.
2. Better understanding of accounts.
3. How we come to have our decimal system.
4. Meaning of per cent.
5. Different kinds of bank accounts.
6. How to open a savings account.
7. How to draw money out of a savings account.
8. How to draw money out of a checking account.
9. Meaning of interest.
10. Some understanding of the meaning of percentage and decimals.

II. Attitudes and appreciations.

A. A better appreciation of the benefits derived through taxation, such as police and fire protection in a city.
B. An appreciation for the value of land and why land differs in value.
C. An appreciation for the number of comforts which have been made possible by mechanical power.
D. An appreciation for the number of comforts which have been made possible by the natural resources of the United States.
E. An appreciation of the importance of conserving our natural resources.
F. An appreciation for the value of the crops of the United States and the part the United States plays in world production.
G. A better appreciation for the ease and accuracy with which we can measure in comparison with ancient times.
H. Better conception of money value.
I. Desire to give and get money's worth in dealings.
J. A better appreciation of accuracy as a time saver.
K. A desire to avoid unnecessary waste of school materials and time.
L. A desire to pay bills promptly.
M. A desire to save money.
N. A willingness to spend money for the good of others.

O. An appreciation of arithmetic as an aid in solving every-day problems.

P. An enjoyment in accomplishing, or attaining skill in various processes.

III. Computational skills.

A. Minimum attainments for average pupil.
  1. Notation and numeration.
     a. Ability to read and write numbers in millions.
     b. Ability to read and write common Roman numerals 1 to 20, by tens to 100, 500, and 1000.
  2. Fundamental processes with integers.
     a. Automatic response to fundamental facts—100 addition, 100 subtraction, 100 multiplication, and 90 division.
     b. Greater speed and accuracy in addition, subtraction, and multiplication containing all types of difficulty.
     c. Increased skill with division enlarged to include ability to divide with two figure divisors.
     d. Greater speed and accuracy with short division now enlarged to include ability to use as short division.
     e. Ability to check all processes.
     f. Increased ability to solve one and two-step problems involving all processes.
  3. Fundamental processes with fractions.
     a. Ability to add, subtract and multiply fractions, including all the specific abilities involved.
     b. Ability to apply these skills in the solution of problems.
  4. Denominate numbers.
     a. Ability to use common units of dry, liquid, linear, avoirdupois, surface, solid, and time measures.
     b. Ability to solve problems involving denominate numbers in United States money and in measures.
B. Attainments for pupils above average.
  1. Mastery of attainments listed above in less time.
  2. Ability to solve more difficult practical problems.
  3. Attainment of more information concerning quantitative aspects of modern living.

Note: The adjustment between the superior and average child has been made in this group largely on a time basis. The superior child devotes less time to arithmetic practice and spends more time in problem solving and in pursuit of information.

IV. Terms.

    A. Familiarity with the following minimum list of terms in the four fundamental processes with integers.

        1. Addition—add, sum, total, column, addends.

        2. Subtraction—subtract, difference, remainder.

        3. Multiplication—multiply, product, multiplier.

        4. Division—divide, divisor, dividend, quotient, remainder.

    B. Familiarity with the following terms in the three fundamental processes with fractions:

fraction	common fraction
fractional part	improper fraction
integer	like fraction
mixed number	unlike fraction
proper fraction	numerator
change	denominator

    C. Familiarity with the following terms in measurement:

pint	pounds	sq. in.
quart	ton	sq. ft.
gallon	inches	sq. yd.
dozen	foot	second
peck	yard	minute
bushel	rod	hour
ounces	mile	day
	year	

    D. Familiarity with the following common terms:

average	width	per
increase	weight	rectangle
decrease	account	square
amount	discount	circle
length	height	triangle
area	perimeter	per cent
	surface	

Arithmetic in Sixth Grade

A. ACTIVITIES

I. **Activities related to room procedure.**

A. Attendance.
1. Recording daily attendance.
2. Finding percent of attendance over a period of time.

B. Program.
1. Deciding on time allotment for units of study.
2. Planning the program for the day or week.
3. Computing the percentage of time each week devoted to certain types of work.
4. Completing a "job" within a specified time.

C. Choosing daily menu, which must contain certain food values, and not exceed a certain price.

D. Taking care of health.
1. Adjusting chairs and desks to sizes of pupils.
2. Computing the percent of each size needed for the group, and comparing with standard.
3. Keeping monthly height and weight record for the group.
4. Computing average height and average weight for the class.
5. Finding percent over or under weight for each member of class.

E. Care of equipment and supplies.
1. Making inventories of supplies on hand.
2. Estimating amount needed.
3. Ordering additional supplies.
4. Mastering combinations on lockers.

F. Spelling practice.
1. Keeping a spelling graph over a period of time.
2. Finding percent of words correct over a period of time.

II. **Activities related to group enterprises.**

A. Enlarging the school library.
1. Selecting books to be purchased from class earnings, with content and price of book considered.
2. Figuring total cost of books purchased.
3. Figuring discounts allowed by publishers and money saved.
4. Computing balance to class credit, and considering further expenditures.

504

EDITING AND MANAGING THE NATIONAL NEWS INVOLVES
MATHEMATICS

B. Publication of magazine.
1. Estimating amount of paper and stencils to order.
2. After approximating cost, deciding on price that would offer a fair profit.
3. Checking number sold and money collected.
4. Depositing money.
5. Decision to spend part of money in framing pictures; and part in subscription to National Geographic Magazine for school library.
6. Receiving bill for framing pictures from school office.
7. Paying bill and receiving receipt.
8. Checking amount left in class treasury.
C. Cooking enterprises in home economics room.
1. Finding $\frac{1}{2}$, $\frac{1}{4}$, or $\frac{3}{4}$ of the recipe, sometimes doubling or trebling amounts.
2. Figuring cost of recipe.
3. Estimating economy or extravagance of recipe.

III. **Activities related to spontaneous interests.**
A. Finding averages and percentages in many situations.
B. Listing all reasons possible for discounts being offered.

IV. **Activities related to social studies.**
  A. Comparing cost and size of ancient and medieval buildings and art treasures with modern productions.
  B. Comparing coins and methods of trading in medieval times with our own.   '
  C. Comparing of medieval methods of book making and number of books available with methods used in modern times.
  D. Placing time of various periods by years and centuries with reference to our present era; making a time-line as a border around three sides of the room.
  E. Finding percentages in comparing modern Europe with our own country.
      1. Percentage of exports and imports.
      2. Percentage of emigration and immigration.
      3. Percentage of United States population from different nationalities.
  F. Measuring in making of maps and in use of maps and globes; measuring and computing costs in making properties and costumes for play of knights.

V. **Activities for explanation and demonstration.**
  A. Explaining steps in a new process on the blackboard.
  B. Outlining on board procedure which will assist in solving reasoning problems.
      1. Read problem carefully.
      2. Try to see in your mind just what the problem describes.
      3. Decide what numbers you should add, subtract, multiply or divide.
      4. Estimate the answer.
      5. Work carefully.
      6. See if your answer agrees with estimate.
      7. See if you can prove your answer to be correct.
  C. Drawing diagrams, such as a large square divided into one hundred small squares, to be used in introducing percentage. Drawing circles and other figures which are divided and shaded.
  D. Marking off on floor measurements which are not well known, such as rods.
  E. Using units of measure in explaining problems involving denominate numbers.
  F. Cutting cardboard figures to be used in finding areas.
  G. Drawing plans of fields, yards and gardens when finding areas.
  H. Drawing graphs.

VI. Use of practice materials (adapted to needs of individuals).
  A. Use of mimeographed practice sheets covering new processes.
  B. Using work book for drill.
  C. Completing exercises in workbooks, usually working by contract method.
  D. Taking curriculum test once a month.
  E. Keeping individual graphs of results of monthly test.

VII. Use of books.
  A. Using books for review and drill after practice has been given.
  B. Using books for diagnostic tests.
  C. Using book as a reference for tables.

VIII. Use of diagnostic tests (by teacher or psychologist).
  A. Finding difficulties of individual children.
  B. Finding difficulties common to the group as a whole.

B. Books and Materials Used

I. Materials for practical experience with number.
  A. Measures: rules, yardstick, tape measure, liquid and dry measures, measuring devices used in cooking, scales.
  B. Cardboard figures used in finding areas.
  C. Cubes used in finding volume.
  D. Height and weight charts.
  E. Attendance records.
  F. Graph paper.
  G. Art and woodwork materials.
  H. Playground materials.
  I. Natural science and social studies materials.
  J. Food and utensils used in cooking.

II. Practice materials.
  A. Mimeographed sheets.
    1. Mimeographed sheets of four fundamental processes to develop greater skill.
    2. Mimeographed sheets covering new processes.
    3. Mimeographed sheets of reasoning problems.
  B. Workbook.

Brueckner, L. J. & others	New Curriculum Workbooks in Arithmetic	1936 Winston

  C. Individual cards for practice in fundamental facts and processes used chiefly in remedial work.

III. Arithmetic books for reference and review.

Brueckner, L. J. & others	New Curriculum Arithmetics	1936 Winston
Knight, F. B., & others	Study Arithmetics	1935 Scott Foresman

IV. Standardized tests.

Metropolitan Achievement Test	World Book Company
New Stanford Achievement Test	World Book Company
Progressive Achievement Test	California Test Bureau

C. Probable Outcomes

I. Information.

A. Necessity of "checking accounts."

B. Better understanding of personal expense accounts and allowances.

C. Correct form for bills.

D. Correct form for receipts.

E. Reasons for discounts.

F. Better understanding of advertising.

G. Knowledge of "good time" to buy.

H. Knowledge of adding machines and automatic devices.

I. Better understanding of uses of graphs.

J. Better understanding of uses of percentage and meaning of average.

K. Better understanding of use of measurement in cooking, and proportion in making or altering recipes.

L. Information about dates and periods in history.

M. Information about size and cost of buildings of different periods.

N. Knowledge of how buying was done in different periods.

O. Knowledge of early coins; how they were made; values in United States money.

P. Information about comparative number and cost of books in different periods.

Q. Knowledge about size of armies and cost of wars in different periods.

R. Statistics about population, immigration, exports and imports in the United States.

S. Information about use of different types of measures.

II. Attitudes and appreciations.

A. Better conception of value of money.

B. Appreciation of need for careful estimating in ordering supplies.

C. Desire to pay bills promptly and hold receipts carefully.
D. Desire to be exact and careful in handling money belonging to a group.
E. Desire to benefit by "bargains" and discounts.
F. Desire to fix price honestly and make fair profit.
G. Desire to avoid unnecessary waste and extravagance.
H. Appreciation of need for accuracy in all accounts.
I. Recognition of need for careful measuring and estimating in using recipes.
J. Readiness to spend money for good of whole school.
K. Desire to spend time to best advantage.
L. Appreciation of contribution of machinery to number of comforts available compared with ancient times.
M. Appreciation of simplicity and convenience of United States decimal system of coinage.

III. Skills in computation.
    A. Attainments for average group.
        1. Fundamental processes.
            a. Mastery of fundamental facts.
            b. Use of four fundamental processes with increased speed and accuracy.
            c. Skill in using process of long division, with some ability to divide by two and three figure divisors.
            d. Increased ability to solve reasoning problems involving all processes.
        2. Fundamental processes with fractions.
            a. Skill in adding, subtracting, multiplying and dividing common fractions.
            b. Ability to solve problems involving these steps.
        3. Decimal fractions.
            a. Ability to read and write decimal fractions accurately.
            b. Ability to add, subtract, multiply and divide common decimal fractions.
            c. Ability to solve problems involving these steps.
        4. Denominate numbers.
            a. Ability to use denominate numbers in the four fundamental processes.
            b. Ability to solve reasoning problems involving these processes.
        5. Percentage.
            a. Ability to use the table of aliquot parts.
            b. Ability to find a percent of a number.

       c. Ability to work all types of percentage problems based on these two processes.

       d. Ability to use percents larger than one hundred.

    6. Finding areas: Ability to find areas of rectangles and triangles.

  B. Attainments for pupils above average.

    1. Mastery of work listed in a shorter period of time.

    2. Time given to more difficult reasoning problems.

    3. Many original problems made by this group based on their own interests.

    4. Attainment of more information concerning the quantitative aspects of modern life.

IV. Terms.

  A. All terms used in the four fundamental processes.

  B. All terms used in the four fundamental processes with common fractions.

  C. All terms used in measurement.

  D. Familiarity with the following terms in decimal fractions: decimal point, decimal fraction, tenths, hundredths, thousandths, ten thousandths, hundred thousandths, millionths.

  E. Terms in percentage: percent, discount, profit, loss, at the rate of, list price, selling price, deposit, interest, commission.

  F. Terms in finding areas: square, rectangle, triangle, base, altitude.

PART V

Individual Records and Their Use

MEETING THE NEEDS OF THE
INDIVIDUAL

IN STUDYING the capacities and interests of each child, the
teachers make use of the various records that are filed at the time
the child is enrolled. In registering the child, the parent is asked
to fill in an experience record and a health history, and to sign a
permit for a physical examination. If a child is enrolled in the
nursery school or one of the kindergartens, the teacher in addition
holds a personal conference with the mother before the child enters,
seeking in this way to gain a more intimate knowledge of the child's
home situation and experience. The records of this and further
conferences are kept on file.

The school physician gives a physical examination each-year,
during the opening weeks of school, and records in the form provided certain physical characteristics. A fuller examination by the
family physician or by a specialist is recommended when the child's
condition seems to need further study. There is also daily health
inspection by the physician assisted by the school nurse, and further
notes and recommendations are made from time to time.

An individual intelligence test is given to each child before he
enters school. The test record is supplemented by the psychologist's
judgment of the physical, mental and social characteristics revealed
during the test. Since the school is not equipped and staffed to take
care of handicapped children, only normal, superior and gifted children are accepted. The child's complete development is considered
in placing him in the group where he can probably attain success.
For purposes of research, an individual intelligence test is given
every two years.

A "key" for studying and guiding the child's responses in the
school situation has been worked out for each field of activity. The
teachers have various ways of keeping individual records. Some
teachers keep daily brief accounts of significant happenings on individual file cards. When a child's behavior seems to need special
study, a diary record is made. Teachers also keep folders for each
child, filing from time to time samples of drawing, writing or other

bits of work. In grades above second, individual progress charts are kept in the acquisition of certain important skills.

At the end of the semester, the teachers prepare a descriptive report for each child, summarizing the various individual records and including recommendations. One copy of the descriptive report is sent to parents and one copy is filed with other permanent records at the school. With the teacher's report a blank is sent to parents, asking for a report of the child's progress and of his needs as seen in the home. While the descriptive reports require much time and study, the results in increased parent cooperation and in the teacher's own understanding of the child's development have been so evident, that teachers have considered them most worth while.

In all grades, beginning with second, achievement tests have been given by a psychologist near the end of each semester, and individual graph records have been made, based on average scores of tests given. Further study of the problem has been provided in a few cases when a child's educational age fell decidedly below his mental age. Grouping within the room and providing individual instruction when needed, take care of individual differences in the mastery of skills so that a child need not fall behind the group where his general development suggests his placement. The school seeks to eliminate failure and repetition of grades, with the accompanying emotional maladjustments.

All the records pertaining to the individual child are kept in his permanent folder in a central office. Teachers draw out these folders at the beginning of the school year in order to study the past experiences of each child in the new group, and also at other times as questions arise. Sometimes the teacher is promoted with her children, and remains with the same group two years. This procedure has been found especially favorable to certain children needing help in social adjustment.

In this section copies are included of actual reports exchanged between parents and teachers, and also the keys for guiding the teacher's study of individual children. To protect the children whose records have been used, names have been omitted or fictitious names have been substituted, and dates have been altered.

THE RELATIONSHIP OF PARENTS
TO THE SCHOOL

ALTHOUGH both teachers and parents prepare records and reports which are exchanged, these do not in any way take the place of individual conferences. Before the child is enrolled, the parents hold an interview with the director of the school or the assistant director, in order that the aims of the school and the parents' purpose in enrolling the child may be fully understood. Usually conferences are held also with the room teacher, the school physician, and the psychologist who gives the initial tests. After the physical examination and the intelligence test, parents are advised concerning the type of work the child is ready to do, and the group where he will probably be most successful. The exact intelligence quotient is not as a rule given out, since this has been found to fluctuate in later tests.

During the year parents hold frequent conferences with the room teachers and special teachers. Two days each week are set aside as parents' visiting days, and informal conversations with teachers often occur following an observation in the room. Prearranged interviews occur also as needs arise in the school and the home. In nursery school and kindergarten it is customary to hold interviews before the child enters, and at all levels interviews are arranged at the close of each semester when semester reports are exchanged. Thus the reports and the recommendations may be fully discussed. Both teachers and parents have found such interviews very helpful, but have been unwilling to omit the written reports, since these may be read many times, may be referred to later as problems arise, and may be shared with relatives at home and other staff members at school who deal with the child.

All the specialists on the staff are ready to give help to parents and teachers in understanding and meeting particular needs. Individual parents frequently ask for conferences with the school physician, the psychologist, the nutritionist, the speech specialist, and the director of the Children's School. Sometimes a conference is arranged with one or both parents present, and two or more members of the staff.

Parents have been interested also in holding group meetings to discuss common problems. Each room group of parents chooses a room chairman, and this officer with the room teacher plans for several meetings of the group during the year. As a rule the room director or some other member of the staff is invited to lead the discussion, and the problem is one of vital interest to the group at the time.

The room officers and room teachers, together with the director of the school, serve on the Executive Board of the Parent-Teacher Council. This Board plans activities for the entire group of parents and teachers. Usually three or more evening meetings are held during the year, presenting speakers of note in the field of education, or providing for forum discussions or panel discussions in which parents and staff members participate. In two different years an All-Day Conference has been held, one on Guidance for Social Growth, and the second on Guidance for Growth in Personality.

In addition to such meetings of general interest, the Council has arranged each year for one or more courses devoted to important problems at particular levels. In these symposium courses several members of the staff and outside lecturers participate. Plans and subjects for these courses vary from year to year so that interested parents may continue their studies for several years. Supervised observation in the Children's School has been a regular part of some of these courses. The following courses have been given successfully in the past few years:

> Child Care and Training in the Early Years.
> Behavior Problems of Early Childhood.
> The Child and His Learning.
> Educative Experiences of Childhood.
> Our Children—Knowing Them and Living with Them.
> Home Guidance of Children.
> The Child and Society.
> Problems of Early Adolescence.
> Adolescence—Its Problems and How to Deal with Them.
> Problems in Child Development from Infancy to Adolescence.
> Progressive Education in School and Home.
> The Specialist Looks at the Child.

CHILD'S ORIGINAL ENROLLMENT RECORD
CHILDREN'S SCHOOL
National College of Education
(Filled by parent for each new child who enters the school)

To the Parent:

We are asking for the following information, so that we may know and understand your child and be able to deal with him as intelligently as possible. We will appreciate your coöperation in filling out this record as completely as you can, recognizing that the information we seek is for the welfare of your child.

Name of Child *Girl*   Date of Birth *January, 1934*
Name of Parent _____   Date of Enrollment *September, 1939*
   Address
   Home telephone
   Business telephone of Father   Picture
                  of Mother   of
   Physician's Name   Child
      Telephone
Previous schools child has attended.
      School   Dates of Attendance   Grades
      None

Physical Environment

Does he live in a house, hotel or apartment? *House*
How many rooms are there in his home? *Seven*
Does he have his own room? *Yes*
Does he sleep alone? *Yes*
Has he his own playroom? *Yes, during the summer only*
Are there shelves or cupboards for his play materials and books? *Yes*
How much responsibility is expected of him in caring for these? *I try to have her put them back after she has had friends in and before she goes to bed. But she never does it unless I tell her to—in other words it is far from a habit.*
Is there yard space where he may play? *Yes*
What play equipment is there in the yard? *Two playhouses—swing —sand pile*
Where does he spend most of his playtime? *Outdoors in our yard and in adjoining yards. Part of each day outdoors; some time playing at home and some time playing at the homes of her friends here in the neighborhood.*

Interests

What toys and play materials does your child have?   Check his favorite ones.

crayons	*dresser*	*iron*
scissors	*table and chair*	*puzzles*
moulding clay	*sewing cabinet*	*blocks*
doll bed	*ironing board*	

What are his favorite books?

Mother Goose	*Millions of Cats*
Cinder	*A Pocketful of Rhymes*
Peter Rabbit	*The Fire Engine Book*

How does he spend his free time when at home?   *Plays outdoors with other children as much as possible.   In winter she cuts, draws a great deal, washes and irons, plays with her dolls once in a while.*
Has he any definite responsibilities or duties to carry out each day, so that he feels that he is coöperating and contributing to the home? Name these. *She must hang up her towel and wash cloth on the rack and put her clothes away—at nap time and at bedtime.   These are practically all of the duties she has to perform other than picking up her toys.*

The Family

Of whom does the immediate family consist? *Father, mother, one sister*
Ages of younger sisters *two years*   younger brothers
       older sisters   older brothers
What other relatives live in the home? *None—grandmother often visits*
How many servants are there? *one*
What has been the education of parents?
Father
   High school graduate? *Yes*   College graduate? *Yes*
   From where?   From where? *N. U.*
Mother
   High school graduate? *Yes*   College graduate? *Yes*
   From where?   From where? *Smith*
Is there any deviation from family life—
   Child adopted?
   Either or both parents dead?
   Parents separated?
   Parents divorced?
   Either or both parents away for long periods?

Who cares for the child most of the time? *Mother*
How much time does he spend with his parents? *Eats breakfast and dinner.*
Mother
Father *Usually the hour after dinner and some time on Saturdays and Sundays.*

Social Contacts and Experiences

With whom does the child play? *There are twelve children ranging in age from two to eight.*
What type of play does he carry on, active or rather quiet? *Very active.*
Is he shy or does he approach others with ease? *Very easy for her to make friends.*
Is he inclined to lead or to follow? *To lead.*
Does he get on happily with companions? *Yes—sometimes directs them too much.*
What contacts does he have with the community? Does he visit the grocery, market, dairy, the beach, forest preserves, railroad station? Name. *Grocery, other stores, beach, railroad station, The Community Kitchen.*
Has he visited a farm, aviation field, train yards, factories of various kinds? Name. *Farm, aviation field.*
By what means has he traveled? Boats, trains, automobile, aeroplane? *Auto, train.*
To what places? Please name. *Indiana and Wisconsin.*
Has he attended Sunday School?
What is his participation in family activities?

Nature Experiences

Has he a garden? *We have a small garden.*
What pets has he? *None*
What responsibility does he take toward his pets or plants? *She helps me pick flowers once in a while. Has planted seeds.*
Has he gone to the woods for picnics, to gather nuts, leaves?
Give other nature experiences.

Aesthetic Experiences

What lessons has your child had outside of school in music, art, dancing? *None*
What are you doing to cultivate an interest in these lines? *We play the piano together and sing. I often play and she and her sister march.*

Needs

What, if any, special help does your child need? Please describe the problem. (discipline, habits of sleep, food, social relationships, physical needs.) *I believe she needs help in forming the habit of neatness. She is not naturally untidy, but likes to get out of picking up. I believe I have erred here and did not insist early enough that she form this habit. I am naturally unmethodical, and have found it easier to pick up after than to start her on the right track herself. I can't rely on her to tell the truth always. Lately she has been very disobedient. I have to tell her three or four times to do a thing.*

What are your reasons for enrolling your child in this school? *I believe she is advanced and needs some kind of intelligent direction. I know she will get it at National College of Education.*

Through whom did you become interested in the school?

Name of person filling out this blank.

INITIAL CONFERENCE WITH PARENTS
NURSERY SCHOOL AND KINDERGARTEN

Date of Conference

Child's Name   Date of Birth

Name of Parent or Guardian

Name of Teacher

General Physical Status

What was the date of the last physical examination? By whom given?
Did it include a blood test? Urinalysis? Footprint?
What diseases has the child had? How recently?
What, if any, operations has he had?
Has he any physical defects—vision, hearing, etc.
Is he left or right handed?
What is his coordination: Can he button? Use scissors? Feed self? Dress self?

Elimination

What terminology does the child use in asking to go to toilet?
Does he take any responsibility for elimination?
Defecation—Time? Conditions? Use of oil, suppository?
Urination—Frequency? Wet bed at nap? At night?
If boy, does he stand or sit?

Sleep

At night—Time in bed? Time asleep? Time awake?
Nap—Time in bed? Time asleep? Time awake?
Condition of sleep?
Does he sleep alone? In room alone?
Is he sensitive to light or dark? To noise?
Does child get out of bed? Sing in bed? Play in bed?
Does he rock? Is he dependent on toy or thumb?
Has he a set position for sleeping?
What is his attitude on waking?

Food

Does child eat alone or with family?
Who supervises child's feeding? Who plans his meals?
Type of appetite?
What are his food dislikes? How dealt with? Allergies?
Abilities—Feed self? Use spoon or fork? Use bib?
Does he vomit at will? Throw food on floor? Get up from table?

A Typical Day's Menu

At what time did he have breakfast this morning?
Of what did it consist?
At what time did he have supper last night?
Of what did it consist?
At what time did he have dinner yesterday?
Of what did it consist?
Is he accustomed to a midmorning feeding? If so, at what time, and
  of what does the feeding consist?
Is he accustomed to a midafternoon feeding? If so, at what time,
  and of what does the feeding consist?
What is the average length of time for breakfast? dinner? supper?

Emotions

Is the child sunny, happy?
What are his special enjoyments?
Does the child cry easily? Often? Why? How treated?
Is he afraid? Why? How treated?
Are there displays of temper? Causes? How treated?
What are his social attitudes—toward parents? servants? brothers and
  sisters? playmates?
What nervous habits does he have; as, biting nails, sucking thumb,
  handling self?
Are you anticipating any homesickness or difficulty in the child's first
  days at school?

Language
What was the age of talking—Using words? Combinations? Sentences?
Speech—Is there any impediment? Letter substitutions? Tendency to
stammer? How treated?
What is the extent of his vocabulary?

Music
Is there music in the home—Piano? Radio? Phonograph?
Do the parents sing? Play an instrument?
Does the child show interest in music?
Does the child sing? Spontaneously? Creatively?
Can he carry a tune? Can he whistle?
Is he rhythmic?

Arrangements
Will the child use the school car? The first day?
If not, who will bring him to school?
Who will call for him?
What will be his schedule on the first day? Later?

What was the attitude of the parent during the conference?

KEY TO TEACHER'S REPORTS AND CHILD STUDY RECORDS

NURSERY SCHOOL AND KINDERGARTEN

Physical Status
A. *General Health*
1. What is the general condition of the child's health?
2. What were the results of the physical examination?
3. Has he defects or disabilities: Poor sight? Defective hearing?
Adenoids? Defective speech? Knock-knees? Bowlegs? Pro-
truding abdomen? Defective teeth? Rachitic symptoms?
4. What illnesses has he had?
5. What was the height and weight at the beginning of term?
6. What is height and weight now?
7. Is he susceptible to colds?
8. Is he hyperactive? Normally active? Lethargic?
9. Is his color good? Are there circles under his eyes?
10. Does he relax?
11. Has he a sensitive skin?

12. Does he run temperature easily?
13. Does he carry himself well? Walk with a spring in his step?

B. *Muscular Coordination*

1. Does he use alternate feet in skipping?
2. Does he alternate feet going up and down stairs?
3. Does he trip often?
4. Can he catch, bounce, throw a ball?
5. Is he right or left handed?
6. Can he button and unbutton?
7. Can he zip fasteners?
8. Can he put on wraps and rubbers alone?
9. How does he manipulate brush, crayon, and scissors?
10. Can he climb on junglegym?
11. Can he carry things without dropping?

C. *Sleep*

1. Total hours of sleep?
2. Time in bed at nap? Asleep? Awake?
3. Does he always sleep?
4. Attitude during nap period?
5. Attitude on waking?
6. Is he dependent upon toys or adults?
7. Has he an habitual way of going to sleep? Any set position? Rolling? Sucking thumb?
8. Is he sensitive to noise? Light?
9. What is the condition of child's sleep? Sound? Restless?

D. *Food*

1. Does child have a good appetite? Indifferent to food?
2. Is he happy during the lunch period?
3. What is his attitude toward new foods?
4. What is his attitude toward disliked foods?
5. What foods does he dislike and why? Allergies?
6. Do the meals which the child has at home balance the meals which he has at school?
7. What is the average length of meal time?
8. What helpful suggestions are effective? Home cooperation?
9. Eating skills: Use of silver? Napkin? Pouring milk? Carrying food? Feeding without spilling?
10. Ability to concentrate on eating?
11. Ability to converse and eat simultaneously?

Emotional Stability

A. *Temperament*

1. Does he adapt to disappointments?
2. Accept criticism?

3. Easily excited?
4. Cry easily?
5. Fearful? What fears if any?
6. Affectionate? Sympathetic? Kindly?
7. Sensitive? Self-conscious?
8. Sensitive to atmosphere and beauty?
9. Is he joyous and free?
10. Has he a sense of humor? Laugh easily? Become silly easily?
11. Is he dependent upon parent, teacher, children, or toys?
12. Are there any physical manifestations of insecurity, such as, biting nails, sucking thumb, handling self, picking lips?

B. *Attitude Toward Work*
1. Does he have emotional drive?
2. Does he show determination?
3. What is his attitude toward failure?
4. Does he show persistence in event of failure?

Social Adjustment

A. *Attitudes Toward Other People*
1. What is the attitude of the child toward the parents? Toward brothers and sisters? Toward the servant?
2. What is the attitude of the child toward the teacher? Toward playmates?

B. *Social Habits and Tendencies*
1. Does he play alone? Does he play with others? If so, how many children?
2. Can he play alone?
3. Is he conscious of other children and their activities? What responses does he make?
4. Does he willingly cooperate in upholding group rules?
5. Does he initiate his own activities?
6. Does he show tendencies toward leadership? Following?
7. Does he attempt to solve his own problems?
8. Do his school and home behavior supplement each other?
9. To what degree does he share?
10. Is he equally interested in both boys and girls?
11. Does he take responsibilities voluntarily: For playthings which he has used? For playthings which others have used? For wraps? For room?
12. Is he dependent upon adults? Does he solicit attention?

Capacities, Appreciations, Interests

A. *General Capacities*
1. What evidence does the child give of: Concentration?

Memory? Imagination? Alertness? Comprehension? Effort? Purpose? Initiative? Perseverance? Reasoning?

2. What attempt has he made to solve his own problems?
3. What is the length of his attention span?
4. Does his interest carry over from day to day?
5. Does he bring things to school which show that his interest has carried over?
6. Does he have few or many interests?
7. What are his special interests: blocks, dolls, creative materials, pets, books, music, nature, etc.?
8. How does he use equipment? Experimentally? Manipulatively? Dramatically? Constructively?
9. What concepts does he have with regard to: Space? Number? Time? Place? Direction?
10. Does he have the ability to count? Name colors? Name the days of the week?
11. Is he observant?
12. Does he use his time wisely? Dependable?
13. Does he ask thoughtful questions?
14. Does he face reality?

B. *Dramatic Play*
1. Is he interested in dramatic play? Does he create his own stories?
2. Is there originality of ideas? Is his play creative? Or imitative?
3. Is he an organizer or a cooperative participant?
4. Is there freedom and joy in expression?

C. *Use of Creative Art Materials*
1. What type of creative materials does he use?
2. Workbench; what is ability to saw? Pound nails? Care for tools? What does he do with the materials?
3. Scissors, crayons, clay, and paint. Responsibility for care of the materials? Discrimination of color and form? Technique in handling materials? Originality? Joy in the doing?

D. *Music*
1. Singing.—Does he have opportunity of hearing members of the family play and sing? Does he participate in singing with the group or alone? Does he create his own songs? What is his voice quality? How accurate is his pitch? Tempo?
2. Rhythms.—Is he creative in his rhythmic response? Does he enjoy rhythmic expression? Is his bodily coordination good?
3. Experimentation with instruments.—Is he interested in experimenting with rhythm and tone by means of bells, gongs, and so forth?

4. Appreciation.—Does he enjoy listening to music? Does he recognize familiar music?

5. Does he enjoy playing the piano himself?

E. *Language*

1. Does he stutter or stammer?
2. Is his enunciation good?
3. Does he use complete sentences? Correct grammatical form?
4. Is he sensitive to new words?
5. Does he play with sounds and words?
6. What is the approximate size of his vocabulary? Extensive? Average? Limited?
7. Does he converse readily? With whom?
8. What is the quality of his voice?

F. *Literary Experience*

1. Does he enjoy stories?
2. What type of stories does he seem to enjoy most?
3. Does he create original stories?
4. Does he enjoy poetry?
5. Does he create original poetry?
6. What is his attention span?
7. Can he relate simple stories, giving main events?
8. Does he show an appreciation of the humorous parts in stories and poems told and read to him?
9. Is he able to comprehend and relate new experiences and facts into his play?

REPORT OF TEACHER

Nursery School and Kindergarten

Name of Child *A.*

Date of birth *June 30, 1935*   Group *Nursery School*

Semester beginning *January 31, 1939*   Days absent *10*

Semester ending *June 2, 1939*   Days present *77*

     Height *38.8*   Weight *37.2*

Physical Status—

A. is a healthy looking boy, apparently in fine physical condition—round rosy cheeks, bright eyes, sturdy, well built little body, and an excellent appetite. He is very active in his play. At times, his eyes look tired, and he becomes easily irritated, depending upon his left thumb for comfort.

His health habits are good, with the exception of afternoon nap. In the beginning, he refused afternoon resting at all, and has had to learn to lie quietly. He rarely falls asleep, but with the help of an adult, he manages to lie pretty quietly for $1\frac{1}{2}$ hours.

His appetite is splendid—always eats several servings—has very few food dislikes.

His motor coordination is well developed, as shown in his walking, running, and climbing, and in his excellent ability in handling wagons and shovels. The finer muscles in his fingers are not as well developed—he becomes impatient in trying to button buttons and lace his shoes.

Emotional Status—

A. has shown some improvement in emotional stability, but he is still far from feeling secure within himself. He has a happy, sunny disposition and a sympathetic, kindly attitude toward the children when everything is going smoothly for him. Upon meeting opposition, he is inclined to dissolve into tears, hit, bite, or grab. He flares into an outburst of temper, but soon quiets down again, using the thumb and twirling of eyelash as his comfort. Biting is very rare now, and he announced with great pride, not long ago, that he no longer grabbed things he wanted. He is making a decided effort to overcome some of these handicaps, and does show much more control in using speech instead of force in settling his problems.

Only recently has he been willing to get into the school car before the teacher in charge is in sight. He still is hesitant to place himself in the charge of people he does not know. He needs a great deal of assurance and reassurance in feeling safe and secure in new situations.

Social Adjustment—

A. is a friendly, sociable child, affectionate towards both children and adults. He can play happily alone, but prefers to play with at least one other child. He both gives and takes suggestions in play and is showing a fine spirit of cooperation. He is learning to share, take turns, and respect the rights of others. He is quick to assert his own rights as well as those of his friends.

In spite of A.'s inclination to hide the toys he likes best at picking up time, he has many generous impulses. One day he brought three powder puffs for three special friends and handed them out with much ceremony. He shows special loyalty for his best friends. His sincerity and friendliness make him a staunch friend of all the children.

Capacities, Attitudes and Interests—

A. is very active in his play. He loves to be out-of-doors where he can use tricycles, wagons, shovels and wheelbarrows, all of which he handles skillfully and adroitly. Dramatic play enters into all his activities and in it he displays a wealth of ideas, a store of knowledge and vivid imagination. He is usually a workman of some occupation or other—"an oil truck man, ice cream cone man, balloon man, fireman, engineer, policeman, garbage man"; some busy active person who engages in an equal amount of conversation and physical activity at the same time.

He shows initiative, originality, and resourcefulness in using whatever materials are at hand. A pail is all that is needed to bring forth the garbage man, two blocks clipped together are an alligator opening and shutting its mouth, pussy willows fallen from the branches or leaves from the trees make good garbage or food, whichever the demand may be.

He is observant and alert to everything in his environment. The advantages and disadvantages of similar toys are all known to A. and if one of the less desirable should be his lot, he exerts persuasive powers in making a more advantageous trade. He is usually successful.

He has been too busy and social to listen to stories at any scheduled time in a group, but is none the less appreciative of books. He prefers informational books and stories full of action. All his knowledge is utilized in his play.

Music is enjoyed as a physically active participant—as a drummer accompanying the piano in almost perfect rhythm, as a marcher playing a trumpet (stick used as such) or, as some animal being dramatized. Singing is a little tame and he generally loses his interest because it does not call for movement from his whole body.

His reasoning powers are excellent when not hampered by immature emotional stability.

His powers of speech are well developed. He enunciates clearly and distinctly, and possesses a good sized vocabulary for one of his age.

A. is a very normal, alive little boy, with real and healthy boy interests.

Recommendations—

A. has been a great asset to the group. He is an unusually healthy, active, well-developed little boy. He does need firm and consistent handling, and at the same time an understanding and appreciation of his ideas and interests in order to become more mature emotionally.

We have appreciated your thoughtful interest and cooperation, Mr. and Mrs. M.

Signed_____

REPORT OF PARENTS

Nursery School

Name of child   *A.*

Date *June 8, 1939*

What school interests has your child most often mentioned at home?

Songs? *He sings Jingle Bells and This Old Man much of the time.*

Rhymes? *I have noticed a greater interest in word sounds and rhyming words.*

Pictures?

Toys and other play materials? *Occasionally speaks of barrels and wagons.*

Pets? *Talks about the guinea pigs and turtles.*

Activities and experiences of the day?

Other children? *Mentions Peter and Dickie frequently. Sometimes speaks of Nancy, wanting to know where she lives.*

Any other persons or things?

He speak of the teachers often, Mr. Olson, the "furnace-man," and Mr. Todd, who drives his school car. He frequently relates happenings, though they have such a fanciful sound that I don't know just how much to believe.

Have you noticed progress at home:

Socially—Attitude toward other children? *Decided.*

Attitude toward parents? *A little less irritable.*

Attitude toward strangers? *No particular change.*

In other ways?

Mentally—Is he alert to things about him? *Very.*

Does he solve his own problems? *Yes, as a general rule.*

How long does he play with one thing? *Long time if outdoors, or playing with cars.*

Other forms of progress? *Shows increased interest in books.*

Physically—Has he improved in health habits? *Yes, more independent.*

Has he gained in coordination? *Yes.*

Other gains?

Has he improved in habits of eating? *He has always eaten well.*

Has he improved in habits of sleeping? *Not in afternoon nap.*

In what forms of work or play does he engage most frequently at home?

Uses small cars, trucks and trains with blocks, making tracks and garages. Out-of-doors with tricycle much of the time. Watches janitor at work repairing odd jobs.

What is the attitude toward coming to school?

Always eager for school car to arrive but does not complain when he stays home on Saturdays. Enjoys using his own toys.

What, if any, undesirable tendencies is your child showing at home just now ?

He says "You dumbbell" to everyone. He fights bed-time and runs off to hide when called, usually dissolving into tears before he is settled for the night. Sucks his thumb when thwarted.

Suggestions or questions:

We have been very gratified that the school has held his interest so unflaggingly.

Do you have any suggestions about making bed-time a more pleasant situation for all concerned? We are willing to try almost anything and are always appreciative of your suggestions.

Signed _____

_____

REPORT OF TEACHER
KINDERGARTEN

Name of Child *S.*

Date of birth *September 20, 1934.*   Group *Senior Kindergarten*

Semester beginning *September 18, 1939.*   Days absent *9*

Semester ending *January 31, 1940.*   Days present *77*

Physical status—

S. has good muscular coordination but does not really enjoy vigorous physical activity; seems to be fearful of adult criticism.

Was decidedly phlegmatic at first but has showed considerable improvement.

Dark rings and puffiness under his eyes at times. Has the cause for this condition been determined?

Relaxes very well when resting.

Weight, Sept.—42.3   Weight, Jan.—46.5.

Emotional status—

He has made very satisfactory improvement in this respect for he was reserved, timid and extremely self-conscious when he first came to Senior Kindergarten. Would become silly, rub eyes and make faces, if attention was focused upon him. There is still need for improvement along this line, but we feel that ignoring him when he feels he is not measuring up is the best method to use with him. Is not willing to accept criticism, but pouts or sulks. We are sure that as he proceeds in school he will overcome this, but criticism should be used very sparingly now.

Has given evidence of real temper, but he keeps this well under control. S. is affectionate and "warms up" to people fairly well if any affection is shown him. Is sensitive to his environment and often comments on things of beauty—color combinations, flowers. Is cautious but not fearful under most circumstances.

Social adjustment—

S. has attained a satisfactory degree of friendliness. He joins in play with others voluntarily and often makes valuable suggestions to their play. At first he would find something to do which did not require any social contact, and in the entire group activities he would hang back and refuse to join. He now presents no social problem, but comes happily.

He follows the lead of others intelligently and in a cooperative manner. He has given a few evidences of leadership, but we can not expect much of him along this line until he forgets self.

Has respect for the property of others.

Will take responsibility when definitely given to him but does not assume it to any degree.

Capacities, attitudes and interests—

S. has excellent ability in concentrating. Is persistent almost to the point of fatigue at times.

Has a long memory span.

He has good reasoning power—often very quick to see through a situation. Needs to be encouraged to do his own thinking. Asks for help when, with a little suggestion or a word to help him feel the problem is not beyond him, he can go ahead. His interests are many. Most of the materials of the kindergarten make an appeal to him. He prefers those activities, however, which do not involve lively physical effort.

He draws and paints with a good deal of skill. His work is meaningful. While he is greatly interested in the doing he is always interested and pleased with his product.

His work with wood and with blocks shows some creative ability. Works with a purpose in mind.

He sings with a sweet voice; has more than average ability. He en-

joys music and will listen intently to piano music. Good sense of rhythm. He was most self-conscious in rhythm work at first and would not participate. After a discussion between S. and myself in private, he has entered into rhythms. I told him he could do anything with his feet and hands that he wished while the others were skipping, etc. Because we have not commented on how he did things, but praised him because he was doing something, he has seemed to feel much more at ease. We are beginning now to work with him alone in helping him to attain greater skill. Freedom in speech is fairly satisfactory when his interest is so high that he forgets himself. Good vocabulary.

Is just beginning to be interested in reading.

Has a good background of information.

Recommendations—

S.'s progress has been satisfactory this term. His greatest need is to feel free, to develop a greater sense of humor and to be less concerned about the opinion of others. I feel sure that he has too close supervision and too much commenting has been made on his shortcomings. I would suggest that he be "put on his own" to a greater degree and that when self-consciousness or spells of stubbornness appear he be joked with and cajoled out of his mood.

REPORT OF PARENTS
KINDERGARTEN

Name of child *S.*

Group   *Senior Kindergarten*   Date   *February 10, 1940.*

What school interests has your child most often mentioned at home?

S. doesn't talk very much about his school work at home unless questioned, but he asks many questions about things, the ideas of which I think he must have obtained at school. When anything special aside from the daily routine comes up he mentions it—auto trips, great interest in the houseboat and Indians. He voluntarily comments on painting, making things of wood and building.

In what phases of our work is his progress most evident?

Most progress has been made in social adjustment, although there is still much room for improvement. Also, has progressed in ability to manipulate things with his hands. He can carry a tune much better but still needs to work on it. Listens more attentively when being read to.

In what forms of work or play does he engage most frequently at home?

When weather requires him to be inside he spends the greater part of his time building with his blocks—all kinds of things; then the mechanical toys—airplane and fire engines, electric train. He and his sister have great times in dramatic play. Out-of-doors he plays much with the neighborhood children, climbs, rides bike, plays with wagon, roller skates. Worked at shovelling snow and will help in the garden later.

During the present year what, if any, changes have you noted:

In habits of eating?

S. always has a good appetite, but is often slow and dreamy. There hasn't been much change here.

In habits of sleeping?

Very little change. I have noticed that he gets along just as well without his afternoon nap and doesn't seem to get more tired on the occasions when he goes without, but these are few and he still takes his nap.

What, if any, changes have you noted:
In attitude toward parents?

Has come to have greater respect for the parent-child relationship and seems to try hard to please. Has become very companionable.

In attitude toward other children?

Has grown more respectful of other children's belongings and more tactful in playing with others. Seems to like to be with them more than before.

What is the attitude toward coming to school?

S. loves to go to school and eagerly anticipates it every morning. It is the one time when he will hurry through dressing and eating in order to be ready to go.

What, if any, undesirable tendencies is your child showing at home just now?

He shows a tendency to be quite silly when asked to repeat anything he has learned. He is very slow about putting on and taking off clothes and wraps and sometimes about eating, showing a tendency to dream.

Suggestions or Questions:

I found the teacher's report very enlightening and helpful in pointing out a way to handle S. more successfully. I do wish that at the times when they are having their physical activities, he could be greatly encouraged. May I have a conference with you after school opens? I'd like to talk about his ability to assume responsibility and about helping him to feel free. Thank you very much for such a detailed and helpful report.

KEY FOR REPORT OF ROOM TEACHER
FIRST AND SECOND GRADES

Physical and Emotional Status

1. Is the general physical condition contributing to success in school work? Is there vitality, energy, robustness?
2. What, if any, physical handicaps hinder the child's progress?
3. Has the child nervous stability, poise, self-control?
4. Are emotional disturbances frequent—laughter, tears, anger, fear?
5. Is there a tendency to self-consciousness, timidity, aggressiveness, obstinacy, over-sensitiveness? Is the child easily discouraged?
6. What is usual attitude or mood at school? Happy, anxious, dreamy, sulky, enthusiastic, serious, eager, ambitious, indifferent?
7. What health habits need special attention: habits of eating, resting, walking?
8. Is there proper care of body and clothing: wraps, handkerchief, hands, nails, teeth?
9. What, if any, nervous habits are there: blinking, handling face or body, chewing nails, tongue, handkerchief.

Social Adjustment

1. Is there a friendly attitude? Is the child broad in choice of friends?
2. Is there proper respect for rights and opinions of others? Is there a sense of fair play?
3. Is there willingness to share experiences and possessions with others?
4. Does the child give and accept help willingly?
5. Does the child show a tendency to work and play in a group or individually?
6. Does he show leadership and ability to coöperate under leadership?
7. What is the attitude toward responsibility?
8. Is there observation of common courtesies?
9. Is there obedience to rules—in schoolroom, on playground, in halls, in bus, in lunchroom?

Social Studies

1. Has there been interest in social studies?
   a. *Housekeeping*—care of room, doll corner, making things for

room or playhouse, cooking, preparation for lunch, picnics, parties.

  b. *Festivals*—significance, planning programs, making gifts, cards, decorations.

  c. *Community activities*—stores, post office, bank, library, art gallery, museum, circus, band, show, concert, newspaper—constructing buildings, properties, costumes, dramatic play.

  d. *Industries*—study of food, shelter, clothing, transportation—making exhibits, posters, booklets.

2. To what extent does the child aid in purposing and planning group activities?

3. To what extent does he show resourcefulness, initiative, independence, originality in working toward a goal?

4. To what extent does he show industry, perseverance, in completing work begun?

5. To what extent can he express attitude and appreciation in art forms?

6. In what degree does he show ability to criticize or judge his own work and the work of the class? Does he profit by suggestions?

Science

1. Has the child exhibited any outstanding interest in nature?—pets, flowers, trees, leaves, birds, insects, shells, stones, weather, seasons?

2. Is there a readiness to nurture; care of pets, garden, plants or flowers in the room?

3. Has the child shown observation or appreciation in creating nature songs or verses, in composing nature stories, in making nature drawings or paintings?

4. Has interest been shown in physical science: causes and effects related to airplanes, steam engine, automobile, radio, electric machines, derricks, light, heat?

5. Is there curiosity about facts; desire to experiment, investigate, ask questions?

Oral Composition

1. Are there voluntary and worth-while contributions? Do they reveal a wealth of first-hand experiences?

2. Is there poise in speaking before a group?

3. What is the quality of voice?

4. Is the choice of English good? Is there normal growth in vocabulary?

5. Is enunciation distinct?

6. Is the child able to give courteous attention in a conversation group?

Written Composition and Spelling
1. What is the attitude toward writing?
2. To what extent does the child show ability to compose his own letters, verses, stories? Is he original?
3. What is the status of handwriting in fluency, uniformity? In what respects is improvement needed?
4. Is the child apt in learning to spell new words and in retaining words learned?
5. Is he conscientious in asking for words that he does not know rather than guessing?
6. What types of errors in spelling does the child make?

Reading
1. What is the attitude toward reading?
2. To what extent is there ability to master vocabulary? Is there a clear understanding of word meanings? •
3. To what extent is there independence in attacking new material?
4. In silent reading are effort, ability to comprehend, and speed, normal for the grade?
5. In oral reading are accuracy, dramatic interpretation, fluency, clear and distinct rendition, satisfactory for the grade?
6. If there is retardation, what are the causes? absence; left-eye dominance; physical defects of the eye, ear, speech; nervousness; immaturity; bad habits, such as spelling or analyzing each word phonetically, memory reading or guessing.
7. What types of errors are made?

Arithmetic
1. Is there interest in numbers? Is there a good number sense?
2. Is there ability to count objects accurately by ones, twos, threes, fives, tens?
3. Is there ability to recognize the number of objects in a small group without counting?
4. Is there ability to make and recognize figures accurately?
5. Is there mastery of number facts required or needed in the grade?
6. Is there ability to apply number facts in concrete situations?
7. To what extent can the child use coins, scales, ruler, clock, calendar, page numbers?
8. What, if any, type of error is frequent?

Outdoor Experiences
1. What is the attitude toward play?
2. How does the child spend his time out-of-doors?

3. Does he play agreeably with others? Does he show a protective attitude toward a younger child?
4. Does he show ability to organize or participate in group play?
5. How well can he handle his body? Is there improvement?
6. How does he react to balls and toys, to apparatus?
7. How well can he adjust to changes in weather?

Recommendations

1. What activities might the child profitably engage in at home?
2. What, if any, special help is needed in order that the child may meet the desired standards?
3. What habits or attitudes need special guidance?
4. Is any change in the child's program suggested?
5. Is the child ready for more advanced work?

REPORT OF TEACHER

FIRST GRADE

Name of child *E.*

Date of birth *September 19, 1933*   Group *First Grade*

Term beginning *September 18, 1939*   Days absent *4*

Term ending *January 31, 1940.*   Days present *82*

Physical and Emotional Status—

E. always appears in the best of health in the schoolroom. She has a great deal of vitality and energy and rarely shows signs of fatigue. She has a sunny temperament and is happy and enthusiastic in her work. She is usually well poised except for self-consciousness with adults. E. requires much encouragement, as she tends to lose interest and becomes easily discouraged. E. is neat in the care of her person and her materials.

Social Adjustment—

E. is generally friendly but with only her special friends. If she takes a dislike to another child she tends to coax others to be unkind to the unfavored one. In this way she has caused unhappiness in the group. She is usually willing to give help, and is always anxious to receive it. E. is usually coöperative with the teachers and other children, and she is for the most part eager to obey the group rules.

Social Studies—

E. is much interested in all room activities. She displays ability in dramatic play in the playhouse and store. She also helped in the construction of the buildings. She has a sense of orderliness and has in several instances shown an interest in the care of the room. She is independent in finding work to do, but she relies too much on adult help and suggestions for planning and executing her tasks. If she is encouraged to carry her work through to completion, it will help her to develop perseverance and willingness to surmount obstacles. She is skillful in basket weaving. She likes to draw and she shows some ability in this field.

Science—

There is a natural childlike interest in nature. E. is interested in watching pets, but she does not like to touch them or care for them. She likes to help arrange flowers. In the fall she composed a pet story telling of her pet at home.

Music—

E. has a clear, sweet voice which she occasionally forces in an effort to excel. She can sing about eight songs without help, carrying the tune and keeping on pitch. She shows excellent rhythmic perception and fine coördination.

Oral Composition—

E. often volunteers suggestions to the group during the conversation period. She has poise in speaking before a group, and the quality of her voice is good. She uses good English. She needs to be encouraged to plan her idea before presenting it, in order to get from her the best solution to a problem, or the most worth-while suggestions. She gives courteous attention unless she sits beside her special friends.

Written Composition and Spelling—

There is keen interest in learning to write. The last month E. has grown in ability to form the letters accurately. She puts forth good effort. She has developed an unusual degree of fluency and she writes with great ease.

Reading—

E. is enthusiastic about learning to read. She learns words easily and usually retains them. She is generally conscientious, but in her zeal to equal the accomplishments of others she sometimes guesses and skims over material. When held to accuracy, she reads well. E. enjoys the stories and she puts forth much effort to do her best.

Arithmetic—

We expect little in number work the first semester, as it is taught incidentally in connection with the room projects. E. does display a background of understanding in numbers especially in the games played during the activity period. She can count accurately by ones, fives, and tens.

Outdoor play—

E. enjoys going to the playground. She prefers few companions as she likes to be a leader. Dramatic play is most frequently entered into. She is always active. She is usually coöperative and willing to conform to the playground rules.

Recommendations—

E.'s progress has been satisfactory. She may read simple primers at home if she is interested, as extra practice gives greater independence and fluency.

REPORT OF PARENTS
FIRST GRADE

Name of child *E.*

Group *First Grade.*

Date *February 10, 1940.*

What school interests has your child most often mentioned at home?

E. speaks frequently of her Music and Reading. The interest seems to be quite evenly divided. Her Music seems to be very much enjoyed, as she claps softly the time of the songs and has us guess the name of the song.

In what phases of our work is his progress most evident?

I feel that E. has made splendid progress in the Reading as well as Writing. She has brought some simple primers home from the school library and is able to read them surprisingly well. She is a good listener and gets a story which is read to her.

In what forms of work or play does he engage most frequently at home?

E. usually plays out of doors with her roller skates or bicycle, as in this, she usually has companionship.

E. enjoys "Old Maid," checkers, and dominoes.

During the present year what, if any, changes have you noted:
In habits of eating?

E. is eating a greater variety of foods. I am happy to have her eating lettuce, and enjoying it for the first time.

In habits of sleeping?

E. sleeps well, and goes to bed cheerfully.

What, if any, changes have you noted:
In attitude toward parents?

There is no great change; perhaps she is a little less dependent upon us.

In attitude toward other children?

I believe that E. is learning to take care of her own interests and depend less upon the intervention of older people. She seems to be fair in her play. She plays with children of all ages happily.

What is the attitude toward coming to school?

She likes her school very much and enjoys going, and loves her schoolmates.

What, if any, undesirable tendencies is your child showing at home?

I would like it if she would obey a little more promptly, but perhaps I expect too much. There is too much of this "wait a minute" to suit me.

Suggestions or questions:

You mention the fact that E. seems to take a dislike to a child and tends to get others to be unkind to this child. I believe that she is imitating an older child with whom she plays a great deal, here on the street. This child will "get mad" at her and then try to coax the other children away from her, so that she will have no one to play with. I have felt for some time that the child's influence was not good. I have questioned E. and I believe that I know where the trouble lies and have told her that she must not make another little girl unhappy. I shall be very glad to know if she persists in this, but I don't believe that you'll have any more trouble. She usually is very sympathetic.

KEY FOR REPORT OF ROOM TEACHER
THIRD, FOURTH, FIFTH AND SIXTH GRADES

Physical and Emotional Status

1. Is the general physical condition contributing to success in school work? Is there abundant energy or does he lack reserve strength? Does this energy vary?
2. What health habits need attention: eating habits, rest habits, walking?
3. Is there proper and orderly care of the body, clothing and other

possessions: wraps, handkerchiefs, hands, nails, hair, toilet, desk?
4. What nervous habits has he: nail biting, playing with face, pencils, masturbation, chewing tongue?
5. What, if any, physical handicaps hinder the child's progress?
6. What is his usual disposition: happy, sulky, dreamy, moody, serious, eager, enthusiastic, passive?
7. What evidence is there of timidity, anger, obstinacy, jealousy, over-sensitiveness, aggressiveness, self-consciousness? Is he easily discouraged?
8. How does he meet a new or unusual situation?
9. Has there been growth in self-control when using halls, lunchroom, toilets, school car? How much adult control is necessary? When?

Social Adjustment

1. Was he slow in adjusting to the group, or does he work well with a group?
2. Is he broad in his choice of friends? What type of personality is annoying?
3. Is he consciously sympathetic in his understanding of others: teachers, pupils, school officers?
4. Is he usually courteous in speech and manner?
5. Does he respect authority?
6. Does he respect property rights?
7. Does he respect differences in opinion on various issues?
8. Is he prompt in accepting and performing his share of group and individual responsibilities?
9. Can he be depended upon both to lead and follow?
10. Is he fair in taking turns; in talking, using tools, in special duties?
11. Does he share his experiences and possessions with others?

Social Studies

1. What evidence is there of interest in social studies?
2. Does he originate new group or individual enterprises?
3. Is there skill in organizing and presenting material? Does he use resources at his command in a creative manner?
4. Is there mastery of facts and clear understanding of units studied?
5. Does he work independently and persistently, completing his work satisfactorily?
6. Does he give and accept help willingly?
7. Does he use his time to advantage?
8. Is he able to criticize constructively himself and others?
9. In what degree does he show skill, artistic ability in constructive activities?

Science

1. In what phases of science is the child interested?
   a. What interest has been manifested in cause and effect as seen in solar system, weather, seasons?
   b. What interest has been manifested in physical science; as, electricity, radio, principles of mechanics?
   c. What interest has been shown in household science: chemistry of foods, composition of textiles?
   d. What evidence of interest is there in the beginnings and development of life, trees, plants?
   e. What is the attitude toward protecting and nurturing life?
2. In which of these fields has there been growth in information and appreciation?
3. Is there curiosity about cause and effect, leading to keen observation, desire to experiment, investigate?
4. Is the interest leading toward creativeness in construction, invention, expression in arts or language?

Oral Composition

1. Are there voluntary and worth-while contributions?
2. Is there mental and physical poise? Does he talk to the point and express himself clearly?
3. Is there good choice of English? Is there normal growth of vocabulary?
4. What is the quality of voice? Is enunciation distinct?
5. Is there interest in dramatization?
6. Is there evidence of dramatic ability?
7. Does he listen to selections read, carefully enough to reproduce important elements?
8. Is he a courteous listener?

Written Composition and Spelling

1. What interest is there in written composition?
2. Is originality and initiative shown in writing?
3. Can he write a simple short story or experience in the order that it occurred?
4. Can he write informal notes, giving all necessary information? Can he write an interesting, friendly letter and a correct business letter?
5. What skill is there in the correct usage of simple marks of punctuation and correct sentence and paragraph construction?
6. What is the quality of form and appearance of written work?
7. What is the condition of handwriting as to speed, form and legibility? In what respects is improvement needed?
8. Is there a spelling consciousness shown?

9. Is mastery of spelling satisfactory for the grade?
10. What are the important errors in spelling?

Reading

1. What is the attitude toward reading?
2. To what extent can the child read books independently and with understanding?
3. Does he know how to use books to find information for himself?
4. Can he select and read aloud stories, interpreting so as to hold the interest of his audience?
5. Can he retell a story read silently?
6. What skill has he in mastering and understanding new words?
7. Does he understand the use of the dictionary, the encyclopedia?
8. Is progress in rate and comprehension in both oral and silent reading satisfactory?
9. If there is retardation, what is the cause: absence; left-eye dominance; physical defects of eye, ear, speech; nervousness; immaturity; bad habits such as spelling or analyzing each word phonetically, memory reading, or guessing?
10. Are there special reading disabilities which need correction; as, omissions, reversals, faulty vowels and consonants?

Arithmetic

1. What is the attitude toward arithmetic?
2. Is the child gaining an understanding and appreciation of the social uses of arithmetic?
3. Is there growth in the application of arithmetic in concrete situations?
4. Is there mastery of the skills in computation needed or required in the grade?
5. Is there appreciation of the need for organization, accuracy and neatness in written work, and effort to attain a high standard?
6. What, if any, type of error is frequent?

Recommendations

1. What activities might the child profitably engage in at home?
2. What, if any, special help is needed in order that the child may meet the desired standards?
3. What habits or attitudes need special guidance?
4. Is any change in the child's program suggested?
5. Is he handicapped by lack of fundamental skills?
6. Is he doing the best work of which he is capable?
7. Is the child recommended for more advanced work?

KEY FOR REPORT OF SPECIAL TEACHERS

Art (Grades I to VI)

1. What is the child's attitude toward art in general and his art work in particular?
2. Is child willing to adventure with materials?
3. Does the child show originality and freedom in expressing ideas?
4. What is the child's development in workmanship and the handling of tools?
5. In what types of work does he show special aptitude: modeling, sketching, painting, design?
6. What individual characteristics does his work show: lightness, neatness, daring, feeling for color and form, accuracy, skill in composition?
7. To what extent does he show persistence in completing work begun?
8. To what degree has the child developed flexibility in analyzing his own work?
9. To what extent does the child show respect for his own finished products? Is his appreciation properly balanced with his own skills?

Crafts (Grades I to VI)

1. What are the child's attitudes with respect to materials and tools?
2. What special interests does he show in construction: articles of utility, articles for play or articles of art?
3. What has his progress been in developing skill in construction?
4. To what extent does he show initiative, independence, originality in constructive enterprises?
5. To what extent does he show industry and persistence in completing work begun?
6. In what degree does he show ability to judge his own work and the work of the group? Does he profit by suggestions?

Music (Grades I to VI. Points starred are not expected below Grade IV)

1. In what ways does the child show interest in music? What evidence does he show of having had contact with good music outside school?
2. How does the child respond to folk or art songs: listening; sensing possibility for rhythmic action and participating in such interpretation; choosing songs for the group to sing; volunteering to sing alone or with small groups?
3. What is the voice quality?
4. What is the child's development in ear training through pitch: difference in pitch; tonal memory; recognition of major and minor modes; *singing in canon form; *singing a second part?

5. What is the child's development in ear training through rhythm: recognition of meter, mood, rhythmic pattern of a suitable piece of music and interpretation of these through bodily movements?

*6. To what extent does the child use notation as an aid in learning new compositions?

7. To what extent has the child developed appreciation: response to general character, tempo, pitch, register; familiarity with a few instrumental compositions and their composers; *interest in attending concerts and recitals; *interest in planning the music period?

*8. Does the child keep any record of the music activities in the form of a diary or notebook?

9. To what extent has creative ability been shown?

Creative Dancing (Grades III to VI)

1. To what extent has the child developed a sense of rhythm and a responsiveness to music?

2. Does the child's work show evidence of interest, freedom, color and originality?

3. What are the individual characteristics of the child's work: daring, lightness, grace, imagination?

4. What has been the child's development in control and coordination of bodily movement?

5. What are the types of work in which the child has shown special creative ability or enthusiasm?

Physical Education (Grades III to VI)

1. What is the attitude toward play and exercise?

2. Does the child play agreeably with others? Does he show a protective attitude toward younger children?

. Does he show ability to organize or participate in group play? To what extent does he show poise, self-control?

4. Is there a tendency to self-consciousness, timidity, aggressiveness, obstinacy, oversensitiveness, discouragement?

6. How is he learning to handle his body?

7. Is he afraid of balls and collision with other children?

8. How does he react to cold weather?

French (Grades III to VI. Questions starred are not used below Grade IV)

1. Does the child show interest and pleasure in the study of language?

2. What has been his progress in oral work: ability to understand and respond to directions or questions; ability to express ideas in phrases or sentences; ability to memorize rote songs or verses; pronunciation; mastery of vocabulary?

*3. What has been the child's progress in written work: accuracy in writing and spelling, neatness, fluency?

*4. What progress has the child made in reading ability: comprehension, fluency, pronunciation in oral reading?

Speech (Individual children needing speech reeducation)

1. To what extent does the child show interest and cooperation?
2. What progress has the child made in gaining relaxation?
3. What progress has the child made in the development of speech consciousness?
4. What has been the child's progress in overcoming his difficulty: voice control and breathing; position and sound of difficult letters and combinations; stuttering?
5. To what extent does his speech work carry over into conversation?

REPORT OF ROOM TEACHER
FOURTH GRADE

Name of child G.

Date of birth *March 27, 1931*   Group *Fourth Grade*

Term beginning *September 18, 1939*   Days absent *1*

Term ending *January 31, 1940.*   Days present *85*

Physical and Emotional status—

G. seems to be well physically. She has grown less tense and nervous, since Christmas. There is better self-control and a happier, freer feeling apparently. She continues however to be a little secretive especially when there is something which she dislikes. She is very sensitive to beauty but would rather not show it, also likes praise but is self-conscious if complimented before the group.

Social Adjustment—

G. is making a marked effort to cooperate with the group, though still feels more at home with one or two chosen friends. She has unusual ability as a leader, and needs to be guided in offering the right sort of leadership. She is helpful whenever her own interests are not too greatly concerned. There is a lovable, sweet, sympathetic quality which we must try to bring more to the foreground.

Social Studies—

G. has been keenly interested in the studies of food and in pioneer life. She has a splendid mastery of the subject matter covered. She is very critical of others, and belittles her own accomplishments, which are usually very original and worth while. She takes much pride in the appearance of her work and is eager that it be the best. She has marked ability in starting new projects, in creating new situations without suggestions from others.

Science—

G. has an unusual interest in the beginnings of life in all forms, eagerly seeks the source and cause of everyday happenings. She has a very keen appreciation of beauty in all forms.

Oral Composition—

G. shares her experiences, but is very timid about speaking before the group. She makes worth-while contributions and is quite dramatic in her approach to any topic. She has a fine command of English, often using lovely descriptive phrases.

Written Composition and Spelling—

G. enjoys writing poems and stories, is often original in her ideas. She uses splendid sentence and paragraph structure as well as the simple marks of punctuation. Her work is usually neat and carefully done. She is well up to grade in spelling.

Reading—

Reading is one of her chief interests. She reads from many fields: history, travel, fairy and folk tales. She finds it difficult to read expressively before the group because of a self-consciousness, but comprehends in a fine way material read silently.

Arithmetic—

There is a growing interest in arithmetic, which needs constant encouragement. When she can do the work with little real effort she enjoys it, but the utter distaste for it noticed in the fall has nearly disappeared. She is able to make fine practical application, but is handicapped by her lack of knowledge of the facts of the four fundamental processes.

Recommendations—

Would be well to encourage G. to finish her Third Grade Arithmetic Book, as it would help to give her the practice needed. Sympathy with firmness seems to yield a desired change in G's attitudes. There is much joy in her improvement.

REPORT OF SPECIAL TEACHERS
FOURTH GRADE

Name of child G.

Semester beginning *September 18, 1939*

Semester ending *January 31, 1940*

Art—

G's Christmas cards showed gain in not overcrowding one thing with too many ideas. I should like to see her gain more in control of herself, as her attitude toward her work and at times toward the group is satisfactory. She has ability and it should give her much happiness.

Manual Training—

Is doing quite well when working alone; needs a better understanding of coöperation. She has initiative but needs help in developing originality and appreciation of group contact.

Physical Education—

At the beginning of the school year, G. objected to playing in group activities; she would run off with a few others, developing an anti-social attitude. Now she seems to enjoy the group play. She has very good control and physical coördination.

Music—

There is no doubt as to G's ability in ear training or singing, nor as to her well-directed taste, but she has not shown as much progress as we would like her to display. Her cliquishness has impeded her progress.

Creative Dancing—

Is in a transitory stage where she wishes to express through movements that are broad and heavy; so I miss the exquisite creative work of last year. When not leading she is tempted to ridicule. I feel that G. has had too much attention.

French—

G's progress has been rather slow this semester; her attitude in class has been too playful at times. Her written work is good. More eagerness and more dependability are wanted.

REPORT OF PARENTS
FOURTH GRADE

Name of child G.

Date *March 1, 1940*

What school interests has your child most often mentioned at home?

G. has shown intense interest in the social studies at school. She has a thirst for historical information, and is getting to be quite an omnivorous reader along many lines. She appreciates any special program at school, such as Rose Fyleman's readings.

In what phases of our work is his progress most evident?

She seems to have grown up amazingly this year. One can almost talk to her as an adult. Her vocabulary is very wide, and she has a store of miscellaneous information. She has an eager interest in learning that I hope she will never lose. I can see progress all along the line, even in arithmetic, but most markedly in the social studies.

In what forms of work or play does he engage most frequently at home?

G. reads a great deal, draws incessantly and is always making things. She is eager to be out-of-doors. She skates a good deal, and plays on our apparatus. She and her little friend play many imaginative games around horses. She collects odds and ends and her pockets are as full as a boy's, all with some imaginative significance. She likes to memorize.

What, if any, changes have you noted:
  In attitude toward parents?

G's attitude toward her parents has improved.

  In attitude toward other children?

G's attitude toward her younger brother is changing from one of hostility to one of indifference—which seems a step in the right direction! She seems too busy and interested in larger affairs to be able to concentrate on him as she has done during the fall and early winter. Her brothers form one unit and she another.

What is the attitude toward coming to school?

G. enjoys school extremely. She is always eager to go. Arithmetic is the only subject that seems difficult for her. I think that G. is a child who might easily dislike school, and it is most gratifying to us to have her enjoy it so thoroughly.

What, if any, undesirable tendencies is your child showing at home just now?

G. is careless of property. She tracks mud over the rugs, strews her belongings on the floor, and loses many things. She is not orderly, even in a rudimentary way. Her mind seems elsewhere.

She indulges often in lies and near lies. "Yes, I brushed my teeth," saves a trip upstairs. "Yes, I washed my hands. Well, at least I wet them." All for convenience. Does not as a rule welcome suggestions. She is jealous of her "free time" and her chances to do as she "pleases." Anything required outside of school she definitely resents. We stopped piano lessons and a class in acrobatic and tap dancing because of the emotional difficulties involved. It has proved to be a wise move. There has been a noticeable lessening in tension. We have come to the conclusion that outside of school the least possible should be required of G. and that she should be let pretty much alone. After all, why not? What are a few extra skills as against a feeling of general "rightness" and ease? I wish G. would oftener do some spontaneous, generous, lovely thing. She seems to have her own interests and comfort well to the fore in her thinking and living.

REPORT OF ROOM TEACHER
FIFTH GRADE

Name of child *R.*   Group *Fifth Grade*

Date of birth *December 14, 1929*   Days absent *2*

Term beginning *September 18, 1939*   Days present *84*

Term ending *January 31, 1940.*

Physical and Emotional Status—

R's physical condition contributes abundant energy for all activities. He is always happy and attacks his work eagerly. He is careful of his personal appearance, but is very disorderly in the care of his possessions. There has been less evidence of boastfulness of late than formerly. There is good self-control in the use of halls, lunch room, except when he encounters his brother. He seems sometimes to take delight in hurting him.

Social Adjustment—

R. is well liked by the group and is friendly toward all. He is very anxious to receive commendation from others. He is courteous in his manner, respects the opinions of others, and willingly shares his possessions and suggestions.

Social Studies—

R. has shown a keen interest in our study of American industries. He gains a great deal of information and collects materials, but has difficulty in organizing his work. There has been a most decided growth, though, in thoroughness. He no longer rushes a piece of work through just for the sake of finishing it. He attacks work with zest and without suggestion.

Science—

R. was very much interested in our study of kinds of power, sources of power, natural resources, and how they help to build a city. This interest led to mastery of facts and creativeness in the form of drawing.

Oral Composition—

R. makes voluntary and worth-while contributions to the class. These are usually in the form of information rather than any solutions to problems which he has thought out. He shows poise both physically and mentally when speaking before a group.

Written Composition and Spelling—

R. seems to enjoy writing stories. He has good ideas and an interesting way of stating them, but his work needs better organization and more logical sequence of events and topics. The appearance of his writing has improved immensely. His class work in spelling is very good.

Reading—

R. has shown an interest in improving his reading, but he gets quite arrogant over any progress he makes. He reads independently for pleasure or information.

Arithmetic—

R. is intensely interested in arithmetic, spending much of his leisure time working in his work book. He is able to handle the four fundamental processes with integers with accuracy except where mistakes are made due to carelessness in writing. He has an understanding of the beginning work in fractions.

Recommendations—

Stories on the history of the United States would be helpful to R. in his work.

REPORT OF SPECIAL TEACHERS
FIFTH GRADE

Name of child *R*.

Semester beginning *September 18, 1939.*

Semester ending *January 31, 1940.*

Art—

R. never wastes time in expressing his ideas. Sometimes his work seems crude because he does not hesitate to put into one picture all that he sees. But the type of work he does promises to develop into an individual thing with charm and originality.

Manual Training—

Has a great respect for materials and tools. Is careful to use them in the right way. Has lately been working on a boat for the mantel. Seems more interested in useful articles than those of play or art. Seems to have progressed in his work. Shows some skill. Has a good deal of initiative—doesn't have to be told to go ahead. Is independent and original. Always anxious to finish a problem and works hard to finish. Is critical of his work and does profit by suggestions.

Physical Education—

Has made a great improvement in the soccer game, and I believe it has made him very much more interested in sports. He is clever at soccer, and the children are beginning to think that he is one of their best players. He plays fair until someone does something he does not approve of; then he will play very hard to make his goal, not being as careful as he usually is.

Music—

Has shown marked growth in interest and abilities. His singing voice is smooth and clear. In ear training he shows development in both pitch and rhythm perception. He has become interested in the group and in its attainments.

Instrumental Music—*Piano*

R's progress is symmetrical. I am very much pleased especially with the creative trend his music seems to be taking. His rhythm, pitch, feeling for harmony, sense of form are good. There now remains the work of developing these to their ultimate possibilities. He should always have the opportunity to take part in some kind of music as he is essentially musical.

French—

R's attitude is excellent in the French class; he shows eagerness and comprehension; his progress is good.

REPORT OF PARENTS
FIFTH GRADE

Name of child *R.*

Group *Grade V*   Date *Feb. 17, 1940*

What school interests has your child most often mentioned at home?

Study of New York.
Book Club.
Woodwork.

In what phases of our work is his progress most evident?

Writing.
Silent Reading: for the first time he reads alone for long periods.

In what forms of work or play does he engage most frequently at home?

Group activity centering around his "Club House" of logs, on which he has worked for several weeks.

What, if any, changes have you noted:
  In attitude toward parents?

Is maturing rapidly. He now considers himself one of the "adults," and so conducts himself.

  In attitude toward other children?

Tries to play mentor to his brother, sometimes assuming discipline if not watched. Is most protective of his younger sister, and seems to be a favorite with his gang.

What is the attitude toward coming to school?

He cannot get there early enough!

What, if any, undesirable tendencies is your child showing at home just now?

We are trying to work out an attitude of self-control over wrath that often is partly at least righteous. R. is probably too fond of defending his rights.

THE FUNCTIONS OF THE HEALTH
DEPARTMENT IN THE CHILDREN'S
SCHOOL

THE medical work of the Children's School, including physical examinations and daily inspection, is directed by a physician and a trained nurse.

The health of the children is safeguarded by a close cooperation between the home and the school, and by the careful examination and daily inspection of all children by an attending physician and graduate nurse. The physician is present daily during the first hour of the morning while the physical inspection of the children is being made. The nurse is in attendance throughout the day. The services of the nurse are many. She assists in the examination of the children, keeps records, and observes the children during the day, taking care of minor hurts. She measures chairs and children so that proper seating will insure correct posture. She keeps height and weight charts. She ascertains the causes of absences by telephoning parents, and she arranges for conferences between the school physician and the parents.

Letters are sent from the school physician to the parents in the early part of the school year giving the policy of the school regarding health and requesting parents to fill in a detailed record of the health of the child from birth. Letters are again sent to parents whenever contagion occurs in the school, with a brief description of signs and symptoms of the disease, for which to watch. Careful health records and observations in the classroom are kept on all children, and significant findings are sent to parents.

Physical examinations are made each year after a written permit has been obtained. Examination and observation of eyes and ears are made on all children of the school. Recording of heights and weights is done throughout the year, and charts are kept on all children of the school. All data are sent to the parents, especially whenever children are not gaining satisfactorily or when for any reason the care of the family physician is indicated.

No child is allowed in school with a cold in the infectious stage, or after contact outside of the school with a contagious disease.

Underlying the plan for medical work is an effort to make the children realize that the possession of health is a privilege and a joy, and that all privileges are secured by self-control and effort. The children respond instantly to this very natural and normal attitude. They easily excel the adults. This idea carried out in their homes, in their classrooms, on the playground, makes health part of a social adjustment and a social responsibility.

Daily inspection of children for colds or other signs of ill health then becomes a cooperative enterprise. Cooperation of parents is part of this plan—a very necessary part. Physical examinations are of great interest to the children, evidenced by a hundred questions.

Histories from parents, frequent observation from the classroom correlated with the intelligence quotient, the achievements and the social responses of the child and the physical findings, are used to determine the best procedure to bring physical and mental health, and to lead parents and children to see that living is an art, not an accident.

Name **Grant, Mary**   Date **September 18, 1939.**
Address   Grade **Nursery School.**
Telephone   Date of Birth **April 19, 1936.**

Please fill out following

Family Record   Number of children in family **One**
   Health of Father **Good** Mother **Good** Children

Infancy Record:
1. Was child born at term? **Yes**   Was delivery normal? **Yes**
2. Birth weight. **7 lbs. 3/4 oz.** Details of any feeding difficulties **Formula changed several times.**
3. Earliest age of following:—
   - Holding Head Up
   Walking **14 months.**
   Talking **13 months.**
   Age of First Tooth **5 months.**

Health Record.
1. Has child control of urine? **Yes**
2. Nervous habits as biting nails, sucking fingers, handling body. **Bites nails. Habit of sucking index**
3. Sleeping habits: **finger upon retiring practically stopped.**
   Number hours at night **Ten**
   Place **Own room.**
   Condition of sleep—. **Usually quiet.**
      Quiet
      Restless
4. Eating habits: **Good**
   Appetite
   Foods that disagree
   Special dislikes **Custards - string beans - fish.**
   Attitude toward meals
5. Bowel habits **Regular**

Please fill opposite side also.

6. Has child ever been ill with any of the following and at what age?
   Diphtheria   German Measles   Mumps
   Scarlet Fever   Measles   Tonsilitis No. of attacks
   Whooping Cough   Frequent colds **Jan. & June, 1939** Chicken Pox
   Glandular trouble   Rheumatism (growing pains, etc)   St Vitus Dance
   Ear trouble   Heart trouble
      Eye condition (red lids, styes etc Tests for eye strain)

7. Injuries, accidents or deformities, Rupture (with description)
8. Operations (including removal of tonsils and adenoids)
9. Weakness or tendency to ill health, nervousness, etc.
10. Has your child been protected against Smallpox by vaccination and when? **Yes - January, 1938.**
11. Has your child been protected against Diphtheria? **Yes**
12. Has your child been protected against Scarlet Fever? **No**
13.

School Data: (Please leave blank)

FILLED BY PARENT FOR ENTERING CHILD.

HEALTH RECORD

NAME **Grant, Mary**

DATE **September 20, 1939** GRADE **Nursery School**	DATE GRADE
PHYSICAL EXAMINATION **Good cooperation - alert.**	PHYSICAL EXAMINATION
GENERAL **Good tissue turgor.**	GENERAL
HEAD AND NECK **Tonsils and teeth normal.** POSTURE **Erect**	HEAD AND NECK POSTURE
CHEST **Heart and lungs** SIGHT **Normal apparently.**	CHEST SIGHT
ABDOMEN **Normal** HEARING **Normal apparently.**	ABDOMEN HEARING
EXTREMITIES **No bowing.** FEET **Good position.**	EXTREMITIES FEET
SUMMARY	SUMMARY

Normal child. No defects.
Letter sent to mother giving data.
Report sent to Demonstration School
office.
Conference with teacher who reports
good cooperation, alertness, good
adjustment.

YEARLY RECORD

DATE **1939-40** GRADE **Nursery School**   DATE   GRADE

MONTH	HEIGHT	WEIGHT	AV. HEIGHT	AV. WEIGHT	MONTH	HEIGHT	WEIGHT	AV. HEIGHT	AV. WEIGHT
SEPTEMBER	39.4	33.4		34	SEPTEMBER				
OCTOBER		34.			OCTOBER				
NOVEMBER		34.5			NOVEMBER				
DECEMBER		35.5			DECEMBER				
JANUARY		36.			JANUARY				
FEBRUARY	39.6	36.		36	FEBRUARY				
MARCH		37.			MARCH				
APRIL		37.4			APRIL				
MAY		37.6			MAY				
JUNE					JUNE				
JULY					JULY				

I. Q. **117**   I. Q.

REMARKS **Physically normal.**   REMARKS

FILLED BY PHYSICIAN FOLLOWING PHYSICAL EXAMINATION.

PHYSICIAN'S REPORT TO PARENTS

The form used in the following letter is the same for all children, from nursery school through sixth grade. The findings inserted in the blanks correspond to those noted on the Health Record, a copy of which is found on page 557.

To the Parents:

We appreciate the cooperation of the parents in maintaining a high standard of health in our school.

Physical examinations have been made of children where permission has been received. Eye tests and ear tests have been made on all children above the Junior Kindergarten and careful observations have been made, relative to defects and health, on all the children of the school. The response of children below Senior Kindergarten in eye and ear tests is usually unsatisfactory.

Weight is an individual matter dependent in part on racial characteristic and family type. Healthier children generally are found to weigh more than the "average weight." This average has been estimated from observations made upon thousands of school children. 20% or more over average weight generally means that the child needs more exercise and needs to eat less sweets. 7% or more under average weight needs special attention. Care should be taken not to worry the child about his weight. It is better to emphasize the positive side. If the child gains steadily and normally, actual weight may be insignificant.

Name: *J. S.*

Physical Examination:

Group: *First Grade*

Date: *Sept. 20, 1939*

Height   *44.8 inches.*   Weight   *42.5 lbs.*   Average Weight   *45 lbs.*

We should like to call your attention to the following findings:
Tonsils show infection—large.
Pallor.
Poor posture.
We advise consultation with your physician concerning these matters.

Signed—

Children's Physician

RECORDS OF THE GUIDANCE LABORATORY

THE personnel of the guidance laboratory includes three educational psychologists. One of these gives intelligence tests to preschool children in the nursery school, junior and senior kindergartens, and observes behavior patterns of children in order to adjust the child to more successful living in both school and home. The specialized training of this psychologist in parent education and mental hygiene has prepared her to conduct classes for parents of the children in the Children's School, to guide them in planning their educational programs and in knowing the policies and principles underlying the management of the school. Following the giving of an intelligence test she may invite the parent or parents to confer with her so that there may be better understanding of the child and his reactions to test items as well as to his general daily routine in school and home. Suggestions are often made to correct negative personal habits and attitudes, and if medical attention seems pertinent, the medical department is consulted. In any case notations are made and placed in the child's permanent file.

The other two psychologists give intelligence tests and achievement tests to children in the grades. Having specialized in learning problems which some children encounter, they spend considerable time creating and giving diagnostic tests and planning instruction of a preventive or corrective nature so that successful learning may result. Parents are periodically advised concerning any progress made. In case children are achieving so rapidly that acceleration seems inevitable an enriched curriculum is strongly advised and the examiner confers with both parent and teacher.

One important aim of all the psychological service is to aid children in growing mentally, emotionally, physically, and academically so that a normal balance is maintained. A psychiatric social worker has been lately added to the staff to aid in maintaining this important balance in living and growing. She interviews the teacher, visits the schoolroom, and occasionally makes home visits

559

with the purpose of knowing individual children more completely. In a few instances, this member of the staff cooperates with a psychiatrist not directly connected with the school but in sympathy with its policies.

Two teachers on the staff in the Guidance Laboratory, expert in the field of the "three R's," give individual instruction to those children who seem to need special guidance for a time.

A visual training expert and her assistant train children and college students to use their eyes more efficiently. The training educates the eyes in conjunction with the brain to fuse images more quickly and accurately; to change focus from the far point to the near point with precision and speed; to see depth when looking at a distance; to follow a slowly moving object with smoothness in fixations; and furthermore to decrease any habits of suppression to a minimum and use all the vision there is. These training experts work in cooperation with the medical department or with family pediatricians or ophthalmologists.

The services of the specialists in the Guidance Laboratory are available to the community, and many children and adults outside the school come in for diagnosis and for periods of training. Guidance is given also to student teachers who wish to specialize in learning problems.

Description of the Laboratory

The main room in this laboratory is divided into sections so that individuals or small groups may be given instruction independent from that given to other individuals or groups. The room is divided by screens, bookshelves or filing cases so that the person giving visual training may have a child use one or the other piece of equipment planned for that purpose; a teacher may be using the kinaesthetic method with the child who needs practice on new or difficult words; another teacher may be guiding a child in his typing of an original composition with primer-sized type to be later read by him to his class. There are two smaller offices adjoining this main room of the laboratory for the director and assistant. When diagnostic tests are given the examiners work in these smaller rooms.

Types of Tests Used in Diagnosis

When diagnosing problems presented by children in the elementary grades, the procedure usually includes an intelligence test; a reading aptitude test for the younger child only; tests to determine preference of hand, foot, eye and ear; tests to ascertain skill of hand and foot and of eye (if the child has learned to read) and ear; a photographic record of eye movements while reading silently for the child who has learned to read; a reading, spelling or arithmetic diagnostic test, and standardized achievement tests which fit the level of learning. Comprehensive letters regarding the findings of each case are written with conclusions and recommendations so that the parents, teachers, psychiatrist, physician, principal, or eye specialist may have a copy of the written report.

MAJOR RESPONSIBILITIES

The responsibilities of this laboratory, which are varied and numerous, are listed below with brief descriptions and later some are described in more detail, so that those particularly interested may understand the methods of guidance, principles and applications.

1. An individual intelligence test is given to each child entering the school and again after an interval of six months to a year, and usually every two years after that. As the child is tested, particular attention is given to emotional disturbances, physical peculiarities, habits of response, or negative habits. These are recorded and slipped into the test booklet.

2. Two booklets of standardized school achievement tests are given at the close of each semester to children from the second grade through the eighth grade. The test results are organized into tabular form with averages computed for each subject and for each child. Copies are given to each teacher, to the director of the school, and to members of the guidance department. Graph reports recording the average test scores are prepared once or twice a year after third grade, so that both parents and children may have an inventory of present attainments and a comparison with previous records in the various school subjects. Reading aptitude tests are given to either first grade applicants or to children in the five-year-old kindergarten group toward the end of the year.

3. Detailed letters are sent to the school to which a child is transferred. These letters state information regarding the intelligence test findings and achievement test results (if the child is in the grades) for several consecutive testing periods. The letters give information concerning the rate and quality of learning of the child, some idea of his social and emotional characteristics, his classroom activities and interests, and his physical development. Any deviations in learning are noted.

4. Interviews with parents, physicians, and visiting educators constitute a major responsibility. The discussions center around a child

and his current problems, recommendations, demonstrations of methods or explanations regarding the use of materials which might be of value to the child. Visits to the home are often planned as an important means of understanding and solving emotional and social difficulties which the child may present. Stimulus-response and diary records are used as a means of evidence to show to parents the need for emphasizing a certain method of attack or to show that improvement has taken place. Lists of positive traits have been organized to use as a key when studying a child. These can be found on page 586.

5. Research studies have been carried on each year to aid in the selection of tests and in the originating of tests so that the diagnosis of children will be more comprehensive. An extensive study has been made of visual factors relative to functioning; data concerning intelligence and achievement tests, attendance, and educational quotients have been computed for the yearly report; special emphasis has been placed upon better methods in learning to spell; and controlled techniques in the teaching of reading have been under way for several years.

6. A considerable amount of supervision is given to student teachers assisting in the Children's School, as they give individual instruction to children encountering learning handicaps, and to college students enrolled in the courses in improvement of academic learning. Children from other schools are also given guidance. Mimeographed material is prepared as an aid in this supervision.

7. A considerable amount of time is spent in answering correspondence, for teachers write for advice concerning tests; school administrators write for recommendations on types of equipment; parents and physicians ask for appointments to bring a child in whom they are interested for diagnosis. Many visitors come throughout the year for brief or extended visits depending upon their purposes and needs.

Studies of Intelligence and Personality

In the nursery school, junior and senior kindergarten, children are given either the Merrill Palmer Scale of Mental Tests, the Minnesota Pre-School Scale, or the Revised Stanford-Binet, Form L and M, all depending upon the ability and interests of the child. The older children are given the Revised Stanford-Binet, the Grace Arthur Performance Scale, the Durrell-Sullivan Capacity Test or the Chicago Non-Verbal Test, according to the age and needs of the child. The two latter tests do not seem fair to children whose eyes are not functioning efficiently, for the pictures are small, crowded with detail, and often too close together. The Binet is not a wise choice for the non-reader who talks very little, whose language development is limited, and who doesn't care to express himself. Since the Children's School does not continue beyond the eighth grade, no mechanical aptitude tests are given. The tests as named above give probably the most reliable indication of the child's mental make-up for academic learning. They do not always indicate the complete innate mental characteristics of a child.

Each child is retested after six or seven months. Very often the test results are questioned because the child being tested may have been emotionally blocked, may have shown a definite language retardation, or may have been physically fatigued. The second or third examination is often given before we attempt to estimate his mental capabilities. In the case of those children whose academic achievement far surpasses their predictions for learning, the intelligence rating is questioned, and a further study may be made of them. We also question intelligence ratings on children who have not been successful in school, since so many test items contain reading or activities including language skills. Recently a twelve-year-old girl raised her intelligence quotient over twenty points after a year's individual instruction in reading. She was apparently released emotionally through successful learning and through the acquisition of more adequate visual efficiency by means of visual training. In fact she reacted more normally in all school situations after a period of a year.

Teachers are given an opportunity to discuss and examine all facts relative to these tests, inclusive of the personality report which accompanies each psychological examination. Samples of these reports are included on pages 566 to 569.

Two lists are prepared for the teacher and director of the school twice a year. One contains an alphabetical list of names (see page 564) with the child's birthday, his chronological age calculated for a day selected near the beginning of each semester, the corrected mental age

FIFTH GRADE

SEPTEMBER 15, 1939

* Name	Date of Birth	C.A.	M. A.	Aver. I. Q.	Individual Ratings in I. Q.
Barns, Jean	5-10-27	10-4	10-9	104	98, 103, 111
Bitler, Anne	3-14-28	10-6	11-3	107	107
Bonner, Jack	10-6-28	9-11	11-7	117	117
Buckly, Frank	1-18-27	11-8	13-1	112	112
Chapin, Mary	1-5-29	9-8	11-5	118	111,126
Deeman, Coral	12-10-26	11-9	10-8	91	92, 91
Gillet, George	1-19-28	10-8	12-1	113	120, 112, 110, 110
Hull, Meredith	11-13-27	10-10	10-2	94	98, 96, 89
Manard, Marie	2-5-27	11-7	12-4	106	96, 125, 96
Nadler, Norman	11-24-28	9-10	11-10	120	120
Reeman, Louise	6-5-28	10-3	11-0	117	116, 117
Roth, John	5-14-28	10-4	12-5	120	105, 125, 131
Schamer, Victor	10-31-28	9-11	11-3	114	114
Seaton, Robert	3-4-28	10-6	12-5	118	112, 124
Whitly, Dan	6-29-28	10-2	12-3	120	116, 115, 128
Whorner, Joan	3-8-30	8-6	12-2	143	133, 152
Woolright, Jim	7-11-28	10-2	12-1	119	118, 120
Zackry, Nancy	1-10-29	9-8	12-1	125	125

* Names are fictitious, but facts are authentic.

(I. Q. times C. A. in terms of months), and all the ratings from intelligence tests which have been given.

The other list (see page 565) is arranged with the class intervals for inclusive corrected mental ages in the horizontal columns and headings for types of minds in the vertical columns as low normal, high normal, superior, very superior, etc. Each child in the class has his name written where it belongs in respect to these criteria. From these two lists the teacher may readily study each child in relation to others in the group if she cares to do so.

The test results are further used to indicate the academic level that the child might attain, providing other factors are not interfering. The mental age is corrected for the time the achievement tests are given, so that it may be compared with the educational age of the child as determined by the achievement tests.

All of these findings are considered with reservations, since none of the tests are perfect instruments of measure and since human beings

* FIFTH GRADE

SEPTEMBER, 1939

Mental Ages	Classifications of Intelligence Ratings				
	Low Normal	High Normal	Superior	Very Superior	Gifted
13–0 to 13–5			Buckly, F.		
12–6 to 12–11		Manard, M.	Gillet, G. Seaton, R. Woolright, J.	Roth, J. Whitly, D. Zachry, N.	Whorner, J.
12–0 to 12–5			Bonner, J.	Nadler, N.	
11–6 to 11–11		Bitler, A.	Chapin, M. Reeman, L. Schamer, V.		
11–0 to 11–5		Barnes, J.			
10–6 to 10–11	Deeman, C.				
10–0 to 10–5	Hull, M.				

* Names are fictitious, but facts are authentic.

react unexpectedly to certain factors which might occur during any one of the testing periods. Evaluations based on tests are always altered by the more complete study of an individual and by knowledge of the environmental factors. However, these intelligence and achievement test data seem to be superior to judgments of any individual teacher, and if used with discretion can be of vital aid in the guidance of an individual child's activities and development. The guide as to our own current policies in a testing and follow-up program is duplicated on pages 570 to 573.

Parents are rarely given the exact numerical finding relative to the intelligence tests but often are told the classification in which the intelligence rating falls as seen by the results of three or four tests. The tester explains the items in which the child was successful and those in which he failed, but guards against details which might lead to coaching. Since most parents are naturally ambitious for their children, they might unconsciously adopt this method of aiding their child for another examination. The psychologist may discuss with the parent personality characteristics as observed during the examination, and feels free to give suggestions for guidance in this field of social-emotional and physical welfare.

Each child enrolled in the school has his own manila folder in which all tests are placed which have been given to him. These are filed according to the grade placement and are available to the teachers.

PERSONALITY STUDIES ACCOMPANYING INTELLIGENCE TEST RECORDS

The following personality studies of children who have been tested recently seem to be fair illustrations of the endeavor to ascertain characteristics of children presenting a variety of problems.

Subject No. 1
Chronological age when tested   7-5
Earned mental age from Binet   8-8
Resulting I. Q.   118
Scatter from the sixth year through the tenth year.

Physical traits

X was a nervous, unstable type of child going through all types of overt actions in the testing periods such as: facial distortions, moving his chair up and down first on the front legs and then on the back; moving knees back and forth; tipping chair forward with his hands. X continued these activities throughout the test. It was suggested he go to the toilet and get a drink of water which he did. We also changed the chairs around and examined a few things in the room as a restful diversion. When observed in the classroom later X was found to be restless and nervous especially in the music period. We understand that the teachers have had conferences with the mother concerning this nervousness but she reports the pediatrician cannot find any cause. He is a right-handed child.

Mental traits

X gave a detailed description of small things in pictures; in making change all of his subtraction facts were incorrect; his drawing of a diamond showed good proportions.

Social and emotional traits

X conversed freely with the examiner and revealed some sense of responsibility when he responded to the question, "What's the thing to do when you have broken something of some one else's?" He said, "Buy another one. Earn money by selling lemonade. Get some stockings, repair them and sell them."

Child's reaction to the test

X was anxious to go with the examiner and was especially curious about the contents of all the envelopes containing the test materials. He said, "What do you ask the children in the seventh and eighth grade to do?" He appeared to enjoy the experience and conversed rather freely about the materials.

Subject No. 2
Chronological age when tested   14-7
Earned mental age   15-0
Resulting I. Q.   107

Physical traits

This subject has gray eyes, dark brown hair, brunette complexion, healthy looking skin. She is physically mature, of medium height and stockily built. She is inclined to be round-shouldered when seated, but carries herself well when standing or walking.

She made many facial contortions such as scowling or contracting the muscles in her face and upper part of her body. X squinted her left eye when drawing or counting and held her head on the left side. Her left hand was used in all writing. Her speech was not as clear as it should be. A possible nasal obstruction might be causal.

Mental traits

The basal age of X was found to be at the fourteen-year level. She failed all tests at the Superior Adult Level I. She passed all tests at the Average Adult Level which involved language but failed to record sentences exactly. She moved her lips while listening. Her attention was excellent throughout the course of the examination. When asked to repeat the digits she said, "There is no connection between these numbers", showing that she sensed difficulty in abstract series.

Social-emotional traits

X felt very much at ease during the entire examination. We understand from the room teacher that her social development is splendid; that she is well poised in most situations and has mature interests. As far as her reactions to the test are concerned, she was interested and tried to do her best. She exclaimed several times, "Gee, that's a sticker," especially when she was not sure of what response to make.

Subject No. 3 (Examined for a reading disability)
Chronological age at the time of the test   10-0
Earned mental age   11-10
Resulting I. Q.   118

X has an attractive personality. She seemed to enjoy the testing program, was friendly and her cooperation was good. The testing was done during two periods with an interval of one week between the giving of the first part of the test and its completion. In the meantime she seemed to have set up a defense but with the first part she seemed much more responsive.

This subject very frequently drawled a self-conscious "Oo——h!" This was followed by a rather high-pitched giggle. When X had taken a few test items she said, "These are tests. Some are reading and I can't read very well."

The Basal age on the Revised Stanford Binet was at the nine-year level and all test items were failed at the Superior Adult I Level. She had difficulty with all tests involving reading but her response to the code (Test 2 at the Average Adult) was given in much less than the allotted time.

The final rating places this subject in the superior classification. This rating might be still higher if the subject had been able to pass items involving reading.

During the entire testing program we noticed that the subject was negatively affected by her mother. Due to the latter's misconception of the reading disability she has become overly anxious and extremely critical of her daughter. She apparently never sees the things that she can do well but constantly indicates her disgust in her daughter's inability to read. The girl was much more relaxed when the mother was not present.

Subject No. 4
Chronological age at the time of test   4-5
Resulting I. Q.   126
     (Minnesota Preschool Scale)

Physical traits

This subject was forty-one and a half inches tall and weighed thirty-eight pounds. She had light blue eyes, light brown hair and a clear color. Her daintiness was outstanding.

Mental traits

She was successful in repeating four digits and was very good in recognizing forms. Her comprehension of word meanings was good. She talked freely and easily, expressing herself clearly. She gave some description in the picture test. Her muscular coordination seemed good for her movements were free and easy in drawing circle and tracing forms. ·

She indicated some weakness in comprehension of absurdities, giving stereotyped answers.

Social-emotional traits

She seemed quite at ease in the testing situation and was happy, cheerful and friendly. She hummed little songs as she worked, often laughed and showed pleasure at success.

She gave eager attention but showed signs of fatigue toward the end. Her cooperation was complete and willing helpfulness was shown. Rapport was immediately established.

Policies Relating to the Evaluation of Achievement and the Improvement of Learning

The Interpretation of Test Results

Intelligence and achievement tests are regarded as valuable aids in measuring progress of individual children in attaining certain academic skills and facts; and in comparing results of an experimental program with results achieved in schools following a more conservative pattern. Extreme care must be exercised in the interpretation of tests, however, that their use does not hinder progress in revising the curriculum in accord with the latest findings in child development and the changing goals of a modern philosophy of education. The following policies are considered important:

A. The school is interested in the development of the entire personality. In this development it is considered highly desirable that:
   1. The curriculum for all children and especially for kindergarten-primary children shall include abundant opportunity for bodily activities such as excursions, outdoor play, rhythms, dramatization, construction, and the like.
   2. The approach to mastery of such skills as reading, arithmetic and spelling shall be gradual with no immediate concern that the child shall reach fixed standards in academic achievement in relation to his mental ability.
   3. The curriculum shall be enriched for superior and gifted children, and overemphasis of "fundamental subjects" shall be avoided. Allowing these children to "work to capacity" in academic subjects is likely to lead to acceleration and the placement of the child in a group where he is physically and socially maladjusted.

B. The school is interested in helping the child develop wholesome attitudes toward learning at each stage and to increase his ability to use what he acquires in situations of everyday living. The following policies are considered in evaluating test results:
   1. In primary reading, the child is believed to have a good foundation if he has developed an interested and enthusiastic attitude and sufficient skill to read new stories independently, however simple the material may be. As his interest leads him to read outside of reading periods, his vocabulary will grow. Teachers, parents, and children should not become discouraged by test results which do not reach

fixed standards, if there is no discovered handicap which would interfere with normal learning.

2. In spelling, it is the teachers' judgment that interest is keener and spelling in written work is more accurate when a considerable percentage of words is taken directly from the child's immediate writing needs, rather than from spelling books or standardized lists. The method of studying words is more important than the particular words being studied. This policy of learning to spell words which are taken from daily needs rather than from recognized lists may tend to lower the child's grade scores in standardized spelling tests.

3. In arithmetic, the Children's School has accepted the new grade placements which postpone certain processes like long division and fractions until the children are more mature. At certain levels test scores in arithmetic computation may fall below the normal grade placement until someone standardizes arithmetic tests geared to the newer grade placements.

4. In social studies, it seems desirable that stress be put on problems of contemporary living—rather than on the far-distant past. History of a particular country or period may prove less interesting and valuable to some groups of elementary children than developmental studies, which trace the development of social customs and scientific inventions from early times to the present; as, development of light and heat, of communication, transportation, architecture, and the like. These trends in curriculum making may tend to lower history and geography scores, since the content of most of the standardized tests includes a great deal of unrelated informational material, of the type found in the older textbooks.

C. The school maintains that in general, facts relating to the child's progress shall be interpreted to parents rather than concealed from them. The age level has its influence upon the character of this interpretation. For instance:

1. In the primary grades, test results may be interpreted to parents in the teacher's descriptive reports or in personal conferences. If some handicapping factor has been found to be present it is thoroughly explained and recommendations given which are the concensus of the opinion of different adults in the school interested in the child.

2. In grades above the third, parents may be shown graph reports during personal interviews after their children have had an opportunity to see their own reports. No graph reports are mailed unless there has been an interview, so that misunderstandings may be avoided.

POLICIES USED IN IMPROVING LEARNING ABILITY

A. It is believed highly desirable that, for children who get their first school experience in the Children's School, factors likely to retard learning shall be detected early and the need for preventive instruction ascertained. The specific plans are as follows:

1. Reading aptitude tests are given near the end of the senior kindergarten or to first grade applicants either during the summer or early in the fall before school opens. The scores are compared with the child's intelligence test rating, the record of visual efficiency, the preference of hand, foot, eye, and ear, and the report from the school physician.

2. Children who show marked mental and emotional immaturity are given experiences preparatory to reading, but systematic instruction in reading is withheld until there is evidence of greater readiness. The school has few mentally immature children.

3. Children who reveal either in the testing or in the initial learning that some persistent handicap is retarding progress, such as low auditory acuity, difficulty in sound discrimination, visual anomalies, confusion in directional movement, or non-interest in learning to read, are given further diagnostic tests.

B. When special individual instruction seems desirable to prevent or correct disabilities, conferences between the teacher, guidance worker, principal and parent are planned, so that recommendations for particular children may be efficiently carried out. Basic policies include the following:

1. Since children often find it difficult to adjust to a number of personalities, individual instruction is carried on in the room by the regular teachers whenever possible.

2. If the child's difficulty suggests the use of special equipment or special methods in the Guidance Laboratory, these steps are taken:

a. The school physician is informed of the nature of the difficulties and the type of treatments recommended.

b. The parents are asked to sign a permit allowing individual instruction to be given.

c. The child is taken from the room at an individual work period or study period, so that he will not miss group activities of special value or interest to him. Individual instruction in middle and upper grades may be set at the period for French, since children who have difficulty with English usually do not enjoy learning a foreign language.

d. The teacher cooperates by permitting the child to leave at the time set and by visiting the Guidance Laboratory frequently to see the methods actually tried out, and to report on the room interests which might be used in the reading material prepared by or for the child.

e. Reports are sent to parents and teachers of the child's progress at frequent intervals.

f. Student teachers in the Children's School are encouraged to enroll in college classes stressing improvement of learning ability, so that special help may be given to any child needing it by one of the student assistants in the room rather than by an outsider.

Records of Achievement

Since some of the faculty members wished to check the educational growth of their pupils, a graph record based on the results of educational tests standardized in American public schools was organized, and has been in use for six or seven years. Two batteries of tests are selected and given to children enrolled in grades three through eight. One list from the Morrison-McCall Spelling Scale is chosen so that three spelling tests may be averaged. Four silent reading tests, two arithmetic reasoning tests, and two arithmetic computation tests are used. In grades five to eight tests in English, literature, language and grammar, history and geography are added. Oral reading tests are given to children in grades two, three and four, and to any children in higher grades who continue to have difficulty in learning to read well. Different colors on the graph indicate the test scores from various semesters, since tests are given in January and May in grades two, three, four, seven and eight. In grades five and six tests have been given in April, since children at this age do not seem to show significant gains per semester. Scores of the preceding May are recorded on the graph for the current year so that progress may be noted from May to the following January. New children are tested in the fall. Public school norms are used.

Tests in English, history, geography, literature or language are not introduced until the last month of the fourth grade. The organization of graphs for third and fourth grades is different from those prepared for the older children. Copies of some of these graphs prepared during 1939 are duplicated on pages 582 to 585.

Most children are very eager to see their graph reports, since progress is easily discerned. If there has been little or no progress, the graph is an incentive to put forth more effort on the part of many individuals. A teacher or a member of the Guidance Laboratory has a conference with each child who has taken the tests so that he may see his own report before his parents see it. A conference afternoon for parents and teachers of each group is planned so that individual parents may discuss learning and emotional-social or developmental problems of their children with the room teachers, the special teachers, and the director of the guidance staff. The physician is present if possible. The graphs are thoroughly explained and interpreted to those parents who have attended the conference.

During these informal but personal conferences, with either pupil or parent, stress is placed upon the child's academic growth, his strength and needs, rather than upon any comparison with anyone else in the class. In other words rivalry is never encouraged.

In order that individual growth from year to year may be conveniently shown in the files, a cumulative record card has been organized for recording all the grade placements the child has earned by semesters in each subject during one year. Total scores are included with educational age, achievement quotient and his educational quotient.

Various factors have determined the selection of the tests used; as, type of content, organization of content, size of type, length in line of print, sufficient range in grade norms, evenness in the increase of grade norms, and range of difficulty in the content. Power tests have been preferred to timed tests because speed is not particularly emphasized in the daily work of the children. Teachers are not informed as to just which tests shall be used, and new tests are tried out as they are available.

It is recognized that these tests do not test the specific information which any particular teacher has covered with a group of children and that newer ideas in curriculum making of necessity must be tried out before they become general enough to warrant their inclusion into tests. For instance, in arithmetic computation some schools include fractions in fourth grade, while others defer this teaching until the latter part of fifth grade or the sixth grade. There seems to be little uniformity as yet as to which arithmetic processes to teach, and when to teach them. Geography and history are included in social studies units by some teachers, as they undertake to study certain social problems. Thus the type of problem determines the amount or kind of history and geography taught rather than the outline of a textbook. Most children show vital interest in reading the historical and geographical information necessary to a complete understanding of the problem under study. However, the general information gained may be quite different from that found in the usual textbook. Teachers who carry on original studies or "units of work" frequently compile newer type examinations on the specific material covered and give these examinations at the close of the enterprise so that individual learning may be determined, needs and strengths of both individual and class discovered, and parents may know outcomes of the project as well as the teacher.

Standardized achievement tests, as a rule, are given by the members of the Guidance Laboratory, and all the scoring and checking is supervised by the staff of this department. A typewritten listing of the grade scores earned by individual children in each test from both batteries of tests is prepared for the different teachers including average rating by subjects, average total scores, average educational ages, each child's chronological age at the time of the testing, his corrected mental age, his average I. Q., the achievement quotient, educational quotient, and percentage of attendance. These same facts are also organized on another sheet with all horizontal lines representing inclusive grade placements according to these tests from the lowest score made in each subject to the highest in terms of a ten-months school year. The vertical columns are used for each main academic subject and one at the extreme right is reserved for total grade placements and achievement and educational quotients for each child. Each child's name is then recorded for each subject exactly where his average grade score places him, as 6.3 or three months in the sixth grade in reading, or 4.5 or five months in the fourth grade in spelling. By studying this listing, the teacher may immediately see the ability groupings by subjects and by keeping in mind the calibre of the daily work of the pupil can arrange her class into more homogeneous groupings and plan the instruction accordingly. This sheet is at least one basis for grouping pupils so that instruction is more efficient. However, it is merely a guide and children should be adjusted and readjusted as the need arises. A typical inventory of test results with the accompanying interpretation can be found on pages 577 to 579.

The Gray Oral Reading Paragraph test is given to second, third, and fourth grade children and to those children in grades above the fourth who do not read and spell with the sufficient skill. It is found that scores made on an oral reading test agree very well with the scores which children make in spelling, and it is therefore believed that children who fail to make normal progress in either of these subjects should be thoroughly diagnosed.

In the last few years the following tests have been given to the children in the various grades. All available forms are used over a period of two or three years so that no form is repeated within that time unless, of course, there is only one form, as the Gray Oral Reading Paragraph Test.

First Grade—Metropolitan Achievement Test—Primary Battery I, Forms A, B and C. Testing is done at the end of the year.

Second Grade—Third Grade—Metropolitan Achievement Test, Primary Battery I to those not achieving rapidly, and Primary II to those who are learning at a normal pace or above. These children are also given the New Stanford Achievement Test, Primary Battery, and a list from the Morrison-McCall Spelling Scale. Tests are given at the end of each semester.

Fourth Grade—New Stanford Achievement Test, Primary Battery, and Metropolitan Achievement Test, Primary Battery II, to those progressing slowly, or the Progressive Achievement Primary Battery, in January and May; Advanced New Stanford and Progressive Elementary Battery or the Metropolitan Intermediate to those achieving at a normal rate or rapidly, in January and May. The organization of arithmetical computational tests is satisfactory, from our experience, in the Progressive Elementary Battery. A list from the Morrison-McCall is also given at each testing period.

Fifth and Sixth Grades—New Stanford Advanced Battery, Metropolitan Intermediate Battery, or Progressive Achievement Elementary Battery are used interchangeably. The National Achievement Test, Municipal Battery (Acorn Publishing Company, Rackville Center, New York) is another possibility.

*FIFTH GRADE

September, 1939

Achievement Test Inventory

Grade Levels	Reading	Spelling	Arith. Reason.	Arith. Comp.	Eng. Lit. & Lang.	History	Geog.	Total	A.Q.	E.
6.8	Bonner	Chapin			Whorner		Roth	Roth	99	1
6.6	Bitler					Whorner		Whorner	103	1
6.4	Whitly	Roth	Whorner							
6.2	Gillet			Roth	Reeman			Chapin	102	1
6.0										
5.8	Reeman		Reeman		Gillet			Whorner		
	Schamer	-			Bitler					
					Bonner					
					Schamer					
5.6	Nadler	Nadler	Gillet		Zackry			Reeman	96	1
	Zackry				Whitly		·	Gillet	92	1
5.4			Hull		Hull		Bitler	Bonner	94	1
5.2	Hull	Reeman	Manard		Deeman		Nadler	Whitly	89	1
	Deeman	Bonner	Chapin	Roth	Nadler	Gillet		Bitler	95	1
5.0		Zackry	Barns	Reeman		Schamer	Chapin	Zackry	86	1
								Nadler	88	1
4.8				Zackry		Chapin		Deeman	97	
			Deeman	Chapin		Whitly	Bonner	Hull	104	
			Whitly	Whorner		Barns		Schamer	93	1
		Hull	Bitler	Hull		Zackry	Hull			
4.6	Barns	Schamer	Bonner	Barns	Barns	Bitler	Schamer			
	Manard	Gillet	.	Schamer	Buckly	Hull	Reeman			
4.4	Buckly		Zackry	Gillet		Bonner	Gillet	Barns	86	
			Nadler	Bitler			Whitly			
				Deeman		Reeman	Buckly	Buckly	74	
4.2			Schamer	Nadler	Manard	Nadler	Deeman	Manard	80	
			Buckly	Bonner		Buckly	Zackry			
				Buckly						
4.0		Bitler		Manard						
				Whitly						
3.8							Manard			
		Deeman					Barns			
3.6	Barns									
3.4	Whitly					Deeman				
	Manard					Manard				
3.2	Buckly									
3.0										
2.8										
2.6										
2.4										
2.2										
2.0										

*Names are fictitious, but facts are authentic.

As a rule a member of the Guidance Staff scores the tests first, and the room teacher or an assistant checks this scoring. After the test for each child is recorded, this recording is checked before averages in grade placement are obtained by another person. These averages are used for the Profile Graphs and for the inventory sheet which has already been described. Children are never shown their test booklets after they have been graded, but those above grade three are told their grade scores and types of needs and strengths are pointed out to them. Often a child's percentage of accuracy for each test is explained to him especially if he has attempted too much and has not done anything well. The teachers examine each child's booklets and record findings of a general nature which will affect the content and calibre of instruction following the testing period. Specific problems or paragraphs are not taken from the test booklets for drill purposes but similar problems are often used to explain the needs of individuals or of the class.

During the testing period notations are made concerning the work habits of individual children, their application to the task, their persistence, their absorption, their willingness to try even though the problem is difficult, their judgment as to time values. Following the testing period, individual conferences are had relative to these notations or even as the testing proceeds. Occasionally a child is allowed to work alone in a small office if he is too annoyed by behavior of others or becomes too tense in the group situation. Children are often urged to do their best, but aid is not given, and an atmosphere of seriousness concerning the testing period prevails. Since the children know that they will be informed of the results, they are more willing to cooperate and seem to be doing their best.

INTERPRETATION OF FIFTH GRADE ACHIEVEMENT TEST INVENTORY

The beginning fifth grade group is reading silently very well if one may judge by their test scores. Daily responses, however, would aid a teacher in determining those children who need further direct experiences, more concrete contacts, a richer meaning vocabulary, or emphasis upon wider reading. The scores in history and geography indicate that more factual reading might be done.

The boy who has the lowest score in reading has recently entered the school and has had individual instruction for only a semester, but is taking hold very well because of his persistence, ambition and splendid physical background. Two other children who are not reading well are also receiving individual instruction. One has many emotional difficulties to iron out. Two other children are new to the group. They come from classes close to forty in size, but are responding readily to the present program. One child has already become more relaxed, is eating better, and to the surprise of his parents gets himself ready for school before the scheduled time.

Some of the group can well spend more time learning how to spell. What words are learned is not as much the problem as the method to be emphasized. If purely visual methods with some auditory approach have not been successful, the kinaesthetic method plus the use of the tactile sense is recommended. Some of these children may need careful analyses of words so that they may gradually learn to recognize vowel and consonant digraphs, silent letters, final e's, murmur diphthongs, prefixes and suffixes, etc. Each child might appreciate having his own filing box to use to file away the words which have been of interest to him and words which were difficult for him to spell. An alphabetical arrangement is the most efficient. Word meanings should be included for each word, synonyms or antonyms, and the word should be used in a sentence.

Because of the newer grade placements in arithmetic, the class as a whole may be learning in accord with the instruction. However, there are in most classes some children not interested in arithmetic who might need to solve some of their own original problems, others who do not read problems accurately or who cannot judge as to the process pertinent to the solving of the problem, others who have habituated themselves to inefficient habits in adding, subtracting, etc., and who need to recite orally to the teacher as they work a problem so that she in turn will know what instruction is needed.

Surely, some of these children who are still eight and nine years of age as Chapin, Bonner, Nadler, Schamer, Whorner, and Zachry, should have considerable time in which to carry out their own purposeful activities, to enlarge their scope of learning by adding instrumental music, drama, speech, art or nature study. They need to spend their time, too, in real concrete learning, in seeing first-hand methods of production, of distribution or selling, to learn vicariously by having a sufficient amount of visual education aids planned for them. One child, Roth, should be carefully watched so that her placement in this class or another will be correct for her.

LETTERS OF TRANSFER

The following letter of transfer is a typical letter. In this case a brother and sister left the Children's School at the same time and transferred to the same school.

Similar letters are written for all children who leave our school, and a copy of each letter is kept for the school files. Such letters are written for school administrators and teachers only.

Miss _____ _____, Principal,

_____ School,

_____ Public Schools,

My dear Miss _____:

In regard to your letter of September 26, 1939, I am very happy to know that both B____ and S____ have entered your school.

The following facts concern B____. She has attended the Children's School since September, 1933, when she entered the nursery school. At one time she attended a public school for one semester. Her academic record has been superior since the beginning. Following are the average grade scores from two achievement test booklets given last May 18 to 22, 1939.

Silent Reading	6.6	Arithmetic Reasoning	6.2
Oral Reading	7.0	English, Literature, Language	6.0
Spelling	6.4	History and Geography	4.9
Arithmetic Computation	4.7		

Her average grade placement from these two booklets was 5.8 with a comparable educational age of 11-4. Her chronological age at the time of the testing period was eight years and seven months, and from the average I. Q. of 127, the approximate mental age was ten years and eleven months. The resulting achievement quotient of 104 is typical of B's____ record. She is well ready for fifth grade, even though she is young. Because of the social maturity of this girl an acceleration in room placement for her years seems almost inevitable although we do not wholeheartedly approve. Her small stature is typical of the family.

In regard to intelligence tests, we have the following I. Q. ratings: 137, 117 and 136. The examiner noted during the last examination when she was eight years and seven months, "When she seemed in doubt her facial expressions were very serious, almost appearing distressed. However, when she was positive of her ability she had a joyous expression, smiling happily. She said, 'I don't know' frequently, but always after consideration of the problem."

During the years which B____ has spent with us her health has been splendid. She is very artistic, very graceful, and well trained socially. We are sorry to have her leave our school.

The following facts concern S____. He started in the senior kindergarten and has had first grade and a semester of second grade in this school. There is a possibility that he is left-handed. He prefers his left eye, his left ear and left foot very consistently, but he has been almost ambidextrous in his use of hands as we have tested or observed him. Whether some decision has been made during the summer we do not know. In tests of hand skill he is slightly better with his left hand and slightly left-footed in the test for foot skill. He has not learned to read as readily as his sister.

The intelligence tests as we have them on file, show I. Q. ratings of 122 and 132. Upon entering first grade, his percentile rankings on the Monroe Reading Aptitude Test ranged from 87 to 98 with an average of 95. We have tested his visual equipment several times because of the extreme near-sightedness characteristic of the mother. This boy's vision is normal but he fails to fuse images at the reading distance. His eye movements are rather sluggish and moreover very faulty as they follow a light. This is especially true as the eyes follow from left to right. The bony area above the eyes is very sensitive to the touch. Had he continued in our school we would have watched the functioning of his eyes very carefully.

Since S_____ is really a midyear student, the following facts should be considered with this in mind. His birth date is February 16, 1932. The average grade scores from the tests given last May, 1939, are as follows:

Silent Reading	2.6	Arithmetic Computation	3.0
Oral Reading	2.3	Arithmetic Reasoning	2.9
Spelling	2.7		

The average grade placement was 2.8 with an equivalent educational age of eight years and one month. At the time of this testing period, S_____ was chronologically seven years and three months, and based on an average I. Q. of 127, his approximate mental age was nine years and two months. The resulting achievement quotient of 88 is somewhat low, indicating that because of his indecision in handedness plus faulty visual functioning, he may not succeed as well academically as his sister. However, S_____ with more physical and social development may work closer to his prediction.

If you feel that we can be of service to S_____ in the future, I am sure that his parents would appreciate knowing this.

Sincerely yours,

_____

Director of Guidance and Research

INDIVIDUAL PROFILE GRAPH

National College of Education

Name of Child ...R. B.. Grade....4.....................

Key to Report:

Percent of Days Present:

Sept. to Feb. 19.39................95%   ▨ Red....May.18,.1938....

Feb. to June 19.39................94%   ■ Blue..Jan.,.17,.1939....

                                         ▦ Green..May.20,.1939...

Grade Levels	Fundamental School Subjects						
	Reading				Arithmetic		Spelling
	Silent		Oral				

This report is based upon a ten months school year and represents average results of standardized tests given throughout the United States.　　　(over)

Comments on progress for First Semester

R. has progressed at more than a normal pace in silent reading, oral reading and spelling. The gains in all fields during the semester have been very satisfactory, or more than we had anticipated.

In the future, R. might spend more of his school time in arithmetic. He should recite some of his solutions to problems to the teacher so that she can diagnose any peculiar methods of work or incorrect thinking.

Signed _____
Director of Measurement

Signature of Parent

_____

Comments on progress for Second Semester

Considering the fact that R. has had a sinus infection and is allergic to many different foods, his continued progress in three of the four subjects is commendable. R. is young for the group, and yet is achieving at a superior rate for his years.

We feel that R. is being sufficiently challenged and that although he did not continue to improve in spelling, he has a normal gain through the year from 4.2 to 5.1, representing nine months.

Signed _____
Director of Measurement

Signature of Parent

_____

INDIVIDUAL PROFILE GRAPH

National College of Education

Name of Child ....H...R..Grade....6..........................

Key to Report:

Percent of Days Present: ······· Red....May..18,..1938....

Sept. 1938. to Feb. ..1,...19.39.............................. ——— Blue..Jan,..20,..1939...

Feb. .1939. to June ..1,...19.39.............................. - - - - Green..May..20,..1939....

Grade Levels	Fundamental School Subjects							
	Reading	Spelling	Arith-metic Problems	Arithmetic Funda-mentals	English	History	Geog-raphy	Aver. Test Grade
Above								
10.5								
10.0								
9.5								
9.0								
8.5								
8.0								
7.5								
7.0								
6.5								
6.0								
5.5								
5.0								
4.5								
4.0								
3.5								
3.0								
Below								

This report is based upon a ten months school year and represents average results of standardized tests given throughout the United States.   (over)

Comments on progress for First Semester

This semester H. has made the following gains from standardized school achievement tests: reading and spelling, eight months; arithmetic problems, seven months. In English there is a lower score this semester. No doubt this is due to the test itself or to some factor concerning the child's reactions to the testing situation.

Scores in spelling and arithmetic fundamentals lag behind other attainments. We hope H. can be influenced to expend a greater amount of time and energy in both these skills this coming semester. Personal drive and consistent ambition are essential to any learning, combined with good teaching and wise stimulation.

We have no comparable scores for either history or geography, as no tests were given covering these fields this semester.

---------------------------------------   ---------------------------------------
Signature of Parent   Signature of Examiner

Comments on progress for Second Semester

H.'s record for the second semester is very gratifying. His greatest gains have been made in arithmetic fundamentals and spelling. The first semester his lowest scores were in these fields of learning. He has made a year's gain in spelling and approximately two years' gain in arithmetic fundamentals. In arithmetic problems he has made outstanding progress.

In all of the academic skills, with the exception of history, he is doing work well above average. His average score from two booklets of achievement tests is now 7.4. Interest in reading content which has a historical background would no doubt prove beneficial.

---------------------------------------   ---------------------------------------
Signature of Parent   Signature of Examiner

Studies of Reading Readiness

The senior kindergarten children and the first grade applicants have been given the Reading Aptitude Test by Marion Monroe, which is one of the most comprehensive reading readiness tests available at the present. The results are tabulated according to the separate tests so that the percentile rankings of individuals and the group may be carefully observed and studied. Each child has his visual efficiency checked by a visual expert and his preference of hand, foot, eye and ear determined by tests given by some member of the staff. A preventive program is set up immediately so that the method of instruction may fit the individual need. The child's chronological age, his approximate mental age, his social development, the efficiency of his visual and auditory senses, his ability to express himself, his physical condition and development, the type of physical and social response, are all given consideration.

A list of positive traits has been compiled which is used as a key for the teacher as she studies each child. This list may be found on pages 586 to 589. Conferences are held with the parent or parents near the beginning of the first grade and at intervals after that so that co-operation of a precise nature may materialize. If the teacher feels the need of a special type of medical examination for an individual child or if the examiner notes questionable findings, parents are asked to give co-operation. If more rest is required for a particular child, if his diet does not seem to be sufficient or of the correct balance, if some habits need to be definitely established, parents are again requested to give earnest and willing cooperation. Waiting for maturity is the easy way out for both teachers and parents with many children. If careful analyses were only made, at the time when learning does not materialize, later agonies would be prevented.

Positive Traits of Children Basic to Learning

To be used by teachers as a key.

I. Cooperation in the Classroom

Gets ready for work quickly when it is work time.

Keeps voice well modulated.

Does his part to maintain a quiet working atmosphere.

Uses materials quietly, correctly, economically; uses good judgment in selecting materials.

Contributes to class discussions:

Talks so that all may hear.

Keeps to the topic at hand.

Accepts positive suggestions open-mindedly.

Acts upon these suggestions so that improvement results.

Brings pertinent contributions to the class.

Listens courteously to others.

Gives helpful suggestions to others in a friendly and positive way.

Shows enthusiastic approval to successes of others.

Has sympathetic and helpful attitude toward unsuccessful attempts of others.

Gives assistance to others when it is wise to do so.

Is able to enter wholeheartedly into a group situation—is not too retiring.

Remains open-minded, until able to judge a varying point of view.

II. Self-control

Keeps toys and trinkets where they will not interfere with others or their own activities requiring concentration.

Keeps hands to himself.

Is willing to sit near those whose influence upon him is positive.

Is able to enjoy a good rollicking time without getting unduly excited; can calm down rather quickly.

Hunts for lost articles instead of immediately getting upset emotionally.

Leaves the family circle willingly.

Shares his own personal belongings willingly.

Stands up for his own rights when the situation warrants it.

Asks for help only when necessary.

Does not interrupt thoughtlessly.

Is willing to uphold important group standards of conduct.

Has average ability to control himself in most situations without constant supervision of adults.

III. Responsibility

Remembers where various materials belong.

Puts materials back into place.

Remembers to take materials home when requested to do so.

Puts waste materials in their proper places.

Keeps personal belongings in good order.

Can carry messages correctly or go on simple errands efficiently.

Knows how to use books properly:

Sees that his hands are clean.

Turns pages carefully.
Asks for help in mending books.
Leaves marker in book.
Leaves book on table or in bookcase when through.
Closes book quietly.

IV. Persistence and Ambition

Sticks to the task begun if it is wise to do so.
If interrupted, returns to the task with enthusiasm and vigor.
Has his own inner drive—does not need constant adult stimulation.
Disregards routine distractions.
Enjoys working industriously.
Tries to find ways of overcoming obstacles.

V. Work Habits

Gets materials, books, papers, etc., ready.
Uses scrap materials in working out initial plans.
Keeps work neat if in final form.
Checks over work with teacher.
Is willing to correct errors.
Changes method if original method is not satisfactory.
Keeps extraneous motor activities at a minimum.
Attacks work with zest.
Works independently when prepared for the task.
Uses time to good advantage.

VI. Intellectual Curiosity

Asks questions as to meanings of words or activities of others.
Observes and examines new materials or objects in environment.
Is sincere about his desire for knowledge.
Attends to responses to questions.
Performs wise experiments..
Raises valuable questions for discussions.
Seeks opportunities to learn.
Engages in wholesome worth-while interests.

VII. Originality and Creativity

Has sufficient background upon which to be resourceful.
Is independent in his thinking.
Creates work of an artistic nature.
Has sufficient background to appreciate the beautiful.
Has ability to think and act originally when new ideas are essential.
Is not self-conscious when he can contribute original ideas.

VIII. Self Criticism

Is eager to improve—sets many goals for himself.

Is dissatisfied with only fair results.

Asks for help when a real need is felt.

Questions himself as to his own objectives so that selection results.

Recognizes when he has improved.

Is happy over improvement even though not recognized by others.

Is contented with results only when they represent best efforts.

IX. Emotional Tone

Meets new situations with ease.

Does not show fear of new or strange experiences.

Faces handicaps constructively.

Faces unpleasant experiences wholesomely and courageously.

Competes with self rather than with group or other individuals.

Tries not to offer alibis.

Research Studies in the Status and Improvement of Learning

Upon the type of research studies which this department has conducted during the past few years several goals have exerted influence.

Data are collected each year for the yearly report to the President of the College regarding intelligence ratings, educational quotients, average gains made in subjects by grades, as determined by standardized achievement tests.

As a second goal of research the staff has been ambitious to select or originate tests which would combine to make an efficient diagnosis of children meeting learning handicaps of an academic nature. A study in collaboration with Dr. William S. Gray and Mrs. Helen M. Robinson of the University of Chicago has been in progress for four years.

Since about one-third of the children encountering these learning handicaps have been found to have inadequate functioning of a visual nature, a visual expert and an assistant have been added to the staff to test eyes of college students and children who cannot read or spell with ease, those children and adults who experience discomfort of a visual nature while studying or reading, and entering first grade pupils who are given a discriminating series of visual tests as a screening out process before recommending that they see an eye specialist. Some of these children and adults have later been given visual training with the Tel-Eye-Trainer, the Squint Korrector, or Rotary Prisms. The work has been done in each case with the consent of an ophthalmologist.

Another goal at the present time is to make a detailed study of methods to correct deficiencies in spelling. Members of the staff endeavor to set the stage in the learning of the spelling of a word so that both eyes will be trained to fuse images. In this way it is thought that both eyes will have to cooperate, and that if they learn to travel consistently in the left-to-right direction plus catching some main characteristic of the word, correct spelling will result. Obtaining the main characteristics means that some of the phonetic components are noted; as, vowel and consonant digraphs, silent letters, root elements with prefixes and suffixes and their meanings, murmur diphthongs.

Since some children apparently need to be controlled in their visual mechanisms, at least temporarily, much of the laboratory equipment available from various companies has been tried out. Since the school is not organized as an experimental school no controlled experiments are conducted. The method used is one of running records with individual children used as subjects. A considerable amount of mimeographed material is obtained from such observations, which in turn is given to the teachers who teach the children. The diagnosis of individuals aids in the selection of the instrument which will be pertinent to the needs.

In the supervision of college students specializing in laboratory methods of instruction we endeavor to determine whether the student knows the facts as stated in the original diagnosis of the child, whether she has sensed current problems in his learning and planned for lessons which might aid in solving the difficulty, what her methods are which will result in success for the child, her general rapport, the knowledge which she has of the child's interests, his home, type of companions, etc. Mimeographed material is prepared as a guide to these students. This will appear in the monograph, "Reeducation in the Three R's" to be published in the near future.

Summary Record of Pupil Attending School
for Eight Years

As a final report of the Guidance Laboratory a survey of records for a recent eighth grade graduate of the Children's School is included. This boy who attended for eight years is typical of many of our graduates.

Since X's birthday was December 15, 1922, he entered first grade quite young—five years and nine months. As the I. Q. rating at that time was only 104, considerable doubt might well have been felt as to his success. He graduated when he was thirteen and a half—a correct age for high school learning with more of a prediction for academic success, for the I. Q. rating had increased to 118 or thereabouts.

The various examiners commented on considerable self-consciousness and nervousness as evidenced by grotesque facial expressions (C. A. 5-9 and 6-9). Later as a nine-year-old his speech was not as distinct as it might have been; he seemed quite happy; was sociable but extremely nervous. His eyes and mouth twitched and he played with his glasses continually. In spite of constant bodily motion he showed good power of concentration, was intellectually honest, and gave quick responses. As a twelve-year-old the examiner found him cooperative and business-like with his responses very much to the point. If he could not answer some items he was immediately aware of his inability but returned to the task very willingly when asked to try again. The average I. Q. from several tests given at intervals of two years was 112, which undoubtedly was not correct because of his consistently higher educational quotient of 120 or better.

The mother's yearly report emphasized the fact that X as a six-year-old was interested in school learning but preferred to play out-of-doors; he was stubborn in not doing the things he did not wish to do; he did not get acquainted easily with other children or show much interest in them. As a seven-year-old X argued more than formerly, was less timid, but slow, always putting off doing the thing that needed to be done if he was engaged in doing something he liked to do. As a fourth grader, his manners were sadly in need of correction, but he was most enthusiastic about school. He was still never ready to do the necessary things. Because the tests tired him out, the parents had his eyes examined and found that he was completely suppressing the vision in his right eye. The doctor excluded the left eye while he dressed (X is a left-handed person) and also asked him to read headlines with his right eye. In sixth grade, the mother wrote that X still was interested in playing out-of-doors and often made excuses to stay home from school. His poor handwriting disturbed his parents.

The room teachers found X to be physically quite well in spite of frequent colds. He lacked fine muscular coordination while in first grade and had to be given assistance in posture. He needed to learn how to relax. Although delicate looking, he seemed to have plenty of energy and vitality. The third-grade teacher thought he was very nervous because of constant bodily movement especially when he talked. The fourth-grade teacher considered him in excellent physical condition, showing good self-control. His sense of humor, jokes, fine poise, enthusiasm and self-confidence were comments that the fifth-grade teacher gave concerning his emotional status. The seventh-grade teacher indicated that he was alert and quick in action, but added that he displayed a few nervous mannerisms.

In social adjustments these traits were listed by the various room teachers:

Positive	*Negative*
Primary Grades	*Primary Grades*
Friendly toward all children, cooperates well, is courteous and always obedient to school rules. Has many friends, children admire him. Has a good sense of fair play. Gives good suggestions.	Not a leader as a younger child, is not eager to assume responsibility. Does not always play with boys who enjoy very strenuous activities. Is quiet.
Positive	*Negative*
Intermediate Grades	*Intermediate Grades*
Dependable, has great respect for others. Is a general favorite and well-liked by both boys and girls. Is democratic, friendly and unselfish. He assumes responsibility. Is more self-assertive and confident of his abilities to excel and achieve. Displays unusual executive ability. Has a fine sense of humor.	Is still a follower.

In regard to academic learning, the first-grade teacher was afraid that X's reading ability would progress far beyond his skills along other lines—especially motor skills. Lack of skill in handwriting was noted. By third grade X gave interesting contributions to the class, although some difficulty was seen in both spelling and handwriting. By fifth grade he was using his time to advantage; he spoke easily and fluently before the group, though not always distinctly; had splendid mastery of all the fundamental skills, while in sixth grade his written work showed good organization and originality of expression, and his work habits were excellent.

The following record of average test scores from second grade through the eighth includes most of the subjects tested and average grade scores with equivalent educational ages:

Grade	Silent Read.	Spell.	Arithmetic Fund.	Prob.	Eng. Lit. Lang.	Hist.	Geog.	Total Grade Pl.	Age
5-15-36	8th	10.3	8.5	10.0	10.0	9.3	10.3	9.3	10.0	15- 3
1-22-36	8th	10.2	9.0	8.8	9.3	8.8	8.6	9.6	9.4	14- 9
5-23-35	7th	9.3	8.9	8.0	9.2	8.2	9.6	9.5	9.0	14- 8
5-21-34	6th	8.6	7.9	7.7	8.3	8.3	7.9	8.7	8.2	13-11
1-20-34	6th	7.4	6.6	7.1	7.7	8.2	8.6	8.4	7.6	13- 2
5-15-33	5th	7.7	6.4	7.6	7.9	6.8	7.0	7.3	7.2	12- 8
1-25-33	5th	7.1	6.3	5.5	6.5	6.6	6.6	6.7	6.5	11-11
5-15-32	4th	5.4	5.9	5.2	5.7	7.0	7.6	5.4	5.0	11- 0
1-20-32	4th	5.9	4.9	4.8	4.9	6.4	5.8	5.8	5.6	11- 5
5-12-31	3rd	5.1	4.7	4.3	4.9					
3-24-31	3rd	4.3	4.6	4.1	3.4				4.1	10- 0
5-26-30	2nd	3.6	3.4	2.6	2.8				3.2	8-11
2- 4-30	2nd	3.3	3.0							

Except in two instances X made satisfactory progress in silent reading, arithmetic fundamentals and arithmetic problems. As with most children the average scores in history and geography are quite erratic because the content is of such a general nature. X seemed to get on plateaus in his learning to spell. Even though many different standardized achievement tests were used the average total scores show good progress. X entered high school with a record somewhat better than normal except in spelling.

A.Q.	E.Q.
114	125
111	121
116	127
115	125
109	121
107	119
110	122
109	121

According to the A.Q.'s listed to the left, X always achieved beyond our predictions for him. His educational quotient (E.Q.) was definitely better than his I.Q. Rarely did this quotient fall below 120, a figure showing very superior learning for one of his years.

The special teachers found a good singing voice; poor coordination in art work while in the primary grades, due to lack of proper muscular control and color blindness. He was good in French and gained in manual training skills. As an older child the art teacher said he had gained much in independence and had done several charming sketches with colored chalk; he was fair in manual training; had fine pitch and rhythmic perception in music, and made excellent progress in French.

A good sampling of his attendance indicates a range of 56% to 100% in attendance per semester, but an average for eleven semesters of 85%.

The letter written at graduation time by the director of the Junior

High School sums up this boy's total personality so well that it is included here:

"Not long ago one of the speakers at National College casually mentioned that he believed a wise person was one who did the things now that he will be glad he did twenty years hence. In many ways this thought characterizes the activities of X; it suggests a kind of 'wisdom' that is interwoven in the responses the boy makes to the obligations and requests in the school community life of a junior high school boy. Displaying none of the 'complexes' commonly attached to children by conscientious pedagogues, the boy has done his work and has done it well and apparently with the best of his ability most of the time. Friendly in spirit and action, X has been one of the outstanding members of the junior high school class. President of the student cabinet, chairman of committees, and one who willingly assumes responsibility without seeking reward and recognition, X has graduated from the eighth grade representing what we consider a boy well adjusted in social relationships.

"On the playground the boy is fair in every respect and has that wholesome attitude of reasonableness and consideration of the wishes of others in group activity. Often the boy has been accused of living within himself with that troublesome silence concerning his personal thoughts and activities; however, X has seemed quite capable of adjusting his own affairs and hasn't found a great need for employing the confidence of others. In this respect he has that admirable desire to use his abilities to adjust his own affairs, and his enthusiasm and judgment haven't yet bubbled over into the problems of his classmates. The boy is always willing to listen to reason and to make adjustments upon the suggestions of those he respects, but he doesn't seek protection or rely upon advice. His keen sense of humor guides him from making mountains of molehills; yet his seriousness of purpose is not impaired in the relative importance of everyday affairs.

"It might be suggested that X does not always and at all times make the best use of his abilities, but it is very possible that some of these 'relapses' contribute to the development of his fine personality and his recognition of the achievements and shortcomings of others in his community. In this respect it is a pleasure to emphasize that X is genuine and seldom, if ever, has been known to resort to subterfuge. He is always willing to assume the 'damages' for any of his misjudgments and is equally willing modestly to accept recognition of his achievements. In the classroom and on the playground he is willing to cooperate and exhibits a fine degree of aggressiveness that is neither designed to promote the ego nor arouse the antipathy of his associates. It seems apparent that these responses of X are not the result of careful planning but are rather spontaneous reactions, and in some circles he might be described as 'natural' in these respects.

"X exercises some care in the selection of his friends. Respectful and cordial to all, he selects his immediate and close associates with some care or at least with some discrimination. His attitude toward life in general seems to be happiness, without the objective of being domineering or striving to rise to great heights. It is some of these characteristics that have brought leadership to X and have gained for him the respect and good will of others.

"In academic work he does not show the characteristics of genius, but he does possess the ability to cope with the classroom assignments and master them in a commendable way. He displays at times a degree of sensitiveness and unwillingness to seek help when help might be very beneficial. He would rather assume the outcome of his own achievement with the hope of improvement the next time.

"While well developed mentally and physically, X is just reaching the social era of adolescence. He is somewhat embarrassed when in the presence of his immediate family at social functions, an attitude which isn't at all unusual for a boy of his temperament. However, in this stage of his development, it might be well to assume a natural attitude and an acceptable feeling towards his activities which will promote opportunities to invite his confidence.

"In graduating X from the eighth grade, his teachers and associates are happy to point to him as a product of the principles of our school. He may experience some difficulty in adjusting himself to a large school, but when these adjustments are made there seems to be little doubt that he will establish himself acceptably in his new environment. We hope that X will return from time to time and recount the happy hours which we feel he has spent in the classrooms and on the playground at National."

———

The Children's School has just received from the Evanston Township High School the certificate of secondary-school credits for X, recorded on the uniform blank adopted by The Department of Secondary-School Principals. At the end of three years in high school, X was rated in the highest quarter of his class. A letter from an instructor says, "X was a very faithful student in my class in third year Latin and showed keen ability. His rating on our Honor Roll for last year's first semester was Cum Laude. He attained Magna Cum Laude rating at the first marking period this fall."

Bibliography for Teachers

Curriculum and General Methods

Adams, Fay	The Initiation of an Activity Program into a Public School	1934 Teachers College
Andrus, R., and others	Curriculum Guides	1936 Reynal
Bain, Winifred E.	Parents Look at Modern Education	1935 Appleton
Brueckner, L. J., and others	The Changing Elementary School	1940 Thor
Caswell, H. L., and Campbell, D. S.	Curriculum Development	1935 American Book
Clapp, Elsie R.	Community Schools in Action	1939 Viking Press
Dewey, John	Experience and Education	1938 Macmillan
Harap, Henry, and others	The Changing Curriculum	1938 Appleton
Hockett, J. A., and Jacobsen, E. W.	Modern Practices in the Elementary School	1938 Ginn
Hopkins, L. T.	Curriculum Principles and Practices	1930 Sanborn
Hopkins, L. T.	Integration—Its Meaning and Application	1937 Appleton
Kallen, Miriam	A Primary Teacher Steps Out	1936 Lothrop
Kilpatrick, W. H.	Remaking the Curriculum	1936 Newson
Lane, Robert	The Progressive Elementary School	1938 Houghton Mifflin
Lee, J. Murray, and Lee, Dorris	The Child and His Curriculum	1940 Appleton
McGaughy, J. R.	An Evaluation of the Elementary School	1937 Bobbs-Merrill
Mead, Cyrus, and Orth, Fred	The Transitional Public School	1934 Macmillan
Melvin, A. G.	Activated Curriculum	1939 John Day
Minor, Ruby	Early Childhood Education	1937 Appleton
Monroe, W. S., and Streitz, R.	Directing Learning in the Elementary School	1932 Doubleday
Mossman, Lois C.	Principles of Teaching and Learning in the Elementary School	1929 Houghton Mifflin
National Society for the Study of Education	Thirty-Third Year Book, Part II: The Activity Movement	1934 Public School
Norton, J. K., and Norton, M. A.	Foundations of Curriculum Building	1936 Ginn
Oberholtzer, E. E.	An Integrated Curriculum in Practice	1937 Teachers College
Otto, H. J., and Hamrin, S. A.	Co-Curricular Activities in the Elementary School	1937 Appleton
Rugg, Harold	American Life and the School Curriculum	1937 Ginn
Rugg, H., and Shumaker, A.	The Child-Centered School	1928 World Book

Teaching of Social Studies

California Curriculum Commission	Teachers'. Guide to Child Development in the Primary Grades	1930 Dept. of Education

California Curriculum Commission	Teachers' Guide to Child Development in the Intermediate Grades	1936 Dept. of Education
Clouser, L. W., and Millikan, C. E.	Kindergarten-Primary Activities Based on Community Life	1929 Macmillan
Clouser, Robinson and Neely	Educative Experiences through Activity Units	1932 Lyons & Carnahan
Everett, S., and others	The Community School	1938 Appleton
Gustin, M., and Hayes, M. L.	Activities in the Public School	1934 Univ. of No. Carolina
Horn, Ernest	Methods of Instruction in Social Sciences	1937 Scribners
Hughes, Avah W.	Carrying the Mail	1933 Teachers College
Lane, Robert	Teachers' Guide Book to the Activity Program	1932 Macmillan
Michener, James A., and others	The Future of the Social Studies	1939 National Council for the Social Studies
Porter, M. D.	The Teacher in the New School	1930 World Book
Reed, M., and Wright, L.	Beginnings of the Social Sciences	1932 Scribners
Sherer, Lorraine	Their First Years in School	1939 Los Angeles County
Smith, D. V., and Frederick, R. W.	Live and Learn	1938 Scribners
Stevens, M. P.	The Activities Curriculum in the Primary Grades	1931 Heath
Storm, Grace	Social Studies in the Primary Grades	1931 Lyons & Carnahan
Stott, L. V.	Adventuring with Twelve-Year-Olds	1927 Greenberg
Stott, L. V.	Eight-Year-Old Merchants	1928 Greenberg
Tippett, James S., and others	Curriculum Making in an Elementary School	1927 Ginn
Tippett, James S., and others	Schools for a Growing Democracy	1936 Ginn
Wesley, Edgar B.	Teaching the Social Studies	1937 Heath
Wright, Lulu	A First Grade at Work	1932 Scribners

Teaching of Reading and Literature

Bessey, M., and Coffin, I. P.	Reading for Understanding	1936 Appleton-Century
Betts, E. A.	Prevention and Correction of Reading Difficulties	1936 Row, Peterson
Cole, Luella W.	The Improvement of Reading	1938 Farrar & Rinehart
Depew, Ollie	Children's Literature	1938 Ginn
Gates, A. I.	Improvement of Reading	1935 Macmillan
Gray, W. S., and Whipple, G.	Improving Instruction in Reading	1933 University of Chicago
Gray, W. S., and others	Recent Trends in Reading	1939 University of Chicago
Gray, W. S., and Leary, B. E.	What Makes a Book Readable	1935 University of Chicago
Harris, Albert J.	How to Increase Reading Ability	1940 Longmans
Harrison, M. Lucille	Reading Readiness	1939 Houghton Mifflin

Hildreth, Gertrude	Learning the Three R's	1936 Educational Pub.
Kirk, Samuel A.	Teaching Reading to Slow-Learning Children	1940 Houghton Mifflin
MacClintock, P. L.	Literature in the Elementary School	1928 University of Chicago
McCallister, J. M.	Remedial and Corrective Instruction in Reading	1936 Appleton-Century
McKee, Paul G.	Reading and Literature in the Elementary School	1934 Houghton Mifflin
Monroe, Marion	Children Who Cannot Read	1932 University of Chicago
Monroe, Marion, and Backus, B.	Remedial Reading	1937 Houghton Mifflin
National Society for the Study of Education	Thirty-Sixth Year Book Part I: The Teaching of Reading	1937 Public School
Patterson, S. W.	Teaching the Child to Read	1930 Doubleday
Pennell, M. E., and Cusack, A. M.	Teaching of Reading for Better Living	1935 Houghton Mifflin
Smith, Nila B.	American Reading Instruction	1934 Silver Burdett
Starbuck, E. D.	A Guide to Literature for Character Training	1929 Macmillan
Stone, Clarence, and Witty, Paul	Better Advanced Reading	1937 Webster
Stone, Clarence R.	Better Primary Reading	1936 Webster
Storm, Grace E., and Smith, Nila B.	Reading Activities in the Primary Grades	1930 Ginn
Weekes, Blanche E.	Literature and the Child	1935 Silver Burdett
Witty, Paul, and Kopel, David	Reading and the Educative Process	1939 Ginn

Teaching of Science

American Nature Association	The Nature Almanac	1931 American Nature Association
Comstock, Anna B.	Handbook of Nature Study	1939 Comstock
Croxton, W. C.	Science in the Elementary School	1937 McGraw
Curtis, Francis D.	Digest of Investigations in the Teaching of Science	1939 Blakiston
Haupt, G. W.	Experimental Application of a Philosophy of Science Teaching in the Elementary School	1935 Teachers College
Hunter, G. W.	Science Teaching	1934 American Book
Lynde, C. J.	Science Experiences with Inexpensive Equipment	1939 International Textbook
Lynde, C. J.	Science Experiences with Home Equipment	1937 International Textbook
National Society for the Study of Education	Thirty-First Year Book: A Program for Teaching Science	1932 Public School
Noll, V. H.	The Teaching of Science in Elementary and Secondary Schools	1939 Longmans
Palmer, E. L.	Field Book of Nature Study	1930 Comstock
Russell, David W.	Teaching Science in the Elementary Grades. (Doctor's Thesis)	1938 Western Reserve University

Slavson, S. R., and Speer, R. K.	Science in the New Education	1934 Prentice Hall
Stevens, Bertha	Child and Universe	1931 John Day
Wells, Harrington	The Teaching of Nature Study	1936 Christopher

Teaching of English Composition

Auslander, J., and Hill, P. E.	The Winged Horse	1927 Doubleday
Barnes, E. A., and Young, B. M.	Plays: Dramatizations by Sixth Grade Children	1932 Teachers College
Blaisdell, T. C.	Ways to Teach English	1930 Doubleday
Brown, Corrine	Creative Drama in the Lower School	1929 Appleton
Chubb, Percival	The Teaching of English	1929 Macmillan
Cobb, Stanwood	Discovering the Genius Within You	1932 John Day
Cobb, Stanwood	The New Leaven	1928 John Day
Ferebee, June, and others	They All Want to Write	1939 Bobbs-Merrill
Francis W. Parker School	Experiment in English Composition and Literature	1934 Francis Parker
Hartman, G., and Shumaker, A.	Creative Expression	1932 John Day
Jenkins, Frances	Language Development in Elementary Grades	1936 Thomas Nelson
McKee, Paul	Language in the Elementary School	1939 Houghton Mifflin
Mearns, Hughes	Creative Power	1929 Doubleday
Mearns, Hughes	Creative Youth	1926 Doubleday
Mountsier, Mabel	Singing Youth	1927 Harper
National Council of Teachers of English	An Experience Curriculum in English	1935 Appleton
Troxell, Eleanor	Language and Literature in the Kindergarten and Primary Grades	1927 Scribner

Teaching of Spelling

Breed, F. S.	How to Teach Spelling	1930 F. A. Owen
Foran, T. G.	The Psychology and Teaching of Spelling	1934 Catholic Education
Hildreth, Gertrude	Learning the Three R's	1936 Educational Pub.
Miller, Helen, and others	Creative Teaching in the Field of Spelling	1931 Wallace
Russell, D. H.	Characteristics of Good and Poor Spellers	1937 Teachers College
Sartorius, Ina C.	Generalizations in Spelling	1931 Teachers College
Schonell, Fred J.	Essentials in Teaching and Testing Spelling	1932 Macmillan
Thompson, R. S.	The Effectiveness of Modern Spelling Instruction	1930 Teachers College
Watson, Alice E.	Experimental Studies in the Psychology and Pedagogy of Spelling	1935 Teachers College
Wickey, Rose, and Lambader, M. B.	Teaching of Spelling	1932 Webster
Zyve, C. T.	An Experimental Study of Spelling Methods	1931 Teachers College

Teaching of Handwriting

Conard, E. U.	Trends in Manuscript Writing	1936	Teachers College
Corser, Jean	Manuscript Writing	1931	Harter
Freeman, F. N.	An Evaluation of Manuscript Writing	1936	Zaner Bloser
Gillingham, Anna, and Stillman, B.	Remedial Work for Reading, Spelling and Penmanship	1936	Sackett & Wilhelms
Orton, Samuel T.	Reading, Writing and Speech Problems in Children	1937	Norton
Varty, J. W.	Manuscript Writing and Spelling Achievement	1938	Teachers College
Voorhis, T. G.	The Relative Merits of Cursive and Manuscript Writing	1931	Teachers College
West, P. V.	Changing Practice in Handwriting Instruction	1927	Public School
Wise, Marjorie	The Technique of Manuscript Writing	1924	Scribner

Teaching of Arithmetic

Brueckner, L. J.	Diagnostic and Remedial Teaching in Arithmetic	1930	Winston
Clark, John R., and others	Primary Arithmetic through Experience	1939	World Book
Godfrey, Charles, and Siddons, Arthur W.	Teaching of Elementary Mathematics	1932	Macmillan
Klapper, Paul	Teaching Arithmetic	1934	Appleton-Century
Morton, Robert L.	Teaching Arithmetic in the Elementary School Vol. I. Primary Grades Vol. II. Intermediate Grades Vol. III. Upper Grades	1937-9	Silver Burdett
National Council of Teachers of Mathematics	Tenth Year Book: The Teaching of Arithmetic	1937	Teachers College
Thorndike, E. L.	Psychology of Arithmetic	1927	Macmillan
Wheat, H. G.	Psychology and Teaching of Arithmetic	1937	Heath
Wilson, G. M.	Teaching the New Arithmetic	1939	McGraw

Teaching of Fine and Industrial Arts

Bonser, Frederick G.	Industrial Art in the Elementary School	1930	Teachers College
Dobbs, Ella V.	First Steps in Art and Handwork	1932	Macmillan
Eng, Helga K.	The Psychology of Children's Drawings	1931	Harcourt
Fine Arts Staff	Art Education Today	1937	Teachers College
Mathias, M. E.	Art in the Elementary School	1929	Scribner
Mathias, M. E.	Teaching of Art	1932	Scribner
Perinne, Van Dearing	Let the Child Draw	1936	Stokes
Porter, Martha	The Teacher in the New School	1930	World Book
Tannahill, S.	Fine Arts for School Administrators	1932	Teachers College
Todd, Jessie M., and Gale, Ann	Enjoyment and Use of Art in the Elementary School	1933	University of Chicago
Wiecking, A. M.	Education through Manual Activities	1928	Ginn

| Wilson, Della F. | Primary Industrial Arts | 1935 Manual Arts Press |
| Zeshaugh, Helen A. | Children's Drawings of the Human. Figure | 1934 University of Chicago |

Teaching of Physical Education

Baker, Gertrude M., and others	Graded Lessons in Fundamentals of Physical Education	1938 Barnes
Bancroft, Jessie H.	The Games	1938 Macmillan
Brock, G. D.	Health through Projects	1932 Barnes
Elson, James C.	Social Games and Group Dances	1927 Lippincott
Farwell, Louise	Reactions of Kindergarten, First and Second Grade Children to Constructive Play Materials	1930 Clark University
Forbush, W. B., and Allen, H. R.	Book of Games	1927 Winston
Fretwell, E. K.	Extra Curricular Activities	1931 Houghton Mifflin
Heaton, K. L.	Character Building through Recreation	1929 University of Chicago
Horrigan, Olive K.	Creative Activities in Physical Education	1929 Barnes
Jacks, L. P.	Education through Recreation	1932 Harper
La Salle, Dorothy	Play Activities for Elementary Grades	1926 Barnes
Lehman, H. C., and Witty, P. A.	The Psychology of Play Activities	1927 Barnes
Lies, E. T.	The New Leisure Challenges the Schools	1933 National Education Association
Macombes, Mable E.	Playground Mystery Box	1927 Badger
Mitchell, E. D., and Mason, B. S.	The Theory of Play	1934 Barnes
Mitchell E. D., and Mason, B. S.	Active Games and Contests	1934 Barnes
Nash, J. B.	Physiological Health	1931 Barnes
Neilson, H. C., and Van Hag, N. W.	Physical Education for Elementary Schools	1936 Barnes
Rodgers, J. E.	The Child and Play	1932 Century
Schneider, Edward	Physiology of Muscular Activity	1933 Saunders
Steiner, J. F.	America at Play	1933 McGraw
Tanner, Jessie R.	A Game Program in Physical Education	1929 Ginn
Witty, Paul A.	Study in Deviations in Versatility and Sociability of Play Interests	1931 Teachers College

Teaching of Music

Aitken, Geraldine	Music Before Lessons Begin	1931 Carl Fischer
Coleman, Satis	Creative Music in the Home	1928 Lewis E. Myers
Foresman, Robert	Manuals to Accompany Book of Songs	1927 American Book
Gehrkens, K. W.	Music in the Grade Schools	1934 Birchard
Glenn, Leavitt, and Rebmann, Baker	Manuals to Accompany The World of Music Series	1936 Ginn
Jaques, Dalcroze E.	Eurhythmics, Art and Education	1930 Barnes
Kwalwasser, Jacob	Problems in Public School Music	1932 Witmark

McCauley, Clara J.	Professional Study of Public School Music	1932 J. E. Avent
McGehee, Thomasine	People and Music	1931 Allyn & Bacon
McKinney and Anderson	Discovering Music	1934 American Book
Mohler, Louis	Teaching Music from an Appreciative Basis	1927 Birchard
Mursell and Glenn	Psychology of School Music Teaching	1931 Silver, Burdett
Mursell, James L.	Human Values in Music Education	1934 Silver, Burdett
Mursell, James L.	Psychology of Music	1937 Norton
National Society for the Study of Education	Thirty-Fifth Year Book, Part II: Music Education	1936 Public School
Pennington, Jo	The Importance of Being Rhythmic	1925 Putnam
Perham, Beatrice	Growing Up with Music	1937 Neil A. Kjos
Redfield, John	Music—A Science and an Art	1928 Knopf
Rusette de, Louie	Children's Percussion Bands	1930 Dutton
Scholes and Earhart	The Complete Book of the Great Musicians	1931 Oxford
Storr, M.	Music for Children	1930 Schirmer
Surette, T. W.	Music and Life	1927 Houghton Mifflin
Thorn, Alice	Music for Young Children	1929 Scribner
Waterman, Elizabeth	The Rhythm Book	1936 Barnes
Zanzig, A. D.	The Concord Teachers' Guide	1929 Schirmer
Zanzig, A. D.	Music in American Life	1932 Oxford

Testing and Schoolroom Procedure

Boynton, Paul L.	Intelligence, Its Manifestations and Measurements	1933 Appleton
Broom, M. E.	Educational Measurements in the Elementary School	1939 McGraw-Hill
Brueckner, L. J., and Melby, E. D.	Diagnostic and Remedial Teaching	1931 Houghton Mifflin
Buhler, Charlotte, and Hetzer, Hildegarde	Testing Children's Development from Birth to School Age	1935 Farrar
Garrett, Henry E., and Schneck, Matthew R.	Psychological Tests—Methods and Results	1933 Harper
Gilliland, A. R., and others	Educational Measurements of the Classroom Teacher	1931 Century
Greene, H. A., and Jorgensen, A. N.	Use and Interpretation of Elementary School Tests	1935 Longmans, Green
Hildreth, G. H.	Psychological Service for School Problems	1930 World Book
Hunt, Thelma	Measurement in Psychology	1936 Prentice-Hall
Lincoln, E. A., and Workman, L. L.	Testing and the Use of Test Results	1935 Macmillan
McCall, W. A.	Measurement	1939 Macmillan
National Society for the Study of Education	Thirty-ninth Yearbook: Intelligence—Its Nature and Nurture	1940 Public School
Nelson, M. J.	Tests and Measurements in Elementary Education	1939 Cordon
Noble, H. C. S.	Practical Measurements for School Administrators	1939 International Textbook
Rinsland, H. D.	Constructing Tests and Grading	1937 Prentice-Hall

St. John, C. W.	Educational Achievement in Relation to Intelligence	1930	Oxford
Sandiford, Peter	Foundations of Educational Psychology	1939	Longmans, Green
Skinner, Charles (Editor)	Educational Psychology	1936	Prentice-Hall
Stutsman, R.	Mental Measurement of Pre-School Children	1931	World Book
Terman, L. M., and Merrill, M. A.	Measuring Intelligence	1937	Houghton Mifflin
Tiegs, E. W.	Tests and Measurements for Teachers	1931	Houghton Mifflin
Webb, L. W., and Shotwell, A. M.	Standard Tests in the Elementary School	1939	Farrar
Woody, D., and Sangren, P. V.	Administration of the Testing Program	1933	World Book
Wrightstone, J. W.	Appraisal of Newer Practices in Selected Public Schools	1935	Teachers College

Nursery School Education

Baruch, Dorothy	Parents and Children Go to School	1939	Scott, Foresman
Blatz, William E.	Nursery Education, Theory and Practice	1935	Morrow
Forest, Ilse	The School for the Child from Two to Eight	1935	Ginn
Foster, J. C., and Headly, N. E.	Education in the Kindergarten	1936	American Book
Foster, J. C., and Mattson, M. L.	Nursery School Procedure	1929	Appleton
Haxton, J. N., and Wilcox, E.	Step by Step in the Nursery School	1936	Doubleday
Iowa Child Welfare Research Station	Manual of Nursery School Practice	1934	University of Iowa
Johnson, Harriet	School Begins at Two	1936	New Republic
McMillan, Margaret	Nursery School	1930	Dutton
Poppleton, Marjorie, and Blatz, William	We Go to Nursery School	1935	Morrow
Updegraff, Ruth, and others	Practice in Preschool Education	1938	McGraw-Hill

Child Development

Arlitt, A. H.	Psychology of Infancy and Early Childhood	1929	McGraw-Hill
Bacmeister, Rhoda W.	Caring for the Runabout Child	1937	Dutton
Bartlett, F. H.	Infants and Children	1932	Farrar
Bott, Helen M.	Personality Development of Young Children	1935	University of Toronto
Chase, Lucille	Motivation of Young Children	1932	University of Iowa
Curti, M. W.	Child Psychology	1938	Longmans Green
De Kok, Winifred	Guiding Your Child through the Formative Years	1935	Emerson
Faegre, M., and Anderson, J. E.	Child Care and Training	1929	University of Minnesota
Gesell, Arnold	Infancy and Human Growth	1928	Macmillan
Isaacs, Susan S.	Social Development in Young Children	1933	Harcourt Brace

Jack, Lois M.	Behavior of the Preschool Child	1934	University of Iowa
Jersild, A. T.	Child Psychology	1933	Prentice Hall
Johnson, Buford J.	Child Psychology	1932	Thomas
Kawin, Ethel	Children of Preschool Age	1934	University of Chicago
Kawin, Ethel	Problems of Preschool Children	1933	University of Chicago
Kenyon, Josephine H.	Healthy Babies Are Happy Babies	1934	Little Brown
Kugelmass, I. N.	Growing Superior Children	1935	Appleton
Langdon, Grace	Home Guidance for Young Children	1931	John Day
Lowenburg, Harry	Care of Infants and Children	1938	McGraw-Hill
Lowenburg, M. E.	Your Child's Food	1939	McGraw-Hill
Mannin, Ethel Edith	Common Sense and the Child	1932	Lippincott
McGraw, Myrtle B.	Growth; a Study of Johnny and Jimmy	1935	Appleton
Monash, Louis	Know Your Child	1931	McGraw-Hill
Morgan, J. B.	Child Psychology	1931	Richard E. Smith
Nimkoff, Meyer F.	The Child	1934	Lippincott
Prescott, Daniel A.	Emotion and The Educative Process	1938	Am. Council of Education
Rand, Sweeney, Vincent	Growth and Development of the Young Child	1930	Saunders
Renz, C., and M. P.	Big Problems on Little Shoulders	1934	Macmillan
Reynolds, Martha M.	Children from Seed to Saplings	1939	McGraw-Hill
Richards, Esther L.	Behavior Aspects of Child Conduct	1932	Macmillan
Rivlin, H. W.	Educating for Adjustment	1936	Appleton
Scheidemann, N. V.	The Psychology of Exceptional Children	1931	Houghton Mifflin
Shirley, Mary M.	The First Two Years, 3 vols.	1931	University of Minnesota
Stoddard, G. D.	Child Psychology	1934	Macmillan
Strang, R.	An Introduction to Child Study	1930	Macmillan
Stuart, H. C.	Healthy Childhood	1933	Appleton
Thom, D. A.	Everyday Problems of the Everyday Child	1930	Appleton
Wagoner, Lovisa C.	Development of Learning in Young Children	1933	McGraw-Hill
Wexburg, E., and Fritsch, H. E.	Our Children in a Changing World	1937	Macmillan
Wittels, Fritz	Set the Children Free	1933	Norton

Character Education

Adler, Alfred	Guiding the Child	1930	Greenberg
Andrus, Ruth, and Peabody, M. A.	Parent-Child Relationships	1930	John Day
Betts, George H.	Foundations of Character and Personality	1937	Bobbs-Merrill
Blatz, W. E., and Bott, H.	Management of Young Children	1930	Morrow
Cabot, Richard C.	The Meaning of Right and Wrong	1933	Macmillan
Department of Superintendence	Tenth Year Book: Character Education	1932	National Education Association

Forest, Ilse	Child Life and Religion	1931 Williams and Norgate
Germane, C. E., and Edith F.	Character Education	1929 Silver, Burdet
Hartshorn, Hugh, and Mark A.	Studies in Organization of Character	1930 Macmillan
Hartshorn, Hugh, and Mark A.	Studies in Service and Self Control	1929 Macmillan
Jones, Vernon	Character and Citizenship Training in the Public School	1936 Chicago University
McLester, Amelia	Development of Character Traits	1931 Scribner
Pendry, Elizabeth, and Hartshorn, Hugh	Organizations for Youth, Leisure Time and Character Building	1935 McGraw-Hill
Sears, L.	Responsibility; Its Development	1932 Columbia University

Teaching Aids for Teachers

Teaching aids of great value, including periodicals, bulletins, leaflets, book lists, booklets, motion pictures, stereopticon slides, posters, pictures, and exhibits, are available from many sources. Excellent materials may be obtained at little or no cost from Federal Government agencies and from various noncommercial organizations.

For the Federal agencies, detailed information about teaching aids may be obtained from the following sources:

(1) A comprehensive list of Government publications which may be purchased for 25 cents from the Government Printing Office.

(2) Catalogs available without charge from the Office of Education in the Department of Interior, and from the information or publication offices of other departments and services.

(3) Current lists of publications from specific bureaus and offices.

Following are a few of many professional and noncommercial organizations which are able to supply bulletins and other teaching aids at slight cost:

American Federation of Arts, Barr Bldg., Washington, D. C.
American Forestry Association, 1713 K Street, N. W., Washington, D. C.
American Humane Education Society, 180 Longwood Ave., Boston, Mass.
American Junior Red Cross, Washington, D. C.
American Library Association, 520 No. Michigan Ave., Chicago, Ill.
American Museum of Natural History, 77th St. and Central Park West, New York, N. Y.
American Nature Association, 1214—16th St., N. W., Washington, D. C.
Association for Childhood Education, 1201—16th St., N. W., Washington, D. C.
Child Study Association of America, 221 W. 57th St., New York, N. Y.
National Association for Nursery Education, 71 East Ferry St., Detroit, Mich.
National Association of Audubon Societies, 1775 Broadway, New York, N. Y.
National Education Association, 1201—16th St., N. W., Washington, D. C.
National Safety Council, 20 No. Wacker Drive, Chicago, Ill.
National Society for the Prevention of Blindness, 50 W. 50th St., New York, N. Y.
Progressive Education Association, 310 W. 90th St., New York, N. Y.
The Woodcraft League of America, Inc., Santa Fe, N. Mex.
Wild Flower Preservation Society, Inc., 3740 Oliver St., N. W., Washington, D. C.
World Peace Foundation, 40 Mount Vernon St., Boston, Mass.